Between the Psalms and the Twelve

Between the Psalms and the Twelve

Exploring the Nature and Shape of Composition

EDITED BY
Matthew I. Ayars
AND
Peter C. W. Ho

FOREWORD BY
David M. Howard Jr.

PICKWICK Publications • Eugene, Oregon

BETWEEN THE PSALMS AND THE TWELVE
Exploring the Nature and Shape of Composition

Copyright © 2025 Wipf and Stock Publishers. All rights reserved. Except for brief quotations in critical publications or reviews, no part of this book may be reproduced in any manner without prior written permission from the publisher. Write: Permissions, Wipf and Stock Publishers, 199 W. 8th Ave., Suite 3, Eugene, OR 97401.

Pickwick Publications
An Imprint of Wipf and Stock Publishers
199 W. 8th Ave., Suite 3
Eugene, OR 97401

www.wipfandstock.com

PAPERBACK ISBN: 979-8-3852-2047-2
HARDCOVER ISBN: 979-8-3852-2048-9
EBOOK ISBN: 979-8-3852-2049-6

Cataloguing-in-Publication data:

Names: Ayars, Matthew I, editor. | Ho, Peter C. W., editor. | Howard, David M., Jr., foreword writer.

Title: Between the Psalms and the twelve : exploring the nature and shape of composition / edited by Matthew I. Ayars and Peter C. W. Ho ; foreword by David M. Howard Jr., Ph.D..

Description: Eugene, OR: Pickwick Publications, 2025 | Includes bibliographical references.

Identifiers: ISBN 979-8-3852-2047-2 (paperback) | ISBN 979-8-3852-2048-9 (hardcover) | ISBN 979-8-3852-2049-6 (ebook)

Subjects: LCSH: Bible.—Minor Prophets—Criticism, interpretation, etc. | Bible.—Psalms.

Classification: BS1560 A93 2025 (paperback) | BS1560 (ebook)

VERSION NUMBER 02/12/25

מַה טּוֹב

. . .

עֲשׂוֹת מִשְׁפָּט
וְאַהֲבַת חֶסֶד
וְהַצְנֵעַ לֶכֶת
עִם־אֱלֹהֶיךָ

Micah 6:8

כִּי טוֹב יְהוָה
לְעוֹלָם חַסְדּוֹ
וְעַד דֹּר וָדֹר אֱמוּנָתוֹ

Psalm 100:5

Contents

List of Contributors | ix
Foreword by David M. Howard Jr. | xiii
Acknowledgments | xv
List of Abbreviations | xvi
Introduction | xxiii
—Matt Ayars and Peter C. W. Ho

Part 1: Methodological, Compositional, and Hermeneutical Approaches

1 Shaping "Books" in the Second Temple Period: Preliminary Observations on the "Canonical" Reading of the Psalms and the Twelve | 3

 —Marco Pavan

2 Can an Integrative Reading of the Masoretic Psalter Stand in the Presence of Variants Discovered Around Qumran with a Different Canonical Order? | 60

 —Peter C. W. Ho

3 Toward the Originally Authored Book of the Twelve: Testing the Coherence of the Variant Shapings of the Twelve Prophets | 89

 —Craig S. Petrovich

4 Hope for the Ideal David and Temple: Eschatology as a Hermeneutical Frame for Interpreting the Shape of the Psalter | 132

—Matt Ayars

5 A Methodology for the Cohesion of the Psalms: Psalms 15, 19, and 24 as a Test Case | 158

—Carissa M. Quinn

Part 2: Thematic Approaches

6 The Conceptualization of the Eternal Covenant in the Book of the Twelve in Dialogue with the Understanding of the Covenant in the Book of Psalms | 185

—Marvin A. Sweeney

7 "Take Away from Me the Noise of Your Songs" (Amos 5:23): The Divine Desire for Justice and Righteousness in the Book of Amos and the Book of Psalms | 203

—J. Clinton McCann Jr.

8 Wrestling with the Absence of God: Theodicy as a Problem within the Psalter and Habakkuk | 218

—David G. Firth

9 "In That Day": Holism and the Eschatologies of the Book of the Twelve | 237

—Daniel C. Timmer

10 The Choir of the Nations in the Psalter: An Intertextual Characterization of "the Nations" in the Book of the Twelve and the Psalter | 261

—Nathan Maxwell

11 Micah the Prophet's Psalm (7:14–20) and Its Basis in the Psalter | 281

—Ernst R. Wendland

List of Contributors

Matt Ayars is the former President and Assistant Professor at Wesley Biblical Seminary. Matt holds a PhD in Old Testament from the University of Chester. His doctoral research was on Hebrew poetry and discourse analysis, and he continues to research and publish on the Psalms and Christian pneumatology. Matt is now pastoring at Wellspring Church in Madison, Mississippi. He is married with five children.

David G. Firth is Tutor in Old Testament and Undergraduate Programme Leader at Trinity College Bristol and a Research Associate of the University of the Free State. His doctoral research was on the Psalms, and he has continued to research and write on them throughout his career alongside his work on the Old Testament's historical books.

Peter C. W. Ho is Academic Dean and Associate Professor of Old Testament at Singapore Bible College. His PhD is from the University of Gloucestershire, UK, and his publications include *The Design of the Psalter: A Macrostructural Analysis* (2019) and *Habakkuk and Zephaniah* (2024). Besides the Psalms, his research interests include the Book of the Twelve and Hebrew poetry.

Nathan Maxwell grew up in Chugiak, Alaska. Since 2009, he has been at Palm Beach Atlantic University, where he currently serves as an instructional designer and online instructor. He lives in Kansas City with his wife, Kathy, and two sons, Caius (8) and Leo (6). Nathan is passionate about literary-critical approaches to the Old Testament, particularly with regard to poetics in the Hebrew Bible.

J. Clinton McCann Jr. is the Evangelical Professor of Biblical Interpretation at Eden Theological Seminary in Webster Groves, Missouri. He is the author of numerous essays and several books on the Psalms and other biblical material, including the Psalms commentary in *The New Interpreter's Bible* and *Judges* in the Interpretation commentary series.

Marco Pavan is an adjunct professor of Old Testament at the Pontifical University of St. Thomas in Rome and at the Theological Faculty of Florence. His PhD is from the Pontifical Biblical Institute (2014), and it is devoted to the Third Book of the Psalter: *"He Remembered that They Were but Flesh, a Breath that Passes and Does Not Return" (Ps 78,39): The Theme of Memory and Forgetting in the Third Book of the Psalter (Pss 73–89)*. His research focuses on the study of the Psalter as a book, biblical Hebrew poetry, and the reception history of the Psalms. He is currently working on an extensive Psalms Commentary with Gianni Barbiero. His writings include *The Formation of the Hebrew Psalter: The Book of Psalms Between Ancient Versions, Material Transmission and Canonical Exegesis* (2021), edited with Gianni Barbiero and Johannes Schnocks.

Craig S. Petrovich is a graduate of Biola University's Talbot School of Theology, where he received an MA in Old Testament. His master's thesis was "Toward the Originally Authored Book of the Twelve: Testing the Coherence of the Variant Shapings of the Twelve Prophets." After originally receiving a BS in Aerospace Engineering from UCLA, he realized that his true passion lay in biblical languages and the study of the compositional shape and messianic strategy of the biblical canon.

Carissa Quinn is a scholar, author, educator, and trained holistic coach. She is the former Director of Scholarship at BibleProject, an EdTech Animation studio located in Portland, Oregon. Carissa holds a PhD in Biblical Studies, where she focused on literary patterns and connections in the Psalms. She also holds a Masters in Teaching and is a certified constellations facilitator. Driven by a lifelong interest in how people learn and grow and a commitment to the wellbeing of others, her work bridges educational design and human transformation.

Marvin A. Sweeney is Professor of Hebrew Bible at the Claremont School of Theology. He is the author of some eighteen volumes in biblical and Jewish studies, such as *1–2 Samuel* (2023); *The Twelve Prophets* (2000);

Isaiah 40–66 (2016); and *Jewish Mysticism* (2020). He is currently writing commentaries on Exodus and Jeremiah (forthcoming).

Daniel C. Timmer (PhD, Trinity International University) is Professor of Biblical Studies for the Doctoral Program at Puritan Reformed Theological Seminary, Grand Rapids, and Professeur d'Ancien Testament at the Faculté de théologie évangélique, Montreal. He is the author of *Nahum* (2020), *The Non-Israelite Nations in the Book of the Twelve* (2015), and *Creation, Tabernacle, and Sabbath* (2009).

Ernst R. Wendland is an instructor at Lusaka Lutheran Seminary and a graduate thesis supervisor at South African Theological Seminary. His PhD is from the University of Wisconsin, USA. His writings include *Studies in the Psalms* (2017) and *Prophetic Rhetoric* (2009), and his research interests focus on literary-structural analysis, poetics, orality, and Bible translation.

Foreword

When I began graduate studies in the Old Testament in the mid-1970s, the dominant approach in mainstream scholarship was the historical-critical method. In his 1981 book *The Art of Biblical Narrative*, Robert Alter brilliantly characterized this as an "excavative" approach, the double *entendre* referring to literal excavations (archaeology) and figurative ones (peeling away supposed layers of texts to uncover the putative—and pristine—*Vorlage* behind them). Alter's work was foundational in opening up biblical studies—in both OT and NT—to literary approaches, not just "excavative" ones.

A related endeavor came from a different direction in the work of Brevard Childs, especially his *Introduction to the Old Testament as Scripture* (1979). Childs's work emphasized the ultimate ("canonical") *unity* of texts and books. His chapter on the Psalms formed the basis for his student Gerald Wilson's landmark book, *The Editing of the Hebrew Psalter* (1985), which has been the single most influential book on the Psalms in the last forty years. Childs's chapters on the individual books among the Twelve analyzed each of them on their own, but he did not consider the larger corpus of the Twelve.

It was left to James Nogalski to bring such approaches to the study of the Twelve in his own landmark works, *Literary Precursors to the Book of the Twelve* and *Redactional Processes in the Book of the Twelve* (both 1993). Like Wilson's in the Psalms, Nogalski's work has animated study of the Twelve as a unified collection in the last three decades—though we must stress that much more energy has been expended in Psalms studies than in "Book of the Twelve" studies.

Therefore, the current work is to be welcomed by scholars in both fields of study. The essays herein are mature, serious reflections on the parallels in both corpora, with insights to be had each from the other. I recommend it highly.[1]

David M. Howard Jr.

Professor of Old Testament
Bethlehem College and Seminary
Minneapolis, Minnesota USA

Professor of Old Testament, Emeritus
Bethel University
St. Paul, Minnesota USA

---

[1]. Much of my own work over the years has been dedicated to study of the Psalter's unity, so I make so bold to mention here my recent essay (with Michael K. Snearly) on "Reading the Psalter as a Unified Book: Recent Trends" (in D. M. Howard, Jr. and A. J. Schmutzer, eds., *Reading the Psalms Theologically* [Lexham, 2023], pp. 1–35), which does not appear in this volume but which parallels much in several of the essays herein.

Acknowledgments

THE INITIAL IDEA OF this project came about during the early days of the COVID-19 pandemic in early 2020, when Matt and Peter met in an online class at Wesley Biblical Seminary. Besides an interest in Hebrew poetry and the passion to understand the Word of God, both Matt and Peter shared a common point of contact between them—David Firth, who is one of the contributors in this volume, was Matt's PhD supervisor and Peter's PhD examiner. All these led Matt and Peter to work on this project together. Interestingly, after many Zoom meetings, texts, email correspondences, and an edited volume of some 100,000 words, Matt and Peter have yet to meet each other in person!

Matt and Peter are deeply encouraged by and grateful to all the contributors who believed in this project and have given their time and energy to participate in this volume. Matt and Peter are humbled and indebted to the careful and insightful scholarship by the contributors. They are also thankful to the editors of Wipf & Stock, who saw the value of this project.

For Matt and Peter, God is the driver and sustainer of this project. Specifically, Matt would like to thank his coworkers at Wesley Biblical Seminary, who were always supportive of his academic work while he was serving as the President of WBS. Peter would like to thank his family and his coworkers at the Singapore Bible College for giving him the encouragement and space to complete this project. He would also like to extend a special thanks to Priscilla Ho and Sharyn Ng for their help to proofread this work. May this volume be a blessing to all who seek to understand the Psalms and the Book of the Twelve.

Matt and Peter
USA and Singapore
July 2024

List of Abbreviations

ABD	*Anchor Bible Dictionary*
ad loc.	*ad locum,* at the place discussed
AIL	Ancient Israel and Its Literature
ANEP	*The Ancient Near East in Pictures Relating to the Old Testament*
AOAT	Alter Orient und Altes Testament
ATANT	Abhandlungen zur Theologie des Alten und Neuen Testaments
BBB	Bonner biblische Beiträge
BBR	*Bulletin for Biblical Research*
BEATAJ	Beiträge zur Erforschung des Alten Testaments und des antiken Judentum
BETL	Bibliotheca Ephemeridum Theologicarum Lovaniensium
Bib	*Biblica*
BibInt	*Biblical Interpretation*
BibInt	Biblical Interpretation Series
BibSem	The Biblical Seminar
BJSUCSD	Biblical and Judaic Studies from the University of California, San Diego
BLS	Bible and Literature Series
BN	*Biblische Notizen*
BTB	*Biblical Theology Bulletin*
BThS	Biblisch-theologische Studien

BWA(N)T	Beiträge zur Wissenschaft vom Alten (und Neuen) Testament
BZAW	Beihefte zur Zeitschrift für die alttestamentliche Wissenschaft
CahRB	Cahiers de la Revue Biblique
CBQ	*Catholic Biblical Quarterly*
CCSL	Corpus Christianorum: Series Latina
CEB	Commentaire Évangélique de la Bible
CRM	Classroom Resource Material
CurBS	*Currents in Research: Biblical Studies*
CurBR	*Currents in Research*
DCH	*Dictionary of Classical Hebrew*
DJD	Discoveries in the Judaean Desert
DSI	De Septuaginta Investigationes
DSD	*Dead Sea Discoveries*
DSS	Dead Sea Scrolls
EBR	Encyclopedia of the Bible and Its Reception
EvT	*Evangelische Theologie*
ExpTim	*Expository Times*
FAT	Forschungen zum Alten Testament
FOTL	Forms of the Old Testament Literature
HAT	Handbuch zum Alten Testament
HebBAI	*Hebrew Bible and Ancient Israel*
HB	Hebrew Bible
HBM	Hebrew Bible Monographs
HS	*Hebrew Studies*
HThKAT	Herders Theologischer Kommentar zum Alten Testament
Int	*Interpretation*
IVP	InterVarsity Press
JETS	*Journal of the Evangelical Theological Society*
JHebS	*Journal of Hebrew Scriptures*
JBL	*Journal of Biblical Literature*
JNSL	*Journal of Northwest Semitic Languages*

JSOT	*Journal for the Study of the Old Testament*
JSOTSup	Journal for the Study of the Old Testament Supplement Series
JTS	*Journal of Theological Studies*
KAT	Kommentar zum Alten Testament
LD	Lectio Divina
LHBOTS	The Library of Hebrew Bible/Old Testament Studies
LXX	Septuagint
MNTS	McMaster New Testament Studies
Ms(s)	Manuscript(s)
MT	Masoretic Text
N.B.	*nota bene*, note carefully
NICOT	New International Commentary on the Old Testament
NovTSup	Supplements to Novum Testamentum
NSBT	New Studies in Biblical Theology
NT	New Testament
OBO	Orbis Biblicus et Orientalis
ÖBS	Österreichische Biblische Studien
ORA	Orientalische Religionen in der Antike
OTE	*Old Testament Essays*
OT	Old Testament
OTL	Old Testament Library
OtSt	*Oudtestamentische Studiën*
PRSt	*Perspectives in Religious Studies*
RB	*Revue Biblique*
RBSem	Rhetorica Biblica et Semitica
RevExp	*Review and Expositor*
RivB	*Rivista Biblica Italiana*
SBFLA	*Studii Biblici Franciscani Liber Annus*
SBL	Society of Biblical Literature
SBLDS	Society of Biblical Literature Dissertation Series
SBLMS	Society of Biblical Literature Monograph Series
SBLSP	Society of Biblical Literature Seminar Papers

ScEs	*Science et Esprit*
SHS	Scripture and Hermeneutics Series
SJOT	*Scandinavian Journal of the Old Testament*
SK	*Skrif en Kerk*
SOTSMS	Society for Old Testament Studies Monograph Series
SSBT	Studies in Scripture and Biblical Theology
SSN	Studia Semitica Neerlandica
StBibLit	Studies in Biblical Literature (Lang)
STDJ	Studies on the Texts of the Desert of Judah
STI	Studies in Theological Interpretation
Tg.	Targum
TLZ	*Theologische Literaturzeitung*
TOTC	Tyndale Old Testament Commentaries
TR	Textus Receptus (received Masoretic tradition of 150 psalms)
TSAJ	Texts and Studies in Ancient Judaism
TynBul	*Tyndale Bulletin*
VF	*Verkündigung und Forschung*
VT	*Vetus Testamentum*
VTSup	Supplements to Vetus Testamentum
XII	The Book of the Twelve
YJS	Yale Judaica Series
ZAW	*Zeitschrift für die alttestamentliche Wissenschaft*

Mishnah, Talmud, and Rabbinic Literature

b.	Babylonian
bar.	baraita
B. Bat.	Baba Batra
Ber.	*Berakot*
Gem.	Gemara
Kid.	Kiddushim
Midr.	Midrash

Deuterocanonical Works and Septuagint

Sir   Sirach/Ecclesiasticus

Qumran Texts

1QM   Milḥamah or War Scroll
1QpHab   Pesher Habakkuk
1QS   Serek Hayaḥad *or* Rule of the Community
CD   Cairo Genizah Copy of the Damascus Document
Ḥev   Naḥal Ḥever
Mas   Masada
Mur   Murabbaʿat
Q   Qumran

Greek and Latin Literature

Civ.   *De civitate Dei*
Hist. eccl. *Historia ecclesiastica*
C. Ap.   *Contra Apionem*

Modern English Versions

ESV   English Standard Version
NET   New English Translation
NIV   New International Version
NRSV   New Revised Standard Version

Symbols

†ᵀ Lexical term involved in this point of coherence occurs nowhere else in the LXX Twelve Prophets; if the qualifier is in parentheses (i.e., †⁽ᵀ⁾), not all instances are shown in this pileup display, and/or not all instances are accounted for by this pileup (in which case the

remaining instances are accounted for in other related pileups between the same books)

†ᶠ Lexical term involved in this point of coherence occurs nowhere else in the five-book sub-group, LXX Joel+Obadiah+Jonah+Nahum+Habakkuk; if the qualifier is in parentheses (i.e., †⁽ᶠ⁾), not all instances are shown in this pileup display, and/or not all instances are accounted for by this pileup (in which case the remaining instances are accounted for in other related pileups between the same books)

#ᵀ Grammatical, syntactical, or collocational combination involved in this point of coherence occurs nowhere else in the LXX Twelve Prophets; if the qualifier is in parentheses (i.e., #⁽ᵀ⁾), not all instances are shown in this pileup display, and/or not all instances are accounted for by this pileup (in which case the remaining instances are accounted for in other related pileups between the same books)

#ᶠ Grammatical, syntactical, or collocational combination involved in this point of coherence occurs nowhere else in the five-book sub-group, LXX Joel+Obadiah+Jonah+Nahum+Habakkuk; if the qualifier is in parentheses (i.e., #⁽ᶠ⁾), not all instances are shown in this pileup display, and/or not all instances are accounted for by this pileup (in which case the remaining instances are accounted for in other related pileups between the same books)

Introduction

The intent of this book is to initiate conversations between two seemingly similar corpora of the Hebrew Bible / Old Testament the scholarship of which has developed independently in the last few decades and remained separate.[2] To our knowledge, there is currently very little scholarship that sustains conversations between the Psalms and the Twelve (XII).[3] We believe this volume will fill a gap in the scholarship of the Psalms and the XII.

Our modest aim is to demonstrate that insights gained from reading the two corpora, even if done separately, can productively inform the reading of both when brought together in conversation. The value of allowing one mature research field to affect the other to spark new growth is too great to ignore. As such, we have gathered several specialists who have worked extensively with either one of these corpora, or both, to initiate and engender conversations.

These contributors hail from five countries (USA, Italy, UK, South Africa, and Singapore) and their essays adopt a particular approach, which can be methodological, scribal, thematic, theological, or literary.

---

2. Consider the BZAW series, which has produced at least twelve volumes relating to the Book of the Twelve (XII) or the Psalms (vols. 217, 218, 260, 325, 340, 360, 389, 428, 433, 437, 472, 505). Several in the FAT series (vols. 89, 111, 133, 149, 151, 160) and FAT II series (vols. 52, 88, 91, 114) from Mohr Siebeck are important as well. See also the specific publications from SBL AIL (vols. 19, 20, 29), SBLDS (vols. 148), JSOTSup/LHBOTS (vols. 20, 102, 159, 252, 258, 624), VTSup (vols. 99, 169, 180, 184), and BETL (vols. 163, 238, 295).

3. About two decades ago, Gerstenberger noted the liturgical and sociological links between similar hymn-like content in both the Psalms and the XII. This was because the "cultic situations may have produced the prophetic pronouncements and literature" (Gerstenberger, "Psalms," 83). Nonetheless, such intertextual reflections between the Psalms and the XII remain few and far between.

xxiii

We believe that this volume has achieved meaningful conversations between specialists of the Psalms and the XII and has raised new possibilities in the scholarship of both corpora.

Scholarship related to both corpora has progressed significantly in the past century and there has been a general shift from historical-redactional to integrative approaches. More specifically, in the past few decades, there has been an increase in the number of essays and monographs wrestling with more coherent approaches to the Psalms or the XII.[4] However, contentions relating to the (in)coherence and unity/diversity of these two collections remain.[5] As such, this is an important angle that this volume will address.

There are several reasons why we decided to study the Psalms and the XII together. First, we observe the surface similarity in their compositional textures as collections. Both corpora consist of largely independent text units (individual psalms/books) originally written by different authors, which were later assembled and transmitted as a larger "book," or collection.[6] Both corpora likely reached their final form in the Second Temple period, and studies concerning their composition naturally ask questions about redaction, formation, manuscripts, and history. Moreover, the order of text units within each corpus sometimes differs across manuscript versions (e.g., LXX, Qumran, MT) with occasional text additions or subtractions.

It is also important to note that the two corpora are primarily poetic in genre. This parallel is more significant than initially perceived. Much literary analysis of how lyrical texts can be read holistically is argued based on poetic features (e.g., inclusio, large-scale palindrome). Insights gained from studying the poetic techniques found in the Psalms can be transferred to the XII and vice versa. Yet surprisingly, theoretical scholarship on biblical poetics (which includes linguistic studies and rhetoric) remains largely detached from biblical studies of these two corpora. For instance, although scholars have noted how individual poems can form a

---

4. Recent monographs on the XII and the Psalter taking a holistic approach include Choi, *Patterns*; Ayars, *Shape*; Ho, *Design*; Timmer, *Non-Israelite*; Cuffey, *Literary*.

5. On methodology, see especially the several essays on "coherence" and "incoherence" of a text in Teeter and Tooman, "Standards of (In)coherence"; Samely, *Profiling*. Consider also the debates in Gertz et al., *Formation*; Wenzel and Fischer, *Book*; Ben Zvi and Nogalski, *Two Sides*; Landy, "Three Sides"; Di Pede and Scaiola, *Book*; Scaiola, "Le Livre"; Tiemeyer and Wöhrle, *Book*.

6. See Willgren, *Formation* for a detailed discussion of the notion of "book" as it relates to the discussion here.

larger integral compositional unit made up of two or more poems, poetics studies of biblical poetry have largely limited the discussion of poetic techniques to a single poem.[7] While poetics studies observe, describe, and theorize poetic features, biblical studies seek to understand how the poetic features serve a larger theological message.

This volume does not plumb every one of these issues mentioned, but we think that this book contains sufficient value to initiate conversations between these separate fields of study. An overview of this volume is detailed below.

In Part I of the volume, five essays initiate the conversation from a more methodological, compositional, and hermeneutical approach. A survey of these issues is first taken up by Marco Pavan. He traces, in exhaustive detail, the interpretive history of both corpora. Pavan identifies three major methodological challenges currently confronting scholarship on both corpora. First, there remains an unresolved methodological debate on the cogency of editorial devices (such as repeated lexemes or superscriptions) that conjoin or demarcate discrete units. A coherent reading logic for either corpus may still be elusive. Second, there is a larger ongoing debate between scholars who adopt editorial/redactional approaches and those who adopt a more historical/reader-oriented reading. In the study of both the Psalms and the XII, we encounter distinct voices representing methodologically opposing perspectives. A third issue that Pavan raises concerns published Qumran findings in the past few decades. Emerging formational theories that challenge the canonical readings of the MT in both corpora are on the rise.

Immediately following Pavan's final point, Peter Ho interacts with several of the emerging formational theories and oppositions to the canonical readings of the MT Psalter, especially concerning the debates of differing orders of psalms in the DSS manuscripts and deviations in superscriptions/delineation of medieval MT Psalms manuscripts. Ho responds to the recent works of Drew Longacre, David Willgren Davage, William Yarchin, and Alma Brodersen, and concludes that it is hard to qualify the observed differences in these variant manuscripts as the

---

7. Consider Lugt and Meynet, who argue how several consecutive poems cohere poetically beyond the individual poem. Meynet's prodigious volumes (forty-one of them!) are found in the Rhetorica Biblica et Semitica series. One of his most recent titles, *The Psalter* (RBSem 41), consolidates his earlier works on the Psalms. See also Lugt, *Hebrew Poetry I-III*. Older poetic studies often limit their analyses to the single poem. Consider Alter, *Biblical Poetry*; Berlin, *Dynamics*; Alonso Schökel, *Manual*; Watson, *Classical*; Kugel, *Idea*.

same kind of editorial or compositional changes in the formational period of the Hebrew Psalter. In other words, while the currently available manuscript evidence of the Psalms does not allow the MT the privilege of an unchallenged position of textual authority prior to the turn of the millennium, Ho argues that it is neither possible nor necessary to preclude the Psalter (or the XII) from having undergone an integrative and coherent shaping by a single or a small group of final editors at the final stages of the formational process to produce a *sepher* with a coherent theological and thematic logic.

This search for an original shaping logic by comparing textual streams is also picked up by Craig Petrovich, who offers a very interesting alternative to the MT tradition of the XII. Petrovich's essay is built on several years of his earlier work of retroverting a Hebrew version of the Greek LXX XII manuscript. He seeks to answer the question of the coherency of the shaping of biblical books as unified texts, despite the presence of multiple arrangements. Essentially, he argues that the LXX XII, rather than the MT, is likely the originally authored shape (pre-MT) and offers a cogent proposition to the logic and coherence of the order of books in the LXX XII. Petrovich argues that the core of this logic is the place of Jonah and its focus on the salvation of gentiles through a suffering servant of YHWH. He proposes that the current order of the MT XII and Qumran variants (4QXII[a]) are possibly derivative textual streams that sought to displace the gentile-centricity of an earlier original Hebrew Vorlage.

As Petrovich offers a gentilic shaping of the entire LXX XII, Matt Ayars argues for an eschatological shaping of the Psalter. He supports his thesis with arguments both external and internal to the text. Externally, he notes how the New Testament reflects an extant Palestinian-Jewish view of messianic psalms as future-predictive. The Qumran Psalms scrolls and several commentaries on the Psalms in the DSS also reflect deep eschatological commitments. The 4Q174 and 4Q177 commentaries on Pss 1, 2, 5, 11, 12, and 13 are cases in point. Ayars has amassed evidence from the LXX, Peshitta, Targum of the Psalms, and Midrash Tehillim, all of which express a future-predictive orientation. Internally, the prologue (Pss 1–2), superscriptions, thematic shifts from lament to praise, strategic placement of royal psalms, and focus on an unrealized ingathering of God's people at an ideal Zion in Book V of the Psalter are reflective of an eschatological shaping. He argues that the Book of Psalms is an instructional praise book, at a time without the temple, that anticipates the fulfillment of God's promises for the ideal Messiah and Zion temple.

All four contributions above have raised concerns when discussing or applying lexical and/or thematic repetitions as a cohesive shaping technique. The essay by Carissa Quinn offers a helpful statistical method to measure patterned repetitions between text units, which she applies to Psalms 15–24 as a test case. Perhaps some literary critics would balk at the mathematical complexity of her work, but Quinn's methodology allows one to read cohesion (whether lexical, morphological, thematic, structural, or superscriptional links) with a definable level of confidence. The application of her method on the test case has successfully verified earlier purely literary observations (e.g., links between Pss 15, 19, and 24). Perhaps to the delight of the same literary critics, Quinn's method can easily be applied to verify more "intentional correlations" in other text units of the Psalter or the XII with some level of confidence. It can be applied intertextually, for instance, between Amos and the YHWH kingship psalms (Pss 93–100) in McCann's study below. Quinn's methodology could also directly address Pavan's concern for the coherency and cogency of editorial devices to conjoin or demarcate discrete units.

Taken together, the five essays above surface important and recent textual, formational, methodological, and interpretive issues common to the scholarships of both the Psalter and the XII.

In Part II of the volume, another six scholars join the conversation in discussing specific themes and topics. These scholars focus on a particular theological motif of the text that displays remarkable resonance in both corpora. Significant thematic motifs such as the covenant, justice, Zion temple, Torah, the people of God, the nations, and eschatology are often explored for macro-textual coherence. These topics move beyond the individual corpus, which means that these scholars are often able to find common threads across corpora. Their concerted voices evidence a common theological telos.

In the first of these essays, Marvin Sweeney examines the conceptualization of the covenant in both the Psalms and the XII and argues that both corpora envision an ultimate permanent and unconditional covenant. For the XII, the compilers placed Hosea and Malachi as compositions of introduction and closing via their use of the marriage and divorce metaphors to exemplify YHWH's eternal covenantal pledge to his people. For the Psalter, a development in the understanding of the concept of covenant as one moves from earlier to later books is seen. Only from

Book IV of the Psalms is there an unambiguous assertion of an eternal and unconditional covenant. And it is only in Book V of the Psalter (esp. Ps 132) that the distinction between the conditional covenant with the Davidic House and the eternal covenant with Zion is clarified. Sweeney posits that these corpora have reflected deeply on the concept of covenant and are thus an important resource for intertextual dialogue.

The topic of YHWH's covenant in Sweeney's essay inevitably raises the problem of the people's rebellion and how God would deal with his people. Reflections on the nature of God and how he deals with his people are taken up by the next two scholars. J. Clinton McCann Jr. gives attention to the motif of YHWH's justice (or the lack thereof in God's people) in the book of Amos and the Psalms. McCann's main thesis is that both corpora are congruent in their portrayal of YHWH's will for justice. In Amos, the focus on God's justice and righteousness has a creation-oriented and universal thrust. This is reflected by its shape, both at the center of the book (Amos 5) and its enveloping frames (Amos 1:3–2:16 and 9:7–8). In a similar way, he suggests that the "theological heart" of the Psalter is a universal manifestation of YHWH's righteousness and justice through his kingship in Book IV (esp. Pss 93–99). In this way, both editorial cores of the Book of Amos and the Psalter heighten the expression of justice and righteousness for the flourishing of Israel and the world. Both corpora show that expressions of justice and righteousness must begin with the most vulnerable, the poor, and the needy in Israel, and be extended outwards towards the nations. McCann concludes with a poignant reflection on the lack of justice we continue to perpetuate in our own time and space.

The notion of the lack of justice is given further contemplation in David Firth's essay. Firth wrestles with the seeming absence of God in a world of violence. His essay addresses three separate collections of psalms and the book of Habakkuk. Firth begins by noting that Psalms 1–2 harmonize with several similar Torah psalms. These psalms emphasize God's promises to the righteous and anticipate how these "reassurances might be problematized." The problem—the apparent flourishing of the wicked—necessitates theodicy to be a perennial issue the psalms must address. In two psalm collections (Pss 9–14 and 52–55), Firth shows the struggle of the psalmist and the wicked holding both ideas of divine absence/presence concurrently. In a third collection, the Asaph psalms (esp. Pss 73, 79), Firth argues that this dilemma is now pondered at the corporate level of the nations. Moving to Habakkuk, Firth sees this book as an "important extension to the Psalter." Like the Psalms, Habakkuk holds God to account but offers an eschatological perspective that gives hope to the righteous and faithful in a world that remains beset by violence.

The topic of eschatology is alluded to in the various essays above. Daniel Timmer shows how the eschatologies in the XII and the Psalter can express coherence and unity. Methodologically, a text is said to have a degree of unity if the reader infers that the linguistic features that hold the text together are stronger than those that fragment it. Such linguistic features can include "reference, causation, and semantic relations." Timmer argues that when "complementarity or similarity" is observed, there is a "sufficient criterion of coherence." From this method, he revisits four books of the XII (Amos, Micah, Zephaniah, and Malachi) through the lens of eschatology. He argues that the eschatologies within these four books are consistent and there is a global coherence across them despite their different historical contexts. Essentially, the common trajectory begins with a focus on YHWH's relationship with his people (Israel and non-Israelite), followed by their sin, punishment, and subsequent deliverance. Among these people, some will become remnants who will enjoy God's full eschatological deliverance. What we have heard earlier, especially about injustices (McCann) and an absent God (Firth), is further addressed in this essay by Timmer. He concludes by noting that the similarity across the four books of the XII finds "fundament alignment" with the Psalms, the rest of the Old Testament, and the New Testament.

At this stage in this volume, Maxwell's contribution assumes that the individual corpus of the Psalter or the XII can be interpreted as a unity. Following Timmer's discussion of God's eschatological deliverance among the nations, Maxwell further elaborates how the fate of a given nation is a source of the coherence of these books. For him, there is a sense that the nations need to move from judgment to salvation—a trajectory of the missio Dei—which serves to unite the texts. Like the XII, the Psalms carry a significant repetition of the theme of the nations. There is a concerted voice at the heart of the Psalms, especially the YHWH kingship psalms (Pss 93–100), that depict YHWH's rule over all the nations for their deliverance and flourishing with clear intertextual links to Amos, Haggai, Zechariah, and Malachi. Again, like the XII, the fate of the nations has an instrumental role in the eschatological vision of the Psalter.

In the final contribution, Wendland shows how Micah, especially through the "Prophet's Psalm" of 7:14–20, manifests "three prominent psalmic macro-characteristics with respect to discourse structure, literary style, and thematic significance." Methodologically, this essay is a poetics tour-de-force. Exercising a ten-step discourse-analysis process he developed over years, Wendland gives attention to strophic structure, conversations, metaphors, rhetorical devices, morphology, intertextual allusions, and more. He argues that Micah 7:14–20 is a three-strophe unit that moves from prayer to judgment and finally to praise. The first strophe (7:14–15) heightens motifs that are associated with the YHWH-as-shepherd metaphor, a motif that resonates well with the Psalms (e.g., Pss 23, 29, 74, 80, 95, 100). The second strophe (7:16–17) depicts the nations' response and submission to God's victorious and salvific acts in history. This, again, finds resonance in the Psalms (e.g., Pss 18, 98, 126). The final strophe (7:18–20) is a confessional doxology of God's steadfast love and compassion—a significant covenantal motif of the Psalms as well (Pss 86, 103, 145). Wendland concludes by noting that not only do we see such thematic resonances between Micah 7:14–20, the XII, and the Psalter, but the strophic, poetic, dictional, stylistic, and emotive parallels are clear between these corpora.

The volume begins with Petrovich's and Ayars's foci on the gentilic and eschatological shaping of the XII and the Psalter respectively, and we return to these common thrusts with Timmer's, Maxwell's, and Wendland's contributions at the end of the volume. This shows that when independent investigations are conducted in view of one another, meaningful conversations will take place. We hope this volume will spark new insights as mature scholarship in one field is brought into conversation with the other.

A final word on this volume: we are privileged to have experienced specialists and important scholars of the Psalms and the XII contributing to this volume at a time when new conversations of these texts are needed. Although our intended audience is the academic community, the volume will benefit all who are looking for resonance among the corpora of Scripture. At such a time as this, when wars and unrest continue unabated around the world and as oppression and injustice reigns, the words of the Psalter and the XII are much needed—what is good? What is required?—but to do justice, love mercy, and humbly walk with your God (Micah 6:8).

Bibliography

Alonso Schökel, Luis. *A Manual of Hebrew Poetics*. Rome: Editrice Pontificio Istituto Biblico, 1988.

Alter, Robert. *The Art of Biblical Poetry*. New York: Basic, 2011.

Ayars, Matthew Ian. *The Shape of Hebrew Poetry: Exploring the Discourse Function of Linguistic Parallelism in the Egyptian Hallel*. SSN 70. Leiden; Boston: Brill, 2018.

Ben Zvi, Ehud, and James D. Nogalski. *Two Sides of a Coin: Juxtaposing Views on Interpreting the Book of the Twelve / the Twelve Prophetic Books*. Analecta Gorgiana 201. Piscataway: Gorgias, 2009.

Berlin, Adele. *The Dynamics of Biblical Parallelism*. Bloomington: Indiana University Press, 1985.

Choi, Yung Hun. *Patterns of Movement in the Hebrew Psalter: A Holistic Thematic Approach with an Exemplar, Psalms 69–87*. StBibLit 174. New York: Peter Lang, 2021.

Cuffey, Kenneth H. *The Literary Coherence of the Book of Micah: Remnant, Restoration, and Promise*. LHBOTS 611. London: T&T Clark, 2015.

Di Pede, Elena, and Donatella Scaiola, eds. *The Book of the Twelve—One Book or Many? Metz Conference Proceedings, November 5–7, 2015*. FAT II 91. Tübingen: Mohr Siebeck, 2016.

Gerstenberger, Erhard S. "Psalms in the Book of the Twelve: How Misplaced Are They?" In *Thematic Threads in the Book of the Twelve*, edited by Paul L. Redditt and Aaron Schart, 72–89. BZAW 325. Berlin; Boston: de Gruyter, 2012.

Gertz, Jan C., et al., eds. *The Formation of the Pentateuch: Bridging the Academic Cultures of Europe, Israel, and North America*. FAT 111. Tübingen: Mohr Siebeck, 2016.

Ho, Peter C. W. *The Design of the Psalter: A Macrostructural Analysis*. Eugene, OR: Pickwick, 2019.

Kugel, James L. *The Idea of Biblical Poetry: Parallelism and Its History*. New Haven: Yale University Press, 1981.

Landy, Francis. "Three Sides of a Coin: In Conversation with Ben Zvi And Nogalski, *Two Sides of a Coin*." JHebS 10 (2010) 1–21.

Lugt, Pieter van der. *Cantos and Strophes in Biblical Hebrew Poetry: With Special Reference to the First Book of the Psalter*. OtSt 53. Leiden; Boston: Brill, 2006.

———. *Cantos and Strophes in Biblical Hebrew Poetry II: Psalms 42–89*. OtSt 57. Leiden: Brill, 2010.

———. *Cantos and Strophes in Biblical Hebrew Poetry III: Psalms 90–150 and Psalm 1*. OtSt 63. Leiden; Boston: Brill, 2013.

Meynet, Roland. *The Psalter: The Whole of the Book of Praises*. RBSem 41. Leuven: Peeters, 2022.

Samely, Alexander. *Profiling Jewish Literature in Antiquity: An Inventory from Second Temple Texts to the Talmuds*. Translated by Alexander Philip et al. Oxford: Oxford University Press, 2014.

Scaiola, Donatella. "Le Livre des Douze: Une Unité? Quelques éléments méthodologiques de réponse." In *The Books of the Twelve Prophets. Minor Prophets—Major Theologies*, edited by Henz-Josef Fabry, 315–28. BETL 295. Leuven: Peeters, 2018.

Teeter, David A., and William A. Tooman. "Standards of (In)coherence in Ancient Jewish Literature." HebBAI 9.2 (2020) 94–129.

Tiemeyer, Lena-Sofia, and Jakob Wöhrle, eds. *The Book of the Twelve: Composition, Reception, and Interpretation*. VTSup 184. Leiden; Boston: Brill, 2020.

Timmer, Daniel C. *The Non-Israelite Nations in the Book of the Twelve: Thematic Coherence and the Diachronic-Synchronic Relationship in the Minor Prophets*. BibInt 135. Leiden; Boston: Brill, 2015.

Watson, Wilfred G. E. *Classical Hebrew Poetry: A Guide to Its Techniques*. JSOT 26. Sheffield Academic, 2009.

Wenzel, Heiko, ed. *The Book of the Twelve: An Anthology of Prophetic Books or the Result of Complex Redactional Processes?* Osnabrücker Studien Zur Jüdischen Und Christlichen Bibel 4. Göttingen: Vandenhoeck & Ruprecht, 2018.

Willgren, David. *The Formation of the "Book" of Psalms*. FAT II 88. Tübingen: Mohr Siebeck, 2009.

PART 1

Methodological, Compositional, and Hermeneutical Approaches

CHAPTER 1

Shaping "Books" in the Second Temple Period

Preliminary Observations on the "Canonical" Reading of the Psalms and the Twelve

Marco Pavan

The rise of the so-called "canonical exegesis" in the late 1970s[1] marked a turning point in the study of the Old Testament, one that caused a shift towards the (synchronic and/or diachronic) analysis of the final form of biblical texts.[2] The influence of canonical exegesis may be detected in some areas of OT scholarship. The study of the Psalter experienced an increasing shift after the publication of the groundbreaking monograph of G. H. Wilson—one of Childs's students—in 1985.[3] In the same vein, the study of the twelve Minor Prophets[4] was profoundly affected by the

---

1. Above all, see Childs, *Introduction*; cf. Auwers and Jonge, *Canons*; Seitz and Richards, *Scripture*.
2. Clines, "Beyond," 52–71.
3. Wilson, *Editing*.
4. In this contribution, I will refer to the so-called "Minor Prophets" always with the term "the Twelve," regardless of whether I am referring to the "group" of the twelve prophets from Hosea to Malachi or to the book as a literary unity. Similarly, I will also use the terms "book(s)" and/or "writing(s)" to denote the individual prophetic work(s) that belong(s) to the collection of the Twelve.

publication of two monographs in 1993 by James D. Nogalski,[5] whose methodological premises were, at least partially, influenced by the shift from the person of the prophet to prophetical texts caused by the rise of the canonical approach.

The "new" approach fostered by the canonical shift could also be considered a first step in approaching the issue of the formation of "canonical" collections in a comparative way.[6] In the following pages, I will try to compare the Psalter and the Twelve from different points of view. The two groups of compositions seem to stem from distinct traditions and editorial activities and can appear to be nearly incomparable. It is possible, however, to conduct such a comparison based on the significant points of contact between the literary shapes of the two books identified by scholars who investigated them canonically in a relatively independent way.[7] Both areas of scholarship worked on the basis of similar assumptions and data, faced similar methodological issues, and reached similar conclusions. Moreover, in both fields of study, the canonical approach[8] experienced strong criticism, based on a new evaluation of manuscript evidence[9] and the adoption of different methodological approaches. It is likely that one of the reasons for the independent development of the two fields of study on this point is the widely recognized specialization of the study of the different OT corpora.

---

5. Nogalski, *Literary*; *Redactional*.

6. From this point of view, the comparison between the Twelve and Isaiah may be instructive. See below.

7. There are some exceptions, notably, Steinberg, *Ketuvim*; see also Niemeyer, *Het probleem*. Recently an integrated view of the canon has been proposed that attempts to bring together independent research on the different parts of the canon: see deClassé-Walford, "Canon," 121–38; Zenger, "Salterio," 11 ("above all, there are surprising analogies between the redaction of the Psalter and that of the prophetic books, especially the book of Isaiah" [our translation from Italian]); cf. Zenger, "Zwölfprophetenbuch," 630–35.

8. In this contribution, I will use the phrase "canonical approach" or "exegesis" as a general reference to an approach that considers the Psalter and/or the Twelve as an organized, edited book, that can and should be read as a complex, unified literary work. From this point of view, the above phrase is used even though scholars use different designations, each having a different perspectives on the matter. Some variants include: "holistic exegesis" (Zenger, "David," 57–72); "editorial criticism" (Snearly, *Return*); "contextual exegesis" (Murphy, "Reflections," 21–41; cf. Millard, *Kompostion*); "Endtext-Exegese" (Zenger, "Psalmenexegese," 246).

9. The influence of the "new philology" should also be mentioned here. See Schnocks, "Psalterexegese," 309–30.

The starting point of my analysis can be summarized by the following question: is a thorough comparison of both books able to confirm or reject the hypothesis that they are products of intentional and meaningful editorial work—that they must be read as "books" and not just anthologies comprising loosely connected units? While this question is far too complex to be dealt with thoroughly in the space constraint of a single contribution, I will attempt, nevertheless, to offer some insight into the issue for future research. For this reason, I will limit myself mainly to methodological questions, bringing forth only a small number of examples of textual analyses.

I will first sketch an answer to the basic question: is it possible to compare the literary shapes of the Psalter and the Twelve? More specifically: is it possible to identify similar literary features in both books? The background of this question is the formation of "anthologies" or "collections" in the Second Temple period, or the scribal and editorial habits prevalent in this period.[10] Since a full-scale comparative work involving the Psalter and the Twelve is yet to be done, I will limit myself to some fundamental observations. Secondly, I will compare the development of scholarship surrounding the Psalter and the Twelve. In fact, it is important to reconstruct how scholars worked out the raw data taken up from the analysis of the text and how they methodologically framed them. Since I tried to offer elsewhere a thorough reconstruction of the modern canonical reading of the Psalter,[11] I will devote more attention to the development of the study of the Twelve as a book here.

In the final paragraph, I will attempt to summarize the data that have come to light in the analysis and draw some preliminary conclusions and suggestions for future research.

1. Comparing the *Text* of the Psalter and the Twelve

The first part of my analysis is a preliminary comparison between the *text* of the Psalter and that of the Twelve. This comparison aims to highlight similarities and differences between the literary shape of each book, namely, similarities and differences in the way both texts are arranged

---

10. In other words, the issue addressed here is whether it is possible to compare the "literary structure" of the Psalter and the Twelve. Such a comparison can pinpoint the basic assumption that they were both edited as "books."

11. Pavan, "Psalter," 11–82.

with regard to their form, content, and other literary devices.[12] Such a comparison should highlight if similar editorial techniques were at work during the redactional process of both books, or if similar literary phenomena in the final forms of both collections can be detected. The focus on the editorial techniques should also account for a comparison of the two books with redactional histories under different contexts, which will be distinct in many ways.[13]

A comprehensive comparison of the two books is the first step to establishing a firm ground for the discussion about the editorial work responsible for the formation of both books. It offers the raw data for evaluating the possibility of distinct editorial processes carried out by different *Trägerkreise* but, at the same time, accomplished using a *common stock* of editorial techniques. In the final analysis, such a comparison can also be considered an "extension" of the methods implemented in reading the Psalter and the Twelve as books.[14]

Differences

At first sight, the differences concerning the literary shape between the Psalter and the Twelve outnumber their similarities. In general, such differences may be summarized as follows:

1. **Oracles vs. Poems.** The writings contained in the Book of the Twelve are organized as collections of *oracles*, whose editorial process can be aptly described as collecting, reworking, and editing of small literary units into more complex and larger "books."[15] The Psalter, instead, was most likely edited from independent *poems*,

---

12. A comparison between the Psalter and the Twelve should be made, in the first instance, only on the basis of the literary shape of the two books. This essentially means focusing on the literary devices the editor(s) used to shape their own books. Such devices include superscriptions, lexemic links, shared themes, etc.

13. The Psalter and the Twelve are apparently to be ascribed to different traditions and *Trägerkreise* and, therefore, it does not seem legitimate to compare them in a simplistic way.

14. In other words, comparing the Psalter and the Twelve is a task with the goal of identifying some shared literary features, which the interpreter could track, and they will be attributed to the common *editorial processes* undertaken behind the two books.

15. Krispenz, *Scribes*.

reworked, and selected from a larger *corpus* of the First and Second Temple psalmody.[16]

2. **Prophecy vs. Liturgy.** The Twelve are usually ascribed to the "genre" of the *prophetic book*, whose purpose[17] and editorial history are clearly distinguished from that of the Psalter, which was probably formulated as a *liturgical book* or, at least, as a support for *meditation*.[18] This is true even if we consider the possible parallels between Psalms and Isaiah and, in general, the blending of the boundaries between *prophetic* and *liturgical* in some passages.[19]

3. **Historical References.** The writings contained in the Book of the Twelve give the reader a good number of "historical" references (i.e., names of places, peoples, historical characters, etc.). Such references may play a role in the overall organization of the book.[20] In the Psalter, instead, historical references are scanty and scattered. This difference could be rooted in the overall distinction between prophecy and cult, the first being a mode of speech "rooted" in history, whereas the second is, to some extent, "timeless."

4. **Superscriptions.** Because of what has just been highlighted, the *shape* of the superscriptions in both books generally overlap but are also different. In the Twelve, the titles of the individual writings give the reader pieces of information about the individual books (author, genre, historical situation, etc.); Psalms' superscriptions contain similar information but with a different value.[21]

5. **Textual Units.** Finally, a substantial difference can be detected also in considering the *individual* units of both books. The Twelve was edited as a collection of *books*, each bearing the name of its "author" and information about time and place of origin, whereas the Psalter was conceived as a collection of individual shorter *poems*.

Overall, the major distinction between the Twelve and the Psalter is rooted in their different "macro-genres." The Twelve can be conceived

16. Leuenberger, *Konzeptionen*, 1–68.
17. Ben Zvi, "Key Form," 276–97; "Concept," 73–95.
18. Cf. the paragraph on "The Psalter as Book" below.
19. Tuell, "Psalm," 262–74.
20. Compare the analysis of the superscriptions below.
21. See also Wilson, "Use," 404–13; Culley, "David," 153–62; Nihan, "David," 193–208.

as a prophetic collection or, at least, as part of the more general "prophetic literature," while the Psalter is the product of liturgy and other influences. At first sight, therefore, it seems reasonable to distinguish the two books and avoid the risk of "leveling" the differences for the sake of finding arguments on behalf of the canonical reading. However, despite the above differences, it is possible to detect similar literary phenomena, such as: lexemic links, superscriptions, sequences, and special formulas. Detecting similar literary elements in both collections stirs the reader to identify, classify, and evaluate if such elements could be ascribed to a specific kind of editorial work.

Shared Features

At first glance, the Psalter and the Twelve share an important common feature. They can both be read as collections of independent literary pieces and as a "macro-composition," having an overall structure and message.[22] This feature can be considered the strongest shared trait between the two books and the most controversial one at the same time—the *crux* of the methodological approaches as adopted by scholars of the two fields. From this point of view, it is possible to detect both macrostructural (e.g., superscriptions)[23] and microstructural (e.g., lexemic links) devices in both books.[24]

Superscriptions are widely recognized as a macrostructural marker in Psalter scholarship,[25] as clear superscription distribution trends indicate micro-collections (or subgroups) of psalms within the larger framework of the individual "books."[26] This is, above all, true with regard to Psalms 3–89 and their inner composition, even if superscriptions are also present to some extent in Psalms 90–150:

---

22. Seitz, "Unique," 37–48.

23. In this context, the issue of sequence should be mentioned. Sequence is one of the key issues in contemporary Psalms scholarship, mainly because of the Qumran debate. Sequence also plays an important role in the scholarship of the Twelve. See Ayars's chapter in this volume for more details on sequences of psalms collections at Qumran.

24. Pavan, "Psalter," 26–35.

25. In Psalms scholarship, Wilson must be credited as among the first to have highlighted the macrostructural function of superscripts.

26. In Psalms scholarship, the five "books" division is the major structural divide created by the so-called "doxologies"; cf. Leuenberger, "Psalterdoxologien," 166–93.

1. Books I–II (Pss 3–72) are mainly marked by the phrase לדוד in superscriptions and the inner articulation is created by the interplay of לדוד and "genre" information.

2. In the same vein, Book III (Pss 73–89) is marked mainly by the phrases לאסף and לבני קרח in superscriptions.[27]

3. Books IV (Pss 90–106) and V (Pss 107–150) are characterized only in a limited way by superscriptions: לדוד (Pss 108–110; 101; 103; 138–145);[28] שיר המעלות (Pss 120–134).[29]

According to some scholars, superscriptions are the most important organizing principle of the Psalter and an important clue to its process of formation.[30] However, the macrostructural function of superscription has recently been challenged on different grounds.[31]

In the scholarship of the Twelve, superscriptions are considered by some scholars to be a macrostructural marker, even if in a limited way.[32] All twelve books contain a title and has formulaic language that highlights some specific features of the individual writings:[33]

1. Most of the writings are introduced by the דבר-formula[34] while others are characterized as חזון (Obad 1; cf. Nah 1:1) or משא (Nah 1:1; Hab 1:1; cf. Zech 9:1; 12:1; Mal 1:1). See also תפלה (Hab 3:1).

2. Historical references are given in Hos 1:1; Amos 1:1; Mic 1:1; Zeph 1:1; Hag 1:1; Zech 1:1 (cf. Nah 1:1).[35]

3. Roughly speaking, the sequence of books and superscriptions reveals a linear, chronological pattern, from pre-exilic (cf. Hos 1:1; Amos 1:1; Nah 1:1; cf. Jonah) to post-exilic (Hag 1:1; Zech 1:1) times.

---

27. In Pss 84–89, however, the situation of superscripts is somewhat complex and enigmatic. See Pavan, *"He Remembered."*

28. The phrase לדוד is also present in Pss 122:1; 124:1; 131:1; 133:1; cf. 132:1, 11, 17.

29. Consider the framing function of הללו יה in Pss 106–150.

30. See, for example, Wilson, *Editing.*

31. See, for example, Willgren, *Formation.*

32. Watts, "Superscriptions," 110–24.

33. According to Watts, "Superscriptions," 112, only three of the writings of the Twelve bear no superscription: Jonah, Haggai, and Zechariah.

34. Hos 1:1; Joel 1:1; Amos 1:1; Mic 1:1; Zeph 1:1; Hag 1:1; Zech 1:1; cf. Mal 3:1. The specific formula, דבר יהוה אשר היה is used in Hos 1:1; Joel 1:1; Mic 1:1; Zeph 1:1; Zech 1:1 (cf. Jonah 1:1; Mal 1:1).

35. See also the references in Jonah.

Some books have up to "three separate superscriptions piled on top of each other."[36] The form of the title reveals, according to Watts, different compositional layers and, therefore, different stages of the redactional process of the Twelve.[37] Six superscriptions provide the chronological framework to the Twelve (Hosea; Amos; Micah; Zephaniah; Haggai; Zechariah) and are arranged in chronological order.[38] In Hosea 1:1, Amos 1:1, Micah 1:1, and Zephaniah 1:1, the chronological framework is established through the mention of the kings and the kingdoms of the eighth to seventh century BCE.[39] Haggai and Zechariah contain a different presentation of chronological data. All in all, the chronological framework created by the six above-mentioned superscriptions reveals how the historical perspective was deemed by the editors of the Twelve an essential pattern.

The phrase משא דבר יהוה in Zechariah 9:1, 12:1, and Malachi 1:1 plays a significant role in the Twelve.[40] Nogalski highlights how such a phrase introduces oracles related to Ephraim and Judah (Zech 9–11), Judah and Jerusalem (Zech 12–14), and the post-exilic community (Mal 3:16–18). The other superscriptions are more difficult to evaluate. Superscriptions are mainly considered by some scholars only as *distinctive markers*, meant to demarcate individual writings.[41] Nevertheless, their formulaic language and arrangement may reflect some kind of editorial work. From this point of view, the superscriptions of the Psalms and the Twelve may be compared, despite their differences.

The main microstructural devices are the so-called "lexemic links," which is the use of individual lexemes or key phrases to create special links between the individual units of the book. In Psalms scholarship, one of the first to acknowledge this phenomenon and its possible editorial function was F. J. Delitzsch.[42] He defined the "law of analogy" and "law of the internal homogeneity" as the criteria used by the editor(s) of the Psalter to organize sequences of Psalms.[43] Delitzsch specifically highlighted how the lexemic links create sequences of adjacent poems and,

---

36. Watts, "Superscriptions," 112–13.
37. Watts, "Superscriptions," 113–17.
38. Nogalski, "Intertextuality," 119.
39. Nogalski, "Intertextuality," 119–20.
40. The phrase appears only here in the OT canon.
41. Ben Zvi, "Twelve Hypothesis," 64–72.
42. See Delitzsch, *Symbolae*.
43. Delitzsch, *Symbolae*, 45.

therefore, how they affect the entire structure of the Psalter.⁴⁴ Delitzsch's emphasis on the "lex analogie" is rooted in the rabbinic principle of the סמיכות and, in general, in the idea that a kind of Midrashic process governed the redaction of the Psalter.⁴⁵

Delitzsch's view on the matter was taken up almost a century later by C. Barth. In 1976, Barth wrote a thorough analysis of a specific form of lexemic links which he named "concatenatio" (*Verkettung*).⁴⁶ He lists seventeen different forms of *concatenatio* by detecting all the lexemic links between adjacent and non-adjacent psalms. In the same year, J. P. Brennan highlighted the targeted and intentional repetition of keywords and phrases within Psalms 1–8. He named the main organizing principle of the Psalter "juxtapositio," that is, the juxtaposing of psalms that share common lexemes, formulas, expressions, etc. It is worth noting that, according to Brennan, the lexemic links allow a fresh insight into the mind of editor(s) of the book and their way of interpreting older material in a different context.⁴⁷

After the publication of the monograph of G. H. Wilson in 1985, much work has been devoted to the study of lexemic links between adjacent and non-adjacent psalms.⁴⁸ Even though some scholars have strongly objected to the results and the methodological premises of this approach,⁴⁹ there is a consensus about the existence, at least in a limited way, of intertextual links between adjacent or even non-adjacent psalms.

Mainly based on the influence of Nogalski's works, in the 1990s, the method of *catchwords* became crucial in the scholarship of the Twelve. The US scholar, in fact, should be credited for the major development of this methodological approach.⁵⁰ Nogalski detects several catchwords that "seam" together the different writings of the Twelve. The examples he brings into the discussion include Hosea 14:5–10 and Joel 1:1–12; Joel 4:16 and Amos 1:2; Amos 9:12 and Obadiah 1–9; Jonah 4:2, Micah 7:18–19 and Nahum 1:2–3; Nahum 1:1 and Habakkuk 1:1; and

---

44. Delitzsch distinguishes between *Echopsalmen*, *Constrastpsalmen* and *Fortschrittpsalmen*. See Delitzsch, *Symbolae*, 70.

45. See also an overview in Pavan, "Psalter," 14–18.

46. Barth resumed insights from Delitzsch, *Symbolae*, and ancient rhetoric. The name *concatenatio* derives from ancient rhetoric. Barth, "Concatenatio," 30–32.

47. Brennan, "Hidden Harmonies," 126–58.

48. Pavan, "Psalter," 31–32.

49. Brodersen, *End*.

50. Nogalski, "Intertextuality."

Habakkuk 2:20 and Zephaniah 1:7. The debate on the Twelve focused on the methodological issues involved in the search for catchwords. In this respect, the competing views of Nogalski and E. Ben Zvi reflect the two different stances on the issue.[51]

Part of the discourse on catchwords and *Stichwörter* is the study of thematic threads within the Twelve, a methodological option that seemed more suitable to some authors than Nogalski.[52] In fact, such thematic threads are mainly detectable through the repetition of keywords and phrases, together with images and, more generally, "content."[53] In some cases, it seems significant that special phrases (e.g., "the Day of the Lord," יום יהוה) play a specific function within the Twelve as a whole.[54] The criticism notwithstanding, in general, it is possible to say that lexemes of phrases are the literary tools used by the editors of both books, even if in a limited way.

A further shared point between the Twelve and the Psalter is the intertextual links to common "reference" texts. This is the case, for example, in Exodus 34:6–7, which is tagged as a significant "intertext" both for the Psalter[55] and the Twelve.[56] Moreover, the book of Isaiah seems to have had a significant influence on the Psalter[57] and the Twelve alike.[58] Finally, possible parallels between Habakkuk 3 and the Psalter can be mentioned here.[59]

2. Comparing Scholarship: The Psalter and the Twelve

The raw data mentioned above were, in different ways, recognized by scholars working in the two fields of study, but they were also understood within somewhat different methodological frameworks. This section,

---

51. See below.
52. See LeCureux, *Thematic*.
53. LeCureux, *Thematic*, 24–31.
54. Goldingay, "Twelve," 171–91.
55. Coniglio, "Gracious," 29–50.
56. Leeuwen, "Scribal," 31–49. See also Bosman, "Paradoxical," 233–43. Exodus 34:6–7 is quoted or alluded to in Hos 1:6, Joel 2:13, Jonah 4:2, Mic 7:18–20; Nah 1:3.
57. Clements, "Psalm 72," 333–41; Lyons, "Psalm 22," 640–56; Berges, "Singt," 11–33.
58. Bosshard-Nepustil, *Rezeptionen*.
59. Flitz, *Gott*.

then, presents a comparison of the development of the canonical approach in the studies of the Psalter and the Twelve, while also shedding light on the key methodological issues involved. As noted, both fields of research developed independently. However, it is possible to detect multiple points of contact and mutual influences. In the following, I will summarize my study of the history of the canonical approach of the Psalter and focus mainly on the study of the Twelve.[60]

The Psalter as a "Book"

The prehistory of the canonical exegesis of the Psalter begins with the already-mentioned work of Delitzsch, which should be credited as the first to highlight the structural function of lexemic links for the entire Psalter.[61] This perspective was taken up more or less one century later by C. Barth and J. P. Brennan, two authors who identified the often-quoted techniques of *concatenatio* and *juxtapositio*, both of which are connected in different ways to the phenomenon of *lexemic links*.[62]

Conventionally, the beginning of the canonical exegesis of the Psalter is credited to the already-mentioned monograph of Wilson.[63] Following the premises of Childs's canonical approach,[64] Wilson set out to describe the final form of the MT Psalter, operating on the hypothesis that the arrangement of the psalms is both meaningful and deliberate. The North American author aims to demonstrate this hypothesis first by comparing the MT Psalter to ANE material (i.e., Sumerian Temple Hymns and Catalogues of Hymnic Incipit) and to psalms collections at Qumran.[65] Then he identifies in the MT Psalter certain markers that possibly reveal the editorial program behind the arrangement of the book. He writes, "The passage from *literary form* to *editorial intention* allows [one] to identify the *global message* (*synchrony*) and, to some extent, the *formation* process of the

---

60. See Pavan, "Psalter."
61. Mitchell, *Message*, 46–49; Auwers, *Composition*, 22–26. See above.
62. Niemeyer, *Het probleem*, 7–56.
63. For a full treatment of Wilson's methodological stance, see Pavan, "Psalter," 27–32.
64. On the relationships between Childs's and Wilson's approaches, see Nasuti, "Editing," 13–20.
65. Wilson, *Editing*, 25–138. The comparative overview of Wilson is deemed to be "an incontrovertible historical argument for recognizing this canonical shape [i.e., of the Psalter]" (Jacobson, "Imagining," 234).

book (*diachrony*)."⁶⁶ Wilson focuses his attention on the macro indicators such as superscriptions, postscripts, doxologies, and specific key phrases (הללויה; הודו).⁶⁷ Consequently, he ascribes only a secondary function to lexemic links.⁶⁸ Wilson's reading of the Psalter is linear. He also posits that the book's purpose is meditation rather than performance.⁶⁹

Methodologically, Wilson's work suffers from a "tension" between *synchronic* and *diachronic* approaches. In fact, it is possible to detect a complex and not easily solved interrelation between the study of the *shape* of the MT Psalter and the attempt at reconstructing its *shaping*.⁷⁰ At the same time, Wilson shifts the main focus of the analysis of the book of Psalms from micro indicators to macro indicators, raising the question regarding the hierarchy of the structural markers of the book.⁷¹ In any case, Wilson's work set the stage for subsequent research on the final form of the MT Psalter and the study of its formation.

Among the numerous "canonical" studies devoted to the Psalms, the works of the German scholars E. Zenger and F.-L. Hossfeld are considered standard reference in Psalms studies.⁷² Zenger and Hossfeld root their analysis of the Psalter in the same perspective as Wilson's, namely, the hypothesis that the Psalter is "a book structured according to clear redactional and compositional criteria" and, therefore, "it has to be read and heard *also* as a book."⁷³ The two German scholars, however, take a different stance on the *starting point* of the "canonical" analysis of the Psalter. They specifically concentrate on micro-level indicators, analyze lexemic connections between consecutive psalms (*concatenatio*), and more broadly, examine the arrangement of similar psalms placed next to each other (*juxtapositio*). Macro indicators such as superscriptions and

---

66. Pavan, "Psalter," 28.

67. Wilson, *Editing*, 193–98.

68. Wilson, *Editing*, 194–97. See also Wilson, "Understanding," 42–51; "King," 391–406.

69. "In its 'final form' the Psalter is a book to be *read* rather than to be *performed*; to be *meditated over* than to be *recited from*" (Wilson, *Editing*, 207).

70. Pavan, "Psalter," 29–30.

71. A detailed review of the issue may be found in Ho, *Design*, 35–40.

72. See Pavan, "Psalter," 32–38, for further references.

73. Zenger, "Dai Salmi," 155–57 (our translation from Italian). Moreover, "the book [has to be] read according to the *lectio currens* . . . that is as a continuous text, . . . as a well-structured whole" (189; our translation).

doxologies are secondary to the research of the intention and literary tools developed by the editors of the book.[74]

At the same time, Zenger and Hossfeld take a different approach to the complex interplay between synchronic and diachronic analyses. In fact, they develop a "synchronic, diachronically reflected reading of the Psalter," in which "the attention to the final form of the text does not exclude, but rather requires the analysis of the editorial process of the text."[75] The two authors try to avoid a simplistic approach that levels all the differences[76] and overemphasizes the synchronic dimensions of the text.[77] Zenger and Hossfeld, therefore, propose a detailed redactional model in which the process of adapting a preexisting psalm to fit the literary context of the Psalter plays a significant role.[78] From this point of view, "the additions that can possibly be found in the Psalms are ... signs of the editorial activity of the formation of the *Psalter*."[79]

Wilson's works, on one hand, and Zenger and Hossfeld's, on the other, can be considered two of the most representative orientations of the canonical exegesis of the Psalter.[80] The redactional models and the methodological premises of these authors, however, were recently challenged by some on various grounds.

The starting point of contemporary criticism is the somewhat complex picture of the textual history of the Psalter, especially when one considers the so-called "Psalms scrolls" found at Qumran and other sites of the Judean Desert (see Ho's chapter 2 in this volume). To some the codicological variations of Psalms manuscripts calls for

---

74. Zenger, "Dai Salmi," 178. See also the criticism of Millard, *Komposition*, 315–17.

75. "Es geht also um eine diachron reflektierte synchrone Lektüre der Texte, die deren gegebenfalls komplexe Textwerdung als gerade im Endtext zu entdeckende Multiperspektivität wahrnehmen und theologisch auslegen will" (Zenger, "Psalmenexegese," 244). See also Hartenstein, "Schaffe," 235.

76. Hossfeld and Zenger, "Neue," 332.

77. In this sense, "die diachrone Fragestellung sowohl heuristische wie kritische Funktion gegen eine exzessive Synchronlektüre hat" (Zenger, "Psalmenexegese," 248).

78. Zenger, "Psalmenexegese," 247. Elsewhere, he notes, "Es kommt bei der Psalmenexegese darauf an, sowohl das Eigenprofil der einzelnen Psalmen als auch die Einbindung dieser Psalmen in ihrem unmittelbaren und weiteren Buchkontext zu reflektieren. Die Alternative Einzellieder bzw. Einzelgebete oder Buchzusammenhang ist eine falsche Alternative" (Zenger, "Psalmenforschung," 430).

79. Pavan, "Psalter," 37.

80. Moore, "Review of A. Brodersen," 520.

a more adequate conceptual framework to describe and evaluate the editorial formation of the Psalter.[81]

Around three hundred fragments of psalms have been found at Qumran and in other sites of the Judean Desert, belonging to 39–41 scrolls and dated between the second century BCE to the first century CE. Because of the degree of deterioration, the fragments range from a few words to much more extensive text, such as 11Q5. The scrolls are characterized by a great variety of formats, layouts, and configurations. Scholars are mainly focused on the *text* witnessed in the fragments and in the *sequences* in which the psalms are arranged, where they can be reliably reconstructed.

The debate originally centered around the so-called "Qumran Psalter Hypothesis."[82] After the completion of the official edition of the psalms fragments in 2000,[83] there was a need to revise the common theories and develop a new interpretation of the psalms fragments, based more on textual and codicological data. A. Lange reclassifies the reconstructed scrolls as "Psalms-collections" (*Psalmen-Sammlungen*) and categorizes them[84] as proto-MT,[85] 11Q5-type,[86] 4Q88-type, 4Q83 and 4Q98-type, 4Q84-type, and 4Q92-type.[87] Furthermore, he highlights the fragmented nature of the findings and the ambiguity surrounding the original purpose of the scrolls. E. Jain moves a step further, highlighting the almost exclusive research focus of 11Q5 and the fact that a considerable number of manuscripts cannot be reconstructed, nor defined in terms of global

---

81. For a preliminary overview of the issue, see Pavan, "Psalter," 31–59. The fragments of the Judean Desert can be considered a snapshot of the process of tradition and probably also of the formation of the Psalter. Brütsch, *Israels Psalmen*; Fabry, "Der Beitrag Qumrans," 429–50.

82. This hypothesis has been worked mainly out by Flint, *Psalms Scrolls*, 237–40. Flint assumes that the Psalter gradually stabilized out of a "fluid" phase. Before the general acceptance of the MT as *textus receptus*, "two or more Psalter are represented among the scrolls of the Judean Desert" (Flint, *Psalms Scrolls*, 239). 11Q5, which contains the latter part of a "true scriptural Psalter" (Flint, *Psalms Scrolls*, 240), in particular, may be considered the "Qumran Psalter," an alternative and competing *edition* of the book of Psalms. For the criticism of Flint's position, see Pavan, "Psalter," 22–23.

83. The year 2000 was when the second volume of Hossfeld and Zenger's commentary (*Psalmen*) and Auwers's monograph (*Psautier*) were published.

84. Lange, *Handbuch*, 418–20.

85. Mas1f and probably 4Q85 (until Ps 53), Mas1e, 5/6Ḥev1b. See also 11Q7.

86. 4Q87, 11Q6, cf. 4Q95.

87. Lange, *Handbuch*, 419–20 rightfully notes that only the following manuscripts could originally contain a quantity of psalms comparable to that of the MT: 4Q98a, Mas1f, 4Q98b, 11Q7, 4Q83, 4Q85, Mas1e, 4Q98, 8Q2, 5/6Ḥev1b, 11Q5, 4Q88.

content, purpose, and function.⁸⁸ Jain argues that it is challenging to determine whether the fragments belonged to scrolls exclusively containing psalms. Consequently, in some cases, it is impossible to ascertain whether the scroll in question aligned with the proto-Masoretic Psalter.⁸⁹ Lastly, the fragmentary state of the findings also implies that the textual variations and the internal relationships between the various manuscripts cannot be adequately explained.

Willgren resumes previous studies on the psalms fragments at Qumran and pays more attention to their chronological arrangement and the sequences they attest.⁹⁰ He then categorizes at least six different arrangements of Psalms sequences and locates the sequences that disagree with the MT around Pss 103–106 (109), 118–119 and 133–150,⁹¹ that is, Davidic psalms or psalms that are framed by הללויה. Willgren, based on his analysis of the Qumran psalms fragments, offers a comprehensive critique of the Qumran Psalter Hypothesis. He emphasizes the fluidity of the psalms' sequences between the second century BCE and the first century CE and dismisses the notion of "multiple" or "competing" editions of the Psalter. The general impression is that individual psalms are arranged in varying orders, often "more or less randomly,"⁹² to create collections. Willgren refers to the result of this process of selection and compilation as an "anthology."

Overall, the primary insight gained from a renewed examination of the Psalter's textual history, according to proponents of the "new" critique of the canonical approach, is the recognition that the redactional focus was not on the book itself—an anachronistic concept—but rather on groups or (micro) collections of psalms, assembled based on various criteria or even randomly.⁹³ This is why no "canonical" or "fixed

---

88. In this group, Jain includes fifteen scrolls: 1Q10, 1Q12, 2Q14, 3Q2, 4Q91, 4Q96, 4Q97, 4Q98b, 4Q98c, 4Q98d, 4Q98e, 4Q98f, 4Q98g, 6Q5, 8Q2. 4Q89 only included Ps 119. Jain, *Psalmen*. At the same time, the author highlights how, in the fragments published in Pinke, Skinner, *Qumran Cave*, there are at least twenty nine scrolls that likely included psalms.

89. For these and the following observations, see Jain, *Psalmen*, 221–98. The fragments taken into consideration are only partially representative of the situation of the psalms in the "libraries" of the Judean Desert.

90. Lange, *Handbuch*, 411–39. Within the "Psalms" scrolls have also been identified sixteen compositions that have been wrongly labelled as "apocryphal." See remarks in Pajunen, "Differentiation," 264–76. See also Flint, *Psalms Scrolls*, 243–51.

91. Willgren, *Formation*, 111.

92. Lange, "Collecting," 297–308. See also Lange, *Handbuch*, 434–36.

93. Willgren, *Formation*, 37–82.

sequence" ever existed before the stabilization of the MT Psalter.[94] In this context, Wilson's macrostructural markers have to be reframed as *paratexts*, that is, as help to the reader or loose markers that can be conceived as suggestions of *trajectories of use*.[95] Similarly, the question of lexemic links is reconsidered within the broader discussion of intertextuality, focusing on the specific criteria by which readers or interpreters can discern intentional lexemic connections between different psalms, whether adjacent or non-adjacent.[96]

The second outcome of a renewed consideration of ancient textual witnesses of the Psalter is the "displacement" of the MT Psalter as a point of reference of the research.[97] Wilson, along with Zenger and Hossfeld, took the MT as the basis of their analysis, while the evidence offered especially by Qumran findings points to a more fluid and complex picture.[98] Since no canonical Psalter sequence existed before the first century CE, the MT has to be considered a *textus receptus*, a somewhat random outcome of the process of transmission of the Psalter that—at a certain point in time—was welcomed by some communities of faith as "their" Psalter so that all competing or alternative sequences were just superseded.[99]

The Twelve as a "Book"

The study of the Twelve as a book can be conceived mainly as a progressive evolution of methodological understanding.[100] From this point of view, we may distinguish at least three major phases in Twelve

---

94. Yarchin, "Authoritative," 355–70; "Collections," 775–89; cf. Davage, "Canon," 196–205.

95. Willgren, *Formation*, 30–33. On this term, see Genette, *Seuils*, 5–6.

96. Brodersen, *End*. The author refers specifically to *diachronic intertextuality*, "the search for links that an author has intentionally created between the text for which he is responsible and others, written or otherwise, which are available to him" (Pavan, "Psalter," 58).

97. Willgren, *Formation*, 116–30; Brodersen, *End*, 18–21.

98. Pavan, "Psalter," 55–57.

99. Pajunen, "Perspectives," 139–63.

100. General overviews: Kaiser, "Dodekapropheton," 103–7; Kessler, "Twelve," 207–23; O'Brien, *Handbook*, xix–xxix; Stovell and Fuller, *Twelve*. See also Schart, "Reconstructing," 34–48; Redditt, "Research," 47–80; "Formation," 1–26; Scaiola, "Dodici," 65–75; Schmid, "Zwölfprophetenbuch," 363–65; Schart, "Section," 138–52; DiPede and Scaiola, *Book*; Nicol, "Research"; Firth and Melton, "Reading." See also Jeremias, "Tendenzen," 122–36.

scholarship, each corresponding to an advance in the organization and systematization of methodological issues: (a) ancient witnesses to the unity of the Twelve, (b) nineteenth- to twentieth-century "precursors" to the contemporary debate, and (c) scholarship after Nogalski's 1993 monographs.[101] In this context, of course, advancement in methodological awareness refers to the works of clarification of basic terms or ideas (e.g., "book," "anthology," "writing," etc.) and the development of exegetical tools. This process goes along with the gathering of essential data, such as catchwords, analysis of superscriptions, etc.

The earliest mention of "the Twelve" can be found in Sir 49:10:[102]

> And let the bones of the Twelve prophets [καὶ τῶν δώδεκα προφητῶν τὰ ὀστᾶ] sprout anew from their place because they comforted Jacob and they ransomed him in the faith of hope [ἐν πίστει ἐλπίδος].

The mention of the twelve prophets as a group is interpreted by Nogalski and others[103] as evidence of the unity of the "Book" of the Twelve. It is, however, unclear if the passage refers to the *texts* of the Twelve or the *person* of the twelve prophets.[104] According to Nogalski, the Jewish tradition that influenced the text of Ben Sira is also present in other sources. For example, Jerome clearly states that the Twelve is one book, that there are two orders of the prophets (MT and LXX), and that the prophets that are not dated are to be assigned to the same period as the last previously dated prophet:[105]

---

101. Sweeney, "Minor Prophets," 267–78.

102. According to LeCureux, ancient witnesses provide "a historical foundation for a unified approach" to the Twelve (LeCureux, *Thematic*, 4). See also Sieges, "One Book," 29–38. The importance of the "historical" data offered by ancient witnesses is underscored also by Nogalski, "Intertextuality," 120.

103. Nogalski goes as far as to state that "ancient traditions irrefutably establish that the writings of the twelve prophets were copied onto a single scroll and counted as a single book from at least 200 BCE" (Nogalski, "Intertextuality," 120).

104. Petersen, "Book," 3–4; Guillaume, "Reconsideration," 10, considers this witness "insufficient."

105. Klinger, "Skylla," 5–22. In the Latin tradition, Augustine is credited for the designation "Minor Prophets," a designation that is based on the mere length of the works. "The twelve prophets . . . are called the minor from the brevity of their writings, as compared with those who are called the greater prophets" ["(Isaias propheta non est) in libro duodecim Prophetarum, qui propterea dicuntur minores, quia sermones eorum sunt breves, in eorum comparatione, qui maiores ideo vocantur"] (*Civ* 18:29; *PL* 41, 585).

> The order of the Twelve prophets is not the same among the Jews as it is among us.... I would only you were warned this, o Paula and Eustochium: the book of the Twelve prophets to be one.... And those [books] in which the time is not set down in the title, under those kings which they were to have prophesied under, they also prophesied after those which have titles.[106]

Another often-quoted Jewish source is b. B. Bat. 13b–15a, a rather complex Talmudic passage that deals with scribal practices.[107] The starting point of the discussion is the issue of copying the different parts of Hebrew Bible in one or different scrolls. At a certain point, the Gem. states:

> When different books are included in the scroll, four empty lines of space should be left between each book of the Torah, and similarly between one book of the Prophets and another. But between each of the books of the Twelve prophets only three empty lines should be left [ובנביא של שנים עשר שלש שיטין].[108]

The difference between the general rule of placing four blank lines between different books copied in a single scroll and the special case of the books of the Minor Prophets is often interpreted as an allusion to the special status of the Twelve.[109] A discussion then arises about the special status of Hosea that it should be considered the first prophet of the pre-exilic period and part of the Book of the Twelve. Moreover, it cannot be separated from the Twelve, as the Talmud states,[110] "Let the

---

106. "Prologus duodecim prophetarum; non idem est duodecim prophetarum apud hebraeos qui et apud nos ... et quia longum est nunc de omnibus dicere, hoc tantum uos, o paula et eustochium, admonitas uolo unum librum esse duodecim prophetarum ... in quibus autem tempus non praefertur in titulo sub illis eos regibus prophetasse sub quibus et hii qui ante eos habent titulos prophetauerun" (Jérôme, *Préfaces*, 468–69). See also the famous statement in *Ep.* 53, where Jerome seems to the consider the Twelve as a single book: "[My commentary on the] Twelve prophets was crammed in the limits of one volume" ["duodecim prophetae in unius uoluminis angustias coartati"] (*PL* 22, 547). Mileto of Sardis refers to the Minor Prophets as "the Twelve in one Book" (τῶν δώδεκα ἐν μονοβίβλῳ). *HE* IV, 26, 14: cf. Eusèbe, *Histoire*, 211.

107. For the text of the Talmudic passage, see Even-Israel Steinsaltz, *Bava Batra*, 74–83.

108. b. B. Bat. 13b.

109. Nogalski, *Literary*, 2. The denomination "the Twelve" is further mentioned in B. Bat. 14b and 15a (שנים עשר).

110. b. B. Bat. 14a. Lee, "Canonical Unity," 3, observes that "the book of Hosea is larger than either Ruth or Ecclesiastes, the latter two being handed down as individual works. Moreover, the Megilloth are never deemed as one book as the XII are."

book of Hosea be written separately and let it precede the others. [But] were it written separately, since it is small it would be lost" (וליכתביה לחודיה וליקדמיה איידי דזוטר מירכס: b. B. Bat. 14b).[111]

The Talmudic test reflects specific scribal practices, already attested, according to some authors, in 4QXII^b and Mur XII and GreekXII.[112] The rabbinic tradition witnessed in b. B. Bat. 13b–15a can be identified also in the manuscript of Masoretic tradition. For example, in *Codex Leningradensis* the count of verses at the end of Malachi indicates Micah 3:12 as the center of the single Book of the Twelve.[113]

In later Jewish tradition, Isaac Abravanel or Abarbanel (1437–1508/9) is probably the strongest supporter of the idea of the unity of the Twelve.[114] He especially considers the chronological arrangement of the writings and tries to justify the somewhat odd placement of Obadiah.[115] He also considers, in a limited way, catchwords and cross-references, and is probably the first to have analyzed catchwords in the Twelve.[116] According to him, the Twelve were collected because they were too small to stand alone.

Some of the ancient Jewish and Christian witnesses, therefore, seem to suggest that the Twelve were read and interpreted as a single book at the beginning of both traditions.[117] This suggestion, however, has been questioned based on a different reading of the sources and a renewed analysis of the Dead Sea Scolls.[118]

In modern scholarship,[119] the idea of the unity of the Twelve gained gradual consensus among scholars from the 1970s.[120] This idea

111. Josephus, *C. Ap.* 1:8, mentions the twenty-two-book canon, a number that involves apparently the Twelve being counted as one book. See also 2 Esd 14:45 and Ego, "Repentance," 155–64.

112. Petersen, "Book," 4–5.

113. Nogalski and Sweeney, *Reading and Hearing*, ix.

114. Lawee, *Abarbanel's Stance*, 9–58; cf. Abarbanel, *Pîrûfsh*.

115. Nogalski, *Literary*, 2–3. In his commentary he considers the order of the Twelve and highlights the *chronological* arrangement of the writings. Obadiah is the oldest, but he was not the first because he was a proselyte. Joel and Amos both quote Obadiah, thus, Obadiah is appended to the first generation of prophets within the Twelve.

116. According to Schneider, "Unity," Abravanel should be credited for being the first to analyze catchwords in the Twelve.

117. Nogalski, "Intertextuality," 120.

118. See below.

119. Sweeney, "Minor Prophets," 267–78.

120. Nevertheless, House states, "Most note that the twelve prophecies have long been considered one book" (House, *Unity*, 9).

was especially fostered by the shift that occurred in Europe and North America from the study of the prophets as historical figures to their *texts* as products of complex editorial activity.[121] This shift can be represented as a two-step process below.

Roughly from Wellhausen to the beginning of the 1970s, the dominance of historical-critical approaches and the focus on the person of the prophet apparently discouraged scholars from considering the idea of the unity of the Twelve or, more generally, studying the prophetic corpus as a literary product. Nevertheless, in pre-1970s scholarship, some occasional or scattered observations on the unity of the Twelve may be found.[122]

J. G. Eichhorn in his *Einleitung in das Alte Testament* briefly mentions that the Twelve were considered a single book by ancient sources.[123] G. H. A. Ewald goes further and tries to reconstruct the process by which the *Book* of the Twelve was shaped.[124] According to Schneider, it is "the first attempt [in modern scholarship] to depict the origin of the book in any detail."[125] Ewald's theory is based solely on the analysis of superscriptions, which are evidence of the editorial process. At the same time, he shows how certain additions may reveal editorial activity as well. The model used by the German scholar to explain the redaction of the book is that of *(sub)collections* gradually added to an original core.[126]

In approximately the same period, C. F. Keil assumed that *chronology* may have played a role in the formation of the first six books of the Twelve[127] but he also recognized other factors, such as catchwords.[128] This element was further identified by F. Delitzsch who briefly dealt with it in an article on Obadiah.[129] Delitzsch identified associations of words, phrases, or themes as the key factor of the formation of at least the first nine writings of the Twelve and pinpointed his position on the basis of

---

121. House, *Unity*, 9–29; Schart, "Redaktionsgeschichte," 893–908. The interest of scholars, in other words, gradually shifted from the prophets as authors and/or historical characters and the quest for his *ipsissima verba* to the process of formation of prophetic literature. Ben Zvi, "Historical," 4–16.

122. Nogalski, *Literary*, 3–11.

123. Eichhorn, *Einleitung*. A fuller presentation of Eichhorn's stance may be found in Sweeney, "Minor Prophets," 268–70.

124. Ewald, *Jeremia*, 74–82; Sweeney, "Minor Prophets," 270–71.

125. Schneider, "Unity," 7.

126. Sweeney, "Minor Prophets," 271.

127. Keil, *Propheten*.

128. Schneider, "Unity," 7. See also Kuhl, *Entstehung*, 217–18.

129. Delitzsch, "Obadja," 92–93. See also Schart, *Entstehung*, 16.

his previous research on the Psalter ("das Princip, dem er [*sc.* der Sammler] folgt, ist das von mir in meinen *Symbolis ad Psalmos illustrandos isagogicis* [1846] für die Anordung der Psalmen").[130] Unlike Keil, Delitzsch rejects chronology altogether as a factor that played a role in the composition of the book. Delitzsch's approach can be found in U. Cassuto, who wrote a century later an influential article on the sequence and arrangement of biblical sections.[131]

In sum, at the beginning of the twentieth century, scanty and scattered observations on the unity of the Twelve could be found in prophets scholarship, though they were yet to be integrated by a unified methdological vision.[132]

The path opened by Ewald was followed in 1912 by C. Steuernagel, who developed a seven-stage model for the redaction of the Twelve, almost entirely based on superscriptions.[133] In 1922, K. Budde developed a unique theory of the formation of the Twelve.[134] According to the German scholar, the editors of the book systematically removed "all that was merely human, all the mere background,"[135] that is, all references to the context of the writings themselves.[136] In this period, according to LeCureux, "scholars began to argue that the oneness of the Twelve was located in the history of the Book's growth."[137]

One of the first articles devoted solely to the unity of the Twelve was published in 1935 by Rolland E. Wolfe.[138] Wolfe adopts a redactional mod-

---

130. Delitzsch, "Obadja," 92.

131. Cassuto, "Sequence," 5–6.

132. See Jepsen, "Beiträge." Sweeney notes that in the nineteenth century, "given the Protestant character of early critical scholarship . . . attempts to understand the formation of the Book of the Twelve did not originate in an interest in Jewish readings of the book." In fact, according to Sweeney, "Jewish scholars read the Twelve Prophets as a single book that had twelve constitutive elements" (Sweeney, "Minor Prophets," 273–74).

133. Steuernagel, *Lehrbuch*, 669–72.

134. Budde, "Redaktion," 218–29; cf. Sweeney, "Minor Prophets," 272–73.

135. Schneider, "Unity," 11.

136. LeCureux, *Thematic*, 5–6. The exceptions to the rule listed by Budde "are by no means exhaustive, a fact that helps account for the lack of serious attention this article received" (Nogalski, *Literary*, 5).

137. LeCureux, *Thematic*, 6. The author goes on and states that "bits and pieces of Hosea, Amos, Joel, and the rest may have existed, but it was later editors who took all of the pieces, edited them, moved them around, and placed them together."

138. Wolfe, "Editing," 90–129. He also wrote an unpublished dissertation, Wolfe, *Editing*. According to Schneider, "Unity," 8, the most significant work of the first decades of the twentieth century on the Twelve is Wolfe's article. See also LeCureux, *Thematic*, 6.

el ("strata hypothesis" in Wolfe's own words[139]) that Schneider describes as "a documentary hypothesis which extends across the XII."[140] The author identifies different additions/layers, ascribed to different editors, actually, up to thirteen layers, piled on top of the few verses that Wolfe deems to be authentic in the prophets' books. From the methodological point of view, Wolfe builds his argument solely on a personal judgment about the data and identification of the different layers—a point that is aptly criticized by Schneider.[141] Wolfe does not seem to take up any of the points highlighted by Ewald, Keil, and Delitzsch. In any case, "Wolfe's work is one of the first to see the Twelve, not as a random collection of unrelated writings, but a purposefully organized book."[142]

Even if Wolfe's article "killed interest in the question of the XII,"[143] some twenty years later, Niemeyer, in his study of the Psalter's order, also considered the issue of the unity of the Twelve and concluded that no single criterion could explain the order of the book or reconstruct the editors' work.[144] His analysis deals with chronology, catchwords, material parallels, similar form and size, and alliteration.[145] The issues of the process of *formation* of the book and the *meaning* of its unity are left out of consideration.[146]

To some extent, the publication of Wolfe's contributions and Niemeyer's monograph can be considered a first shift towards a more methodologically mature approach to the unity of the Twelve.[147] Such

---

139. Wolfe, "Editing," 91.

140. Schneider, "Unity," 11.

141. Schneider criticizes some of Wolfe's flaws and states that "Wolfe has killed interest in the question of the XII" (Schneider, "Unity," 12).

142. LeCureux, *Thematic*, 7. See also the OT introductions mentioned by Schneider, where he complains that "it was taken for granted that the Book of the XII was a creation of the late scribes (c. 350–250 BC), that it was assembled in a few generations by a more or less established class of scribes." These authors "also tended to assume that the XII were placed together simply to preserve the small books" (Schneider, "Unity," 13).

143. Schneider, "Unity," 12.

144. Niemeyer, *Het probleem*, reviews also the Mishnah, the Qur'an, Exodus 21–23, and Proverbs 25–29.

145. Niemeyer, *Het probleem*, 7–56.

146. Niemeyer, *Het probleem*, 7–35.

147. Rudolph, *Hosea*, 25–34. In his commentary, Rudolph devotes three pages to the issue and states that the order is basically chronological but other two principles, book size, catchwords, were at work.

a shift began to take on more defined contours, as mentioned above, in the 1970s, a period when greater attention to prophetic collections as products of scribal and editorial activity started to surface.[148]

In 1979, Dale A. Schneider wrote an unpublished dissertation about the unity of the Twelve that can be considered one of the most comprehensive works on the subject before Nogalski.[149] Schneider offers one of the first thorough reviews of previous scholarship on the Twelve and concludes that "investigation of the cross links among the books themselves (citations, catchwords, common topics, common traditions) turned out to be the most fruitful study."[150] His approach demonstrates the strong influence of Cassuto and Delitzsch.[151] Schneider interprets verbal/lexemic links as signs of redactional activity and develops a four-stage model for reconstructing the formation of the Twelve, based on the idea that "the prophets authored their own works and collected the works of earlier prophets influential to them."[152] It is worth noting that, according to Schneider, in the third stage, "Joel (late seventh century)[153] and Obadiah are incorporated into Hosea-Amos-Micah on the basis of catchwords/topical connections."[154] Schneider does not limit himself to catchwords but also considers "the level of literacy in Israel, the various superscriptions of the books, and relationships with the major prophets."[155] According to Schneider, the location of the book in the overall composition also plays a significant role since it is one of the tools used by its editor(s). The placement of Joel and Jonah represents, from this point of view, a case in point.[156]

In the same year, Brevard S. Childs published his groundbreaking *Introduction to the Old Testament as Scripture*, which addresses the unity of the Twelve.[157] The American scholar assumes that the Twelve should

---

148. House, *Unity*, 28–29.
149. Schneider, "Unity."
150. Schneider, "Unity." See also Sweeney, "Minor Prophets," 274–75.
151. Schneider, "Unity," 1–18.
152. Nogalski, *Literary*, 7.
153. Schneider was one of the first to place Joel's redaction or composition in pre-exilic period. LeCureux, *Thematic*, 7.
154. Schneider, "Unity," 90.
155. Schneider, "Unity," 17. Among the ancient witnesses, Schneider mentions the DSS and early Jewish and Christian tradition. He seeks to investigate the *literary context* and to work out a new model of the way prophetic books were formed.
156. Scheinder, *Unity*, 237–39.
157. Childs, *Introduction*, 308–10. Childs mentions "R. E. Wolfe, K. Budde, W.

be considered a literary unity, even if explaining "how twelve independent prophetic collections were united into a single book has remained unresolved."[158] This is why, according to House, "Childs asserts that the various orders of the major prophets in the canon argue against any discernible purpose for the present configuration of the 15 prophetic books."[159] Childs never addresses the structure of the twelve,[160] and the role of canonical exegesis is limited to a broad affirmation of the book's canonical unity, without delving deeply into the editorial processes that shaped it or their significance for the reader.[161]

Schart rightly attributes to Childs's influence a significant shift in prophetic scholarship, moving the focus from the individual prophets to their texts.[162] Such a shift paved the way for considering the prophetic collections both as canonical and literary works, whose redactional history involve a far more complex activity than just collecting oral-written oracles. Together with Childs's works, a major influence on the study of prophetic corpora was that of the "literary study" of the Bible, a field of research whose beginnings can be traced back to the late 1970s.[163]

Following the above-mentioned shift, R. Clements suggests, in the late 1980s, a new approach to the issue of the unity of the Twelve. The author endeavors to identify the thematic coherence of the book and the binding elements that reveal its cohesiveness.[164] In the same period, a thematic approach to the issue may be found also in Pierce,[165] and above all, in the unpublished dissertation of A. Y. Lee, who investigates the salvation passages in the Twelve, and how they contribute to the

---

Rudolph and others" as those who tried to investigate the issue before him (309). See also Childs, "Canonical."

158. Childs, *Introduction*, 309.

159. House, *Unity*, 26–27; cf. Childs, *Introduction*, 310.

160. Childs comments on the individual writings of the Twelve. See Childs, *Introduction*, 373–500.

161. House, *Unity*, 63–110. According to Schart, "Redaktionsgeschichte," Childs's approach contributed to the shift of interest from the person of the prophet to the text. In this regard, House, *Unity*, 19–20, also quotes the literary commentary of Watts, *Isaiah 1–33*.

162. "Die prophetischen Worte sind von den Herausgebern so gestaltet worden, daß sie für die entsprechende Glaubensgemeinschaft als heilige Schrift anerkannt werden konnen" (Schart, "Redaktionsgeschichte," 15).

163. See Marks, "Twelve," 207–33.

164. Clements, "Patterns," 189–200. See also Clements, "Prophetic Canon," 42–55.

165. Pierce, "Connectors," 277–89, highlights thematic correspondences between Haggai, Zechariah, and Malachi. See also Pierce, "Development," 401–11.

overall structure of the collection.[166] Lee takes the canonical approach and states that "the scroll of the Twelve should be interpreted as a canonical entity," having a "deeper theological unity . . . as the whole is greater than the sum of its parts."[167] Lee's canonical analysis offers a thorough investigation of the unifying function of the theme of hope for the Twelve.[168]

In 1990, P. House published a thorough investigation of the unity of the Twelve that can be considered, together with Schneider's, as two of the most important monographs on the issue.[169] House reviews previous scholarship on the Twelve and denounces the lack of sensitivity to the *literary* shape of the book.[170] Being quite skeptical about the editorial value of catchwords,[171] he decided to take his cues from a purely synchronic approach, assuming that the Twelve is indeed a complex literary unity (a "book"), with a plot and a structure, and belonging to a specific genre.[172] House here adheres to the Aristotelian view of a comedy and ascribes to the Twelve a U-shaped plot structure, that is, a three-stage development (sin, punishment, restoration), mirrored in the tripartite division of the Twelve (Hosea–Micah; Nahum–Zephaniah; Haggai–Malachi).[173] All in all, according to House, the collection could and should be read as a single, literary construction whose original intention supposes a single plot, genre, and structure. As such, he divides the Twelve into three main sections following the MT order (Hosea–Micah; Nahum–Zephaniah; Haggai–Malachi), each respectively corresponding to three stages of sin-punishment-restoration noted above. The plot is well developed, complete with characters, a narrator (the prophets), an implied audience, among other plot devices.

A different perspective can be found in Odil H. Steck's works on Isaiah, which serve, according to F. Landy, as a model for the study of the Twelve as a book.[174] Steck compares the history of the redaction of

---

166. Lee, "Canonical Unity."
167. Lee, "Canonical Unity," 11.
168. Lee draws from Clements, "Patterns."
169. House, *Unity*.
170. House does not mention Marks, "Twelve."
171. House, *Unity*, 66.
172. House, *Unity*, 111–62.
173. House, *Unity*, 111–62. Gottwald assumes an implied narrative in the Latter Prophets, one that can be characterized as a comedy. Gottwald, "Tragedy," 83–96.
174. Landy, "Three Sides," 11. See also Steck, *Heimkehr*; *Tritojesaja*; *Gottesknecht*;

the Twelve and of Isaiah, arguing that these books could no longer be read in isolation, but had to be read as redacted compositions.[175] Steck develops a model for reconstructing the redactional history of prophetic corpora that is based on the idea of *Fortschreibung* and *innerbiblical interpretation*.[176] Prophetic collections are the product of scribal activity (*schriftgelehrte Prophetie*) whose main premises include the editor(s)'s responsibility of re-reading the prophetic collections and re-interpretation of older material to accommodate new contexts, and their arrangement of the "new" composition into a coherent whole.[177] The task of the reader of prophetic collections is to detect the links within the final form of the text and from them, deduce the redactional processes responsible for the different layers of the text. The model used by Steck was taken up by his student, Nogalski, and was also influential for the work of Utzchneider,[178] Bosshard-Nepustil,[179] Schart,[180] and Zapff.[181]

In the same vein, T. Collins[182] and R. J. Coggins[183] suggest that the Twelve ought to be read as a unified book, similar to Isaiah. According to Collins, the editorial processes of Isaiah and the Twelve are similar,[184] and therefore, in the Minor Prophets it is possible to find the division between pre-exilic, exilic, and post-exilic material, which have been observed in Isaiah.[185] He notes, "The same historical process that was at work in the Twelve was also at work in Isaiah, and as result, Isaiah's division of material . . . roughly mirrors the Twelve's historical development."[186] This material was collected, expanded, and edited into an organized whole.[187] The main difference between the Twelve and Isaiah is that "in *the Twelve* the various

---

"Abfolge," 249–53; "Eigenart," 357–72; "Frage," 157–66; Kratz, "Steck," 467–80; Hossfeld and Zenger, "Psalmenauslegung," 237–58.

175. Steck, *Abschluss*. See also Sweeney, "Minor Prophets," 274–75.
176. Schmid, "Schriftauslegung," 1–22. See also Steck, *Exegese*.
177. Berry, "Design," 269–302.
178. Utzchneider, *Künder oder Schreiber?*; "Schriftprophetie," 377–94.
179. Bosshard-Nepustil, "Beobachtungen," 30–62; *Rezeptionen*.
180. Schart, *Entstehung*.
181. Zapff, *Studien*; "Völkerperspektive," 86–99.
182. Collins, *Mantle*.
183. Coggins, "Prophets," 57–68.
184. "The techniques of composition and presentation are the same in both books, and so are the basic elements in their contents" (Collins, *Mantle*, 64–65).
185. Collins, *Mantle*, 60.
186. LeCureux, *Thematic*, 12.
187. Collins, *Mantle*, 61. See also LeCureux, *Thematic*, 12–13.

sections were allocated to different names preserved by traditions."[188] The final product is a coherent literary unity and, therefore, "fragmentation of *The Twelve* is a mistake, just as fragmentation of *Isaiah* is a mistake, and for the same reasons."[189] Coggins bases his approach to the unity of the Twelve on the same assumption: that both Isaiah and the Twelve were considered books.[190] Collins notes also the thematic connections within the Twelve: "Covenant-election, fidelity and infidelity, fertility and infertility, turning and returning, the justice of God and the mercy of God, the kingship of God, the place of his dwelling (Temple/Mt Zion), the nations as enemies, the nations as allies."[191]

The works of House, Collins, and Coggins were, according to LeCureux, influential for the subsequent scholarship on the Twelve: "Almost all scholarship that deals with this topic[192] is, at least in some way, responding to these early works."[193] Apart from the scholars mentioned by LeCureux as influential for the following development of the study of the Twelve, the methodological framework developed by Steck and his school should also be considered.

James D. Nogalski

The publication of James Nogalski's two monographs in 1993[194] represents a turning point in the history of the interpretation of the Twelve.[195] Nogalski acknowledges the influence of studies on the final form of the text (structuralism, canonical criticism, rhetorical criticism, and new literary criticism) as well as inner-biblical exegesis, intertextuality, and

---

188. Collins, *Mantle*, 64–65. Collins goes as far as to say that the only difference between Isaiah and the Twelve is that the Twelve maintained their separate headings. The author adds: "This is, however, really only a superficial difference. The techniques of composition and presentation are the same in both books, and so are the basic elements in their contents" (65).

189. Collins, *Mantle*, 60.

190. Coggins, "Prophets," 62.

191. Collins, *Mantle*, 65.

192. That is, the unity of the Book of the Twelve.

193. LeCureux, *Thematic*, 15.

194. Nogalski, *Literary*; *Redactional*. Several significant contributions of the author have been recently collected in Nogalski, *Book*.

195. Nogalski "is indeed largely responsible for what he calls the consensus . . . in favour of the thesis" of the unity of the Twelve (Landy, "Three Sides," 3).

Schriftprophetie on his work.¹⁹⁶ In general, however, the model that lies behind his research is what Steck and his students had developed for Isaiah. Nonetheless, Nogalski should be credited with providing a clear methodological framework to the issue of the unity of the Twelve and paving the way for the development of an emerging field of research.¹⁹⁷ Nogalski's influence became evident in 1994 during the SBL's Seminar on the Formation of the Book of the Twelve.¹⁹⁸ According to LeCureux, this seminar provoked a major turning point in Twelve scholarship.¹⁹⁹

Nogalski offers a critical review of the previous attempts to justify the idea of the unity of the Twelve. Specifically, he tackles the following points:

1. The analysis of the superscriptions only, according to Nogalski, does not yield an agreement between scholars and, therefore, cannot be considered a suitable way to work out the unity of the Twelve.[200]

2. The redactional models of Budde and Wolfe "failed to receive acceptance" because of their lack of methodological clarity.[201]

3. The works of Delitzsch, Cassuto, and Schneider demonstrated the presence and importance of catchwords in the Twelve but they "assume *apriori* that the shape of the writings was unaffected by these catchwords."[202] Nogalski offers a "corrective" to such a supposition.

4. The "purely synchronic" approach of House fails to clearly identify the unity of the Twelve: "House offers no solid *criteria* for arguing that one must view these writings as a literary unity."[203]

Point 3 of the above list explains one of the main tenets of Nogalski's approach, which can be defined as a *diachronic* exegesis based on the

---

196. Nogalski refers to Fishbane, *Interpretation*; Utzschneider, *Künder oder Schreiber?* See also Bergler, *Joel*; Nogalski and Sweeney, *Reading and Hearing*, vii–viii.

197. Today, a growing number of scholars accept this perspective, and in the 2021 *Handbook* the issue runs throughout the whole volume. See O'Brien, *Handbook*.

198. The contributions of this working group can be found in different collective volumes: Watts and House, *Literature*; Nogalski and Sweeney, *Reading and Hearing*; Redditt and Schart, *Thematic Threads*. See also Collins, *Mantle*, 59–87.

199. LeCureux, *Thematic*, 2.

200. Nogalski, *Literary*, 4–5.

201. Nogalski, *Literary*, 5–6.

202. Nogalski, *Literary*, 11.

203. Nogalski, *Literary*, 11–12.

synchronic analysis of the final form of the Twelve.[204] Nogalski declares that he endeavors to "understand the foundational stimuli behind the compilation of the Book of the Twelve,"[205] that is, the intention of the editors of the compilation. The starting point of the author's analysis is clearly the MT and the basic assumption of his approach may be summarized as follows: the Book of the Twelve was purposefully composed as a unified book through a complex and chronologically layered editorial work. The task of the interpreter should be to identify the clear markers of the editors' activity.[206] In this respect, Nogalski considers that recurring themes and placement of the individual prophetic books played a significant role in the compositional process of the collection.[207] However, the real cornerstone of the editorial analysis of the Twelve is catchwords (or *Stichwörter*), the "linking words which close one writing and begin another."[208] Catchwords are the main tool used by the editors of the Twelve to create a unified book out of twelve different individual compositions.[209] From this point of view, "an editor has revised portions of one book to enable it to be connected to another book, next to which it sits."[210] A crucial aspect of Nogalski's approach is that catchwords were created by the editor(s) and did not predate them.[211] In any case, they "played a significant role in

---

204. Nogalski distinguishes between synchronic and diachronic approaches. A purely synchronic approach is that of reading the Twelve as if they were one book. Petersen, "Book," 8. Petersen underscores that this approach does not account for either ancient manuscripts or redaction-critical issues and that the term "book" is primarily meant to denote a literary unity possessing *theme*, *plot*, and so on.

205. Nogalski, "Intertextuality," 103.

206. "In order to speak meaningfully of 'unity' with respect to the Book of the Twelve, one must first establish that the texts of the Twelve relate to one another" (Nogalski, "Intertextuality," 102).

207. Nogalski, *Literary*. See also Nogalski, "Intertextuality," 116–18.

208. LeCureux, *Thematic*, 8. The German word, "Stichwort," is used in Nogalski, *Literary*, 23.

209. Example are given in Nogalski, *Literary*, 24–25. Here the author states, "Catchwords offer a springboard into the editorial work of the Book of the Twelve. One cannot, however, concentrate upon these words myopically and exclude other editorial factors" (25).

210. Petersen, "Book," 7.

211. For example, Amos 9:12a // Obad 16, 17–21. Also, Hosea 14:8a // Joel 1. Therefore, "catchwords have been deliberately (redactionally) implanted into existing texts to highlight" the connections between neighboring writings of the Twelve (Nogalski, "Intertextuality," 112).

the arrangement of developing collections" such as "wisdom sayings, legal saying, psalms, and prophetic logia."[212]

Nogalski's primary approach to reconstructing the editorial process of the Twelve can be seen in his adoption of intertextuality as a key methodology. Nogalski defines intertextuality as "the interrelationship between two or more texts which evidence suggests (1) was deliberately established by ancient authors/editors or (2) was presupposed by those authors/editors."[213] Five types of intertextuality may be detected in the Twelve: "quotations, allusions, catchwords, motifs, and framing devices."[214] In general, catchwords are redactionally significant when they appear in a passage probably added to the original layer by a later hand.[215]

According to Nogalski, another significant marker of the editorial activity responsible for the Book of the Twelve is what he calls "framing devices," which include superscriptions, genre similarities,[216] structural parallels,[217] juxtaposition of catchwords, and canonical allusions.[218] They all reveal, according to Nogalski, the works and the intentions of the editors of the Twelve, even if "much work" has to be done "before making definitive statements" on the issue.[219]

Nogalski worked out a model for the redactional process of the Twelve essentially based on the so-called "Joel-related layer,"[220] which functioned to join the "Deuteronomistic" (Hosea-Amos-Micah-Zephaniah)[221] with the post-exilic Haggai-Zechariah *corpora*.[222] Nogalski goes as far as to label Joel "the literary anchor" of the Twelve, putting

---

212. Nogalski, "Intertextuality," 112.
213. Nogalski, "Intertextuality," 102. See also Bosshard-Nepustil, *Rezeptionen*.
214. Nogalski, "Intertextuality," 103.
215. Nogalski, *Literary*.
216. Nogalski, "Intertextuality," 121–22.
217. Nogalski, "Intertextuality," 122–23, brings up Amos 9 to Obadiah and Nahum 3 to Habakkuk 1 as examples.
218. Nogalski, "Intertextuality," 118. Here "framing devices" correspond roughly to "macroindicators." Canonical allusions play a significant role in Zech 13:9; 14:1–21; Mal 3:22–24. They allude to the beginning of the Former Prophets (Mal 3:22 // Josh 1:2, 7), the beginning of the Latter Prophets (Zech 14 // Isa 2, 66) and the beginning and the end of the Twelve (Hos 2:25 // Mal 3:3).
219. Nogalski, "Intertextuality," 124.
220. Nogalski, *Literary*, 275.
221. Nogalski, *Literary*, labels this corpus "the precursors" of the Twelve.
222. Nogalski, *Literary*.

together and defining various images in the book.²²³ The "Joel layer" is dated by Nogalski to 400–350 BCE whereas Obadiah, Nahum, Habakkuk, and Malachi were considered "Joel-related" additions. Jonah and Zechariah 9–14 belong, according to Nogalski, to the final layer of the book.²²⁴ It is important to note that the two precursors of the Twelve are seen by Nogalski as sources of a single, time-developed literary composition. The composition of the collection should be credited to the Levites "on the grounds of their proximity to the Temple; their literacy and teaching function; their role in the shifting power politics of the Second Temple period; and finally . . . their responsibility for the composition and performance of cultic poetry, like Psalms."²²⁵

Nogalski's works have sparked a broader and ongoing debate within prophetic scholarship regarding the Twelve. One of the cornerstones in the debate is the publication, in 2009, of a volume Nogalski co-edited with Ben Zvi,²²⁶ where the main tenets of his method are re-stated and criticism addressed.²²⁷ The works of Nogalski put several issues on the table that would come to dominate the following research, for example:

1. Intertextuality.
2. Synchronic vs. diachronic approaches.
3. The "macrogenre" of the Twelve (book, anthology, etc).
4. The differences between MT and LXX sequences and the place of Qumran findings.
5. Redactional models used by scholars to reconstruct the formation of the book.
6. Alternative ways of framing the issue of the unity of the book (thematic approaches, superscripts, sequence, etc.).

The extensive range of studies published following Nogalski's monographs cannot be summarized here. I will limit myself to mentioning some of the most important studies on the "genre" of the book, the different redactional models, the thematic approach, the study of superscriptions and sequence, and the intertextual connections with Isaiah.

223. Nogalski, "Joel," 91–109.
224. Nogalski, *Literary*.
225. Landy, "Three Sides," 18; cf. Nogalski, "Twelve Books," 11–46.
226. Ben Zvi and Nogalski, *Two Sides*.
227. Nogalski, "Doubts," 16–22.

Beck assumes that the Twelve are to be conceived as an anthology. He specifically compares the Twelve with Greek anthologies—previously independent texts brought together and ordered according to certain principles. As an anthology, the Twelve can be read as a single composition and, at the same time, the works can be approached as discrete, independent works.[228] Guillaume suggests that the anthology was compiled in Alexandria at the time of the translation of the Minor Prophets into Greek.[229]

In 1997, Schart, under the influence of Nogalski, developed an alternative model for the history of the redaction of Twelve. Schart bases his analysis on the superscriptions and redactional criticism. The outcome is a six-step model. Schart's model is similar to Nogalski's (cf. "Deuternomist *corpus*") but he does not identify a "Joel layer."[230] He highlights how it is impossible to discern the reason for the call to repentance in Joel without assuming Hosea.[231] Jakob Wöhrle published another explanation in 2006 and 2008,[232] developing a third model for the formation of the Twelve. His methodology is based on redactional critical analysis of each individual writing of the Twelve. The outcome is an eight-step model.

LeCureux, in 2012, developed a thematic model to read the Twelve as a literary unity. This approach is rooted in the very idea of intertextuality and thematic analysis.[233] The theme is, according to LeCureux, the unifying element of the Twelve. The theme "gives reason for the ordering and selection of the material into the work."[234] A prophetic theme is "a recurring idea, communicated by word or phrase, which supports the main thrusts of the prophecy and gives theological shape and meaning to the work."[235] The theme is "part of the grammatical codes embedded in the text by the authors/editors of the Twelve."[236]

---

228. Beck, "Dodekapropheton," 558–81. See also Sweeney, "Concerns," 21–33.

229. Guillaume, "Reconsideration."

230. Schart, "Redactional Models," 893–908; "Redaktionsgeschichte," 893–908. See also Schart, *Entstehung*, 304–6.

231. Schart, "Section," 138–52.

232. Wöhrle, *Sammlungen*; "Future," 608–27.

233. Cf. LeCureux, *Thematic*, 26–28.

234. LeCureux, *Thematic*, 31. "This is perhaps its most significant function in regard to the Twelve."

235. LeCureux, *Thematic*, 33.

236. LeCureux, *Thematic*, 38.

His proposal is based on "word repetition, as well as the position of Hosea-Joel and Zechariah-Malachi."[237] He tries to identify the unifying and controlling theme of the book—that of *return*, connected to the root שוב and the phrase שובו אלי ואשובה אליכם, "return to me and I will return to you." He uses not only statistics (high number of occurrences of the root in the Twelve) but "the distribution of those occurrences."[238] LeCureux resumes Bowman's article and highlights that the root שוב opens and closes the Twelve. Finally, "using constant repetition and the position of the writings, the MT editors of the Twelve hoped to instill the necessity of the imperative call to return into the mind of all who read the Twelve."[239]

Rendtorff suggests that the mention of the "Day of the Lord" is the unifying theme of the Twelve.[240] There are strong grounds for supporting this hypothesis,[241] which has garnered considerable scholarly attention.[242] Bowman argues that the root שוב is the unifying theme of the Twelve.[243] He bases his argument on the hypothesis that Hosea and Malachi form the framework of the book, where the uniting features of the book should appear.[244] Since the theme of the "Day of the Lord" is absent from Hosea 1–3, it cannot form the uniting theme of the Twelve.[245]

The structural function of superscriptions is explored by Watts.[246] The author highlights how the Twelve's superscriptions are used as means to unify the book in a much more complex way than Jeremiah or Ezekiel and, to some extent, Isaiah.[247] A careful study of superscriptions allows one to gather evidence about the redactional history of the book. According to Watts, Haggai, Zechariah 1–8, and Jonah are the literary precursors to the Twelve.[248] Moreover, "the process of build-

---

237. LeCureux, *Thematic*, 22.

238. LeCureux, *Thematic*, 23.

239. LeCureux, *Thematic*, 23.

240. Rendtorff, "How to Read," 75–87; cf. Rendtorff, "Day," 186–97.

241. Nogalski, "Day(s)," 192–213.

242. Nogalski, "Themes," 125–36; Schwesig, *Rolle*; Barton, "Day," 68–79.

243. Bowman, "Reading," 1–18.

244. See Watts, "Frame," 209–18. See also, Tooze, "Framing."

245. Bowman, "Reading," 9.

246. Watts, "Superscriptions," 110–24.

247. Watts, "Superscriptions," 122.

248. "The Amos superscription suggests that Amos should be viewed in this light although redactional work was performed to tie Amos into the larger whole" (Watts, "Superscriptions," 123).

ing" the Twelve "accounts for the development of superscriptions" in Joel, Micah, Nahum, Habakkuk, Zephaniah, and Malachi.[249] Finally, Watts emphasizes that the significance of the linguistic elements in the superscriptions can differ from one book to another. Above all, "the use of these superscriptions to separate units does not produce twelve writings" but a unified book.[250]

Sweeney takes a broader approach, focusing on the position of the writings.[251] The various sequences of the LXX and the MT reveal different purposes. Specifically, "the sequence points to hermeneutics by which the individual prophetic books are both received and presented as constitutive components of the 'Book of the Twelve' as a whole."[252] The book is thematically organized around two "programmatic books," Hosea and Joel. The LXX and MT sequences both emphasize different themes. LXX reflects the Christian communities while MT is linked to the Jewish communities. "Repeated thematic links . . . bring a unifying feature across the whole of the Book while at the same time allowing the writings to develop their own unique understanding of such themes."[253] These authors build on the observations of Collins, focusing specifically on a single unifying theme.

Seitz emphasizes the canonical sequence and argues that there is intentionality behind the ordering of the book.[254] In fact, "the earliest tradents were themselves concerned, not with individual historical prophets and their message in this or that period, but with the correlation of these prophets and these messages, in the name of a large-scale account of YHWH's dispensation of history, under his providential care and sovereignty."[255]

Bosshard-Nepustil investigates the intertextual connections among the prophetic books and their importance for the reconstruction of the development of the prophetic corpus. He sees correlations between the Major and Minor Prophets and two exilic redactions in Isaiah 1–39 that both read Jeremiah sequentially as consecutively

---

249. Watts, "Superscriptions," 123.
250. Watts, "Superscriptions," 123–24.
251. Sweeney, "Sequence," 49–64; cf. Sweeney, *Twelve*, xxvii–xxxix.
252. Sweeney, "Sequence," 55.
253. LeCureux, *Thematic*, 16.
254. Seitz, "Lesson," 443–69; "Letting a Text," 151–72; *Prophecy*.
255. Seitz, *Prophecy*, 196.

ordered books. The latter redaction alludes to Isaiah 40–66.²⁵⁶ In contrast, Conrad highlights the meaning of the canonical composition "that emerges from the reader's interaction with the canonical text, quite apart from any intentionality, which may or may not have been a factor in the work of the various editors responsible for the production of the texts."²⁵⁷ Conrad mostly focuses his work on the intertextual links between superscriptions in the prophetic books.

Ehud Ben Zvi

The interpretation of the Twelve as a single book gained widespread support but also faced criticism. Ehud Ben Zvi is widely recognized as the most vocal of the critics of the approach fostered by Nogalski.²⁵⁸ Besides the arguments that Ben Zvi brought forth to counter Nogalski, the main difference between the two authors is methodological. The approach of Nogalski is redactional while Ben Zvi focuses on a reader-oriented analysis of the texts.²⁵⁹ Landy summarizes the issue as follows: while Nogalski's approach is redaction-critical, Ben Zvi focuses "on the readerships (or, in his parlance, *rereaderships*) of the texts."²⁶⁰ It is, in fact, impossible to ascertain when the Twelve were compiled onto a single scroll or whether ancient readers perceived them as a unified work. Therefore, instead of tracking back the intention of the editors through the identifiable literary markers, the reader/interpreter of the Twelve should investigate how the intended audience of the writings would have read them.²⁶¹ This is why Ben Zvi focuses on memory studies²⁶² and highlights the lack thereof in the studies devoted to the Twelve. Instead of being "author/redactor centered," his own reading is based on careful consideration of the community of readers.²⁶³

---

256. Bosshard-Nepustil, *Rezeptionen*. See also Bosshard-Nepustil, "Beobachtungen."
257. Hadjiev, "Anthology," 91. Hadjiev refers to Conrad, "Forming," 90–103.
258. See especially Ben Zvi, "Is the Twelve," 64–72.
259. Landy. "Three Sides," 9.
260. Landy, "Three Sides," 6. He quotes Ben Zvi, "Is the Twelve," 53.
261. Ben Zvi, "Shades," 37–54; *Memory*.
262. Ben Zvi *Memory*, 28–79.
263. Ben Zvi, "Is the Twelve," 85–86.

Starting from this fundamental premise, Ben Zvi brings forth several arguments against the hypothesis of a unified Book of the Twelve:[264]

1. He contends that there were different sequences of the books.[265]

2. He also contends that it is impossible to discern editorial activity because editorial activity is aimed at assimilating earlier versions into a new one without being detected. Therefore, it is hypothetically impossible to identify the "signs" of the editors' activity.[266]

3. Ben Zvi notes that the hypothesis of the Twelve as a book has many versions.[267] Since redactional models for the Twelve abound,[268] it is better to focus on the Persian period readers (or *literati*) of the final form of the individual writings. This option can give the analysis a firm ground.

4. From this point of view, the strongest objection against the reading of the Twelve as a book is that ancient readers looked for access to the prophet himself and not to the book. There could be no Book of the Twelve because there was no one called "the Twelve."[269]

5. The preservation of the headings is proof that the writings of the Twelve were conceived as individual books.[270] Furthermore, authority was granted to a text on the basis of the authority of the text's author.[271] "The most significant and unequivocal internal evidence, namely that of the titles (or incipits) of the prophetic books, sets them on the same level with Isaiah or Jeremiah or Ezekiel, namely as separate prophetic books."[272]

---

264. Ben Zvi, Nogalski, *Two Sides*.
265. Ben Zvi, "Is the Twelve," 47–53.
266. Ben Zvi, "Concept," 58–63.
267. Ben Zvi, "Is the Twelve," 47–96.
268. Sieges, "One Book."
269. Ben Zvi, "Is the Twelve," 82–83.
270. Ben Zvi, "Is the Twelve," 80. Superscriptions may have had a macrostructural function, but only if one assumes the reading of the Twelve as a book in advance. Ben Zvi, "Twelve," 77.
271. Ben Zvi, "Is the Twelve," 80.
272. Ben Zvi, "Twelve Prophetic Books," 137.

6. Furthermore, the ending of books often demarcates them.[273] Moreover, the Twelve as such has no "general" superscription that can identify it to the readers' eyes.[274]

7. Finally, the writings themselves are so diverse as regards to style, purpose, genre, and theology that they lend to the idea that they are to be read individually.[275] Moreover, it is not possible to detect anywhere in the Hebrew Bible anything comparable with the Twelve regarding literary genre. It could be categorized as an anthology but if so, it differs from other biblical anthologies because it is not attributed to a particular character, like David or Solomon.[276] In any case, Ben Zvi thinks that the Twelve is only an anthology made up for convenience.[277]

The study of openings and endings is, according to Ben Zvi, the point where his own approach and "the one that characterizes much research supporting the TH [i.e., the Twelve Hypothesis] differ more markedly, and with far reaching consequences."[278] For example, Ben Zvi contends that Hosea and Joel are not linked through catchwords as Nogalski states, but instead, they are separated by ending (Hos 14:10) and superscription (Joel 1:1).[279] Moreover, the catchwords identified by Nogalski are, according to Ben Zvi, common words or themes in prophetic literature. Ben Zvi notes, "It is most unlikely, and . . . unthinkable, that the intended and primary readers of [Hosea and Joel] . . . thought that such a repetition created a sense of textual bond between these two texts that outweighed the most salient and overt differences between the two texts."[280] Finally, even successful links "do not constitute evidence that the relevant books were read as parts of a whole."[281] Ben Zvi puts every individual book of the Twelve in the "model of fifteen prophetic books

---

273. Ben Zvi, "Key Form," 286.

274. The book as such *has no superscription*, it is therefore impossible to answer the question: how is it possible to ascertain that the editors wanted to give the readership a book with a single, comprehensive message?

275. Ben Zvi, *History*; Ben Zvi, "Message," 269–90.

276. Ben Zvi, "Is the Twelve," 79–80.

277. Ben Zvi, "Twelve Prophetic Books," 125–56.

278. Ben Zvi, "Is the Twelve," 86.

279. Ben Zvi, "Is the Twelve," 87.

280. Ben Zvi, "Is the Twelve," 88–89.

281. Ben Zvi, "Is the Twelve," 90.

within a larger repertoire of authoritative books" where "it does not matter whether the cross-reference or allusion involves books within the twelve, or within the fifteen, or for that matter, within the entire authoritative corpus available to the literati."[282]

Ben Zvi underscores the *linear sequential reading* model used by Schart to justify the reading of the Twelve as a book.[283] Ben Zvi also proposes a web, branched discursive model. In fact, he argues that "every book is an equal participant in the repertoire of the community and engages freely with all others."[284] The linear sequential model of reading is "not an essential feature of the TH."[285] In the last analysis, according to Ben Zvi, all arguments point towards a conceptualization of the Twelve as a loose compilation of individual texts, connected thematically in some cases but not bearing any single message.[286]

Along with Ben Zvi, other scholars criticized some of the methodological premises of the approach advocated by Nogalski. Jones rejects the identification of catchwords as a literary marker[287] since he finds a weakness with the catchwords surrounding Joel and Obadiah in the MT that can be solved by the LXX sequence.[288] Petersen deems it misleading to call the Twelve "a book" and prefers "book-scroll" (Haran) or "thematized anthology."[289] In general, he finds the argument of Nogalski weak and sees the Twelve as an anthology that has been secondarily configured into twelve books and linked to other portions of the Hebrew Bible. The dominant theme of such an anthology, if any, is "Lord's day."[290] Petersen also emphasizes that from the point of view of the scribes, the Twelve were written on a single scroll. However, "the most such practice might allow would be the claim that these books provide an anthology or collection,

---

282. Ben Zvi, "Is the Twelve," 93–94. At that time the Twelve would have reached its final form and would have been seen as authoritative. The Persian period *literati* interpreted their own situation in the light of the words of the (more) ancient prophets.

283. Ben Zvi, "Is the Twelve," 90–91.

284. Ben Zvi, "Is the Twelve," 92.

285. Ben Zvi, "Is the Twelve," 94.

286. Ben Zvi, "Twelve Prophetic Books," 125–56.

287. Jones, *Formation*.

288. Nogalski, *Literary*, 24–25.

289. Petersen, "Book," 10.

290. Petersen, "Book," 3–4. According to Petersen, ספר occurs only in Nahum 1:1 in the prophetic *corpus*. Apart from this passage, the individual texts are labeled as "words" [דברי] (Amos 1:1), "word" [דבר] (Hos 1:1; Joel 1:1; Mic 1:1; Zeph 1:1), "vision" [חזון] (Obad 1), "oracle" [משא] and "book of the vision" [ספר חזון] (Nah 1:1).

not necessarily 'a book.'"²⁹¹ "That different orders achieved fixity in diverse canonical traditions *does not . . . suggest* that these books constitute 'a literary unity.'"²⁹² According to Petersen, "The key issue is what critical vocabulary is salient—plot, point of view, imagery—and whether it is to be found in the text or imposed upon it."²⁹³ Finally, from the point of literary analysis, Landy underscores that the Twelve Hypothesis should counterweigh the overwhelming "centripetal" tendency of the book—one that focuses on individual books rather than on the collection itself. Moreover, a literary unity is made of concordances and antitheses as well and Nogalski's approach is apparently unconcerned about this aspect.²⁹⁴

Criticism against the unified reading of the Twelve was also raised by Cuffey based on his analysis of superscriptions.²⁹⁵

Additional criticism of Nogalski's approach was raised by some scholars based on the analysis of material evidence. Nonetheless, copying the text of the Twelve on a single scroll may be assumed as proof of the literary unity of the composition. Moreover, ancient manuscripts may offer a more precise picture of the internal order(s) of the writings belonging to the Twelve than the external evidence of ancient witnesses such as Ben Sira, Jerome, or the Talmud. This is why the study of the Twelve as a book—or a criticism of Nogalski's approach—may be supplemented by considering the textual data offered mainly by the findings of the Judean Desert.²⁹⁶

According to Fuller, manuscript evidence ranges from the second century BCE (4QXII$^{a\text{-}b}$) to the second half of the first century CE (Mur 88).²⁹⁷ Seven scrolls were found in Cave 4 that can be dated to the Hasmonean period (150–130 BCE). They were probably complete scrolls of the Twelve.²⁹⁸ Fuller evaluates that two of seven are aligned with the MT, two with the *Vorlage* of the LXX, and two are non-aligned.²⁹⁹ The *pesharim* on some of the writings of the Twelve should also be mentioned. Passages

291. Petersen, "Book," 4–5.
292. Petersen, "Book," 7.
293. Petersen, "Book," 8.
294. Landy, "Three Sides," 6.
295. Cuffey, "Remnant," 185–208. See also Floyd, "מַשָּׂא," 401–22.
296. Pajunen underscores how the analysis of the Twelve as a book and the study of Qumran findings are strictly interwoven. Pajunen, "Bible," 373–74. On Hebrew manuscripts of the Twelve, see Glenny, "History."
297. Fuller, "Form," 86–87. See also Fuller, "Minor Prophet."
298. For an overview of the preserved material in the DSS, see Fuller, "Form," 99–101; "Minor Prophets," 606–10. See also Fuller, "Twelve," 221–318.
299. "One is too small to ascertain its textual character" (Fuller, "Form," 87).

from the Twelve are also quoted in 4QCatena[a-b], 4QFlorilegium, CD, 1QS, and 1QM. Besides Qumran proper, the Murabbaʿat Minor Prophets scroll has to be mentioned here (Mur 88): it is dated to the second half of the first century CE and it is virtually identical with the MT. Scholars have long noticed that Mur 88 contains several "corrections" probably meant to bring the text as close as possible to the consonantal MT.[300]

In the same vein, LeCureux states, "The writings of Hosea-Malachi have been transmitted on one scroll from very early in the transmission process despite the lack of an overall introductory heading."[301] According to LeCureux, 4QXII[a-b] (150 BCE) contains a section of Malachi-Jonah while 4QXII[b] shows the sequence Zephaniah-Haggai.[302] No less than six other first-century BCE scrolls, both Greek and Hebrew, attest to the collection of these writings onto a single scroll.[303] All in all, Fuller summarizes the data offered by the DSS as follows:

1. "All seven [of Cave 4 scrolls] are quite fragmentary, much more so than . . . Mur 88. . . . This means that our conclusions must remain tentative."[304]

2. The oldest manuscript evidence seems to confirm that already at about 150 BCE the Twelve was completed as a collection.[305] Fuller underscores how the evidence from Qumran includes all of the Twelve Prophets, although "none of the scrolls which originally contained the entire collection preserves fragments of more than nine of the books (4QXII[g]) and usually fewer than that."[306]

3. According to Tov, however, only three manuscripts (Mur XII; 4QXII[b]; 4QXII[g]) "show that the entire collection of the Twelve was copied on one scroll."[307] Brooke considers as complete Twelve scrolls only 4QXII[c], 4QXII[e], and possibly 4QXII[d].[308]

---

300. Fuller, "Form," 89.
301. LeCureux, *Thematic*, 3.
302. LeCureux, *Thematic*, 3.
303. Fuller, "Form," 98–99.
304. Fuller, "Form," 95.
305. See also 4QMal (i.e., 4QXII[c] frg. 35); Shoyen 4612/1; 5QAmos. Guillaume, "Reconsideration," 1–2.
306. Fuller, "Form," 91.
307. Cf. Guillaume, "Reconsideration," 3. See also Tov, "Texts," 142.
308. Brooke, "Twelve," 19–44.

4. The Dead Sea manuscripts also preserve some transitions between individual writings: Malachi–Jonah (4QXII^a);[309] Zephaniah–Haggai (4QXII^b); Joel–Amos (4QXII^c);[310] Amos–Obadiah (4QXII^g). Mur XII (Jonah–Micah; Micah–Nahum; Habakkuk–Zephaniah; Zephaniah–Haggai; Haggai–Zechariah) preserves more than one joint.[311]

5. The transition that may be attested in 4QXII^a is unique, since it is not attested in the MT, nor in the LXX sequence.[312] In general, however, the order attested in these scrolls aligns with that of the MT.[313]

6. Variations between the MT and the LXX order exist only as regards the first six books. 4QXII^g and maybe 4QXII^c confirm the antiquity of the MT sequence. The same is true for books VII–XII as evidenced in 4QXII^b.

Oesch showed that the internal division of Mur 88 agrees with that of MT. One cannot but notice that the scribe of this scroll left *three* blank lines between the individual writings of the Twelve.[314] In any case, "the agreement [of Mur XII] with the system of division and placement of division of later Masoretic manuscripts is very strong."[315] Among the seven Cave 4 scrolls, it is possible to detect multiple systems of internal division of text.

The number of copies of the Twelve at Qumran may indicate "a great deal of interest in this material."[316] The inclusion of pesharim on writings from the Twelve may indicate the significant esteem these works held in the eyes of their authors. Quotation from the Twelve in "sectarian" texts further strengthens this assumption.[317]

Recent research on Qumran findings questioned some of the above-mentioned points as follows:

309. This joint is uncertain.

310. This joint is uncertain.

311. See 8ḤevXIIGr (Jonah–Mic; Nah–Hab; Hab–Zeph; Hag–Zech). A somewhat different picture is offered by Guillaume, "Reconsideration," 9–10.

312. Jones, *Formation*.

313. Fuller, "Form," 92.

314. More precisely, "in Mur 88 the scribe also consistently marked the division between compositions (or books) by leaving three lines uninscribed if the transition occurred on the same column but leaving five lines blank at the top of a column if the preceding book ended at the end of a column" (Fuller, "Form," 93–94).

315. Fuller, "Form," 94.

316. Fuller, "Form," 96.

317. Fuller, "Form," 97.

1. A careful investigation of the seven Cave 4 scrolls of Qumran yields a different picture from the above-mentioned,[318] since "the fact that a scroll contains fragments of several Minor Prophets does not prove it was a scroll of the Twelve."[319]

2. In fact, only two manuscripts transmit, according to Guillaume, more than two writings (4QXII[c-g]). From this point of view, "it should be clear that no second-century BCE Hebrew scrolls deserve the 4QXII label and that the probability that scrolls transmitting more than one Minor Prophet would have been scrolls of the entire collection of the XII increases as the date of their Hebrew script gets closer to the turn of the era."[320]

Based on the above-mentioned statements, Guillaume claims that the Twelve may have originated at Alexandria.[321] He supports his hypothesis by revisiting Diana Edelman's statements about the catchword links between Jonah and Nahum,[322] and adopts McKechnie's hypothesis that Sir may have been composed in Egypt.[323] Furthermore, Guillaume brings as argument the fact that the LXX is "the clearest evidence for the existence of the Twelve."[324] For these reasons, the Twelve should be considered an anthology[325] composed in Alexandria before the second century BCE. Therefore, the manuscript evidence is, according to Guillaume, "a far cry from James Nogalski's claim" about the irrefutability of ancient evidence with regard to the reading of the Twelve as a book.[326]

Another issue raised by the Qumran findings is the alleged different order of the writings of the Twelve witnessed in 4QXII[a], the oldest manuscripts of the book (second century BCE). In this scroll, Jonah seems to be appended to an original collection which ended with Malachi.[327] If this is the case, which is the oldest sequence: MT, LXX, or 4QXII[a]? For

---

318. Guillaume, "Reconsideration." See also Pajunen, "Bible," 373–74.
319. Guillaume, "Reconsideration," 2.
320. Guillaume, "Reconsideration," 4.
321. Guillaume, "Reconsideration," 10–14.
322. Edelman, "Jonah," 150–67.
323. McKechnie, "Career," 3–26.
324. Guillaume, "Reconsideration," 11.
325. Here, Guillaume takes up Beck, "Dodekapropheton."
326. Guillaume, "Reconsideration," 5. See also the quoted statement of Nogalski, "Intertextuality," 102.
327. Fuller, "Form," 86–101.

some MT is the original one.³²⁸ Others believe that LXX is the original.³²⁹ According to Jones, the sequence attested in 4QXII^a is the original³³⁰ and Jonah was the last to be added to the Twelve. The MT is dependent on the LXX, rather than the reverse. According to Jones, the Twelve grew from a book of nine (without Joel, Obadiah, and Jonah), to a book of eleven (without Jonah).³³¹ 4QXII^a can be considered the last stage of the formation process and LXX and MT followed in this order the Qumran scroll. Jones's position was criticized mainly because it had no explanation of how the MT came into being.³³²

The issue was again tackled by Guillaume and Brooke from a more codicological point of view. In fact, the seam between Malachi and Jonah is uncertain, and its reconstruction has raised several questions. Above all, Guillaume's analysis of the issue highlighted the speculative nature of reconstructing the fragments that reflect the joining of Malachi and Jonah.³³³ The same caveat comes from Brooke's analysis of the question.³³⁴ The conclusion seems therefore inevitable: "The notion of a widely accepted literary unit already in the second century BCE is not supported by the evidence" and the claim that Sir 49:10 and the contemporary 4QXII^a,b both support the ancient reading of the Twelve as a unity is not demonstrated by material evidence.³³⁵ The passage in Ben Sira does not specify the order of the Twelve and therefore "before the turn of the era, the Twelve constituted no more than an anthology gathered in a somewhat flexible order, which later on became fixed."³³⁶ Finally, according to Guillaume, the material evidence is a strong case on behalf of Ben Zvi's approach rather than Nogalski's.³³⁷

---

328. Schneider, "Unity," 224–25; Nogalski, *Literary*, 2.
329. Jones, *Formation*, 218–20.
330. Jones, *Formation*.
331. Jones, *Formation*, 129–69.
332. Schart, "Redactional Models."
333. Guillaume, "Malachi-Jonah," 1–10.
334. Brooke, "Twelve," 22.
335. Guillaume, "Malachi-Jonah," 10.
336. Guillaume, "Malachi-Jonah," 10.
337. Petersen, "Book," 4–5, also highlights that the Book of the Twelve as a scroll would have been relatively long: Naḥal Ḥever XII is more than ten meters long (1QIsa^a runs almost seven and one-half meters).

3. Conclusions

The analysis carried out so far should be considered only a preliminary exploration of a wider and more complex issue. However, analyzing the text of the two books alongside a comparative study of Psalter and Twelve scholarship can provide valuable insights for forming a tentative conclusion and identifying potential breakthroughs for future research.

The Psalter and the Twelve share some literary features that give them a kind of cohesiveness. This is true especially when one considers the superscriptions and the lexemic links.[338] Both devices can be interpreted as editorial tools, used by the editor(s) of the books to organize the material and, to some extent, to give it a book-like shape. Both features can be considered the starting point and the basis of every exploration of the unity of the books and the identification of the possible link between the final form of the text and the intention and scribal work of the editor(s) as one of the key issues in both scholarships.[339] Regarding superscriptions and intertextuality, scholars face the following problems:[340]

1. The superscriptions may be interpreted as editorial devices used to give the book a specific profile or as markers meant to demarcate the discrete units and, therefore, to shape a collection or anthology rather than a book.[341]

2. The study of *intertextuality* is affected by the difficulty of ascertaining the *intentionality* of lexemic links. For this reason, some scholars strongly underplay the role of such links as editorial markers.

The decision about the interpretation of both features may be influenced by multiple factors.

The study of the textual tradition of the books may offer "historical proof" to the claim that both the Psalter and the Twelve were composed as books.[342] The same is true, to some extent, for external witnesses,

---

338. From this perspective, a terminological similarity among scholars working in both fields can be observed. The term, "seam," is used in a similar way by Wilson and Nogalski.

339. Willgren Davage, "Agree," 85–87.

340. A further issue faced by both areas of scholarship involves the identification of the chronological end of the process of redaction of the books and, consequently, of the identity of the final editors.

341. Apparently, this is the reason why Willgren, *Formation*, conceptualizes the superscriptions as paratexts.

342. As mentioned, Wilson's 1985 monograph opened a new avenue in Psalter

like quotations or allusions in early Jewish and Christian writings. In this regard, Qumran findings have been scrutinized to ascertain whether or not they confirm the basic assumption of the canonical approach, but the outcome is somewhat disputed. It seems that for both the Psalter and the Twelve the manuscripts witness a late stabilization of the books. As for the Psalter, the fluidity of the textual transmission seems to confirm the idea that the sequences of Psalms were copied and transmitted in different forms, even randomly.[343] The methodological issue at stake here can be summarized as follows: what is the relationship between what the manuscripts reveal about the transmission of the books and what the books themselves say about their formation?[344] This is a question needing further investigation.

A problem of method, as highlighted in the scholarship of the Twelve by Ben Zvi, is the difference between an editorial or redactional approach and a (historical) reader-oriented one.[345] The first approach is focused on the final form of the text and attempts to identify the intention(s) of the editor(s) of the book, while the second is focused on reconstructing the original audience of the book and whether they would have been able to decipher the markers inserted into the text by its editor(s). The methodological approach worked out by Ben Zvi finds a somewhat loose parallel in E. Mroczek's claim about the abuse of the term "book" for ancient textual artifacts.[346] Both Ben Zvi and Mroczek conclude that the Psalter and the Twelve were not conceptualized as books by the original or intended audience. From this point of view, another "historical" proof is, so to speak, stripped of any validity.[347] In my opinion, however, neither

---

research because it offered some "historical" evidence about the canonical shape of the book. Perhaps, Nogalski's emphasis on the ancient witnesses of the unity of the Twelve may be considered in a similar way.

343. In this regard, it is interesting to note that in Willgren, *Formation*, the issues of the literary unity of the book and that of the *canon* seem to overlap and blur together.

344. See Pavan, "Psalter," 65–68. "The resolution of the conflict and the integration of the data offered by manuscripts with the models worked out by the *Literarkritik* are yet to be achieved" (66). The distinction between "external" (i.e., manuscripts) and "internal" data is correctly proposed by Hensley, *Relationships*.

345. I add the adjective "historical" to highlight that the original audience is here at stake.

346. Mroczek, *Imagination*. The author claims that, prior to the emergence of the printed "book," textual artifacts were conceived not as a closed entity but rather as something that could always be improved and modified over time.

347. A similar observation comes from Landy, "Three Sides," 9–10, when he asks what literary unity in antiquity is.

the study of the original audience of the books nor Mroczek's criticism[348] are conclusive, but more research is needed in the study of the scribal practices and ideology in Second Temple period.[349]

A third problem that emerges in both fields of study is connected to the distinction between the notions of "book" versus "anthology." Each term can be considered a different way to conceptualize the unity of the Psalter and the Twelve. The term "book" conveys the idea of linear reading with a strong internal coherence created by perspective, plot, character development, etc.[350] On the contrary, an anthology is a collection of individual writings, loosely connected, whose parts can be read independently from the whole without losing essential meaning. Regarding the Psalter, the term "anthology" involves the idea of a flexible collection, meant for personal use—an ensemble of texts without a specific order and carrying different perspectives.[351] The difference between the two perspectives is linked to the combination of parts and whole and—to put it in Landy's words—centripetal and centrifugal tendencies.[352]

All in all, the discussion about the interpretation of the superscripts and lexemic links cannot overshadow the striking parallels between the Psalter and the Twelve. These parallels are somewhat reflected in the points of contact between the two fields of research, both with regard to the canonical reading of the books and its criticism. From this point of view, it is true that the canonical approach is a matter of "vast and careful labor" and that "it is also the result of a *choice*."[353] Such a choice is a result of a decision made by an interpreter based on different evidence. In the case of the Psalter and the Twelve, the parallels considered above and the methodological discussion developed in both fields of research *strengthen* the idea that the two books were not—at least partially—the product of random processes of redaction and transmission of texts.

---

348. Willgren, *Formation*, contends that the manuscript evidence from Qumran does not warrant the idea that that Psalter may have been written *on a single scroll*. Another proof, in his opinion, is that the very idea of a "book" of Psalms is anachronistic. See also Jain, *Psalmen*.

349. For example, Carr, "Rethinking"; "Background"; Longacre, "11Q5 Psalter."

350. See Janowski, "Tempel," 279–326.

351. Pavan, "Psalter," 52–53.

352. "Each book . . . is strongly marked as an individual entity; centripetal tendencies overwhelm centrifugal ones." In his opinion, therefore, the canonical approach "would have to provide sufficient counterweight to this dynamic" (Landy, "Three Sides," 14).

353. Landy, "Three Sides," 12 (emphasis added).

Despite the undeniable differences between the Psalter and the Twelve, the presence of common editorial elements in two different kinds of collections may reveal a shared scribal background, whose profile is still waiting for a more careful and comprehensive study.[354] It seems that a similar "impulse" and similar techniques were used by the scribes responsible for both books to create not only a loose archive or an anthology but rather an organized whole, a book that could offer an overall "structure of meaning" to its different parts.

Bibliography

Abarbanel, I. *Pîrûsh ʿal neviʾim ûketûvîm*. Tel Aviv: Hôṣaʾat Tôrâ wedaʿat, 1960.

Auwers, Jean-Marie. *La Composition Littéraire Du Psautier: Un État de La Question*. CahRB 46. Paris: Gabalda, 2000.

Auwers, Jean-Marie, and Henk J. de Jonge, eds. *The Biblical Canons*. BETL 163. Leuven: Peeters, 2003.

Barth, Christoph. "Concatenatio im ersten Buch des Psalters." In *Wort und Wirklichkeit. Studien zur Afrikanistik und Orientalistik*, edited by Brigitta Benzing et al., 30–40. Meisenheim am Glan: Hain, 1976.

Barton, John. "The Day of Yahweh in the Minor Prophets." In *Biblical and Near Eastern Essays: Studies in Honour of Kevin J. Cathcart*, edited by Carmel McCarthy and John F. Healey, 68–79. JSOTSup 375. London: T&T Clark, 2004.

Beck, Martin. "Das Dodekapropheton als Anthologie." *ZAW* 118 (2006) 558–81.

Ben Zvi, Ehud. "Balancing Shades of 'Historical,' 'Historically-Blurred' and 'Trans-Historical' Contexts and Temporal Contingency in Late Persian/Early Hellenistic Yehudite Memories of YHWH's Words and Prophets of Old in the Prophetic Book Collection and Its Subcollections." In *Profeti Maggiori e Minori a confronto—Major and Minor Prophets Compared*, edited by Guido Benzi et al., 37–54. Rome: Libreria Ateneo Salesiano, 2019.

———. "The Communicative Message of Some Linguistic Choices." In *A Palimpsest: Rhetoric, Ideology, Stylistics, and Language Relating to Persian Israel*, edited by Ehud Ben Zvi et al., 269–90. Piscataway: Gorgias, 2009.

———. "The Concept of Prophetic Books and Its Historical Setting." In *The Production of Prophecy: Constructing Prophecy and Prophecy in Yehud*, edited by Diana V. Edelman and Ehud Ben Zvi, 73–95. London: Equinox, 2009.

———. "From 'Historical' Prophets to Prophetic Books." In *The Oxford Handbook of the Minor Prophets*, edited by Julia M. O'Brien, 4–16. Oxford: Oxford University Press, 2021.

———. *History, Literature and Theology in the Book of Chronicles*. London: Routledge, 2006.

———. "Is the Twelve Hypothesis Likely from an Ancient Readers' Perspective?" In *Two Sides of a Coin. Juxtaposing Views on Interpreting the Book of the Twelve / the Twelve Prophetic Books*, edited by James D. Nogalski and Ehud Ben Zvi, 64–72. Analecta Gorgiana 201. Piscataway: Gorgias, 2009.

---

354. Pavan, "Psalter," 64–65.

———. "The Prophetic Book: A Key Form of Prophetic Literature." In *The Changing Face of Form Criticism for the Twenty First Century*, edited by Marvin A. Sweeney and Ehud Ben Zvi, 276–297. Grand Rapids: Eerdmans 2003.

———. *Social Memory Among the Literati of Yehud*. BZAW 509. Berlin; Boston: de Gruyter, 2019.

———. "Twelve Prophetic Books or 'The Twelve': A Few Preliminary Considerations." In *Forming Prophetic Literature: Essays on Isaiah and the Twelve in Honor of John D. W. Watts*, edited by James W. Watts and Paul R. House, 125–57. JSOTSup 235. Sheffield: Sheffield Academic, 1996.

Ben Zvi, Ehud, and James D. Nogalski. *Two Sides of a Coin: Juxtaposing Views on Interpreting the Book of the Twelve / the Twelve Prophetic Books*. Analecta Gorgiana 201. Piscataway: Gorgias, 2009.

Berges, Ulrich. "'Singt dem Herrn ein neues Lied': Zu den Trägerkreise von Jesajabuch und Psalter." In *Trägerkreise in den Psalmen*, edited by Frank-Lothar Hossfeld et al., 11–33. BBB 178. Göttingen: Vandenhoeck & Ruprecht, 2017.

Bergler, Siegfried. *Joel als Schriftinterpret*. BEATAJ 16. Frankfurt: Lang, 1988.

Berry, Donald K. "Malachi's Dual Design: The Close of the Canon and What Comes Afterward." In *Forming Prophetic Literature: Essays on Isaiah and the Twelve in Honor of John D. W. Watts*, edited by James W. Watts and Paul R. House, 269–302. JSOTSup 235. Sheffield: Sheffield Academic, 1996.

Bosman, Jan P. "The Paradoxical Presence of Exodus 34:6–7 in the Book of the Twelve." *Scriptura* 87 (2004) 233–43.

Bosshard-Nepustil, Erich. "Beobachtungen zum Zwölfprophetenbuch." *BN* 40 (1987) 30–62.

———. *Rezeptionen von Jesaja 1–39 im Zwölfprophetenbuch: Untersuchungen zur literarischen Verbindung von Prophetenbüchern in babylonischer und persischer Zeit*. OBO 154. Fribourg: Vandenhoeck & Ruprecht, 1997.

Bowman, Craig. "Reading the Twelve as One: Hosea 1–3 as an Introduction to the Book of the Twelve (The Minor Prophets)." *Stone-Campbell Journal* 9 (2006) 1–18.

Brennan, J. P. "Some Hidden Harmonies of the Fifth Book of Psalms." In *Essays in Honor of Joseph P. Brennan*, edited by Robert F. McNamara, 126–58. New York: St Bernard's Seminary, 1976.

Brodersen, Alma. *The End of the Psalter: Psalm 146–150 in the Masoretic Text, the Dead Sea Scrolls, and the Septuagint*. BZAW 505. Berlin; Boston: de Gruyter, 2017.

Brooke, George J. "The Twelve Minor Prophets and the Dead Sea Scrolls." In *Congress Volume Leiden 2004*, edited by André Lemaire, 19–43. Leiden; Boston: Brill, 2006.

Brütsch, Matthias. *Israels Psalmen in Qumran: Ein textarchäologischer Beitrag zur Entstehung des Psalter*. BWA(N)T 193. Stuttgart: Kohlhammer, 2010.

Budde, Karl. "Eine folgenschwere Redaktion des Zwölfprophetenbuchs." *ZAW* 39 (1921) 218–29.

Carr, David M. "Background and Aims of a Scroll Approach to the Formation of the Hebrew Bible." In *Advances in Ancient, Biblical and Near Eastern Research* 3 (2023) 9–79.

———. "Rethinking the Materiality of Biblical Texts: From Source, Tradition and Redaction to a Scroll Approach." *ZAW* 132 (2020) 594–621.

Cassuto, Umberto. "The Sequence and Arrangement of Biblical Sections." In *Bible*, 1–6. Vol. 1 of *Biblical and Oriental Studies*. Jerusalem: Magnes, 1973.

Childs, Brevard S. "The Canonical Shape of the Prophetic Literature." *Int* 32 (1978) 46–68.

———. *Introduction to the Old Testament as Scripture.* Philadelphia: Fortress, 1979.

Clements, Ronald E. "Patterns in the Prophetic Canon." In *Canon and Authority: Essays in Old Testament Religion and Theology*, edited by George W. Coats and Burke O. Long, 42–55. Philadelphia: Fortress, 1977.

———. "Patterns in the Prophetic Canon: Healing the Blind and the Lame." In *Canon, Theology, and Old Testament Interpretation: Essays in Honor of Brevard S. Childs*, edited by Gene M. Tucker at al., 189–200. Philadelphia: Fortress, 1988.

———. "Psalm 72 and Isaiah 40–66: A Study in Tradition." *PRSt* 28 (2001) 333–41.

Clines, David J. A. "Beyond Synchronic/Diachronic." In *Synchronic or Diachronic? A Debate on Method in Old Testament Exegesis*, edited by Johannes C. de Moor, 52–71. OtSt 34. Leiden; Boston: Brill, 1995.

Coggins, Richard J. "The Minor Prophets—One Book or Twelve?" In *Crossing the Boundaries: Essays in Biblical Interpretation in Honour of Michael D. Goulder*, edited by Stanley E. Porter et al., 57–68. BibInt 8. Leiden; Boston: Brill, 1994.

Collins, Terence. *The Mantle of Elijah: The Redaction Criticism of the Prophetical Books.* BibSem 20. Sheffield: JSOT, 1993.

Coniglio, Alessandro. "'Gracious and Merciful is YHWH . . .' (Psalm 145:8): The Quotations of Exodus 34:6 in Psalm 145 and Its Role in the Holistic Design of the Psalter." *SBFLA* 67 (2017) 29–50.

Conrad, Edgar W. "Forming the Twelve and Forming Canon." In *Thematic Threads in the Book of the Twelve*, edited by Paul L. Redditt and Aaron Schart, 90–103. BZAW 325. Berlin; Boston: de Gruyter, 2003.

Cuffey, Kenneth H. "Remnant, Redactor, and Biblical Theologian: A Comparative Study of Coherence in Micah and the Twelve." In *Reading and Hearing the Book of the Twelve*, edited by James D. Nogalski and Marvin A. Sweeney, 185–208. SBL Symposium Series 15. Atlanta: SBL, 2000.

Culley, Robert C. "David and the Psalms: Titles, Poems, and Stories." In *The Fate of King David: The Past and Present of a Biblical Icon*, edited by Tod Linafelt et al., 153–162. LHBOTS 500. London: T&T Clark, 2010.

deClaissé-Walford, Nancy L. "The Canon of Psalms." In *Canon Formation. Tracing the Role of Sub-Collections in the Biblical Canon*, edited by W. Edward Glenny and Darian R. Lockett, 121–38. London; New York: T&T Clark, 2023.

Delitzsch, Franz J. *Symbolae ad Psalmos Illustrandos Isagogicae.* 2 vols. Leipzig: Carolum Tauchnitium, 1846.

———. "Wann weissagte Obadja?" *Zeitschrift für die gesamnte Lutherische Theologie und Kirche* 12 (1851) 91–102.

DiPede, Elena, and Donatella Scaiola, eds. *The Book of the Twelve—One Book or Many?* Metz Conference Proceedings, November 5–7, 2015. FAT II 91. Tübingen: Mohr Siebeck, 2016.

Edelman, Diana V. "Jonah Among the Twelve in the MT: The Triumph of Torah Over Prophecy." In *The Production of Prophecy: Constructing Prophecy and Prophets in Yehud*, edited by Diana V. Edelman and Ehud Ben Zvi, 150–67. London: Equinox, 2009.

Ego, Beate. "The Repentance of Nineveh in the Story of Jonah and Nahum's Prophecy in the City's Destruction—A Coherent Reading of the Book of the Twelve as Reflected in the Aggada." In *Thematic Threads in the Book of the Twelve*, edited by Paul L. Redditt and Aaron Schart, 155–64. BZAW 325. Berlin; Boston: de Gruyter, 2003.

Eichhorn, Johannes G. *Einleitung in das Alte Testament.* Leipzig: Weidmann, 1803.

Even-Israel Steinsaltz, Adin. *Bava Batra—Part One.* Vol. 27 of *Koren Talmud Bavli. The Noé Edition.* Jerusalem: Koren, 2016.

Ewald, Georg H. A. *Jeremia und Ezecheil mit ihren zeitgenossen.* Die Propheten des Alten Bundes 2. Göttingen: Vandenhoeck & Ruprecht, 1868.

Fabry, Heinz-Josef. "'Mich machte Er zum Herrscher über die Söhne Seines' (Ps 151,11). Der Beitrag Qumrans zu einer Theologie des Psalters." In *Zur Theologie des Psalters und der Psalmen. Beiträge in memoriam Frank-Lothar Hossfeld*, edited by Ulrich Berges et al., 429–50. BBB 189. Göttingen: Vandenhoeck & Ruprecht, 2019.

Firth, David G., and Brittany N. Melton. "On Reading the Twelve Minor Prophets." In *Reading the Book of the Twelve Minor Prophets*, edited by David G. Firth and Brittany N. Melton, 1–6. SSBT. Bellingham: Lexham Academic, 2022.

Fishbane, Michael. *Biblical Interpretation in Ancient Israel.* Oxford: Clarendon, 1985.

Flint, Peter W. *The Dead Sea Psalms Scrolls and the Book of Psalms.* STDJ 17. Leiden; Boston: Brill 1997.

Floyd, Michael H. "The מַשָּׂא (MAŚŚĀ') as a Type of Prophetic Book." *JBL* 121 (2002) 401–22.

Flitz, Judith E. *Gott unterwegs. Die traditions- und religionsgeschichtlichen Hintergründe des Habakukliedes.* ORA 36. Tübingen: Mohr Siebeck, 2020.

Fuller, Russell E. "The Form and Formation of the Book of the Twelve: The Evidence from the Judean Desert." In *Forming Prophetic Literature: Essays on Isaiah and the Twelve in Honor of John D. W. Watts*, edited by Paul R. House and James W. Watts, 86–87. JSOTSup 235. Sheffield: Sheffield Academic, 1996.

———. "The Minor Prophet Manuscripts from Qumrân, Cave IV." PhD diss., Harvard University, 1995.

———. "9.2.2 Minor Prophets: Ancient Hebrew Texts: Masoretic Texts and Ancient Texts Close to MT." In *The Hebrew Bible: Pentateuch, Former and Latter Prophets*, edited by Armin Lange and Emanuel Tov, 606–10. Vol. 1B of *Textual History of the Bible.* Leiden; Boston: Brill, 2016.

———. "The Twelve: 4QXIIa, 4QXIIb, 4QXIIc, 4QXIId, 4QXIIe, 4QXIIf, 4QXIIg." In *The Prophets*, edited by Eugene Ulrich et al., 221–318. Vol. 10 of *Qumran Cave 4.* DJD XV. Oxford: Clarendon, 1997.

Genette, Gérard. *Seuils.* Paris: Éditions du Seuil, 1987.

Glenny, W. Edward. "Textual History of the Minor Prophets: Hebrew Manuscripts and Versions." In *The Oxford Handbook of the Minor Prophets*, edited by Julia M. O'Brien, 40–55. Oxford: Oxford University Press, 2021.

Goldingay, John. "Twelve Books, One Theology?" In *Reading the Book of the Twelve Minor Prophets*, edited by David G. Firth and Brittany N. Melton, 171–91. SSBT. Bellingham: Lexham Academic, 2022.

Gottwald, Norman K. "Tragedy and Comedy in the Latter Prophets." *Semeia* 32 (1985) 83–96.

Guillaume, Philippe. "A Reconsideration of Manuscripts Classified as Scrolls of the Twelve Minor Prophets (XII)." *JHebS* 7 (2007) 1–12. https://doi.org/10.5508/jhs.2007.v7.a16.

———. "The Unlikely Malachi–Jonah Sequence (4QXII^a)." *JHebS* 7 (2007) 1–10. https://doi.org/10.5508/jhs.2007.v7.a15.

Hadjiev, Tchavdar S. "A Prophetic Anthology Rather than a Book of the Twelve." In *The Book of the Twelve: Composition, Reception, and Interpretation*, edited by Lena-Sophia Tiemeyer and Jakob Wöhrle, 90–108. VTSup 184. Leiden; Boston: Brill, 2020.

Hartenstein, Friedhelm. "'Schaffe mir Recht, JHWH!' (Psalm 7,9) Zum theologischen und anthropologischen Profil der Teilkomposition Psalm 3–14." In *The Composition of the Book of Psalms*, edited by Erich Zenger, 229–58. BETL 238. Leuven: Peeters, 2010.

Hensley, Adam D. *Covenant Relationships and the Editing of the Hebrew Psalter*. LHBOTS 666. London: T&T Clark, 2018.

Ho, Peter C. W. *The Design of the Psalter: A Macrostructural Analysis*. Eugene, OR: Pickwick, 2019.

Hossfeld, Frank-Lothar, and Erich Zenger. "Neue und alte Wege der Psalmenexegese: Antworten auf die Fragen von M. Millard und R. Rendtorff." *BibInt* 4 (1996) 332–43.

———. *Psalmen 51–100*. HThKAT. Freiburg-Basel-Wien: Herder, 2000.

———. "Psalmenauslegung im Psalter." In *Schriftauslegung in der Schrift. Festschrift für Odil Hannes Steck zu seinem 65. Geburtstag*, edited by Reinhard G. Kratz et al., 237–58. BZAW 300. Berlin; Boston: de Gruyter, 2000.

House, Paul R. *The Unity of the Twelve*. BLS 27; JSOTSup 97. Sheffield: Almond, 1990.

Jacobson, Rolf A. "Imagining the Future of Psalms Studies." In *The Shape and Shaping of the Book of Psalms: The Current State of Scholarship*, edited by Nancy L. deClaissé-Walford, 231–46. SBLAIL 20. Atlanta: SBL, 2014.

Jain, Eva. *Psalmen oder Psalter? Materielle Rekonstruktion und inhaltliche Untersuchung der Psalmenhandschriften aus der Wüste Juda*. STDJ 109. Leiden; Boston: Brill, 2014.

Janowski, Bernd. "Ein Tempel aus Worten. Zur theologischen Architektur des Psalters." In *The Composition of the Book of Psalms*, edited by Erich Zenger, 279–326. BETL 238. Leuven: Peeters, 2010.

Jepsen, Alfred. "Kleine Beiträge zum Zwölfprophetenbuch." ZAW 56 (1938) 85–110; 57 (1939) 242–55.

Jeremias, Jörg. "Neuere Tendenzen der Forschung an den Kleinen Propheten." In *Perspectives in the Study of the Old Testament and Early Judaism*, edited by Florentino G. Martinez and Ed Noort, 122–36. VTSup 73. Leiden; Boston: Brill, 1998.

Jones, Barry Alan. *The Formation of the Book of the Twelve: A Study in Text and Canon*. SBLDS 149. Atlanta: Scholars, 1995.

Kaiser, Otto. "Das Dodekapropheton oder Zwölfprophetenbuch." In *Die prophetische Werke*, 103–7. Vol. 2 of *Grundriß der Einleitung in die kanonische und deuterokanonische Schriften des Alten Testaments*. Gütersloh: Gütersloher Verlagshaus Gerd Mohn, 1994.

Keil, Carl F. *Biblischer Commentar über die Zwölf kleinen Propheten*. Leipzig: Dörffling und Franke, 1888.

Kessler, Rainer. "The Twelve: Structure, Theme, and Contested Issues." In *The Oxford Handbook of the Prophets*, edited by Carolyn J. Sharp, 207–23. Oxford: Oxford University Press, 2016.

Klinger, Bernhard. "Zwischen Skylla und Charybdis: Hieronymus als Ausleger der kleinen Propheten." *Vulgata in Dialogue* 4 (2020) 5–22. https://doi.org/10.25788/vidbor.v4i0.302.

Kratz, Reinhard G. "Odil Hannes Steck und seine Arbeiten über das Alte Testament." *TLZ* 129 (2004) 467–80.

Krispenz, Jutta. *Scribes as Sages and Prophets: Scribal Traditions in Biblical Wisdom Literature and in the Book of the Twelve*. BZAW 496. Berlin; Boston: de Gruyter, 2021.

Kuhl, Curt. *Die Entstehung des Alten Testaments*. Bern: Francke, 1953.

Landy, Francis. "Three Sides of a Coin: In Conversation with Ben Zvi and Nogalski, Two Sides of a Coin." *JHebS* 10 (2010) 1–21. https://jhsonline.org/index.php/jhs/article/view/11273.

Lange, Armin. "Collecting Psalms in Light of the Dead Sea Scrolls." In *A Teacher for All Generations. Essays in Honor of James C. VanderKam*, edited by Eric F. Mason, 1:297–308. Supplements to the Journal for the Study of Judaism 153. 2 vols. Leiden; Boston: Brill, 2012.

———. *Handbuch der Textfunde vom Toten Meer, Band 1: Die Handschriften biblischer Bücher von Qumran und den anderen Fundorten*. Tübingen: Mohr Siebeck, 2009.

Lawee, Eric. *Isaac Abarbanel's Stance Toward Tradition: Defense, Dissent, and Dialogue*. Albany: State University of New York Press, 2001.

LeCureux, Jason T. *The Thematic Unity of the Book of the Twelve*. HBM 41. Sheffield: Sheffield Phoenix, 2012.

Lee, Andrew Yueking. "The Canonical Unity of the Scroll of the Minor Prophets." PhD diss., Baylor University, 1985.

Leeuwen, Raymond C. van. "Scribal Wisdom and Theodicy in the Book of the Twelve." In *In Search of Wisdom: Essays in Memory of John G. Gammie*, edited by Leo G. Perdue et al., 31–49. Louisville: Westminster John Knox, 1993.

Leuenberger, Martin. *Konzeptionen des Königtums Gottes im Psalter. Untersuchungen zu Komposition und Redaktion der theokratischen Bücher IV–V im Psalter*. ATANT 83. Zürich: Theologischer Verlag, 2004.

———. "Die Psalterdoxologien. Entstehung und Theologie." In *Gott in Bewegung. Religions- und theologiegeschichtliche Beiträge zu Gottesvorstellungen im alten Israel*, 166–93. FAT 66. Tübingen: Mohr Siebeck, 2011.

Longacre, Drew. "The 11Q5 Psalter as a Scribal Product: Standing at the Nexus of Textual Development, Editorial Processes, and Manuscript Production." *ZAW* 134 (2022) 85–111.

Lyons, Michael A. "Psalm 22 and the 'Servants' of Isaiah 54; 56–66." *CBQ* 77 (2015) 640–56.

Marks, Herbert. "The Twelve Prophets." In *The Literary Guide to the Bible*, edited by Robert Alter and Frack Kermode, 207–33. Cambridge: Belknap, 1987.

McKechnie, Paul. "The Career of Joshua Ben Sira." *JTS* 51 (2000) 3–26.

Millard, Matthias. *Die Komposition des Psalters. Ein formgeschichtlicher Ansatz*. FAT 9. Tübingen: Mohr Siebeck, 1994.

Mitchell, David C. *The Message of the Psalter: An Eschatological Programme in the Book of Psalms*. JSOTSup 252. Sheffield: Sheffield Academic, 1997.

Moore, M. S. "Review of A. Brodersen, The End of the Psalter: Psalm 146–150 in the Masoretic Text, the Dead Sea Scrolls, and the Septuagint." *CBQ* 81 (2019) 520–21.

Mroczek, Eva. *The Literary Imagination in Jewish Antiquity*. Oxford: Oxford University Press, 2016.

Murphy, Roland E. "Reflections on Contextual Interpretation of the Psalms." In *The Shape and the Shaping of the Psalter*, edited by J. Clinton McCann, 21–41. JSOTSup 159. Sheffield: Sheffield Academic, 1993.

Nasuti, Harry P. "The Editing of the Psalter and the Ongoing Use of the Psalms: Gerald Wilson and the Question of Canon." In *The Shape and the Shaping of the Book of Psalms: The Current State of Scholarship*, edited by Nancy L. deClaissé-Walford, 13–20. SBLAIL 20. Atlante: SBL, 2014.

Nicol, George G. "Recent Research on the Book of the Twelve Prophets." *ExpTim* 130 (2018) 80–81.

Niemeyer, Cornelis T. *Het probleem van de rangschikking der Psalmen*. Leiden: Luctor et Emergo, 1950.

Nihan, Christophe. "David Superscripts in the Psalms and Concepts of Authorship in the Hebrew Bible." In *Authorship and the Hebrew Bible*, edited by Sonja Ammann et al., 193–208. FAT 158. Tübingen: Mohr Siebeck, 2022.

Nogalski, James D. *The Book of the Twelve and Beyond. Collected Essays of James D. Nogalski*. SBLAIL 29. Atlanta: SBL, 2017.

———. "The Day(s) of YHWH in the Book of the Twelve." In *Thematic Threads in the Book of the Twelve*, edited by Paul L. Redditt and Aaron Schart, 192–213. BZAW 325. Berlin; Boston: de Gruyter, 2003.

———. "Doubts about the Task." In *Two Sides of a Coin: Juxtaposing Views on Interpreting the Book of the Twelve / the Twelve Prophetic Books*, edited by James D. Nogalski and Ehud Ben Zvi, 16–22. Piscataway: Gorgias, 2009.

———. "Intertextuality and the Twelve." In *Forming Prophetic Literature: Essays on Isaiah and the Twelve in Honor of John D. W. Watts*, edited by James W. Watts and Paul R. House, 102–24. JSOTSup 235. Sheffield: Sheffield Academic, 1996.

———. "Joel as 'Literary Anchor' for the Book of the Twelve." In *Reading and Hearing the Book of the Twelve*, edited by James D. Nogalski and Marvin A. Sweeney, 91–109. SBL Symposium Series 15. Atlanta: SBL, 2000.

———. *Literary Precursors to the Book of the Twelve*. BZAW 217. Berlin; Boston: de Gruyter, 1993.

———. "One Book and Twelve Books: The Nature of the Redactional Work and the Implications of Cultic Source Material in the Book of the Twelve." In *Two Sides of a Coin: Juxtaposing Views on Interpreting the Book of the Twelve / The Twelve Prophetic Books*, edited by James D. Nogalski and Ehud Ben Zvi, 11–46. Piscataway: Gorgias, 2009.

———. "Recurring Themes in the Book of the Twelve: Creating Points of Contact for a Theological Reading." *Int* 61 (2007) 125–36.

———. *Redactional Processes in the Book of the Twelve*. BZAW 218. Berlin; Boston: de Gruyter, 1993.

Nogalski, James D., and Marvin A. Sweeney, eds. *Reading and Hearing the Book of the Twelve*. SBL Symposium Series 15. Atlanta: SBL, 2000.

O'Brien, Julia M., ed. *The Oxford Handbook of the Minor Prophets*. Oxford: Oxford University Press, 2021.

Pajunen, Mika S. "Bible." In *T&T Clark Companion to the Dead Sea Scrolls*, edited by George J. Brooke and Charlotte Hempel, 373–74. London: T&T Clark, 2017.

———. "Differentiation of Form, Theme, and Changing Functions in Psalms and Prayers." *SJOT* 33 (2019) 264–76.

———. "Perspectives on the Existence of a Particular Authoritative Book of Psalms in the Late Second Temple Period." *JSOT* 39.2 (2014) 139–63.

Pavan, Marco. *"He Remembered that They Were but Flesh, a Breath that Passes and Does Not Return" (Ps 78,39). The Theme of Memory and Forgetting in the Third Book of the Psalter (Pss 73–89)*. ÖBS 44; Frankfurt: Peter Lang, 2014.

———. "The Psalter as a Book? A Critical Evaluation of the Recent Research on the Psalter." In *The Formation of the Hebrew Psalter: The Book of Psalms between Ancient Versions, Material Transmission and Canonical Exegesis*, edited by Gianni Barbiero et al., 11–82. FAT I 151. Tübingen: Mohr Siebeck, 2021.

Petersen, David L. "A Book of the Twelve?" In *Reading and Hearing the Book of the Twelve*, edited by James D. Nogalski and Marvin A. Sweeney, 3–10. SBL Symposium Series 15. Atlanta: SBL, 2000.

Pierce, Ronald W. "Literary Connectors and a Haggai/Zechariah/Malachi Corpus." *JETS* 27 (1984) 277–89.

———. "A Thematic Development of the Haggai/Zechariah/Malachi Corpus." *JETS* 27 (1984) 401–11.

Pike, Dana M., and Andrew C. Skinner. *Unidentified Fragments*. Vol. 23 of *Qumran Cave 4*. DJD 33. Oxford: Oxford University Press, 2001.

Redditt, Paul L. "The Formation of the Book of the Twelve: A Review of Research." In *Thematic Threads in the Book of the Twelve*, edited by Paul L. Redditt and Aaron Schart, 1–26. BZAW 235. Berlin; Boston: de Gruyter, 2003.

———. "Recent Research on the Book of the Twelve as One Book." *CurBS* 9 (2001) 47–80.

Redditt, Paul L., and Aaron Schart, eds. *Thematic Threads in the Book of the Twelve*. BZAW 325. Berlin; Boston: de Gruyter, 2003.

Rendtorff, Rolf. "Alas for the Day! The 'Day of the LORD' in the Book of the Twelve." In *God in the Fray: A Tribute to Walter Brueggemann*, edited by Tod Linafelt and Timothy K. Beal, 186–97. Minneapolis: Fortress, 1998.

———. "How to Read the Book of the Twelve as a Theological Unity." In *Reading and Hearing the Book of the Twelve*, edited by James D. Nogalski and Marvin A. Sweeney, 75–87. SBL Symposium Series 15. Atlanta: SBL, 2000.

Rudolph, Wilhelm. *Hosea; Joel, Amos, Obadja, Jona; Micha, Nahum, Habakuk, Zephanja; Haggai, Sacharja 1–8, Sacharja 9–14, Maleachi*. KAT XIII: 1–4. Gütersloh: Gütersloher Verlagshaus Gerd Mohn, 1966–1976.

Scaiola, Donatella. "I Dodici Profeti minori: problemi di metodo e di interpretazione." *RivB* 54 (2006) 65–75.

Schart, Aaron. *Die Entstehung des Zwölfprophetenbuchs. Neubearbeitungen von Amos im Rahmen schriftenübergreifender Redaktionsprozesse*. BZAW 260. Berlin; Boston: de Gruyter, 1998.

———. "The First Section of the Book of the Twelve Prophets: Hosea-Joel-Amos." *Int* 61 (2007) 138–52.

———. "Reconstructing the Redaction History of the Twelve Prophets: Problems and Models." In *Reading and Hearing the Book of the Twelve*, edited by James D. Nogalski and Marvin A. Sweeney, 34–48. SBL Symposium Series 15. Atlanta: SBL, 2000.

———. "Redactional Models: Comparisons, Contrasts, Agreements, Disagreements." In *Society of Biblical Literature 1998 Seminar Papers*, edited by David J. Lull, 893–908. SBLSP 37. Atlanta: Scholars, 1998.

———. "Zur Redaktionsgeschichte des Zwölfprophetenbuchs." *VF* 43 (1998) 893–908.

Schmid, Konrad. "Innerbiblische Schriftauslegung: Aspekte der Forschungsgeschichte." In *Schriftauslegung in der Schrift: Festschrift für Odil Hannes Steck zu seinem 65. Geburtstag*, edited by Reinhard G. Kratz et al., 1–22. BZAW 300. Berlin; Boston: de Gruyter, 2000.

———. "Das Zwölfprophetenbuch." In *Grundinformationen Altes Testament: Eine Einführung in Literatur, Religion und Geschichte des Alten Testaments*, edited by Jan C. Gertz et al., 363–65. Göttingen: Vandenhoeck & Ruprecht, 2006.

Schneider, Dale A. "The Unity of the Book of the Twelve." PhD diss., Yale University, 1979.

Schnocks, Johannes. "Die Psalterexegese und die Handschriften: Überlegungen zum IV. Psalmenbuch (Ps 90–106) als Komposition und in Qumran." In *The Formation of the Hebrew Psalter: The Book of Psalms between Ancient Versions, Material Transmission and Canonical Exegesis*, edited by Gianni Barbiero et al., 309–30. FAT I 151. Tübingen: Mohr Siebeck, 2021.

Schwesig, Paul-Gerhard. *Die Rolle der Tag-JHWHs-Dichtungen im Dodekapropheton*. BZAW 366. Berlin; Boston: de Gruyter, 2006.

Seitz, Christopher R. "On Letting a Text 'Act Like a Man'—The Book of the Twelve: New Horizons for Canonical Reading, with Hermeneutical Reflexions." *Scottish Bulletin of Evangelical Theology* 22 (2004) 151–72.

———. *Prophecy and Hermeneutics: Toward a New Introduction to the Prophets*. STI. Grand Rapids: Baker Academic, 2007.

———. "The Unique Achievement of the Book of the Twelve: Neither Redactional Unity Nor Anthology." In *The Book of the Twelve: An Anthology of Prophetic Books or the Result of Complex Redactional Processes?*, edited by Heiko Wenzel, 37–48. Osnabrücker Studien Zur Jüdischen Und Christlichen Bibel 4. Göttingen: Vandenhoeck & Ruprecht, 2018.

———. "What Lesson Will History Teach? The Book of the Twelve as History." In *"Behind" the Text: History and Biblical Interpretation*, edited by Craig Bartholomew et al., 443–69. SHS. Grand Rapids: Zondervan, 2003.

Seitz, Christopher R., and Kent H. Richards, eds. *The Bible as Christian Scripture. The Work of Brevard S. Childs*. SBL Biblical Scholarship in North America 25. Atlanta: SBL, 2013.

Sieges, Anna. "One Book or Twelve Books?" In *The Oxford Handbook of the Minor Prophets*, edited by Julia M. O'Brien, 29–38. Oxford: Oxford University Press, 2021.

Snearly, Michael K. *The Return of the King: Messianic Expectation in Book V of the Psalter*. LHBOTS 624. London: T&T Clark, 2016.

Steck, Odil H. *Der Abschluß der Prophetie im Alten Testament: Ein Versuch zur Frage der Vorgeschichte des Kanons*. BThS 17. Neukirchen-Vluyn: Neukirchener, 1991.

———. *Bereitete Heimkehr: Jesaja 35 als redaktionelle Brücke zwischen dem Ersten und dem Zweiten Jesaja*. Stuttgart: Katholisches Bibelwerk, 1985.

———. *Exegese des Alten Testaments: Leitfaden der Methodik. Ein Arbeitsbuch für Proseminare, Seminare und Vorlesungen*. Neukirchen-Vluyn: Neukirchener, 1999.

———. *Gottesknecht und Zion. Gesammelte Aufsätze zu Deuterojesaja*. FAT 4. Tübingen: Mohr Siebeck, 1992.

———. *Studien zu Tritojesaja*. BZAW 203. Berlin; Boston: de Gruyter, 1991.

———. "Zu Eigenart und Herkunft von Ps 102." *ZAW* 102 (1990) 357–72.

———. "Zur Abfolge Maleachi-Jona in 4Q76 (4QXIII^a)." *ZAW* 108 (1996) 249–53.

———. "Zur Frage der Schlußredaktion des Psalters." In *Der Abschluß der Prophetie im Alten Testament: Ein Versuch zur Frage der Vorgeschichte des Kanons*, 157–66. BThS 17. Neukirchen-Vluyn: Neukirchener, 1991.

Steinberg, Julius. *Die Ketuvim: Ihr Aufbau und ihre Botschaft.* BBB 152. Hamburg: Philo, 2006.

Steuernagel, Carl. *Lehrbuch der Einleitung in das Alten Testament.* Tübingen: Mohr Siebeck, 1912.

Stovell, Beth M., and David J. Fuller. *The Book of the Twelve.* Eugene, OR: Cascade, 2022.

Sweeney, Marvin A. "The Minor Prophets and the Book of the Twelve in Late-Eighteenth through Early-Twenty-First-Century Research." In *The Oxford Handbook of the Minor Prophets*, edited by Julia M. O'Brien, 267–78. Oxford: Oxford University Press, 2021.

———. "Sequence and Interpretation in the Book of Twelve." In *Reading and Hearing the Book of the Twelve*, edited by James D. Nogalski and Marvin A. Sweeney, 49–64. SBL Symposium Series 15. Atlanta: SBL, 2000.

———. "Synchronic and Diachronic Concerns in Reading the Book of the Twelve Prophets." In *Perspectives on the Formation of the Book of the Twelve: Methodological Foundations, Redactional Processes, Historical Insights*, edited by Rainer Albertz et al., 21–33. BZAW 433. Berlin; Boston: de Gruyter, 2012.

———. *The Twelve Prophets.* Vol. 1. Berit Olam. Collegeville, MN: Liturgical, 2000.

Tooze, George A. "Framing the Book of the Twelve. Connections Between Hosea and Malachi." PhD diss., Iliff School of Theology Denver, 2002.

Tov, Emanuel. "The Biblical Texts from the Judean Desert—An Overview and Analysis of the Published Texts." In *The Bible as Book. The Hebrew Bible and the Judean Desert Discoveries*, edited by Edward D. Herbert and Emanuel Tov. The Bible as Book 4. London: British Library, 2002.

Tuell, Steven S. "The Psalm in Habakkuk 3." In *Partners with God. Theological and Critical Readings of the Bible in Honor of Marvin A. Sweeney*, edited by Shelley L. Birdsong and Serge Frolov, 262–74. Claremont: Claremont, 2017.

Utzschneider, Helmut. *Künder oder Schreiber? Eine These zum Problem der "Schriftprophetie" auf Grund von Maleachi 1,6–2,9.* BEATAJ 19. Frankfurt: Lang, 1989.

———. "Die Schriftprophetie und die Frage nach dem Ende der Prophetie: Überlegungen anhand von Mal 1,6–2,16." *ZAW* 104 (1992) 377–94.

Watts, James W., and Paul R. House, eds. *Forming Prophetic Literature. Essays on Isaiah and the Twelve in Honor of John D. W. Watts.* JSOTSup 235. Sheffield: Sheffield Academic, 1996.

Watts, John D. W. *Isaiah 1–33*, Waco, TX: Word, 1985.

———. "Frame for the Book of the Twelve: Hosea 1–3 and Malachi." In *Reading and Hearing the Book of the Twelve*, edited by James D. Nogalski and Marvin A. Sweeney, 209–18. SBL Symposium Series 15. Atlanta: SBL, 2000.

———. "Superscriptions and Incipits in the Book of the Twelve." In *Reading and Hearing the Book of the Twelve*, edited by James D. Nogalski and Marvin A. Sweeney, 110–24. SBL Symposium Series 15. Atlanta: SBL, 2000.

Willgren, David. *The Formation of the "Book" of Psalms: Reconsidering the Transmission and Canonization of Psalmody in Light of Material Culture and the Poetics of Anthologies.* FAT II 88. Tübingen: Mohr Siebeck, 2016.

[Willgren] Davage, David. "A Canon of Psalms in the Dead Sea Scrolls? Revisiting the Qumran Psalms Hypothesis." *BTB* 51 (2021) 196–205.

Willgren Davage, David. "What Could We Agree On? Outlining Five Fundaments in the Research of the 'Book' of Psalms." In *The Formation of the Hebrew Psalter: The Book of Psalms Between Ancient Versions, Material Transmission and Canonical Exegesis*, edited by Gianni Barbiero et al., 83–117. FAT I 151. Tübingen: Mohr Siebeck, 2021.

Wilson, Gerald H. *The Editing of the Hebrew Psalter*. SBLDS 76. Chico: SBL, 1985.

———. "King, Messiah, and the Reign of God: Revisiting the Royal Psalms and the Shape of the Psalter." In *The Book of Psalms: Composition and Reception*, edited by Peter W. Flint and Patrick D. Miller, 391–406. VTSup 99. Leiden; Boston: Brill, 2005.

———. "Understanding the Purposeful Arrangement of Psalms in the Psalter: Pitfalls and Promise." In *The Shape and Shaping of the Psalter*, edited by J. Clinton McCann, 42–51. JSOTSup 159. Sheffield: Sheffield Academic, 1993.

———. "The Use of 'Untitled' Psalms in the Hebrew Psalter." *ZAW* 97 (1985) 404–13.

Wöhrle, Jakob. *Die frühen Sammlungen des Zwölfprophetenbuches: Entstehung und Komposition*. BZAW 360. Berlin: de Gruyter, 2006.

———. "'No Future for the Proud Exultant Ones': The Exilic Book of the Four Prophets (Hos., Am., Mic., Zeph.) as a Concept Opposed to the Deuteronomistic History." *VT* 58 (2008) 608–27.

Wolfe, Rolland E. "The Editing of the Book of the Twelve." *ZAW* 53 (1935) 90–129.

———. *The Editing of the Book of the Twelve: A Study of Secondary Material in the Minor Prophets*. Harvard: Harvard University, 1933.

Yarchin, William. "Is There an Authoritative Shape for the Hebrew Book of Psalms? Profiling the Manuscripts of the Hebrew Psalter." *RB* 122.3 (2015) 355–70.

———. "Were the Psalms Collections at Qumran True Psalters?" *JBL* 134.4 (2015) 775–89.

Zapff, Burkard M. *Redaktionsgeschichtliche Studien zum Michabuch im Kontext des Dodekapropheton*. BZAW 256. Berlin; Boston: de Gruyter, 1997.

———. "Die Völkerperspektive des Michabuches als 'Systematisierung' der divergierenden Sicht der Völker in den Büchern Joël, Jona und Nahum? Überlegungen zu einer buchübergreifenden Exegese im Dodekapropheton." *BN* 98 (1999) 86–99.

Zenger, Erich. "Dai Salmi al Salterio: Nuove vie della ricerca." In *Dai Salmi al Salterio: Orientamenti per le letture nuove*, edited by Eberhard Bons and Angelo Passaro, 169–99. Scripturae 4. Trapani: Il pozzo di Giacobbe, 2014.

———. "Kanonische Psalmenexegese und christlich-jüdischer Dialog: Beobachtungen zum Sabbatpsalm 92." In *Mincha: Festgabe für Rolf Rendtorff zum 75. Geburtstag*, edited by Erhard Blum, 243–60. Neukirchen-Vluyn: Neukirchener, 2000.

———. "Psalmenforschung nach Hermann Gunkel und Sigmund Mowinckel." In *Congress Volume. Oslo 1998*, edited by André Lemaire and Magne Sæbø, 399–435. VTSup 80. Leiden; Boston: Brill, 2000.

———. "'So betete David für seinen Sohn Salomo und für den König Messias': Überlegungen zur holistischen und kanonischen Lektüre des 72. Psalms." *Jahrbuch für biblische Theologie* 8 (1993) 57–72.

———. "Das Zwölfprophetenbuch als Ganzes." In *Einleitung in das Alte Testament*, edited by Erich Zenger and Christian Frevel, 630–35. Stuttgart: Kohlhammer, 2016.

CHAPTER 2

Can an Integrative Reading of the Masoretic Psalter Stand in the Presence of Variants Discovered around Qumran with a Different Canonical Order?

PETER C. W. HO

THE PUBLICATION OF MORE manuscripts from Qumran and the Judean desert in the last few decades has generated renewed interest in the diachronic history of the text development of biblical books. Now, this interest is spurred more by *textual*, rather than biblical-redactional critics, with the latter quickly joining the discussion on the formation and canonization of biblical books.[1] Some scholars suggest that the Qumran text types were competing mainline traditions and there was no single authoritative version in the Second Temple period. This is because the Qumran psalters are observed to include, at times, extrabiblical and varying orders of psalms as compared to the MT. Such compositional variations have led to proposals for an anthological and amalgamative growth process in the formation of psalters, where certain psalms were selected from an existing pool of psalms and collected into a version.

1. See esp. Lange et al., *Textual History*; Jones, *Formation*; Albertz et al., *Perspectives*; Zenger, "Psalmenexegesis"; Willgren, *Formation*.

It is important to note that there is currently neither external material evidence to support such scholarly propositions of the formational process, nor evidence of an existing pool of psalms from which selection was made for a version of the psalter. This latter process is a part of the *anthological compilation theory* and entirely speculative. In contrast, there remain others who consider the earliest inferable tradition of these corpora as proto-Masoretic on which other psalters were dependent during the compositional or formational process.[2]

In view of the data amassed by Marco Pavan earlier, can an integrative reading of the Masoretic Psalter stand in the presence of variants discovered around Qumran with a different canonical order, especially after more than three decades of Psalter exegesis?[3] In this essay, I interact with some of the most recent research arising from the conversation between redactional critics and integrative readers, focusing on key methodological debates in the conversation.[4] I will interact primarily with the works of Drew Longacre, David Willgren Davage, William Yarchin, Alma Brodersen, and several others.[5] My conclusion is that while an anthological compilation theory to the formation of these corpora is plausible, key propositions to the editorial profiling of the growth of the text—regardless of whether it is a DSS, LXX, or MT text type—are still literary constructs and this theory is a deductive endeavor.[6] It remains an open question whether the DSS Psalms scrolls and LXX were dependent and derivative of the MT. The *status quaestionis* almost four decades after Gerald Wilson's *The Editing of the Hebrew Psalter* is that it is neither possible nor necessary to preclude the Psalter (or the XII) from having undergone an integrative and coherent shaping by a single or a small group of final editors at the final stages of the formational process to produce a *sepher* with a theological and thematic logic.[7]

This essay takes a departure from Willgren's "What Could We Agree On?" where he argues against a sequential and coherent reading

---

2. See Longacre's citation for more recent propositions on 11Q5's dependence on the MT: Longacre, "11Q5 Psalter," 88n9.

3. On Psalter exegesis, see Zenger, "Psalmenexegesis," 17–65; cf. Grant, "Editorial," 149–56. For a recent survey on this approach, see Howard and Snearly, "Reading," 1–35.

4. While most of my discussion is in the area of the Psalms study, such methodological concerns can be reckoned with the XII.

5. Pavan, "Psalter," 11–82; Willgren Davage, "Agree," 83–117; Yarchin, "Future," 119–37; Brodersen, "Final Hallel," 369–81; Ballhorn, "Researching," 401–13.

6. Pavan, "Psalter" 11–82.

7. Ho, "Macrostructural," 36–55.

of the Psalter. I will structure this essay along his "five fundaments," which are stated as follows: first, the "Book" of Psalms is not a modern-day book; second, there was no fixed segmentation of the psalms up until the printing press; third, there were no fixed sequences in the Second Temple period; fourth, the "Book" of Psalms has grown out of diverse, non-linear trajectories; and fifth, psalms were not read in light of neighboring psalms in the Second Temple period.[8]

The "Book" of Psalms is not a Modern-Day Book?

Willgren seeks to classify the Psalms as an "anthology," defined as "the independent text which has been actively selected and organized together with other such texts in relation to some present needs . . . [and] anthologies can also have various degrees of coherence."[9] He adds:

> The anthology served as a container of authoritative psalms, . . . The formation of the "Book" of Psalms is not ultimately an issue of shaping of a "book" in the way it is usually conceived, but of the creative preservation of a tradition. Rather than relating the formation of the "Book" of Psalms to the formation of other books in the Hebrew bible, I suggest that a better analogy would be the formation of the Hebrew Bible itself.[10]

Willgren compares the Zà-mì Hymns and the Papyrus Chester Beatty I as anthologies on two ends of a spectrum, with the former having a stronger coherence because poetic lines have similar doxological endings and recurring literary features. Chester Beatty I, on the other hand, is a weak anthology by its lack of common features between juxtaposed compositions in the text. Willgren is correct in seeing a spectrum of coherence, but the value of classifying a text such as the Hebrew Psalter as an "anthology" is more difficult to justify. Using his definition, almost all the books of the Hebrew Bible, by way of source or redaction criticisms, can be considered anthologies. This offers little usefulness for interpretation. Rather, what is crucial in his definition are the terms "selected" and "organized." To what extent were the selection, organization, or editing of the text accomplished? How will we know and to what extent can we

---

8. Willgren Davage, "Agree," 84; cf. "Why Davidic Superscriptions," 71; See also my review of Willgren in Ho, *Design*, 58–61.

9. Willgren Davage, "Agree," 89.

10. Willgren, *Formation*, 386.

justify it? I am not doubting that a highly coherent anthology in its final form could begin as a loosely connected composition. What is open for debate is the interpretation of the data, on which we judge the extent of the process of selection, organization, and editing of the text. Willgren agrees that the selection and organization work include the editing of the original text, but it remains an open question as to how much editorial freedom the author/editors/scribes had in bringing these separate compositions into the final text and how modern interpreters read coherency, or the lack thereof, from it.[11]

From this, it is also important to qualify how poetic discourses cohere.[12] A single poem is often accepted as a unity[13] despite having lines that may not always flow in order. However, as Samely notes:

> Unity is the assumption that shapes the actual methods of close reading. The text is read in the expectation of its end, not conceived as the final sentence, and as the text's status as a finite object. Close reading tends to reread the text, or parts of it, after its end has been encountered, precisely so as to make the meaning adjustments to earlier passages that have become necessary in the light of its ending, that is, in the light of certain knowledge of what the text *contains* and what it does *not* contain.... The reader thus experiences the text's meaning as that of a prima facie bounded, finite verbal entity. This means that the meaning boundaries of the text are constructed *in initial dependence on its de facto boundaries*.[14]

In other words, unity, meaning, and coherence are significantly connected to the boundaries we set for the text. The boundaries we set to the text affect meaning. But why must analyses of poetry be limited to the level of a single poem/psalm/oracle? What is lacking is an understanding of poetic coherence at the macrostructural level, of several poems, or even an entire book—an understanding we have already accepted at

---

11. Yarchin differentiates the role of "author," "editor," and "scribe" in the historical process of the production of the Hebrew Bible. See Yarchin, "(Para)Textual," 311–20.

12. Teeter and Tooman conclude that text must always be afforded a temporary coherence that can be permanently rejected after the whole text is analyzed. See esp., Teeter and Tooman, "Standards," 94–129. They have depended on the work of Samely, *Profiling*, 20–28.

13. Here, unity can be understood as an analytically judged phenomenon of the text by readers—a judgment that is independent and agnostic of authorial/editorial/redactional claims.

14. Samely, *Profiling*, 21.

the level of a single poem.[15] We have stopped at the level of the psalm because we have not really explored beyond the single poem. The quest, therefore, is to understand the *ways of the text* beyond the single psalm. Shifting the discussion from a "book" to an "anthology," as Willgren does, predisposes readers of the psalter, in an a priori manner, to boundaries that disenfranchise any analysis for coherence at the outset. As a label, an "anthology" may be seen as an interpretation of part of the formational process, but as the final text stands, the label, "anthology," adds little to understanding a *book of poems*. The question, rather, is *how* a book of poems can be coherent—a notion we must temporarily afford to the text as we try to read it beyond the single psalm. As Barr notes,

> It is a literary question to what extent the editors of a biblical book, in putting together various sources of pieces of material, have created a meaning in the juxtaposition, as distinct from the meaning of the parts. "The case for meaning must be decided on literary criteria: one must show that a unit is not just an anthology but is an intended structure with meaning."[16]

In my view, the coherence of a poetic text must be decided *beyond* common literary features and semantic content between juxtaposed or consecutive compositions.[17] I think that a mere sequential reading of a limited unit of text does not always reflect coherency. In Psalm 67, the lines are organized around a central tricolon in 67:5 [4], which emphasizes the justice and righteousness of YHWH as the basis of God's blessings to the ends of the earth. Sequentially, the lines do not read smoothly, and repetitions seem random, but the psalm's unity and message can be understood more fully when the entire concentric macrostructure of the psalm is seen. The righteous character of YHWH at the center of Psalm 67 is the basis of praise and blessings to the nations. This important motif is set at the strategic center of the psalm and repetitions are set symmetrically about this theological core. So, a chronological reading of sequential lines may not always appear initially coherent before the whole text is read and reread. Since this hermeneutical process applies for a single psalm, it follows that if we limit our boundary to the single psalm, we will be

---

15. "Cohesion refers to formal connections at the surface structure of a text, and coherence refers to connections in one's mental model formed during the reading process" (Lyons, "Standards," 184).

16. Barr, *Holy*, 160.

17. "Meaning crucially depends on boundaries so that all close readers rely on text boundaries as constraints in the construction of meaning" (Samely, *Profiling*, 19).

unable to see the fuller coherence that could have been intended under a larger pericope. This has happened because classical poetic studies have generally limited their scope to the boundary of a single psalm.[18] I think that macrostructural poetic methodologies should be further integrated with canonical approaches, as currently, macrostructural poetic studies that address large units of poems are few and far between.[19]

In short, the debate is less about definitions but more on how a larger body of apparently individual poetic texts is coherent when seen together. What is lacking is clarity on how ancient macrostructural poetic discourses work across larger swaths of delimited texts beyond a search for lexical similarities in consecutive poems.

No Fixed Delimitation of the Psalms until 1525

On this second point, Willgren depends on Yarchin's work, which shows that only 21 percent of a list of medieval Hebrew psalters have the same segmentations as the received MT tradition (or TR-150).[20] The majority of the Hebrew medieval psalters studied by Yarchin were delimited differently at various points, giving rise to different total number of psalm compositions. The implication that Yarchin and Willgren are raising here is that since psalm delimitations fluctuated in history, psalter exegeses that were built on the TR-150 delimitations have a very small foundation. However, it needs to be highlighted that all these psalters in consideration (by Yarchin) have the same fixed text and content sequence. Only the delimitations, deemed as paratextual elements,[21] are different. That is, two separate psalms were, at times, combined as one, or a single psalm was divided into two.

---

18. For example, see Watson, *Classical*; Alonso Schökel, *Manual*; Fokkelman, *Reading*.

19. Consider Régis, "Fractal"; Meynet, *Rhetorical*; Ayars, *Shape*; Ho, "Pan-Psalter."

20. Willgren Davage, "Agree," 91. Since the Psalms manuscripts in the Masoretic tradition do not always have 150 psalms, we can use Yarchin's preferred term, "TR-150" (Textus Receptus), to indicate the received Masoretic tradition of 150 psalms for our purposes here. On Yarchin's works, see "Future," 125–27; "Authoritative"; "Translated"; "(Para)Textual"; "Were the Psalms."

21. Genette defines *paratexts* of a text as features like the preface, titles, or illustrations. One of the functions of the paratext is to give purpose (illocutionary force) to the text. They always belong to the one who publishes it and are studied as synchronic features. Genette, "Introduction," 261, 264, 267.

Although Yarchin admits that the compositional *Gestalt*, which includes the text itself and the continuous sequence of the semantic content, was fixed by the end of the first century CE, he argues that the paratexts of the psalters were still open to continual changes by the scribes as new psalters were copied. Counterintuitively, it is precisely not the unchanging fixity of the text wherein lies its continuance but by means of the adjustments brought to the text via all manner of paratext, serving to situate the text vis-à-vis the reader and the reader vis-à-vis the text either according to the purposes intended by the author or by other later hands.[22]

Unfortunately, it is not always easy to define what a paratextual feature (such as the psalm delineation) means in these medieval Hebrew psalters. Tov has systematized the kinds of gaps—spacing in the middle, front, or end of a line, or large spacing between lines.[23] On gaps in the middle of a line, Tov reckons that some of them were ascribed to inconsistencies in the scribing process and do not always indicate text divisions. Moreover, some of these divisions were sense-units for calendarized reading. That means the psalms were delineated with a criterion defined much later and not of the same nature or character as the compositional *Gestalt*. This is a significant difference. Elsewhere, Yarchin also notes that the Targums, attested in medieval period, have layouts that serve antiphonal reading practices.[24] But Yarchin is arguing that these delimitation variations are *a form of continuing (re)compositional activity*, and such paratextual fluidity means "there is no such thing as the final form of the text,"[25] and that "the assumption of a single Hebrew psalter-configuration as the only canonical one is false."[26]

Before we address Yarchin's over-assertion, we need to clarify what Yarchin means by a "psalm delimitation."[27] An example of how two psalms are merged into one can be seen in the medieval *Tehillim* Parma

---

22. Yarchin, "(Para)Textual," 313.

23. Besides gaps, signs, enumeration, and red inks were also used as sense divisions. Tov, "Sense," 124.

24. Yarchin, "Translated," 146.

25. Yarchin, "(Para)Textual," 320.

26. Yarchin, "Future," 130; cf. Yarchin, "Authoritative," 355.

27. On this, I am grateful to Yarchin, who has generously shared some manuscript images, directed me to the digital archives of the manuscripts, and explained these features over private emails.

3186.²⁸ In Figure 2.1 below, notice that there is no separation between TR 92 and TR 93. However, a clear spacing after TR 93 and before TR 94 begins on the same line. Yarchin understands this spacing as a psalm delimitation.

Figure 2.1: Parma 3186, Fol. 025r, TR 92/93 and 93/94.

Notice also that consecutive lines alternate in lengths and the shorter lines are centralized in Figure 2.1.²⁹ The beginning and end of these lines are also kept consistent down the column. This is often accomplished by stretching a last text character in the line to fill up empty space. For

---

28. Parma 3186 is an early thirteenth-century CE manuscript written in the Ashkenazic square script. The psalter is divided into 149 psalms. Beit-Arié, *Hebrew Manuscripts*, 45.

29. The digital snapshot of the texts of the manuscripts is from the Biblioteca Palatina of Parma, Ministero per I Beni e le Attività Culturali, Italy; accessible through the "Ktiv" Project, at the National Library of Israel. For a digital version of the manuscript, see https://www.nli.org.il/en/discover/manuscripts/hebrew-manuscripts/partnerpage?PartnerId=987007606088605171.

Parma 3186, the long-short alternating lines in the *Tehillim* are a peculiar feature, likely for aesthetic reasons.

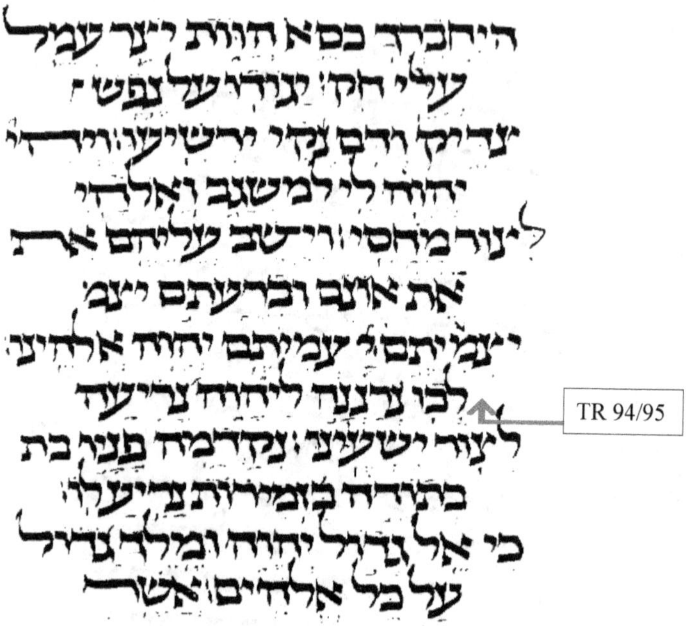

היחבךך בסא הוות יצר עמל
עלי חק יגודו על נפש ׃
צדיק ודם נקי ירשיעו ויהי
יהוה לי למשגב ואלהי
לצור מחסי וישב עליהם את
את אונם וברעתם יצמ׳
יצמיתם ׳ עמיתם יהוה אלהינו
לבו ערנה ליהוה צריעה ← TR 94/95
לצור ישעינו ׃ נקדמה פני בת
בתירה בזמירות נריעלו
כי אל גדול יהוה ומלך צדיל
על כל אלהים אשר

Figure 2.2: Mss Parma 3186, Fol. 025v, TR 94/95.

Figure 2.2 shows the same Parma 3186 but identifies the beginning of a new psalm (TR 95) on the next line.[30] Whether TR 95 is a clearly delimited psalm based on the criteria defined by Yarchin in the absence of any marginal notes is unclear.

Consider Figure 2.3 below. Yarchin points out that TR 116 and 117 are joined as a single psalm because there is no gap between them on the same line. The full line spacing between lines TR 117 and 118, in contrast, is a clear delimitation. Likewise, the line spacing between TR 118 and 119 marks a clear delimitation.

---

30. The source of the digital snapshot of the texts of the manuscripts is from the Biblioteca Palatina of Parma, Ministero per I Beni e le Attività Culturali, Italy; accessible through the "Ktiv" Project, at the National Library of Israel. For a digital version of the manuscript, see https://www.nli.org.il/en/discover/manuscripts/hebrew-manuscripts/partnerpage?PartnerId=987007606088605171.

Figure 2.3: Parma 3186, Fol. 031v, TR 116–119.

Nonetheless, as we have seen at the boundary of TR 93/94 in Figure 2.1, the presence of a space within a line does not always indicate a psalm delimitation. In the left column in Figure 2.3 and somewhere in the middle, notice a space in a line across two words (נא, אנה) within a single verse (TR 118:25).[31] This space does not indicate a sense-unit delimitation. The last word, אנה (instead of אנא) following the gap, is located just below the exact same word, also spelt אנה (with a *heh* and not *aleph*, cf. first word of TR 118:25). This creates a visually common ending for these two lines but breaks the alternating long-short lines vertically down the column. It is unclear why the scribe would deviate from the modus operandi. He could be trying to line up a series of tetragrammatons on the right side of the column as the arrows indicate, not just creating a visually pleasing form, but heightening the semantic emphasis on Yahweh's work of salvation.

---

31. The digital snapshot of the texts of the manuscripts is from the Biblioteca Palatina of Parma, Ministero per I Beni e le Attività Culturali, Italy; accessible through the "Ktiv" Project, at the National Library of Israel. For a digital version of the manuscript, see https://www.nli.org.il/en/discover/manuscripts/hebrew-manuscripts/partnerpage?PartnerId=987007606088605171.

70   PART 1: METHODOLOGICAL, COMPOSITIONAL, AND HERMENEUTICAL APPROACHES

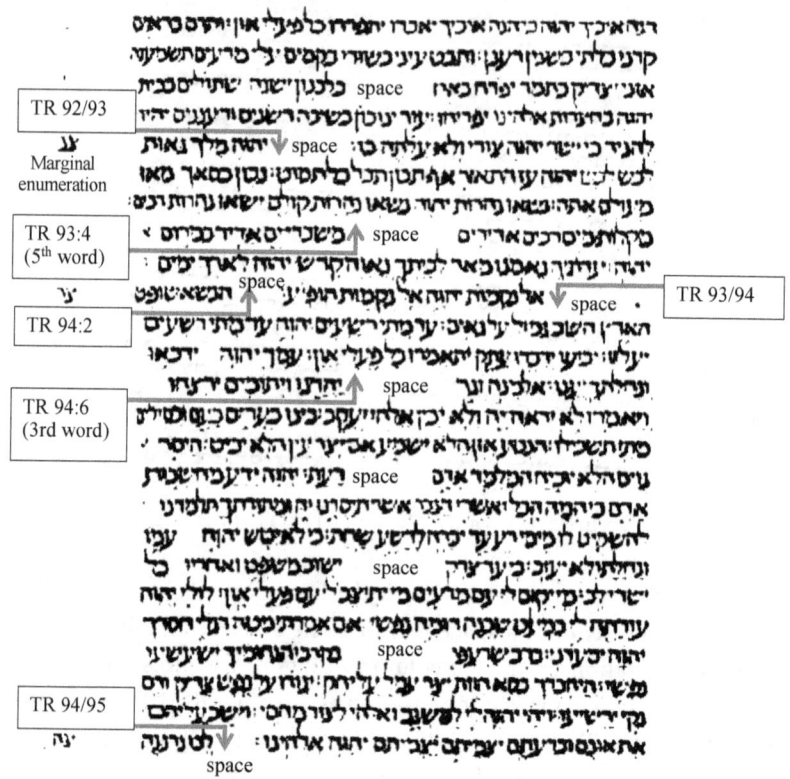

Figure 2.4: Parma 3233, Fol. 029r, Psalms 92–95.

In Figure 2.4, Parma 3233 has an interesting layout that likely combines texts and gaps to form an aesthetic layout pattern.[32] A space roughly in the middle of a line is observed after one to two lines and this pattern continues down the entire column. In this manuscript, the psalm numbering is seen on the margins at the same level where a new psalm begins. So, delineation of psalms is understood by these numberings. When we compare these psalm delimitations with spaces, we see that several of these spaces coincide with the beginning of a psalm. But other

32. Parma 3233 is a thirteenth-century CE manuscript written in Sephardic square script. The psalter is divided into 149 psalms. Beit-Arié, *Hebrew Manuscripts*, 61. The source of the digital snapshot of the texts of the manuscripts is from the Biblioteca Palatina of Parma, Ministero per I Beni e le Attività Culturali, Italy; accessible through the "Ktiv" Project, at the National Library of Israel. For a digital version of the manuscript, see https://www.nli.org.il/en/discover/manuscripts/hebrew-manuscripts/partnerpage?PartnerId=987007606088605171.

spaces are located at syntactically random locations within a psalm (e.g., fifth word in 93:4; third word in 94:6).

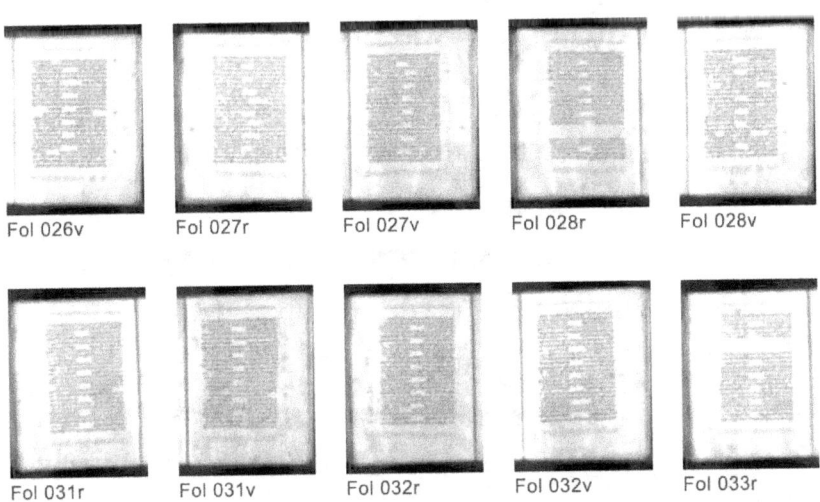

Figure 2.5: Thumbnails of Fol. 026v–028v; 031r–033r in Parma 3233.

When we take a step back and consider the many folios of the *Tehillim* in Parma 3233 as shown in Figure 2.5 (Fol. 026v–028v; 031r–033r; TR84–92; TR103–107),[33] notice how such white spaces that occur in every few lines of a column create a distinctive artistic layout. In other words, the scribe(s) was(were) likely following some sort of visual convention in that *Tehillim* rather than using the spaces to indicate sense-delimitation. Therefore, these delimitations were not functioning with the same compositional sense unit as intended by the original composers. So, spacing, or the lack thereof, was not always a sure indicator of delimitations as we see in Parma 3186 and 3233, which were likely governed by aesthetic requirements. This possibility has also been raised elsewhere.[34]

33. Layout for acrostic Psalms 111–112, 119, 145, and 136 are different. The digital snapshot of the texts of the manuscripts is from the Biblioteca Palatina of Parma, Ministero per I Beni e le Attività Culturali, Italy; accessible through the "Ktiv" Project, at the National Library of Israel. For a digital version of the manuscript, see https://www.nli.org.il/en/discover/manuscripts/hebrew-manuscripts/partnerpage?PartnerId=987007606088605171.

34. Note Moor and Korpel's point: "Finally, some scribes strived after a beautiful layout of poems and lists and this could be achieved by using extra spaces which later scribes might interpret as paragraph markings" ("Paragraphing," 18).

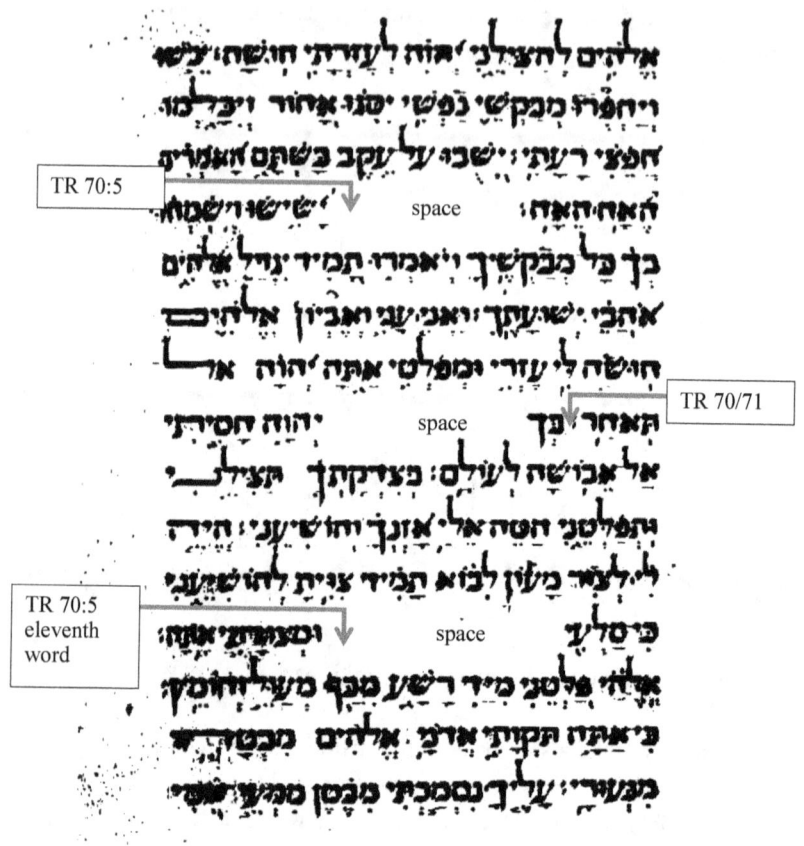

Figure 2.6: Parma 1866, leaf_003, verso, Psalm 70/71.

Such aesthetic use of space is also found in another manuscript, Parma 1866 (Figure 2.6).[35] Again, the use of spacing does not delimit a psalm. Notice that the first word of TR 71 appears just before the space at the center. Like Parma 3233, spaces also break the line without syntactical considerations. What is consistent is the pattern of spaces taking up about one-third of the length of the entire column, occurring at the center of the line, and recurring after an interval of three complete lines.[36]

35. This is a fifteenth-century Sephardic square script. The digital snapshot of the texts of the manuscripts is from the Biblioteca Palatina of Parma, Ministero per I Beni e le Attività Culturali, Italy; accessible through the "Ktiv" Project, at the National Library of Israel. For a digital version of the manuscript, see https://www.nli.org.il/en/discover/manuscripts/hebrew-manuscripts/partnerpage?PartnerId=987007606088605171.

36. Another manuscript, Parma 2189, had also merged TR 70 and 71.

In sum, Yarchin and Willgren were right in concluding that the paratextual delimitations of the medieval psalters remain fluid. However, it is hard to qualify such fluidity as the *same kind* of editorial changes that shaped the *Gestalt* of a text as Yarchin suggests. Seen above, it is difficult for us to systematize the delimitations of psalms as a criterion defined for one manuscript may not work for another. More importantly, if these paratextual variations really indicate genuine compositional fluidity, then they should logically occur randomly in different psalm boundaries across different manuscripts. But cited variations often occur at specific psalm boundaries where superscriptions were lacking (e.g., Pss 70/71, 94/95).[37] It is reasonable to argue that from a transmissional point of view, the lack of a clear heading in the second of two psalms would have had a higher likelihood of the two compositions conflating into one.[38] Likewise, single psalms could have been divided at locations with obvious semantic shifts (e.g., TR 118:1–4/118:5–29 and 115:1–11/115:12–18). In short, much of this supposed "compositional fluidity" appears more likely as non-random scribal activity rather than bona fide compositional fluidity. While it is conceivable that scribes had introduced these changes wittingly or unwittingly at one time in one exemplar, once introduced, these paratextual variations became "stuck" and the transmission process perpetuated these variations across manuscripts.[39] Perhaps Moor and Korpel's point here is applicable, that "the analysis of unit delimitation should be subjected to the same rules as textual criticism,"[40] and should be distinguished from editorial criticism.

Tov offers helpful reasoning for such variations. He thinks that the scribal process of copying repeated text chunks from the source text to the target scroll had included ad hoc decisions by the scribes that gave rise to these space delimitations. Each of these repeated processes of

---

37. Yarchin cites key variations of conflation or division occurring at TR 42/43, 70/71, 90/91, 118:1–4/118:5–29, 114/115, 116/117, 115:1–11/115:12–18. Yarchin, "Future," 131.

38. This has been observed by many others. See Prinsloo, "Delimitation," 232–63; "Psalms 114 and 115," 668–89.

39. Yarchin notes an interesting observation of eleven manuscripts containing the psalms copied by the Italian scribe Isaac ben Obadiah ben David of Forli in the fifteenth century. Although copied by the same scribe, there are at least five different kinds of configurations. Yarchin explains that this is due to Isaac's use of different underlying *sefer Tehillim* exemplars available to him at that point. But this is his interpretive call. Yarchin, "Future," 128.

40. Moor and Korpel, "Paragraphing," 23.

copying—reading, keeping the text in mind, and writing it down in the target scroll—could have introduced spaces that had little to do with the scribe's understanding of the text and its sense division.

> After all, in order to know the exact relation between the various content units, a scribe would have to carry out a close reading of the context and be involved in the literary analysis of several adjacent content units. Since we do not believe that scribes were involved to such an extent in content analysis, it seems that scribal decisions on the type of relation between sense units should be considered *ad hoc*, made upon completing one unit and before embarking on the next.[41]

To return to our contention, the critical point of Yarchin's and Willgren's claim is that the varying delimitations of these medieval Psalms manuscripts are bona fide new compositions. That is, they are to be seen as "newly composed *discrete psalms* comprised of what were, presumably, existing psalmic textual units."[42] And the paratextual activities by these medieval scribes are to be seen alongside the compositional techniques as observed in TR 108, which is made up of the texts of TR 57:7–11 and TR 60:5–12. But as we have shown, these manuscripts have only minor changes that avoid modifying the *Gestalt* of the Psalter. Such paratextual variations in the medieval psalms had likely served other cultural functions such as aesthetics. We do not see any entire new Mss psalms formed by splicing a part of one psalm into a part of another psalm. Willgren and Yarchin may have overstated their case.

There Are No Fixed Sequences in the Second Temple Period; The "Book" of Psalms Has Grown Out of Diverse Trajectories

Willgren's third and fourth points are related to the earlier point on the fixing of content sequences, but he pushes the argument back to the Second Temple period. To substantiate these propositions, he cites the example of 1 Chronicles 16's rearranging of Psalms 105, 96, and 106, and argues that MT sequences were not fixed during the Second Temple period. Willgren also considers the dual transmission of the parallel texts of Psalms 14 and 53 as fluidity in the compositional sequencing of the psalms. He points out that certain psalms with overlapping material (Ps 40:14–18 and Ps 70;

---

41. Tov, "Sense," 123.
42. Yarchin, "Future," 128 (emphasis original).

and Ps 108 using material from Pss 57:8–12 and 60:7–14) are of the same kind of varying arrangement of psalms as seen in the Qumran psalters (4Q171, 4Q83, 4Q98, and 11Q5).

Willgren's argument here can be seen together with Brodersen's study of Psalms 146–150, where she understands 11Q5 and the LXX Psalter to have grown out of a tradition independent from the (proto-)MT.[43] Like Willgren, her method is to compare the differences in text forms of the oldest extant texts available for Psalms 146–150.[44] She highlights the differences in (1) the order of the Qumran Psalms scrolls as compared to the MT; (2) the delimitation of psalm boundaries, and (3) the lack of hallelujah superscriptions.[45] She also applies a set of intertextual criteria to ascertain if there were lexical connections between the five psalms. Her conclusion is that there is little coherence between these last five psalms.[46]

Nonetheless, it must be said that the relationships between the MT, LXX, and Qumran texts remain debated in scholarship. Can we really equate these texts and conflate their compositional techniques on the same plane? Willgren's observations on how psalms were reused or rearranged in 1 Chronicles or within the Psalms itself reflect the compositional stages of the HB before its completion. The *terminus ad quem* for the completion an MT-like *Vorlage* of the Psalms would be earlier than the Septuagint translation of the Bible in the third/second century BCE.[47] During this Qumran period,[48] variations of texts arrangement or reuse were seen in the DSS psalters. But it is questionable if variations seen in this period can be commensurate with the compositional stages of an incomplete Hebrew Psalter. Rather, it is plausible that the variations in the DSS and the LXX were reflecting a methodologically

---

43. Brodersen, *End*, 19–20, for a summary of her argument; cf. Brodersen, "Final Hallel," 369–81.

44. She cites 4Q86, 11Q5, and Mas1f, which are dated to the first centuries on both sides of the millennium, and Codices Vaticanus and Sinaiticus, dated to the fourth century CE. For images of these manuscripts, see https://www.deadseascrolls.org.il/explore-the-archive/manuscript/Mas 1f-1; https://www.deadseascrolls.org.il/explore-the-archive/search#q='psalm'; https://digi.vatlib.it/view/MSS_Vat.gr.1209; https://codexsinaiticus.org/en/manuscript.aspx.

45. Brodersen, *End*, 21.

46. Brodersen, *End*, 28.

47. But the "earliest attestations of the Hebrew canon as a list come from the second half of the first century CE (Josephus, *C. Ap.* 1.38; 2 Esdras 14)" (Toorn, "Constructing," 261).

48. Cargill, *Qumran*, 215–16, Appendix Plate 10.1.

and qualitatively different compositional process. There are scholars who argue for the dependence of the DSS psalters on the proto-MT. And scholars on either side also recognize that "both the Septuagint Psalter and 11QPs^a seem to be aware of the 'final' (proto-)MT arrangement or an arrangement very close to it."[49]

My response to Brodersen's study is that the application of her methods could bring us to a different conclusion when applied to a different group of psalms. Consider her method applied on consecutive Psalms 125–130 instead. We could compare the Masoretic version with the same group of psalms in 11Q5, columns IV–V.[50] Using Brodersen's criteria, we find the presence of framing with the superscriptions of Psalms 126 and 130 preserved, and in accordance with the TR. Likewise, the partly preserved superscription of Psalm 127 also accords with the TR. The first and last lines of Psalms 125, 126, 129, and 130 can be clearly seen.[51] There are also clear intertextual connections. The term, ישראל, occurs nine times in Psalms 120–134 and more than half of them are found in these six psalms (125:5; 128:6; 129:1; 130:7, 8). Words like "Jerusalem," "Zion," or "city" (125:1; 126:1; 127:1; 128:5; 129:5), "bliss," and "peace" (e.g., the use of ברך in 128:2, 4, 5; 129:8), "offspring," and "youth" (127:3–5; 128:3, 6; 129:2), including arboreal and agricultural imageries (cf. 126:5–6; 128:2; 3; 129:3, 6–7), tie these psalms together.[52] In other words, we can arrive at very different conclusions by reusing Brodersen's own method, applied on a different set of psalms. So Brodersen's conclusion can actually vary depending on the choice of psalms her method is applied to. To substantiate this proposition, we note that Hossfeld, Zenger, Ballhorn,

---

49. Pajunen, "Perspectives," 151.

50. Column IV (Plate 976, Frag. 4) is damaged at the right and bottom, with the last line of Psalm 124 at the top and the first line of Psalm 127 at the bottom still visible. Likewise, Column V (Plate 976, Frag. 2) is also damaged at the right and bottom, but the last lines of Psalms 128 and 130 are still observable. For images of 11Q5, col. IV–V, see https://www.deadseascrolls.org.il/explore-the-archive/image/B-371135; https://www.deadseascrolls.org.il/explore-the-archive/image/B-371128.

51. There are minor orthographical variations in several words between 11Q5 and the TR. They include missing single words in the TR (cf. 125:5; 129:8; 130:1, 2, 6), additions or minuses of prefixes and suffixes (cf. 125:1, 2, 4, 5; 129:2, 8), and the use of the tetragrammaton (אדוני or YHWH in 11Q5, but often יהוה in TR Pss 125:2; 128:5; 129:4). For details, see Ulrich, *Psalms–Chronicles*, 703–4.

52. On the compact of the Songs of Ascents, see Hossfeld and Zenger, "Pilgrim Psalter," 286–99; For a spatial perspective, see Prinsloo, "Role," 457–77.

and Neumann have worked on Psalms 146–150 as well and they have also arrived at a different conclusion to Brodersen.[53]

Furthermore, consider several detailed studies that suggest the dependency of the DSS and LXX psalters on an MT-like exemplar.[54] First, we will consider Drew Longacre's recent article suggesting 11Q5's dependency on a Proto-MT exemplar.[55] Second, we will consider Gilles Dorival's study on the differences in the psalms superscriptions between the MT, Qumran, and Septuagint psalters.[56] A third study by Peter Gentry and John Meade compares Psalms 82, 83, and 85 in the Codex Sinaiticus, Codex Vaticanus, MasPs^a, and the MT Aleppo codex.[57] They conclude that the preservation of the MT as seen from these important manuscripts set the MT apart from the DSS psalters, which had a different set of scribal characteristics. We will expand briefly on each one of them below.

Longacre argues that the "11Q5 was created as *a revised version of the psalter, expanded and rearranged from an MT-like* (i.e., Masoretic text) base text to enhance thematic, lexical, and sometimes formal connections between psalms."[58] This is because of the similar content and the general sequence of psalm groupings with their major editorial features (e.g., superscriptions, doxological endings).[59] The formational process of 11Q5, according to Longacre, begins with an exemplar (an MT-like psalter manuscript), on which the "compiler"[60] of 11Q5 would plan and mark selections before transferring those psalms to the new scroll. Some psalms were transferred largely in full, but the compiler could include creative editorial interventions at various points. In total, 11Q5 consists of "two expansions of [MT] psalms, five insertions of supplementary material, eight or nine movements of psalms [from their original MT locations], and a corrective appendix."[61] Longacre

53. Hossfeld and Zenger, "Little Hallel," 605–7; Ballhorn, "Researching," 401–13; Neumann, *Schriftgelehrte*.

54. On views that reject a dependency, see Pajunen, "Perspectives," 139–63.

55. Longacre, "11Q5 Psalter," 85–111; "Scribal," 141–64; "Paleographic," 67–92; "Developmental," 17–50.

56. Dorival, "Titres," 3–18.

57. Gentry and Meade, "MasPs^a," 113–45.

58. Longacre, "11Q5 Psalter," 86 (emphasis added).

59. Longacre, "11Q5 Psalter," 88.

60. By "compiler," Longacre means the "creator of the 11Q5 psalter" (Longacre, "11Q5 Psalter," 85).

61. See especially his Table 1. Longacre argues that the last seven poems (Hymn,

lists several principles in the formational process of 11Q5:⁶² (1) the structure of 11Q5 is largely based on the order of the MT exemplar; (2) rearrangements were for enhancing thematic links between adjacent psalms; (3) non-MT psalms were found only after Psalm 136 in 11Q5; (4) the "Hallelujah" formula likely led to the formation of a "Supplementary Praise Cluster" (Pss 104, 147, 105, 146, 148); (5) authorship attribution was not as important a grouping technique as compared to the MT; (6) thematic concerns for rearrangements trumped group-forming superscriptions like מזמר and שיר המעלות, (7) formulaic terms like הודו ליהוה and ברכי נפשי were likely not used for structuring.

For Longacre, the entire composition of 11Q5 was likely undertaken in a "single, comprehensive revision of the psalter tradition."⁶³ The compiler's work (for 11Q5) remains largely at the arrangement of psalms at the level of individual psalms, and this compilation was dependent on the proto-MT. Observable differences from the MT are deemed as creative interventions based on thematic concerns, on which Longacre offers only brief notes.

It is important to note that these "creative interventions" are subservient to Longacre's larger observation that the compiler composed the 11Q5 psalter on scribal principles of preservation, linearity, and efficiency, and not for any overarching arrangement principles. This observation, too, is worked out from internal arguments. But if internal arguments are provisos to any suggestions of the formational process, the strength or lack thereof of such internal arguments should likewise reject these proposals. Noted above, Longacre provides only limited internal arguments to explain his reasons for the editorial interventions. Longacre made no attempts to analyze the entire 11Q5 thematically. Of course, Longacre cannot be faulted for these, but from a methodological point of view, his rejection of a unifying theme or program is *not* the result of countering some proposals to an overarching logic for the 11Q5 psalter. Since the entire enterprise for the formation of the 11Q5 psalter requires an internal argumentation, without substantiating rejections to internal arguments for more thoroughgoing thematic shaping, claims *against* an overall logic of 11Q5 psalter are largely one-sided.

---

2 Sam 23:1–7, DavComp, 140, 134, 151A, 151B) in 11Q5 were appended (Longacre, "11Q5 Psalter," 86, 106–8).

62. Longacre, "11Q5 Psalter," 108–9.

63. Longacre, "11Q5 Psalter," 90.

What is significant about Longacre's study for our purposes is that the 11Q5 is seen to be dependent on an MT-like exemplar and that the 11Q5 composition is argued to be limited to the rearrangement of individual psalms. This observation may be correct, but more importantly, it is qualitatively different from what we see in the compositional stages of the composition of the Hebrew Psalter as Willgren or Brodersen have suggested.

Dorival argues that differences in the psalms superscriptions (between the MT, Qumran, LXX, and Targums) are to be understood as *interpretive signals* rather than genuine compositional diversity. For him, quantitative differences in the superscriptions can be dated to Hellenistic periods and were interpretations concerning biblical characters (e.g., David) described in the psalm. Dorival points out that there were no psalms superscriptions present in the MT that were correspondingly absent in the Septuagint Psalter. There was also no superscription in the MT that was correspondingly longer in the LXX Psalter.[64] In other words, the Septuagint Psalter seemed to have avoided altering what was in the MT, and had only *added* to the MT superscriptions. On the character of psalms titles represented across these witnesses, Dorival notes:

> The tradition that is least developed is the MT, and the most developed is represented by the LXX. Qumran and the Targum represent intermediate traditions, which are not identical to each other. When did these traditions appear? The testimonies of Qumran and the LXX support the presence of interpretative debates in Jewish circles during the Hellenistic period.[65]

What sort of interpretive debates could have given rise to the differences in the superscriptions? Dorival notes a record of the conflict of interpretation in Justin's *Dialogue with Trypho*. Such interpretive conflicts on the Psalms occurred between the early Christians and the rabbis, with the latter refusing to read Jesus into the Scripture. Moreover, there is a development of the understanding of musical titles in the rabbinic period that furthered the conflict in the interpretation of the Psalms. In other words, psalms superscriptions became an area of interpretive contestation. Most of the qualitative differences in the psalms superscriptions as observed by Dorival fall under this category.[66]

64. Dorival, "Titres," 4.
65. Dorival, "Titres," 9 (translation mine).
66. Dorival, "Titres," 11.

By the Hellenistic period, Christian and Jewish tradents had reckoned superscriptions as paratexts on which minor changes without altering the *Gestalt* of the text were possible.[67] What is important in Dorival's study is to factor in the changing historical contexts when studying the differences in the ancient Psalms manuscripts. Again, Dorival's work raises questions on whether the apparent differences in superscriptions were bona fide compositional diversity. For him, such differences were sectarian responses/interpretations to the MT.

Peter Gentry and John Meade highlight not only the close link between the MT-like Psalms of the Second Temple period (MasPs^a) and the Masoretic Psalms (Aleppo) but a comparative distinction between the MT and the Qumran psalters. Basing their study on Psalms 82, 83, and 85, they show that there is an "almost identical layout between Masada Psalms and the Aleppo codex."[68] The spaces between poetic cola in the MasPs^a correspond closely to the Masoretic terminal markers of its accentuation system. Superscriptions of these psalms in the MasPs^a also accord with the MT. Moreover, when the MasPs^a is compared to the important Greek codices (Sinaiticus and Vaticanus), stichometric agreement in the layout of these poetic texts is found.

> Five hundred years after the original translation, B [Codex Vaticanus] and S [Codex Sinaiticus] have largely preserved the terminal markers of a Hebrew parent text like MasPs^a. The evidence suggests that the original translation into Greek followed the stichometric layout in poetic texts and even in the earliest texts had spaces corresponding to the reading tradition, and that this tradition was preserved for some time.[69]

Gentry and Meade also highlight the superscription of LXX Psalm 151, which states that Psalm 151 is "outside the number" (ἔξωθεν τοῦ ἀριθμοῦ). This is an important *material evidence* suggesting that there were a recognized number of psalms in the Psalter. Gentry and Meade also cite Tov, who thinks that the MasPs^a was probably connected to the Temple and these texts (as opposed to other texts) could have been preserved and protected by priests.[70] Gentry and Meade disagree with

---

67. Separately, Ballhorn also points out that the differences between the psalmic texts of the MT and LXX are the result of "small shifts" or "accents" (Ballhorn, "Researching," 408).

68. Gentry and Meade, "MasPs^a," 123.

69. Gentry and Meade, "MasPs^a," 138.

70. See Gentry and Meade, "MasPs^a," 139–40, notes 33, 34, citing Tov, "Text," 177; Ulrich, "Methodological," 155.

Flint's suggestion of developing "a trajectory from 4QPs[a]—an extremely fragmentary text—to 11QPs[a] and from there to our MT Psalter of 150 psalms."[71] Possibly, the Qumran community had likely "added psalms and arranged them differently due to their solar calendar and the liturgical system based thereon."[72] Such distinctions are also observed by Tov, on the manuscripts of 5/6ḤevPs, MasPs[a] and MurXII, and 8 ḤevXIIgr, which he calls, "luxury scrolls" or "deluxe editions." These manuscripts are characterized by "large top and bottom margins, large intercolumnar margins, tall columns, a low incidence of scribal intervention, and a high degree of proximity to or even identity with MT."[73]

In sum, our response to Willgren's third and fourth "fundaments" is that it is hard to make a definitive methodological case that there were no fixed sequences of psalms in the earlier part of the Second Temple period, prior to the completion of the LXX Psalter. When the kind of comparative differences raised are qualified, they can be explained as interpretive receptions dependent on an MT-like exemplar and were not bona fide authoritative compositions methodologically speaking. Otherwise, cited evidence would belong to the kind of shaping before the completion of the HB. As seen in Brodersen's case, internal arguments used to qualify the differences can also be used to qualify their similarities, depending on the source and scope chosen. The works of Longacre, Dorival, Gentry, and Meade have shown that the Qumran psalters and LXX were more likely derivatives from an MT-like *Vorlage*.

Psalms Were not Read in Light of Neighboring Psalms

In the fifth "fundament," Willgren claims that "a sequential reading of psalms where the interpretation of an individual psalm was informed by the neighboring psalms (or guided by 'book' boundaries) is not found in the Second Temple period."[74] He reasons this via a continuous pesher 4Q171 dated to the first century CE, arguing that the pesher displayed a sequence different from the MT (Pss 37, 45, and 60). This difference in sequence "paints a picture of how the *yahad* [Judah] was living in a period

---

71. Gentry and Meade, "MasPs[a]," 140.
72. Gentry and Meade, "MasPs[a]," 140.
73. Tov, "Luxury," 428.
74. Willgren Davage, "Agree," 95.

of testing and refining . . . to wait for the intervention of YHWH,"[75] and that there would be a happy ending when God's people returned to the land. Note that Willgren is applying an internal argument here. He argues that the reading of these three psalms in the pesher's sequence is justification that their placement within the MT did not have any interpretive significance because they could be taken from their *Sitz im Psalter* and combined elsewhere into a message of hope.[76]

My response to this is threefold. First, methodologically, the presence of an alternative sequence elsewhere does not necessarily mean that Psalms 37, 45, and 60 cannot be read in their *Sitz im Psalter* with *their own* interpretive significance. They could have their interpretive significance in their respective sequences within Books I–III in the MT as well, just not understood.[77] Second, and using Willgren's own approach, does it not more show that the method of reading one psalm in light of neighboring psalms was practiced? In other words, even as Willgren downplays a particular fixed sequence of MT psalms, he has shown that a juxtaposed series of psalms, through their lexical links, can be read in light of each other to provide a thematic message of hope! So, reading one psalm in light of neighboring psalms was actually practiced in the Qumran period. These different sequences show us the *affordance* of psalms, that is, the Qumran community could select and sequence them for a different thematic significance because the psalms afford more than one way of interpretation. Willgren also applies a similar methodology of internal arguments to build a case for the formation of the MT in his published dissertation, where he articulates the various stages of formation of the MT.[78] For more details on how the Qumran community could have sequenced compositions, see Matt Ayars's essay in this volume.

> The conclusion drawn so far should not be interpreted in the sense that psalms have been randomly juxtaposed, rather that the proposed readings of recent scholarship need to be reframed. Since this study has focused explicitly on paratexts, features such as lexical and thematic links between adjacent psalms have not been considered in depth, except for in some cases. *As seen there, and shown in numerous studies, it is quite likely that similar*

---

75. Willgren Davage, "Agree," 95.

76. Willgren Davage, "Agree," 105.

77. Barbiero, "Le Premier," 439–80; Auwers, *Composition*, 47–49; McCann, "Books I–III," 93–107.

78. Willgren, *Formation*.

> vocabulary (etc.) might have served as points of departure when juxtaposing psalms.... Nonetheless, it would be important to note that such features did not imply that such compositions should be read together. A blunt comparison to modern day cookbooks could perhaps be illustrative.[79]

The extended quote above highlights Willgren's methodological fluidity. Notice how Willgren allows the internal techniques to work for the formation of the pesher with the particular theme of hope on the one hand but rejects the plausibility that MT psalms could be read in a particular order on the other. At its core, Willgren's basis for the rejection of any fixed psalms sequences in the MT is due to the presence of variations seen in the DSS or Septuagint psalters. This is what we have seen in Brodersen's argument as well. But if both DSS and Septuagint psalters were dependent on the MT and were historical receptions of the Hebrew Psalter, which Longacre has also suggested, then such variations can be qualified.

At this point Pavan's critical evaluation on the recent research on the Psalter is significant.[80] He concludes that the critical points of the debate include a distinction between internal and external *data*, and a distinction between the *analyses* of each. Internal data relates to the analysis of the final form of the MT Psalter [or of any text] whereas external data relates to how the DSS and LXX, via a "*reconstruction of the ancient scribal praxis*," affects the reading of the MT.[81] Pavan rightly questions if the Qumranic evidence really belongs to "the *formative* period of the psalter rather than to the period of its *reception*."[82] He also highlights the tensions in the methodology espoused by some of the scholars above, noting:

> The study of the manuscripts of the Judean Desert is founded on the same *deductive* base that was used by the scholars of the canonical form of the MT Psalter, since the methodological path of determination on the premises of the scribal activity are the same. At the same time, the uncertainty regarding the function, purpose and origin of the "psalmic scrolls" necessarily makes any conclusion that can be drawn based upon them provisional and incomplete. As a result, the scribal praxis that

---

79. Willgren, *Formation*, 389 (emphasis added).
80. Pavan, "Psalter," 63–68.
81. Pavan, "Psalter," 64.
82. Pavan, "Psalter," 64.

can be deduced, within certain limitations, from the evidence of the Judean Desert lack uniformity in relation to both the origin of the scrolls and their purpose.[83]

Pavan has astutely asked if a deductive methodology based on the given material evidence available to us can "allow the complete exclusion or relativization of the use of conjunctive or disjunctive techniques between adjacent Psalms on behalf of the editors of the Psalter."[84] Ancient scribes "could have acted in the sense of *concatenatio* or *juxtapositio* and not only in the sense of 'pure compilation.'"[85]

Conclusion

The aim of this essay is to identify the *status quaestionis* of the methodological issues associated with comparative discussions of the Psalms (and indirectly of the XII), and to highlight implications for the holistic interpretation of these text corpora. I have also organized this essay as a response to Willgren's five fundaments and countered his propositions.

The important methodological issue is *how* a single poem can be coherent beyond its own boundary. There is a methodological lacuna in understanding how poetic discourse works beyond the individual psalm/poem. The potential for an integrated reading of the MT Psalter (or the XII) must lie beyond simply looking for lexical similarities along consecutive delimited psalms or simply by categorical redefinitions. At the core of the debate, the question of the relationship between the various ancient psalter traditions must also be addressed. Scholars raise issues with the difference in the arrangement of psalms observed in DSS psalters, minor deviations in the superscriptions of the LXX psalters, and fluidity in the delineation of psalms in the medieval psalters. In this essay, I have shown that it is hard to qualify such differences *as the same kind of editorial changes* in the formational period of the Hebrew Psalter. Such differences can be explained as historical receptions rather than bona fide compositional diversity. Paratextual delineation of psalms in the medieval Psalms manuscripts could have served aesthetic reasons that were not always related to semantic or syntactical reasonings. To date, there is neither attestation of any Mss psalters reworked

---

83. Pavan, "Psalter," 65; cf. Ho, *Design*, 60–61.
84. Pavan, "Psalter," 68.
85. Pavan, "Psalter," 67.

to the same extent as seen in the formational stages of the psalter, nor any material evidence to support anthological proposals to the Psalter's formation process. Methodologically, scholars use similar internal and deductive approaches but arrive at different, and sometimes conflicting, conclusions. As such, a consensus remains wanting but the critical points on methodology are becoming clearer.

Bibliography

Albertz, Rainer, et al., eds. *Perspectives on the Formation of the Book of the Twelve: Methodological Foundations, Redactional Processes, Historical Insights.* BZAW 433. Berlin; Boston: de Gruyter, 2012.

Alonso Schökel, Luis. *A Manual of Hebrew Poetics.* Rome: Editrice Pontificio Istituto Biblico, 1988.

Auwers, Jean-Marie. *La Composition Littéraire Du Psautier: Un État de La Question.* CahRB 46. Paris: Gabalda, 2000.

Ayars, Matthew Ian. *The Shape of Hebrew Poetry: Exploring the Discourse Function of Linguistic Parallelism in the Egyptian Hallel.* SSN 70. Leiden; Boston: Brill, 2018.

Ballhorn, Egbert. "Researching Sense at the End of the Psalter: Pss 145–150 and Its Canonical Shapes." In *The Formation of the Hebrew Psalter: The Book of Psalms between Ancient Versions, Material Transmission and Canonical Exegesis,* edited by Gianni Barbiero et al., 401–13. FAT I 151. Tübingen: Mohr Siebeck, 2021.

Barbiero, Gianni. "Le Premier Livret Du Psautier (Ps 1–41): Une Étude Synchronique." *Revue Des Sciences Religieuses* 77 (2003) 439–80.

Barbiero, Gianni, et al., eds. *The Formation of the Hebrew Psalter: The Book of Psalms between Ancient Versions, Material Transmission and Canonical Exegesis.* FAT I 151. Tübingen: Mohr Siebeck, 2021.

Barr, James. *Holy Scripture: Canon, Authority, Criticism.* Oxford: Oxford University Press, 1983.

Beit-Arié, Malachi. *Hebrew Manuscripts in the Biblioteca Palatina in Parma: Catalogue.* Edited by Benjamin Richler. Jerusalem: Jewish National and University Library, 2001.

Brodersen, Alma. *The End of the Psalter: Psalms 146–150 in the Masoretic Text, the Dead Sea Scrolls, and the Septuagint.* BZAW 505. Berlin; Boston: de Gruyter, 2017.

———. "No Final Hallel: Material Sources for Psalms 146–150." In *The Formation of the Hebrew Psalter: The Book of Psalms between Ancient Versions, Material Transmission and Canonical Exegesis,* edited by Gianni Barbiero et al., 369–81. FAT I 151. Tübingen: Mohr Siebeck, 2021.

Cargill, Robert R. *Qumran through (Real) Time: A Virtual Reconstruction of Qumran and the Dead Sea Scrolls.* Piscataway, NJ: Gorgias, 2009.

Dorival, Gilles. "Titres Hébreux et Titres Grecs Des Psaumes." In *Textual Research on the Psalms and Gospels: Papers from the Tbilisi Colloquium on the Editing and History of Biblical Manuscripts,* edited by Christian-B. Amphoux and J. Keith Elliott, 3–18. NovTSup 142. Leiden; Boston: Brill, 2012.

Fokkelman, J. P. *Reading Biblical Poetry: An Introductory Guide.* Louisville: Westminster John Knox, 2001.

Genette, Gérard, and Marie Maclean. "Introduction to the Paratext." *New Literary History* 22.2 (1991) 261–72.

Gentry, Peter J., and John D. Meade. "MasPs^a and the Early History of the Hebrew Psalter." In *From Scribal Error to Rewriting: How Ancient Texts Could and Could Not Be Changed*, edited by Anneli Aejmelaeus et al., 113–45. DSI 12. Göttingen: Vandenhoeck & Ruprecht, 2020.

Grant, J. A. "Editorial Criticism." In *Dictionary of the Old Testament: Wisdom, Poetry & Writings: A Compendium of Contemporary Biblical Scholarship*, edited by Tremper Longman III and Peter Enns, 149–56. Downers Grove, IL: IVP Acadmic, 2008.

Ho, Peter C. W. *The Design of the Psalter: A Macrostructural Analysis*. Eugene, OR: Pickwick, 2019.

———. "The Macrostructural Design and Logic of the Psalter: An Unfurling of the Davidic Covenant." In *Reading the Psalms Theologically*, edited by David M. Howard Jr. and Andrew J. Schmutzer, 36–62. SSBT. Bellingham, WA: Lexham Academic, 2023.

———. "Pan-Psalter Occurrence Scheme of 'Jacob' and 'Covenant.'" *JSOT* 44.2 (2019) 217–32.

Hossfeld, Frank-Lothar, and Erich Zenger. "Excursus: The Composition of the So-called Little Hallel or Concluding Hallel." In *Psalms 3: A commentary on Psalms 101–150*. Translated by Linda M. Maloney, 605–7. Hermeneia. Minneapolis: Fortress, 2011.

———. "Excursus: The Composition of the So-Called Pilgrim Psalter Psalms 120–134." In *Psalms 3: A Commentary on Psalms 101–150*. Translated by Linda M. Maloney, 286–99. Hermeneia. Minneapolis: Fortress, 2011.

Howard, David M., Jr., and Michael K. Snearly. "Reading the Psalter as a Unified Book: Recent Trends." In *Reading the Psalms Theologically*, edited by David M. Howard Jr. and Andrew J. Schmutzer, 1–35. SSBT. Bellingham, WA: Lexham Academic, 2023.

Jones, Barry Alan. *The Formation of the Book of the Twelve: A Study in Text and Canon*. SBLDS 149. Atlanta: Scholars, 1995.

Lange, Armin, et al., eds. *Textual History of the Bible*. Vol. 4. Leiden; Boston: Brill, 2016.

Longacre, Drew. "Developmental Stage, Scribal Lapse, or Physical Defect? 1QIsa^a's Damaged Exemplar for Isaiah Chapters 34–66." *DSD* 20 (2013) 17–50.

———. "The 11Q5 Psalter as a Scribal Product: Standing at the Nexus of Textual Development, Editorial Processes, and Manuscript Production." *ZAW* 134 (2022) 85–111.

———. "Paleographic Style and the Forms and Functions of the Dead Sea Psalm Scrolls: A Hand Fitting for the Occasion?" *VT* 72 (2021) 67–92.

———. "Scribal Treatment of Defective Exemplars: Not Just a Modern Dilemma." In *The Dead Sea Scrolls and the Study of the Humanities*, edited by Pieter B. Hartog, et al., 141–64. STDJ 125. Leiden; Boston: Brill, 2018.

Longman, Tremper, III, and Peter Enns, eds. *Dictionary of the Old Testament: Wisdom, Poetry and Writings*. IVP Bible Dictionary Series 3. Downers Grove: IVP Academic, 2008.

Lyons, Michael A. "Standards of Cohesion and Coherence: Evidence from Early Readers." *HebBAI* 9.2 (2020) 183–208.

McCann, J. Clinton, Jr. "Books I–III and the Editorial Purpose of the Hebrew Psalter." In *The Shape and Shaping of the Psalter*, 93–107. JSOTSup 159. Sheffield: JSOT, 1993.

Meynet, Roland. *Rhetorical Analysis: An Introduction to Biblical Rhetoric.* Edited by Andrew Mein and Claudia V. Camp. Rev. ed. JSOTSup 256. Sheffield: Sheffield Academic, 1998.

Moor, J. C. de, and M. C. A. Korpel. "Paragraphing in a Tibero-Palestinian Manuscript of the Prophets and Writings." In *Method in Unit Delimitation, Pericope 6,* edited by Marjo C. A. Korpel et al., 1–34. Scripture as Written and Read in Antiquity. Leiden; Boston: Brill, 2007.

Neumann, Friederike. *Schriftgelehrte Hymnen: Gestalt, Theologie und Intention der Psalmen 145 und 146–150.* Edited by John Barton et al. BZAW 491. Berlin; Boston: de Gruyter, 2016.

Pajunen, Mika S. "Perspectives on the Existence of a Particular Authoritative Book of Psalms in the Late Second Temple Period." *JSOT* 39.2 (2014) 139–63.

Pavan, Marco. "The Psalter as a Book? A Critical Evaluation of the Recent Research on the Psalter." In *The Formation of the Hebrew Psalter: The Book of Psalms between Ancient Versions, Material Transmission and Canonical Exegesis,* edited by Gianni Barbiero et al., 11–82. FAT I 151. Tübingen, Germany: Mohr Siebeck, 2021.

Prinsloo, Gert T. M. "Psalms 114 and 115: One or Two Poems?" *OTE* 16.3 (2003) 668–89.

———. "The Role of Space in the Shire Hama'lot (Psalms 120–134)." *Bib* 86 (2005) 457–77.

———. "Unit Delimitation in the Egyptian Hallel (Psalms 113–118): An Evaluation of Different Traditions." In *Unit Delimitation in Biblical Hebrew and Northwest Semitic Literature, Pericope 4,* edited by Marjo Korpel and Josef Oesch, 232–63. Scripture as Written and Read in Antiquity. Assen: Van Gorcum, 2003.

Régis, Sébastien. "The Fractal Structure of Biblical Books: A Mathematical Model Explaining and Formalizing the 'Chaotic' Structures of Books of the Bible through the Concepts of Biblical and Semitic Rhetoric." In *Studi Del Terzo Convegno RBS: International Studies on Biblical & Semitic Rhetoric,* edited by Roland Meynet and Jacek Oniszczuk, 381–404. Retorica Biblica et Semitica 2. Roma: Gregorian & Biblical, 2013.

Samely, Alexander. *Profiling Jewish Literature in Antiquity: An Inventory, from Second Temple Texts to the Talmuds.* Translated by Alexander Philip et al. Oxford: Oxford University Press, 2014.

Teeter, David A., and William A. Tooman. "Standards of (In)coherence in Ancient Jewish Literature." *HebBAI* 9.2 (2020) 94–129.

Toorn, Karel van der. "Constructing the Canon: The Closure of the Hebrew Bible." In *Scribal Culture and the Making of the Hebrew Bible,* 233–64. Harvard, MA: Harvard University Press, 2007.

Tov, Emanuel. "'Luxury Scrolls' from the Judean Desert." In *Fountains of Wisdom: In Conversation with James H. Charlesworth,* edited by Gerbern S. Oegema et al., 421–32. London: T&T Clark, 2022.

———. "Sense Divisions in the Qumran Texts, The Masoretic Text, and Ancient Translations of the Bible." In *The Interpretation of the Bible: The International Symposium in Slovenia,* edited by Joze Krasovec, 121–46. JSOTSup 289. Sheffield: Sheffield Academic, 1998.

———. "The Text of the Hebrew/Aramaic and Greek Bible Used in the Ancient Synagogues." In *Hebrew Bible, Greek Bible, and Qumran: Collected Essays,* 171–88. TSAJ 121. Tübingen: Mohr Siebeck, 2008.

Ulrich, Eugene. "Methodological Reflections on Determining Scriptural Status in First-Century Judaism." In *Rediscovering the Dead Sea Scrolls: An Assessment of Old and New Approaches and Methods*, edited by Maxine L. Grossman, 145–61. Grand Rapids: Eerdmans, 2010.

———, ed. *Psalms–Chronicles*. Vol. 3 of *The Biblical Qumran Scrolls: Transcriptions and Textual Variants*. Leiden; Boston: Brill, 2012.

Watson, Wilfred G. E. *Classical Hebrew Poetry: A Guide to Its Techniques*. JSOT 26. Sheffield: JSOT, 1984.

———. *The Formation of the "Book" of Psalms: Reconsidering the Transmission and Canonization of Psalmody in Light of Material Culture and the Poetics of Anthologies*. FAT II 88. Tübingen: Mohr Siebeck, 2016.

Willgren Davage, David. "What Could We Agree On? Outlining Five Fundaments in the Research of the 'Book' of Psalms." In *The Formation of the Hebrew Psalter: The Book of Psalms between Ancient Versions, Material Transmission and Canonical Exegesis*, edited by Gianni Barbiero et al., 83–117. FAT I 151. Tübingen: Mohr Siebeck, 2021.

———. "Why Davidic Superscriptions Do Not Demarcate Earlier Collections of Psalms." *JBL* 139.1 (2020) 67–87.

Yarchin, William. "Is There an Authoritative Shape for the Hebrew Book of Psalms? Profiling the Manuscripts of the Hebrew Psalter." *RB* 122.3 (2015) 355–70.

———. "(Para)Textual Composition on Both Sides of the Canonical Divide." In *Partners with God: Theological and Critical Readings of the Bible in Honor of Marvin A. Sweeney*, edited by Shelley L. Birdsong and Serge Frolov, 311–20. Claremont, CA: Claremont, 2017.

———. "Were the Psalms Collections at Qumran True Psalters?" *JBL* 134.4 (2015) 775–89.

———. "What is the Translated Hebrew Bible? A Paratextual Reflection." *HS* 61 (2020) 143–72.

———. "Why the Future of Canonical Hebrew Psalter Exegesis Includes Abandoning Its Own Premise." In *The Formation of the Hebrew Psalter: The Book of Psalms between Ancient Versions, Material Transmission and Canonical Exegesis*, edited by Gianni Barbiero et al., 119–37. FAT I 151. Tübingen: Mohr Siebeck, 2021.

Zenger, Erich. "Psalmenexegesis Und Psalterexegese: Eine Forschungsskizze." In *The Composition of the Book of Psalms*, 17–65. BETL 238. Leuven: Uitgeverij Peeters, 2010.

CHAPTER 3

Toward the Originally Authored Book of the Twelve

Testing the Coherence of the Variant Shapings of the Twelve Prophets

CRAIG S. PETROVICH

THIS ESSAY IS AN exploration into the nature of biblical authorship.[1] It is motivated by the simple thesis that the Hebrew Bible was authored, in the same sense that any individual book within the Hebrew Bible was authored. Biblical books were not authored in the same way that modern books are typically authored. A modern book is typically written by a named individual "from scratch," resulting in a smooth work from start to finish; a biblical book, on the other hand, consists of various units of text—narratives, poems, letters, etc.—that were already in existence but were then "skillfully arranged and woven into a single, coherent book."[2] The author who stitched together these pieces of text may or may not have been the author of the various pieces themselves. A good example of the former might be the book of Ezekiel, while a classic example of the latter is the anonymously authored book of Chronicles. Either way, the making

---

1. This is a revised and condensed version of the present writer's master's thesis (Petrovich, "Toward"). The thesis was inspired by Dr. John H. Sailhamer, who always encouraged his students to develop a *biblical text theory*.

2. Sailhamer, *Meaning*, 248, 269.

of a biblical book was not a passive, non-invasive bundling of texts; rather, it was an active shaping of existing texts into a single, coherent, final text. This is the way that biblical books were authored.

So then, a biblical book is not fundamentally a *uniform* composition, whose every word was smoothly laid out from start to finish; rather, it is fundamentally a *unified* text, composed from existing texts. It is a *text made of texts*. This, of course, sounds remarkably similar to saying that the Hebrew Bible is a *book made of books*. The only difference is that the units of text used to form the Hebrew Bible were whole books themselves—narrative books, poetic books, etc. In fact, not only is the Hebrew Bible a text made of texts, but so are the various groupings in between. Joshua plus Judges is a text made of texts. Samuel plus Kings is a text made of texts. Joshua plus Judges, combined with Samuel plus Kings, is an even larger, single text.[3]

To validate such a theory of *biblical authorship above the book level*, the main task would be to demonstrate that a particular grouping of books in the Hebrew Bible is coherent, employing the same methods one typically uses to show that an individual biblical book is coherent. Whatever methodology is chosen, it should attempt to explain how all the points of coherence across the grouping of books work together to form a complete semantic structure of hierarchically arranged books. That is to say, more is required to demonstrate authorship than just pointing to one or two connections at the seams between books—inasmuch as pointing to a few connections at the seams between chapters would not be adequate to show that an entire biblical book was coherent.

An obvious objection, at this point, would be the existence of different arrangements for the various groupings of books in the manuscript traditions. How can one claim that a grouping of books had been

---

3. Since the text of the Hebrew Bible was originally recorded on scrolls, which were limited in size, it may sound odd to refer to Joshua plus Judges, combined with Samuel plus Kings, as a single text. Such a book certainly could not have existed on a single scroll. It must be noted, however, that the combination of Genesis, Exodus, Leviticus, Numbers, and Deuteronomy is referred to in the Hebrew Bible as a single book, "the book of the Law" (Josh 1:8) or "the book of Moses" (Neh 13:1), i.e., the Pentateuch. Regarding the Pentateuch, Dempster points out, "The finished Text had no physical unity, since there was no scroll large enough to contain it. Consequently, it was written on five separate scrolls. Yet not even the most radical literary critic would dare to claim that the correct sequence of scrolls was unimportant for interpretation, and that the whole—the Text—was not greater than the sum of its five parts—the texts. Linguistic, stylistic and thematic devices ensured that conceptual unity was established, even if technological limitations precluded physical unity" (Dempster, *Dominion and Dynasty*, 20–21).

authored when more than one arrangement is attested? The solution to this apparent problem is to recognize that a grouping of books is a text-segment like any other biblical text-segment. What happens when a smaller text-segment—a sentence, for example—presents the same kind of problem? If more than one arrangement is attested for the words of a particular sentence, one would be hard-pressed to suggest that there was no originally authored sequence of words for that sentence. Rather, one sequence is original, while all the others are derivative. Though different arrangements of books in the Hebrew Bible involve text-segments at the highest level of the textual hierarchy, it is fundamentally no different than variations in the word order of a sentence. Thus, an added task for validating the theory of *biblical authorship above the book level* is to show that, for a grouping of books with variant arrangements, one arrangement is original, while the others are secondary.

This essay will test its theory of *biblical authorship above the book level* against the twelve books known as the Minor Prophets, or the Twelve. This collection has been the subject of a flurry of studies over the past several decades,[4] not only on whether the collection constitutes a coherent book, but on how this is even possible in the face of differing orders in the manuscript traditions. The three main orders derive from the Masoretic Text (MT), the Septuagint (LXX),[5] and the fragments of the reconstructed scroll 4QXII^a found among the Dead Sea Scrolls (DSS), as shown in Table 3.1 (with books of differing positions italicized in bold).[6]

MT	LXX	4QXII^a
Hosea	Hosea	(?)
Joel	Amos	(?)
Amos	Micah	(?)
Obadiah	*Joel*	(?)
Jonah	*Obadiah*	(?)
Micah	*Jonah*	(?)

4. See the following edited collections: Nogalski and Sweeney, *Reading and Hearing*; Redditt and Schart, *Thematic Threads*; Albertz et al., *Perspectives*; DiPede and Scaiola, *Book*; Wenzel, *Book of the Twelve*; Tiemeyer and Wöhrle, *Book of the Twelve*. See also the following monographs: Schneider, "Unity"; Lee, "Canonical Unity"; House, *Unity*; Jones, *Formation*; LeCureux, *Thematic*.

5. The LXX conceived of in this study is the pre-Christian, Greek translation of the books of the Tanak, the notion of which is hinted at in the Prologue of Sirach.

6. Jones, *Formation*, 2–7.

MT	LXX	4QXII[a]
Nahum	Nahum	(?)
Habakkuk	Habakkuk	(?)
Zephaniah	Zephaniah	(?)
Haggai	Haggai	Zechariah
Zechariah	Zechariah	Malachi
Malachi	Malachi	*Jonah*

Table 3.1: Three main arrangements of the Twelve Prophets (according to the manuscript traditions).

The study will proceed in four stages. First, it will present a methodology both for testing the coherence of a shaping of books and for determining the original shaping among variants. Second, early clues to the original shaping of the Twelve will be sought from a comparison with the Three (i.e., Isaiah, Jeremiah, and Ezekiel), the high-level unit to which the Twelve is attached in the Hebrew Bible. Third, having identified one shaping of the Twelve as the most promising, a demonstration of the depth of its coherence will be offered. Finally, it will be shown how the other shapings of the Twelve might have arisen from the proposed original shaping.

Testing the Coherence of a Shaping of Books amid Variants

The claim of this study is that groupings of biblical books were authored in much the same way that any individual biblical book was authored.[7] If so, a reasonable way to test the coherence of a shaping of books would be to apply the same kinds of techniques used to demonstrate the coherence of a single, biblical book.[8] While commentaries offer a wealth of analysis and reflection on how the various units of a given biblical book cohere together, a model approach can be found in the Semantic and Structural Analysis series produced by the Summer Institute of Linguistics (SIL). Each entry in the series takes a different book of the Greek New Testament and provides an exhaustive analysis of the coherence of all the various

---

7. See the chapter by Quinn in this volume for a thoughtful discussion of *author* versus *editor*.

8. Ho and Quinn similarly argue that the same techniques used to analyze individual psalms should be applied to larger collections in the Psalter; see their chapters in this volume.

units (from greatest to smallest) that make up that particular biblical book. The approach outlined below draws inspiration from that series.

The strongest evidence that particular units of text cohere together to form a larger whole is the patterned *repetition* of words and strings across those units of text, such that the points of repetition share a similar meaning.[9] When a range of such points of coherence pile up around a common set of boundaries between texts, it is a tell-tale sign that an author was at work, intentionally binding those units together into a meaningful whole. In fact, biblical authors use such pileups of patterned repetition repeatedly to bind pieces of text into larger and larger units, until the final result is a hierarchy of textual units constituting a single, coherent text, normally referred to as a book. The following is a representative list of the kinds of patterned repetition one might find between units in a biblical book:

- *simple parallelism*
- *parallel openings*
- *parallel closings*
- *bookends*
- *seams (tail-head links)*
- *pointing forward*
- *pointing backward*

---

9. For repeated *words*, the primary focus would be Hebrew lexical parallels (either the same lexeme or words from the same lexical root); a secondary concern would be synonyms (or even words from the same semantic domain). For repeated *strings*, this would involve parallel grammatical, syntactical, and/or collocational combinations of words.

- *chiasmus*[10]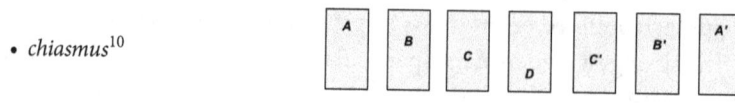

Finding a single instance of such patterned repetition is not adequate for demonstrating coherence, but rather multiple pileups of such parallels are required.[11] These pileups would mark out in no uncertain terms where the boundaries lie for a particular grouping of text-segments, distinguishing that text-segment from all surrounding text-segments, as shown in Figure 3.1.

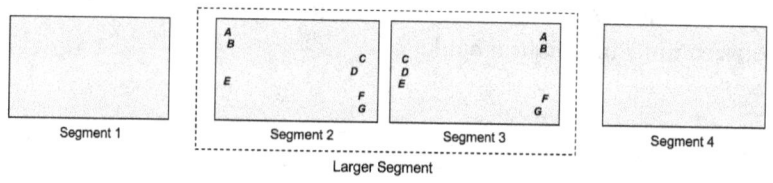

Figure 3.1: Pileups of patterned repetition (*bookends*, *seams*, *parallel openings*, and *parallel closings*).

As text-segments come together to form larger and larger groupings, these arrays of pileups will be found at every level of grouping, as illustrated in Figure 3.2. Applying this methodology to a grouping of biblical books, the text-segments shown in Figure 3.2 would correspond to individual books, while the overall text would be the entire grouping. Thus, to demonstrate the coherence of the Twelve, a search should be made for all instances of patterned repetition across the books—even those instances involving high-frequency words. The goal is not simply to find rare and provocative parallels, but to uncover the depth of connectivity between these books. If multiple pileups of points of coherence should prove to be binding these books together into a hierarchical arrangement of units, it would suggest *authorship above the book level* for the Twelve.

---

10. Technically, *chiasmus* simply refers to *reverse parallelism* (e.g., A-B-C-C'-B'-A'); however, since biblical chiasms often contain a lone textual unit at the center (e.g., A-B-C-D-C'-B'-A'), and since such a phenomenon will prove relevant to this study, the accompanying diagram reflects this variant of *chiasmus*.

11. See Quinn's chapter in this volume for an ingenious way to quantify the intentionality of a set of parallels between textual units.

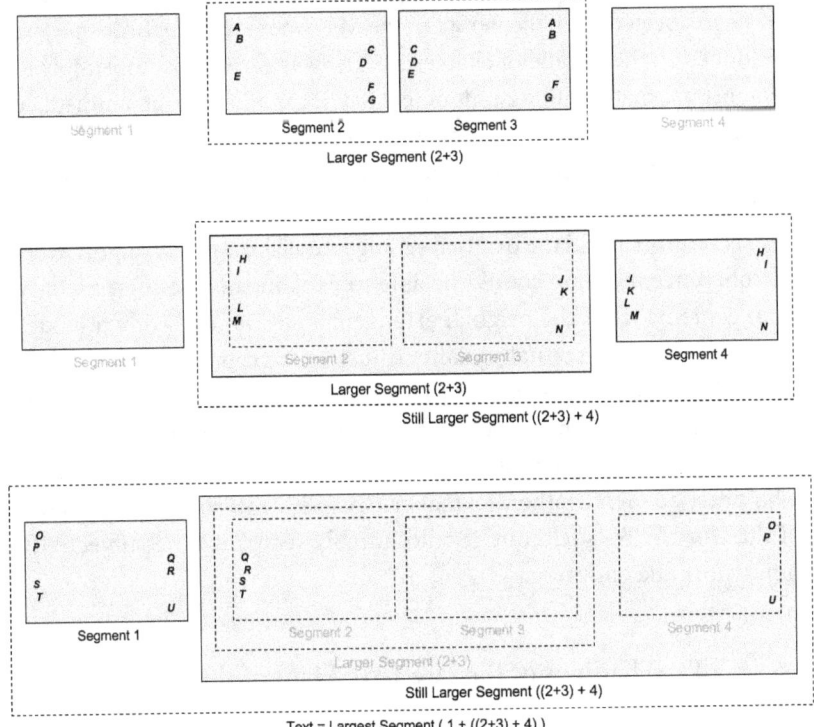

Figure 3.2: Pileups of patterned repetition at each and every level of a sample textual hierarchy.

Since the search for patterned repetition involves specifically Hebrew textual elements, an addendum to the methodology is necessary. If a different arrangement of units is attested in a textual witness from a language other than Hebrew, a Hebrew retroversion of that text should be attempted, in order to give that arrangement the best opportunity to demonstrate its own coherence. Since the LXX arrangement of the Twelve is attested by a Greek text, a Hebrew retroversion of the LXX Greek Twelve was developed for this study, so that the resulting Hebrew text could be fully searched for (potentially) original lexical and grammatical connections.[12]

The final methodological issue is how to compare the coherence of multiple arrangements of a grouping of texts, to determine the originally authored arrangement. This is already a concern within the scope of

12. See Petrovich, "Toward," 189–254, for a detailed presentation of the retroversion.

individual biblical books. For instance, in the case of Jeremiah, chapters 46–51 are located after chapter 45 in the MT, whereas in the LXX they are positioned in the middle of chapter 25. The way forward is not simply to demonstrate that a shifting unit of text has some affinity to its immediate surroundings, whether in one position or the other. The solution is to look at the entire textual hierarchy of units, and to determine which position corresponds to the strongest overall coherence for the whole text.

Not only should the original arrangement show the strongest overall coherence, but one should be able to explain the rise of secondary arrangements from the original arrangement. This well-known guideline for evaluating textual variants is just as appropriate to be applied *above* the book level as *below*. That being said, Emanuel Tov cautions against thinking of this process as a rigid science, whose methods are easy to follow and guaranteed to generate agreed-upon results by all who practice them; rather, textual criticism is "an *art* in the full sense of the word."[13] As such, one should humbly recognize the subjectivity inherent in the endeavor.

The Shapings of the Twelve in Light of the Three

The first step in the pursuit of the originally authored book of the Twelve is to compare the Twelve against the high-level grouping to which it is adjacent in virtually all the manuscript witnesses, namely, the three books of the Major Prophets, or the Three. This step is driven by the expectation that the Twelve—a constituent of the higher-level grouping known as the Latter Prophets—would itself demonstrate coherence with the other constituent of the Latter Prophets, namely, the Three. Looking for high-level points of coherence with the Three might reveal clues as to the internal structure of the Twelve. These clues might even eliminate one or more of the variant orders of the Twelve from consideration as the original shaping.

One feature of the Three that is important to note before comparing it with the Twelve is that in virtually all the early canon lists and manuscript witnesses, Ezekiel follows Jeremiah in close connection.[14] The implication is that Jeremiah and Ezekiel were likely fashioned into

---

13. Tov, *Textual Criticism*, 280.
14. See Beckwith, *Old Testament Canon*, 198–211, especially the section on "Jewish evidence."

a larger unit, "Jeremiah+Ezekiel," to be set alongside Isaiah as a parallel unit within the Three.[15] This is corroborated by the unique duplication of two large narrative blocks from the book of Kings (roughly 2 Kings 18–20 and 2 Kings 25) in the *middle* of the two constituent units of the Three (at Isaiah 36–39 and Jeremiah 52, respectively), as shown in Figure 3.3.

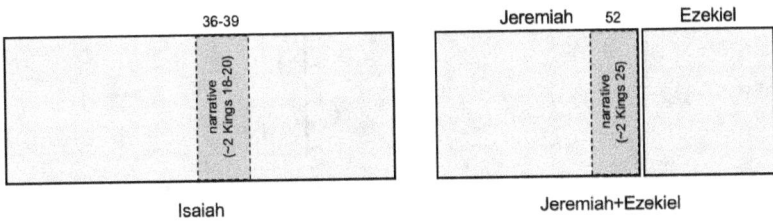

Figure 3.3: Two-part structure of the Three Prophets
(based on narrative insertions).

When comparing the Twelve and the Three, two high-level features immediately stand out: (1) the superscriptions of the individual books, and (2) the unique narrative insertions within these otherwise predominantly poetic texts. An examination of the superscriptions reveals an important set of parallels. The openings of Isaiah and Hosea exhibit the same unique phrase, "in the days of Uzziah, Jotham, Ahaz, and Hezekiah, kings of Judah," while similarly the openings of Jeremiah and Zephaniah share the unique phrase "in the days of Josiah, king of Judah." This suggests a two-part structure for the Twelve in parallel with the Three, as shown in Figure 3.4. "Hosea+" indicates a grouping of books that begins with Hosea, while "Zephaniah+" refers to a grouping that begins with Zephaniah.

---

15. See Petrovich, "Toward," 24–26, for further discussion of the affinity between Jeremiah and Ezekiel.

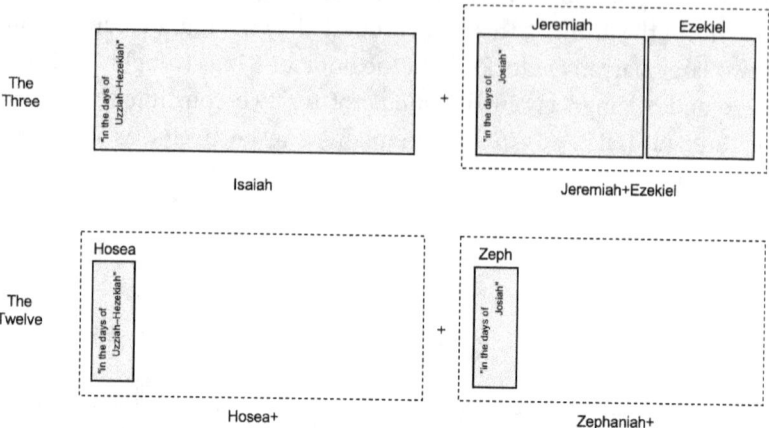

Figure 3.4: Two-part structure of the Three and of the Twelve in parallel (based on superscriptions).

Assuming the Three and the Twelve share this common two-fold structure, then given the earlier observation regarding unique narrative insertions in the Three, one might expect similar narrative insertions in the middle of the two large constituent units of the Twelve. This is precisely what one finds with the LXX and MT arrangements. Only two books in the Twelve are end-to-end narrative texts—Jonah and Haggai. In the LXX and MT orders, Jonah is inserted into the *middle* of Hosea+, while Haggai is inserted into the *middle* of Zephaniah+. This seems to correspond to the insertion of Isaiah 36–39 in the *middle* of Isaiah, and the insertion of Jeremiah 52 in the *middle* of Jeremiah+Ezekiel, respectively, as shown in Figure 3.5.

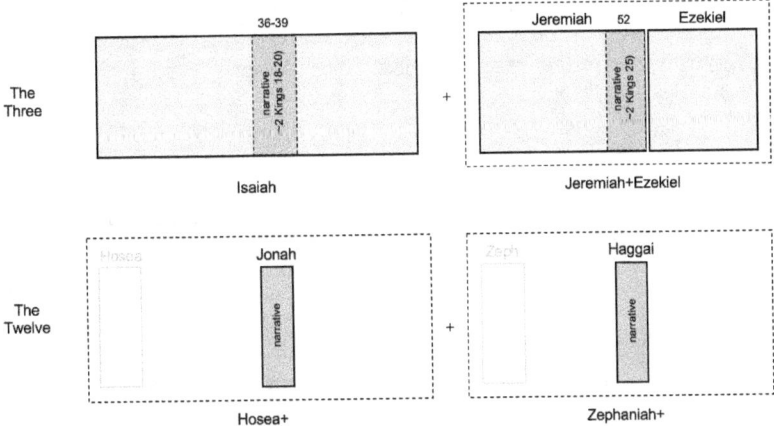

Figure 3.5: Two-part structure of the Three and of the Twelve in parallel (based on narrative insertions).

If this parallel structure is intentional, there should be significant amounts of meaningful repetition between the corresponding narratives.[16] Indeed, a comparison of these insertions reveals spectacular arrays of points of coherence between Isaiah 36–39 and Jonah, as well as numerous significant correspondences between Jeremiah 52 and Haggai. These parallels are often marked by *reversal*, especially as it relates to the *gentiles*. Thus, while the stories and prayers in Jonah echo the stories and prayers in Isaiah 36–39, the role (and fate) of the *Assyrians* is flipped relative to that of *Israel*. Similarly, the fate of Jerusalem and its temple under the *Babylonians* in Jeremiah 52 is reversed under the *Persians* in Haggai. Below are displays of some of the key pileups (P1–P6) of points of coherence between the two sets of narrative insertions.[17]

---

16. Fokkelman offers these insightful words on the role of repetition in the shaping of biblical narratives: "Repetition is used at practically every level of the hierarchy which the text constitutes, from sounds, words, and clauses to stories and groups of stories. It is rarely applied mechanically or inartistically, and usually it features ingenious variations. Thus, a dialectic game of identity and difference is created which challenges us to compare parallelisms at various levels and to ask questions such as: What has remained unchanged and why? What differences occur and what do they mean?" (Fokkelman, "Genesis," 46).

17. Each display features a table of parallel words and parallel strings, along with a rough graphical sketch that shows (by means of dots) where the parallel elements occur in the span of the two texts being compared. Specifically, each horizontal row of dots corresponds to a single set of parallel words or parallel strings from the table. Each table of parallels employs the following formatting scheme:

Isaiah 36–39 and Jonah

P1. Assyrian messenger resembles Israelite prophet

Isaiah   Jonah

Isaiah 36–37   Jonah 3

- (1)<u>the king . . . sent Rab-shakeh . . . to Jerusalem</u>(1)
- (2)<u>Rab-shakeh stood **and proclaimed . . . and said**</u>(2)
- message based on (3)<u>**words of the great king**</u>(3)
- **men**(4) told they should not *trust*(5) in YHWH
- **words**(6) reported to **king**(7) Hezekiah
- tore *clothes*(8), **covered-himself**(9) with **sackcloth**(10)

- (1)<u>(YHWH) said, . . . go to Nineveh!</u>(1)
- (2)<u>Jonah began to enter . . . **and proclaimed and said**</u>(2)
- message based on (3)<u>**word of YHWH**</u>(3)
- **men**(4) *believed*(5) in God
- **word**(6) reached **king**(7) of Nineveh
- removed *robe*(8), **covered-himself**(9) with **sackcloth**(10)

- Each set of parallel words or parallel strings is sequentially tagged with a superscripted number in parentheses; tag number one corresponds to the topmost horizontal row of dots in the graphical sketch, and so on, sequentially.
- Parallel words are followed by a single superscripted tag, e.g., **king**(7).
- Parallel strings are bracketed by matching superscripted tags, e.g., (3)<u>**word of YHWH**</u>(3).
- Strings are always <u>underlined</u>.
- Words in **bold italics** usually signify parallel Hebrew lexical material (either by root or by lexeme); occasionally, they signify parallel artifacts of Hebrew grammatical constructions.
- Words in *normal italics* signify either synonyms or words belonging to the same semantic domain.
- Any words in italics (*normal* or **bold**), and any <u>underlined</u> words, come directly from the biblical text.

P2. Hezekiah's poem-prayer resembles Jonah's poem-prayer

Isaiah   Jonah

Isaiah 38

- (1)*and (Hezekiah) **prayed to YHWH**(1)*
- YHWH says, I **heard**(2) your **prayer**(3)
- (4)*I myself said, . . . I will be deprived*(4)
- (5)*I will see no more the salvation of God . . . , I will look no more on man*(5)
- at gates of **Sheol**(6)
- I was deprived of my remaining **life**(7), but you snatched my **soul**(8) from **decaying**(9)
- you **cast**(10) all my sins behind
- the living will **thank**(11) you, YHWH who **saves**(12) me
- I will play stringed music at (13)*God's house*(13)
- (14)*from **day** to **night***(14) you finished me
- like a **dove**(15) I will mutter

Jonah 2

- (1)*and Jonah **prayed to YHWH**(1)*
- YHWH, you **heard**(2) my **prayer**(3)
- (4)*I myself said, I am driven away*(4)
- (5)*I am driven from your eyes, . . . will I again look to your holy temple?*(5)
- in belly of **Sheol**(6)
- my **soul**(8) was fainting, may the **decay**(9) of my **life**(7) go up
- you **cast**(10) me into the sea
- I will sacrifice with **thanksgiving**(11) for my **salvation**(12)
- will I again look to (13)*your holy temple*(13)?
- (14)*three **days** and three **nights***(14) Jonah was in fish
- Jonah{**Dove**(15)} prayed

- All remaining words (i.e., words not in italics and not underlined) are included to lend context to the parallels—sometimes coming directly from the biblical text, sometimes merely summarizing it.
- Words hyphenated against English convention indicate that a single Hebrew lexeme is in view, e.g., **go-down**; this hyphenation is implemented selectively, usually only for words involved in a lexical parallel.
- Exclamation points signal the presence of an imperative in the biblical text.
- All instances of the biblical text represent the present writer's translation of (a Hebrew retroversion of) the LXX Greek text; the reason for preferring the LXX will soon become apparent.

Note that these displays represent only a subset of the displays found in the present writer's thesis—and are significantly more abbreviated. For full displays of all the parallel words and parallel strings (in chapter-and-verse translational context, though without the accompanying graphical sketches) for each pileup, along with details on the exact nature and relative frequency of each correspondence, see Petrovich, "Toward," 35–47, 255–62.

P3. Assyrian invaders resemble plant (and Ninevite inhabitants)

Isaiah 37

- [1]*and Hezekiah **prayed to YHWH**[1]*
- [2]*in the morning*[2], YHWH's angel **struck**[3] [4]*185,000*[4] Assyrians—king also was **struck**[3] who [5]*dwelt in*[5] Nineveh[6]

Jonah 4

- [1]*and (Jonah) **prayed to YHWH**[1]*
- [2]*when dawn rose*[2], God **struck**[3] the plant; [2]*when the sun appeared*[2], Jonah also was **struck**[3]; shall I not pity [4]*120,000*[4] [5]*dwelling in*[5] Nineveh[6]?

Jeremiah 52 and Haggai

P4. Jerusalem ruined versus rebuilt

Jeremiah 52

- Nebuzaradan **burned**[1] the [2]***house of YHWH***[2], and all **houses**[3] of the king and the city

Haggai 1

- the people rebuilt *desolate*[1] [2]***house of YHWH***[2], after already overlaying their **houses**[3]

P5. Judah judged versus encouraged

Jeremiah 52

- Nebuchadnezzar **spoke**[1] judgments against Zedekiah
- all princes of **Judah**[2], [3]*the chief priest*[3], and sixty men of [4]*people of the land*[4] were slaughtered

Haggai 2

- YHWH **spoke**[1] encouragements through Haggai
- Zerubbabel of **Judah**[2], Joshua [3]*the high priest*[3], and remnant of [4]*people of the land*[4], be strong!

- Nebuzaradan **stands**[5] before Nebuchadnezzar
- Nebuzaradan took from YHWH's house **gold**[6], **silver**[7], and bronze beyond **weight**[8]

- my Spirit **stands**[5] in your midst
- I will fill this house with **gold**[6], **silver**[7], and **glory**[8] from the nations

P6. Jehoiachin's exaltation ressembles Zerubbabel's exaltation

Jeremiah Ezekiel Zephaniah Haggai

Jeremiah 52

- [1]***in the* (first) *year of* (Evil-merodach's) *kingship***[1]
- he ***spoke***[2] good things to Jehoiachin king of ***Judah***[3]
- he set his throne above the [4]***throne of the kings***[4]
- he gave him ***bread***[5] all ***days***[6] of his life, a portion each ***day***[6], in its ***day***[6], until the ***day***[6] of his death

Haggai 2

- [1]***in the*** second ***year of Darius the king***[1]
- YHWH ***spoke***[2] by Haggai to Zerubbabel of ***Judah***[3]
- I will overthrow the [4]***throne of kingdoms***[4] for you
- I will bless your ***grain-bin***[5] from this ***day***[6], from this ***day***[6], ***day***[6] foundation was laid, from this ***day***[6]

These results, combined with the results from the superscriptions, strongly suggest that both the Three and the Twelve were intentionally shaped with a parallel, two-fold structure—Isaiah matching Hosea+, and Jeremiah+Ezekiel matching Zephaniah+, as shown in Figure 3.6. The superscriptions serve as parallel openings for the respective units, while the narrative blocks serve as parallel mid-points.

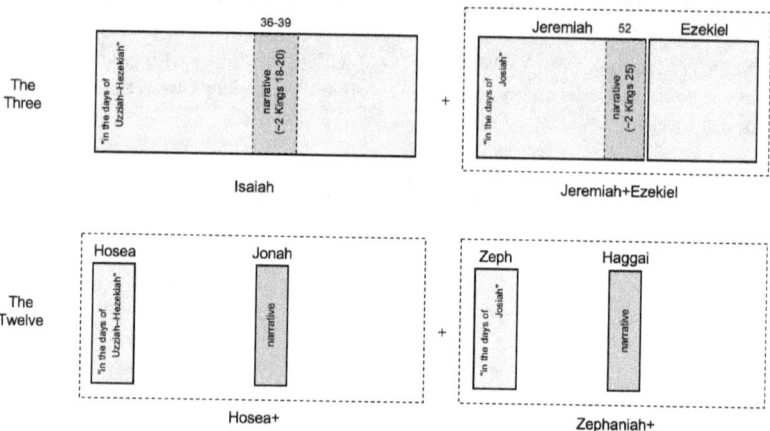

Figure 3.6: Two-part structure of the Three and of the Twelve in parallel (by superscriptions and narrative insertions).

Since Jonah plays a pivotal role in this parallel structure, the 4QXII[a] variant shaping (which has Jonah at the end of the Twelve) is necessarily eliminated from consideration as the original shaping. At the same time, the order of books in Zephaniah–Malachi (previously labeled "Zephaniah+" when the position of Jonah was uncertain) is identical between the MT and LXX orders; as such, the unit of Hosea–Habakkuk (previously "Hosea+") becomes the best place to find further clues as to the most coherent and likely original shaping of the Twelve.

Looking closer at the superscriptions across Hosea–Habakkuk, one finds a strong parallel between Hosea, Amos, and Micah, all of which begin with "in the days of X, king(s) of Judah" (where X is one or more personal names). Such commonality suggests that these three superscriptions serve as parallel openings for three distinct units within Hosea–Habakkuk; however, since the order of books in Hosea–Habakkuk differs between the MT and LXX arrangements, these parallel openings result in divergent textual hierarchies, as shown in Figure 3.7. Because of this, any demonstration of coherence for the LXX unit of "Hosea+Amos+Micah" would also translate into coherence for the overall MT combination of "Hosea+Joel," "Amos+Obadiah+Jonah," and "Micah+Nahum+Habakkuk," since Hosea, Amos, and Micah would function as parallel opening texts for the three main MT units.

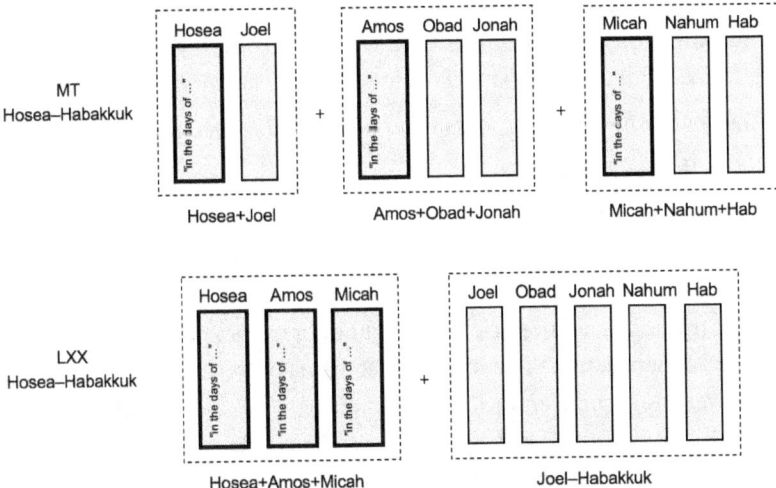

Figure 3.7: MT versus LXX textual hierarchies for Hosea–Habakkuk (based on superscriptions).

Thus, the only remaining unit that is unique between the two arrangements, and therefore deserving of further research, is LXX Joel–Habakkuk. Early examination of this unit, in fact, reveals incredible promise for coherence. Similarities between the superscriptions of Obadiah and Nahum, and between the opening and closing material of Joel and Habakkuk, show signs that the entirety is shaped according to a five-part chiastic structure, with Jonah at the center, as shown below:[18]

> A: Joel—*recounting* an invasion of Israel; God comes to judge the gentiles
>
> > B: Obadiah—*vision of* X; for the gentiles
> >
> > > C: Jonah—should God not have pity on the gentiles?
> >
> > B': Nahum—*vision* of X; for the gentiles
>
> A': Habakkuk—*recounting* an invasion of Israel; God comes to judge the gentiles

---

18. Jones affirms that "the books of Joel and Obadiah do possess significant literary parallels with the books of Nahum and Habakkuk"; yet surprisingly, he believes that the "relatively high degree of literary affinity" between the two groupings is only evident "when one removes the Book of Jonah from consideration" (Jones, *Formation*, 200).

Early research also indicates that "Joel+Obadiah" and "Nahum+Habakkuk" constitute two smaller, more tightly cohering units,[19] suggesting an additional three-part chiastic structure, again with Jonah at the center, as shown below:

X: Joel+Obadiah

Y: Jonah

X': Nahum+Habakkuk

If this is indeed the case, one might even expect pileups of points of coherence between the opening text-segments of the X and X' units (that is, between Joel and Nahum), and also between the closing text-segments of the X and X' units (i.e., between Obadiah and Habakkuk).

In the LXX shaping of the Twelve, Jonah appears to hold a prominent position within the textual hierarchy of Joel–Habakkuk; however, in the MT shaping, Jonah seems almost tangential, dangling incongruously at the end of Amos+Obadiah+Jonah, as shown below:

N: Hosea

A: Joel

N': Amos

B: Obadiah

C: Jonah

N'': Micah

B': Nahum

A': Habakkuk

That is to say, while Hosea and Micah both have exclusively poetic books attached to them (albeit different numbers of poetic books), Amos has one poetic book and one narrative book attached to it. In fact, not only does the MT arrangement lack symmetry, but it breaks the tight coherence of Joel+Obadiah that was noted earlier (although the tightly cohering Nahum+Habakkuk remains unscathed). Consequently, if an exhaustive analysis of LXX Joel–Habakkuk were to confirm this complex chiastic structure (with Jonah as central to its coherence), then the LXX shaping of the Twelve would possess the stronger overall coherence, making it more likely to be the originally authored book of the Twelve.

19. See Jones, *Formation*, 194–203.

The Coherence of the LXX Shaping of the Twelve

The key to establishing the coherence of the LXX shaping of the Twelve is to establish that its most distinctive unit, Joel–Habakkuk, is itself a coherent text. To that end, an exhaustive search was made for all points of coherence that might bind that unit together. The search revealed a wide distribution of multiple pileups of connections, fully confirming the chiastic structures noted above and the role of Jonah as the unquestionable heart of the text. What follows is an abbreviated presentation of the results of that search, beginning with a representative sample of key pileups (P7–P16) of parallels for each pairing of books in the unit's complex chiastic structure.[20]

Joel and Habakkuk

P7. Israel invaded, YHWH answers their cry—annihilates enemy in sea

20. For full displays of all the matchups between these pairings of books (in chapter-and-verse translational context, though without the accompanying graphical sketches), along with details on the exact nature and relative frequency of each correspondence, see Petrovich, "Toward," 82–117, 263–82. As for the present displays, see note 17 for the general formatting scheme. Additionally, two new types of symbols appear in these (and all remaining) displays:

- The symbols †T or †F indicate a lexical matchup (either by root or by lexeme) that appears nowhere else in the LXX Twelve or LXX Five, respectively (where LXX Five refers to Joel, Obadiah, Jonah, Nahum, and Habakkuk).
- The symbols #T or #F indicate matching strings that appear nowhere else in the LXX Twelve or LXX Five, respectively.

If the T or the F ever appears in parentheses (e.g., †(T) or #(F)), it indicates that not all instances of the said word or string are shown in this display, and/or not all instances are accounted for by this particular pileup (in which case, the remaining instances are accounted for in other related pileups between the same books).

108   PART 1: METHODOLOGICAL, COMPOSITIONAL, AND HERMENEUTICAL APPROACHES

Joel 1:1–2:27	Habakkuk 1–3
• ***recount***[(1)†F] what's happening [(2)]***in your days***[(2)#T]!	• won't believe work [(2)]***in your days***[(2)#T] if ***recounted***[(1)†F]
• [(3)]***nation strong***[(4)] ***and*** innumerable[(3)] invading ***land***[(5)]	• mighty[(4)] [(3)]***nation*** bitter ***and*** hurried[(3)] invading ***land***[(5)]
• ***horses***[(6)] and ***horsemen***[(7)] running/leaping[(8)]	• ***horses***[(6)] and ***horsemen***[(7)] riding/swift[(8)]
• [(9)]***great and renowned***[(9)#T] day	• [(9)]***dreaded and renowned***[(9)#T] nation
• they ***devoured***[(10)] and ***desolated***[(11)]	• be ***desolated***[(10)]! they will ***devour***[(11)]
• priests plead, [(12)]***and YHWH answered and said***[(12)#T]	• Habakkuk pleads, [(12)]***and YHWH answered me and said***[(12)#T]
• I will annihilate army of ***nations/peoples***[(13)] in ***sea***[(14)]	• YHWH will trample ***nations/peoples***[(13)] in ***sea***[(14)]
• inhabitants to ***quiver***[(15)†F], seek ***compassionate***[(16)] God	• Habakkuk ***quivers***[(15)†F], seeks ***compassion***[(16)]
• ***fig-tree***[(17)], ***vine***[(18)†F], ***food***[(19)], ***sheep***[(20)], and ***oxen***[(21)] in ***stalls***[(22)†T] languished, but now restored—***rejoice***[(23)]!	• though ***fig-tree***[(17)], ***vine***[(18)†F], ***food***[(19)], ***sheep***[(20)], and ***oxen***[(21)] in ***stalls***[(22)†T] languish, I will ***rejoice***[(23)]

P8. Israel decimated as gentiles decimated (amid signs)

Joel 1:1—2:27	Habakkuk 3
• ***hear***[(1)] this, elders!	• YHWH, I ***heard***[(1)]
• God's army comes with ***horses***[(2)] and ***chariots***[(3)]	• God mounts his ***horses***[(2)] and ***chariots***[(3)]
• [(4)]***peoples will writhe***[(4)#T]	• [(4)]***peoples will writhe***[(4)#T]
• ***heavens***[(5)] and ***earth***[(6)] shake	• splendor covers ***heavens***[(5)] and ***earth***[(6)]
• ***sun***[(7)] and ***moon***[(8)†(F)] darkened, ***brightness***[(9)†(F)] withdrawn	• ***sun***[(7)] lifted, ***moon***[(8)†(F)] still, arrows go forth with ***brightness***[(9)†(F)]
• YHWH [(10)]***utters his voice***[(10)#(F)]	• the deep [(10)]***uttered its voice***[(10)#(F)]

Obadiah and Nahum

P9. Vision of despised Edom resembles vision of dishonored Nineveh

Obadiah 1:1–10

- (1)***vision of** Obadiah*(1)#T (2)*to Edom*(2)
- (3)***thus says** Lord **YHWH***(3)#F
- I (4)***heard a heard-thing***(4) about ***siege***(5)†F
- you became *despised/insignificant*(6) to *nations*(7)
- (8)***declares YHWH***(8), you are ***cut-off***(9) as by ***devastators***(10)

Nahum 1–3

- (1)***vision of** Nahum*(1)#T (2)*concerning Nineveh*(2)
- (3)***thus says YHWH***(3)#F
- all (4)***hearing the heard-thing***(4) of ***siege***(5)†F will clap
- *nations*(7) will see your *nakedness/dishonor*(6)
- (8)***declares YHWH***(8), Nineveh is ***devastated***(10) and ***cut-off***(9)

P10. Lots cast for Jerusalem as for Nineveh

Obadiah 1:11–21

- Jerusalem's ***gates***(1) entered
- (2)***they cast lots over***(2)#T Jerusalem
- strangers ***taking-captive***(3) Jacob's strength—***exile***(4)†F
- Edom, do not ***look***(5) at his destruction

Nahum 2:4–3:19

- Nineveh's ***gates***(1) opened
- (2)***they cast lots over***(2)#T all her honorables
- she by ***exile***(4)†F goes into ***captivity***(3)
- I will make nations ***look***(5) at your nakedness

Joel and Nahum

P11. Israel overrun as Nineveh overrun (while drunk)

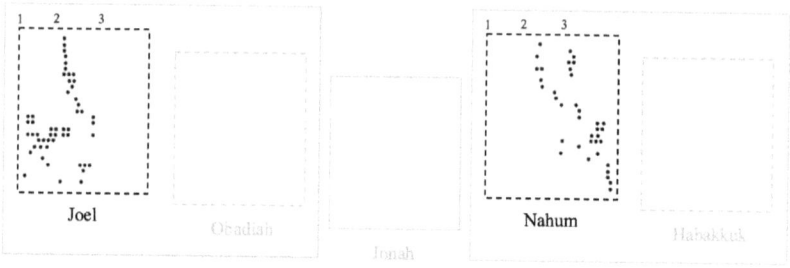

Joel 1:1—2:27

- (1)*its **appearance is like***(1)#T
- ***horses***(2), ***horsemen***(3), ***sound***(4) of ***chariots***(5) ***leaping***(6)†F; invaders ***run***(7), go up the ***wall***(8), ***weighed-down***(9) with shields
- (10)*peoples will **writhe**, all **faces** are like burning of a pot*(10)#T
- (11)***declares YHWH***(11), turn to me!
- ***who***(12) knows if YHWH will ***comfort-himself***(13)?
- ***locust-swarm***(14)†F, ***hopper***(15)†F, and ***fire***(16) ***devoured***(17)
- fields are ***devastated***(18), everything ***cut-off***(19)
- awake, d***runkards***(20)!
- priests, ***spend-the-night***(21) in sackcloth!
- ***gather/collect***(22) the ***people***(23)!
- ***hear***(24), elders! (25)***explode-with-blasting-of***(25)†F trumpet!

Nahum 2:4—3:19

- (1)*their **appearance is like***(1)#T
- ***horses***(2), ***horsemen***(3), ***sound***(4) of ***chariots***(5) ***leaping***(6)†F; chariots ***run***(7), defenders hurry to ***walls***(8), invaders ***weighed-down***(9) with desirables
- (10)***writhing** is in all loins, and **faces** of them all are like burning of a pot*(10)#T
- (11)***declares YHWH***(11), I am against you
- ***who***(12) will grieve? where will I seek ***comforters***(13) for you?
- sword and ***fire***(16) ***devour***(17) like ***locust-swarm***(14)†F and ***hopper***(15)†F
- Nineveh is ***devastated***(18), you will be ***cut-off***(19)
- you will be ***drunk***(20)
- shepherds/nobles *slumbered/laid-down*(21)
- no one was ***collecting***(22) your ***people***(23)
- all ***hearing***(24) will (25)***explode-with-clapping-of***(25)†F hands

P12. Israel avenged on dark day; saved one evangelizes on mountain

Joel 2:28–3:21
- young-ones will see *visions*⁽¹⁾
- *great*⁽²⁾ *day*⁽³⁾ of *darkness*⁽⁴⁾†⁽F⁾, land will *shake*⁽⁵⁾
- YHWH will be a *strength*⁽⁶⁾ to Israel
- I will *avenge*⁽⁷⁾†F, I will not *consider-innocent*⁽⁸⁾
- strangers will ⁽⁹⁾*not pass-through ever*⁽⁹⁾#F
- *delivered-one*⁽¹⁰⁾ on *mountain*⁽¹¹⁾, and those *bearing-good-news*⁽¹²⁾†T
- ⁽¹³⁾*I will reverse the* captivity *of Judah*⁽¹³⁾#F

Nahum 1:1–2:3
- *vision*⁽¹⁾ of Nahum
- YHWH *great*⁽²⁾ on *day*⁽³⁾ of *darkness*⁽⁴⁾†⁽F⁾, mountains *shook*⁽⁵⁾
- YHWH is good to one *showing-strength*⁽⁶⁾ in him
- YHWH is *avenging*⁽⁷⁾†F, I will not *consider-innocent*⁽⁸⁾
- they will ⁽⁹⁾*not ever again pass-through*⁽⁹⁾#F
- *preserved-one*⁽¹⁰⁾ on *mountains*⁽¹¹⁾ *bearing-good-news*⁽¹²⁾†T
- ⁽¹³⁾*YHWH reversed the* pride *of Jacob*⁽¹³⁾#F

P13. Lots cast for Judah as for Nineveh

Joel 2:28–3:21
- *captivity*⁽¹⁾ of Judah and Jerusalem
- ⁽²⁾*they cast lots*⁽²⁾ for my people
- *silver*⁽³⁾, *gold*⁽⁴⁾, *desirables*⁽⁵⁾†F taken
- YHWH will be a *strength*⁽⁶⁾ to Israel

Nahum 2:4–3:19
- Nineveh goes into *captivity*⁽¹⁾
- ⁽²⁾*they cast lots*⁽²⁾ over all her honorables
- *silver*⁽³⁾, *gold*⁽⁴⁾, *desirables*⁽⁵⁾†F plundered
- you will seek a *strength*⁽⁶⁾

Obadiah and Habakkuk

P14. Edom standing and looking resembles Habakkuk standing and looking—toward enemy's ruin

Obadiah 1

- thus says ⁽¹⁾**Lord YHWH**⁽¹⁾ to Edom
- do not **stand**⁽²⁾ and **look**⁽³⁾ at Judah's ruin (gloatingly)
- do not **be-glad**⁽⁴⁾ about Judah's ⁽⁵⁾**day of distress**⁽⁵⁾

Habakkuk 2–3

- ⁽¹⁾**Lord YHWH**⁽¹⁾ is my strength
- I will **stand**⁽²⁾ and **look**⁽³⁾ (for word of invaders' ruin), I *watched*⁽³⁾ it, quivered, and begged for compassion
- I will *rejoice*⁽⁴⁾ in my saving God in ⁽⁵⁾**day of distress**⁽⁵⁾

P15. Edom ensnared as gentiles ensnared (for arrogance and violence)

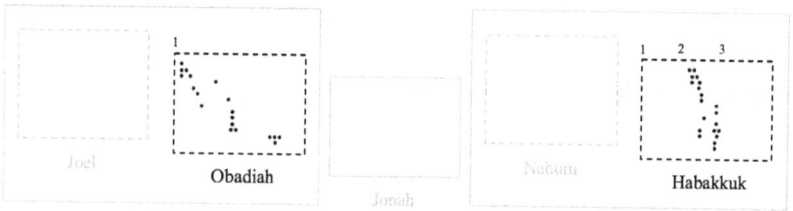

Obadiah 1

- the **vision**⁽¹⁾—**arise**⁽²⁾, **nations**⁽³⁾!
- they ⁽⁴⁾*set a snare beneath you*⁽⁴⁾, Edom
- one **raising-on-high**⁽⁵⁾ his habitation— ⁽⁶⁾*your nest is placed among the stars*⁽⁶⁾#T
- your warriors are **dismayed**⁽⁷⁾†F as by **devastators**⁽⁸⁾

Habakkuk 2

- write the **vision**⁽¹⁾—**nations**⁽³⁾ will **arise**/**awake**⁽²⁾
- those ⁽⁴⁾*plotting against you*⁽⁴⁾, oppressor, will awake
- the oppressor gains an evil gain for his house, ⁽⁶⁾*to place his nest on-high*⁽⁵⁾⁽⁶⁾#T
- **devastation**⁽⁸⁾ from beasts will make you **dismayed**⁽⁷⁾†F

- **shame**⁽⁹⁾ will **cover**⁽¹⁰⁾ you, due to ⁽¹¹⁾**violence against your brother Jacob**⁽¹¹⁾, ⁽¹²⁾**because-of slaughter**⁽¹²⁾
- you will **drink**⁽¹³⁾ the **wine**⁽¹⁴⁾ (of my wrath)

- you devised **shame**⁽⁹⁾—your ⁽¹¹⁾**violence against the land**⁽¹¹⁾ will **cover**⁽¹⁰⁾ you, ⁽¹²⁾**because-of bloodshed**⁽¹²⁾
- **drink**⁽¹³⁾ the **cup**⁽¹⁴⁾ of dishonor from YHWH!

P16. Vision-report about Edom resembles prayer-report about gentiles

Obadiah 1
- ⁽¹⁾**vision of Obadiah**⁽¹⁾
- ⁽²⁾**I heard a heard-thing from YHWH**⁽²⁾#T
- warriors of **Teman**⁽³⁾†F will be dismayed, cut-off ⁽⁴⁾**from mountain**⁽⁴⁾ of Esau
- **nations**⁽⁵⁾ will drink, **saved-ones**⁽⁶⁾ will go up

Habakkuk 3
- ⁽¹⁾**prayer of Habakkuk**⁽¹⁾
- ⁽²⁾**I heard the heard-thing concerning you**⁽²⁾#T
- God will come from **Teman**⁽³⁾†F, the Holy One ⁽⁴⁾**from mountain**⁽⁴⁾ of shady bough
- you will thresh **nations**⁽⁵⁾ to **save**⁽⁶⁾ your people

In some of these arrays of parallels, one book echoes another book in a straightforward manner, affirming the message hinted at earlier (when the chiastic structure was first discovered): God will judge Israel with a gentile invasion, but when Israel calls, YHWH will save them by judging those violent, arrogant gentiles (P7, P9, P12, P15, and P16). In other cases, however, one book echoes another book in the unexpected context of *reversal*—with God's judgment of the *gentiles* in one book bearing a striking resemblance to God's judgment of *Israel* in the other book (P8, P10, P11, P13, and P14).

This use of textual repetition in the context of alternation between Israel and the gentiles is the main way the biblical author brings the topic of gentile salvation to the foreground within the larger text of Joel–Habakkuk.²¹ In essence, the biblical author is engaging the reader

---

21. For a broader look at the complex characterization of the gentiles across the Twelve and the Psalter, see the chapters by Timmer and Maxwell in this volume.

with the following flow of thought: (1) Israel is going to be judged; (2) but Israel will be saved if they repent and call on God for mercy; (3) the gentiles also are going to be judged; (4) their judgment will resemble Israel's judgment; (5) so if the gentiles will be judged in the same manner that Israel will be judged, can the gentiles not also be saved in the same manner? Can they not repent and call on God for mercy? More pointedly, if you who are reading this book of Joel–Habakkuk are longing for the salvation of Israel from terrible judgment, should you not long for the same salvation to be extended to the gentiles, as you read of them facing the same terrifying judgment?

As this flow of thought is constantly triggered through repetition and reversal, it is not hard to see how all of Joel–Habakkuk points toward the book of Jonah as its centerpiece. Not only does the entire story of Jonah confront the reader with gentile salvation, but its story is even shown earlier to be a reversal of Israel's salvation in Isaiah 36–39. Given Jonah's central position in Joel–Habakkuk, one would expect that such reversal would only be further explored and enhanced. According to David A. Dorsey, this is precisely the role of the central element of a chiasm:

> The central unit is the natural location for the turning point, climax, high point, or centerpiece, since it marks the point where the composition reverses its order. Both halves of the symmetry look toward the center unit, making it the natural focal point.[22]

Jonah's role as the centerpiece was borne out by the exhaustive analysis of Joel–Habakkuk, which found remarkable pileups of connections between Jonah and each of the other four books[23]—pileups that exhibit either wholesale or subtle reversals. Space constraints do not allow for a detailing of all that was found, but a sampling of key pileups (P17–P29) are noted below.[24]

---

22. Dorsey, *Literary Structure*, 31.

23. Contra Jones, who argues not only that Jonah disrupts the coherence of LXX Joel–Habakkuk, but that "Jonah and Obadiah, although contiguous in both the LXX and MT, share no verbal ties with one another and only the broad thematic connection of Israel's relationship to the nations" (Jones, *Formation*, 199–200). P20–P23 below reveal a different state of affairs, including three verbal links between Jonah and Obadiah that are unique within the Twelve.

24. For full displays of all the matchups with Jonah (in chapter-and-verse translational context, though without the accompanying graphical sketches), along with details on the exact nature and relative frequency of each correspondence, see Petrovich, "Toward," 117–66, 282–96. As for the present displays, see notes 17 and 20 for the formatting scheme.

Joel and Jonah

P17. Israel's invaders thrown into sea as Jonah is thrown into sea

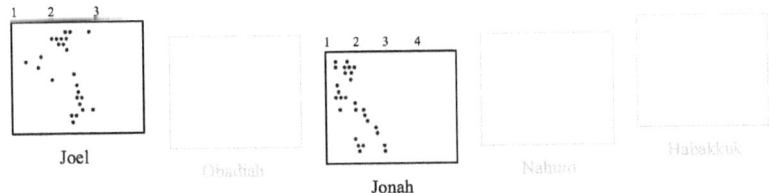

Joel 1:1—2:27

- a ***great***(1) day of *darkness/gloom/cloud/fog*(2), an army will ***move***(3) against Israel—who is ***able***(4)?
- ***cry-out***(5) to YHWH!
- ***awake***(6)! *spend-the-night*(7) in sackcloth!
- the priests will (8)***say, . . . YHWH, . . . do not place***(8) your inheritance as a reproach
- I will ***call***(9) to you, YHWH

- YHWH ***answered***(10)—I will thrust army into *sea*(11), its *stink/stench*(12) will ***go-up***(13)
- YHWH ***dealt***(14) with you wondrously
- YHWH may leave behind *offering/libation*(15) (16)***for YHWH***(16)?

Jonah 1–2

- a ***great***(1) *storm*(2) was ***moving***(3) against the sailors, they were not ***able***(4) to reach dry-land
- they ***cried-out***(5) to their gods
- chief told Jonah, *arise*(6)! why are you *sleeping*(7)?
- the sailors (8)***said, please YHWH, . . . do not place***(8) upon us innocent blood
- they ***called***(9) to YHWH, I ***called***(9) to YHWH
- he ***answered***(10) me—you cast me into the *seas*(11), may the *decay*(12) of my life ***go-up***(13)
- you, YHWH, ***dealt***(14) as you pleased
- they made *sacrifice*(15) and *vows*(15) (16)***for YHWH***(16), I will *sacrifice*(15) and repay *vow*(15) (16)***for YHWH***(16)

116 PART 1: METHODOLOGICAL, COMPOSITIONAL, AND HERMENEUTICAL APPROACHES

P18. Proclamation among gentiles resembles proclamation to Nineveh (for evil and violence)

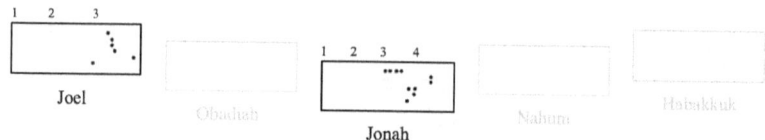

Joel 2:28—3:21

- ***proclaim***[(1)] among gentiles—***there***[(2)] I will ***sit***[(3)] to judge your ***evil***[(4)] and ***violence***[(5)]! yet all who ***call***[(6)] on YHWH will be delivered

Jonah 3–4

- ***proclaim***[(1)] to Nineveh—overthrown! yet they turned from ***evil***[(4)] and ***violence***[(5)], ***calling***[(6)] on God to escape, as ***there***[(2)] ***sat***[(3)] Jonah to see their judgment

P19. God pitying Israel resembles Jonah pitying plant

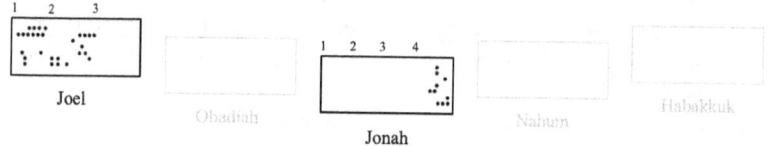

Joel 1:1–2:27

- vines ***dried***[(1)] by ***locusts***[(2)]—YHWH, ***have-pity***[(3)†(T)]!
- ***gladness***[(4)] cut-off—now vines ***sprouted***[(5)], be ***glad***[(4)]!
- invading (locust) army was ***great***[(6)] and ***numerous***[(7)]

Jonah 4

- plant ***dried***[(1)] by ***worm***[(2)], Jonah ***had-pity***[(3)†(T)] on plant
- Jonah ***glad***[(4)] with ***gladness***[(4)] when it first ***rose-up***[(5)]
- should I not pity ***great***[(6)] and ***numerous***[(7)] Nineveh?

Obadiah and Jonah

P20. Edom standing and looking resembles Jonah sitting and looking—toward enemy's destruction

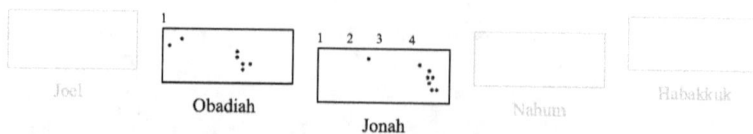

Obadiah 1	Jonah 2, 4
• Edom brags, ⁽¹⁾*who will **bring-down** me to earth*⁽¹⁾#ᵀ? ⁽²⁾***Lord YHWH***⁽²⁾ tells Edom, I will bring you down	• Jonah prayed, you cast me, ⁽¹⁾*I went-down to earth*⁽¹⁾#ᵀ; Jonah prayed, ⁽²⁾***Lord YHWH***⁽²⁾, take my life!
• when ⁽³⁾*you stood from opposite*⁽²⁾ Jerusalem⁽⁴⁾, you should not have **looked**⁽⁵⁾ at their destruction, nor been **glad**⁽⁶⁾ for it	• ⁽³⁾*he sat from before*⁽³⁾ the *city*⁽⁴⁾, so that he might **look**⁽⁵⁾ at what (misery) would befall them, being **glad**⁽⁶⁾ only for the plant

P21. Obadiah hearing report against Edom resembles Jonah receiving word against Nineveh

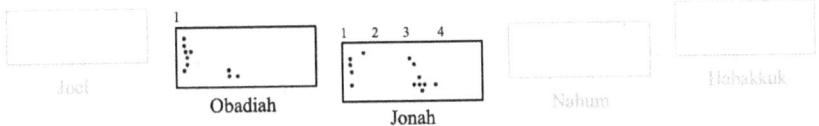

Obadiah 1:1-10	Jonah 1, 3
• Obadiah{⁽¹⁾***Servant-of-YH***⁽¹⁾#ᵀ} heard a *report*⁽²⁾—***arise***⁽³⁾! let us ***arise***⁽³⁾ ⁽⁴⁾***against her***⁽⁴⁾	• Jonah, ⁽¹⁾***servant of YH***⁽¹⁾#ᵀ, received the *word*⁽²⁾—***arise***⁽³⁾! proclaim ⁽⁴⁾***against her***⁽⁴⁾!
• siege *sent-forth*⁽⁵⁾—*Edom*⁽⁶⁾ will be *ruined/cut-off*⁽⁷⁾	• Jonah *went*⁽⁵⁾—*Nineveh*⁽⁶⁾ will be *overthrown*⁽⁷⁾

P22. Lots cast for Jerusalem as for Jonah

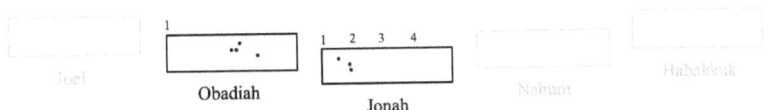

Obadiah 1:10-21	Jonah 1
• ⁽¹⁾*they cast **lots upon** Jerusalem*⁽¹⁾	• ⁽¹⁾*the **lot fell upon** Jonah*⁽¹⁾—hurl me into the sea!
• shame from *violence*⁽²⁾ against Jacob will cover you	• do not place his *blood*⁽²⁾ on us, YHWH
• to you ⁽³⁾*it will be **dealt just as you dealt***⁽³⁾#ᵀ	• YHWH, ⁽³⁾*you **dealt just as you pleased***⁽³⁾#ᵀ

118   PART 1: METHODOLOGICAL, COMPOSITIONAL, AND HERMENEUTICAL APPROACHES

P23. Edom covered in shame as Nineveh covered in sackcloth

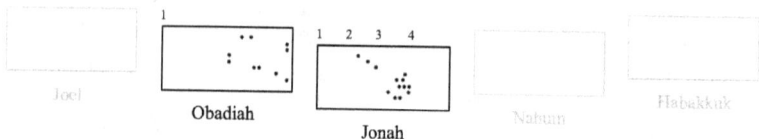

Obadiah 1:10–21

- Jacob in **distress**⁽¹⁾, but **saved-ones**⁽²⁾ will **go-up**⁽³⁾ to judge Esau
- shame from **violence**⁽⁴⁾ will **cover**⁽⁵⁾ Edom
- God will **deal**⁽⁶⁾ with you just as you **dealt**⁽⁶⁾—for YHWH has **spoken**⁽⁷⁾
- the **kingdom**⁽⁸⁾ will be YHWH's

Jonah 2–3

- Jonah in **distress**⁽¹⁾—may my decaying life **go-up**⁽³⁾ **saved**⁽²⁾
- Nineveh **covered**⁽⁵⁾ in sackcloth from **violence**⁽⁴⁾
- God saw their **dealings**⁽⁶⁾ and didn't **deal**⁽⁶⁾ with them as he had **spoken**⁽⁷⁾
- the **king**⁽⁸⁾ and people turned to YHWH

Jonah and Nahum

P24. Lot falling on sleeping Jonah resembles lots cast on slumbering Nineveh

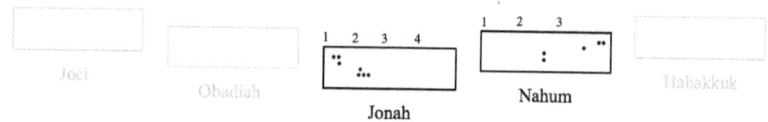

Jonah 1–2

- Jonah **laid-down**†F/**fell-fast-asleep**⁽¹⁾

- ⁽²⁾*the lot fell on Jonah*⁽²⁾, he was hurled into the sea

- Jonah{**Dove**⁽³⁾†⁽F⁾} prayed/called-out/cried-for-help⁽⁴⁾

Nahum 2:4–3:19

- Nineveh's shepherds/nobles slumbered/**laid-down**⁽¹⁾†F

- ⁽²⁾*they cast **lots on** all her honorables*⁽²⁾, she is exiled

- her exiled handmaids were like **doves**⁽³⁾†F twittering⁽⁴⁾

P25. Word from the comforting God resembles message from Comforter (for evil Nineveh)

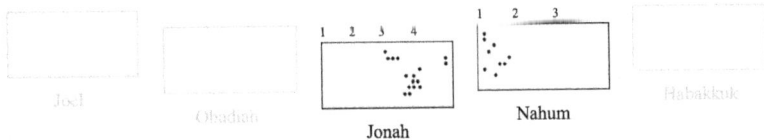

Jonah 3–4

- **word**⁽¹⁾ of YHWH—go to **Nineveh**⁽²⁾†⁽ᶠ⁾! more than 120,000 persons ⁽³⁾**dwelling in it**⁽³⁾
- Jonah said, I knew ⁽⁴⁾**you are . . . slow to anger and *abounding in* kindness**⁽⁴⁾
- they turned from **evil**⁽⁵⁾, God did not **deal**⁽⁶⁾ them the promised misery
- they said, who knows if God will **comfort-himself**⁽⁷⁾ from the ⁽⁸⁾**burning of his anger**⁽⁸⁾#ᵀ? God **comforted-himself**⁽⁷⁾; Jonah said, I knew you **comfort-yourself**⁽⁷⁾ concerning misery

Nahum 1:1–2:3

- *message*⁽¹⁾ for **Nineveh**⁽²⁾†⁽ᶠ⁾—the land and all ⁽³⁾**dwelling in it**⁽³⁾ heaved
- ⁽⁴⁾**YHWH is slow to anger and great *in* power**⁽⁴⁾
- his enemies counsel **evil**⁽⁵⁾, God will **deal**⁽⁶⁾ them a complete-end
- vision of Nahum{**Comforter**⁽⁷⁾}—who can withstand the ⁽⁸⁾**burning of his anger**⁽⁸⁾#ᵀ?

P26. King leads nobles to the comforting God; king leads nobles to exile without comforters

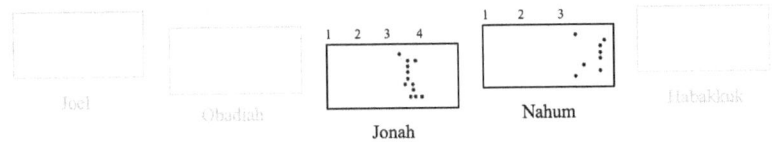

Jonah 3–4

- ⁽¹⁾**(Jonah) said, . . . Nineveh is overthrown**⁽¹⁾#ᵀ
- they turned from **evil**⁽²⁾
- ⁽³⁾**king of Nineveh**⁽³⁾#ᵀ set-aside⁽⁴⁾ **majestic-robe**⁽⁵⁾†⁽ᶠ⁾, had **great-ones**⁽⁶⁾ prohibit **feeding-at-pasture**⁽⁷⁾
- they said, who knows if God will **comfort-himself**⁽⁸⁾? God **comforted-himself**⁽⁸⁾; Jonah said, I knew you **comfort-yourself**⁽⁸⁾ concerning misery

Nahum 3

- ⁽¹⁾**(one) will say, Nineveh is devastated**⁽¹⁾#ᵀ
- their **evil**⁽²⁾ passed-over continually
- ⁽³⁾**king of Assyria**⁽³⁾#ᵀ laid-down⁽⁴⁾ **majestic-ones**⁽⁵⁾†⁽ᶠ⁾, those **leading-to-pasture**⁽⁷⁾ slept, **great-ones**⁽⁶⁾ bound
- where will I seek **comforters**⁽⁸⁾ for you?

Jonah and Habakkuk

P27. Jonah prays about death at sea as Habakkuk prays about death of wicked at sea

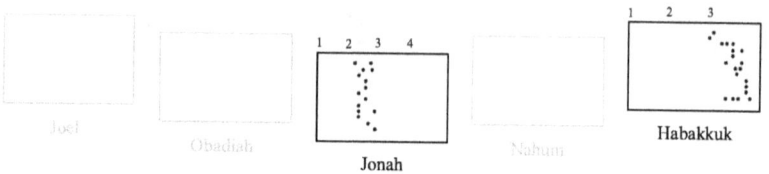

Jonah 2	Habakkuk 2:20–3:19
• may my **prayer**[(1)†(T)] come to [(2)]*your holy temple*[(2)]	• Habakkuk's **prayer**[(1)†(T)]; YHWH is in [(2)]*his holy temple*[(2)]
• **currents**[(3)] and **waters**[(4)] of **deep**[(5)†F] **seas**[(6)] surrounded me, my **head**[(7)] sank into *Sheol*[(8)]	• **currents**[(3)] and **waters**[(4)] of **deep**[(5)†F] **sea**[(6)] were scattered, **heads**[(7)] of wicked shattered in **death**[(8)]
• you heard my **voice**[(9)], I called from **distress**[(10)]—may my decaying life **go-up**[(11)]	• I trembled at my **voice**[(9)]; I will rest amid **distress**[(10)] until **going-up**[(11)] to my people
• I will give-thanks for **saving**[(12)] me	• you will **save**[(12)] us and your anointed

P28. Jonah sits to see outcome as Habakkuk stands to see outcome

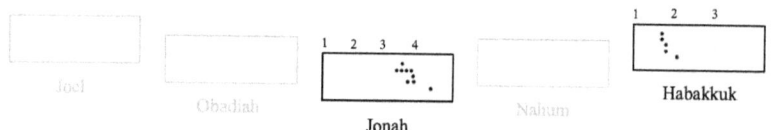

Jonah 3–4	Habakkuk 1:5–2:1
• the king caused his robe to **pass-over**[(1)], and all *put-on*[(2)] sackcloth to signify they *repented*[(2)]	• invader will *change*[(2)] his spirit (as a garment), which will **pass-over**[(1)], as he makes-restitution-for-trespasses
• God **saw**[(3)] them repent from **evil**[(4)]	• YHWH, your eyes are too pure to **see**[(3)] **evil**[(4)]
• [(5)]*(Jonah) sat, . . . he sat . . . , until he should see what will happen with the city*[(5)#T]	• [(5)]*I will stand . . . , I will station-myself . . . , to see what he will speak with me*[(5)#T]

P29. Jonah waits to see misery fall upon his enemies; Habakkuk sees it and quivers

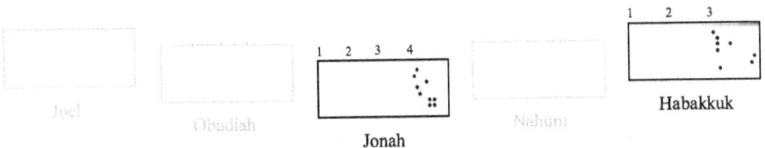

Jonah 4	Habakkuk 3
• Jonah **prayed**^{(1)†(T)}	• Habakkuk's **prayer**^{(1)†(T)}
• ⁽²⁾*Jonah was vexed with great vexation*⁽²⁾	• ⁽²⁾*my spirit quivers with quivering*⁽²⁾
• he sat to **see**⁽³⁾ what (misery) will happen to Nineveh	• I **saw**⁽³⁾ your works—even Cush quivering
• I knew you are **compassionate**⁽⁴⁾	• you will remember **compassion**⁽⁴⁾
• ⁽⁵⁾**Lord YHWH**⁽⁵⁾, take my life!	• ⁽⁵⁾**Lord YHWH**⁽⁵⁾ is my strength
• Jonah was *glad*⁽⁶⁾ (only) about the plant, which **shaded**^{(7)†F} him from misery	• I will *rejoice*⁽⁶⁾ in my saving God, who comes from the mountain of the **shady**^{(7)†F} bough

One of the most exciting discoveries of this study is that whole sections of Joel, Obadiah, Nahum, and Habakkuk regularly mimic the stories and prayers of Jonah—to the point where these four books, taken together, represent a coordinated retelling of the entire Jonah story. Not only does this mimicry of Jonah reveal how deeply concerned each of the four books is with the salvation of the gentiles, but it also allows the larger text of Joel–Habakkuk to explore exactly how it is that the gentiles will be saved, given such dire threats of judgment.

Joel, in its first half, completely mimics the sailor-story from Jonah (P17).[25] Just as Israel (in Joel) calls to God and is saved by the drowning of the (gentile) army at sea, so the (gentile) sailors call to God and are saved when Jonah is drowned at sea. From this complex correspondence (involving Jonah, Israel, and the gentiles), an answer begins to take shape as to how God intends to save Israel from the gentiles, while at the same time showing mercy to those very gentiles: an individual from among them must suffer their fate as a substitutionary sacrifice.

In its entirety, Joel is a large-scale version of the object lesson from the end of Jonah. Just as Jonah was glad for the plant and pitied it when

25. It also mimics the Nineveh-story proper (though not displayed here).

it was destroyed by the worm, so God pitied repentant Israel and restored gladness to them when their vegetation was saved from the locusts (P19). Joel should now pity the gentiles and proclaim to them (as Jonah did) the news of their judgment—so that they too might repent as Israel did and escape judgment (P18).

Obadiah, like Jonah, is the Servant-of-YH, who receives a message intended for a gentile nation regarding their coming destruction (P21). The implication of the parallel is that Obadiah would be sent as an advanced messenger ahead of the siege of Edom (even as Rab-shakeh, also a type of Jonah, was sent ahead of the siege of Jerusalem), in order to trigger repentance in Edom.

Obadiah mimics portions of both the sailor-story and the Nineveh-story proper in Jonah. Even as Edom deals violence to Judah, the sailors deal bloodshed (as it were) to Jonah, throwing him overboard; yet while Edom is to be dealt violence in return, the sailors beg for mercy and are dealt it—just as God pleased (P22). The implication is that, if Edom appeals to God—even trusting in the substitutionary sacrifice of his servant—he will likewise deal mercy to them. Similarly, as Edom is covered in shame for violence, the Ninevites are covered in sackcloth for the same; and while God spoke of dealing violently with Edom, he did not deal the misery he spoke of dealing to Nineveh (P23). Such a parallel has incredible implications for Obadiah, suggesting that its inherent purpose is to trigger repentance unto salvation for Edom (and all gentiles).

Obadiah also briefly echoes both scenes in which Jonah interacts with God (P20). Although Edom thinks that no one will bring him down to earth, God assures him that he himself will bring him down; Jonah meanwhile makes the surprising observation (amidst drowning) that God has brought him down to the earth. This correspondence confirms God's plan for how the gentiles will obtain mercy—the substitutionary death of his anointed. Later, God indicts Edom for positioning himself to watch the destruction of Jerusalem (and for being glad over it); God likewise critiques Jonah for positioning himself to watch for the overthrow of Nineveh (the only outcome that would have made Jonah glad). The echo from Jonah reverberates back to the reader of Obadiah: do not sit and wait for the destruction of Edom, nor be glad over it.

Nahum, like Jonah, receives a message intended for Nineveh regarding their complete destruction (P25). Nahum is also the Comforter who, like Jonah, knows that God is slow to anger and one who comforts himself from dealing the destruction he has promised. According to the parallel,

God's ultimate purpose in giving this message to Nahum would be to stir repentance in Nineveh, thereby bringing comfort to the city.

Nahum also offers fascinating echoes of the sailor-story and the Nineveh-story proper. From the sailor-story, just as Jonah lies down, falls asleep (despite a storm), has lots cast upon him, and is finally hurled into exile at sea, so the Assyrian king (in Nahum) lays down his nobles to slumber (despite a siege), until lots are cast for them, and they are carried away into exile (P24). As for the Nineveh-story, the Ninevite king (in Jonah) lays down his majestic garments and has his nobles proclaim a fast, whereas the Assyrian king (in Nahum) lays down his majestic nobles to sleep, resulting in death or captivity (P26). By this magnificent interplay with Jonah, Nahum's comforting message to Nineveh becomes clear: despite looming judgment, one only needs to wake up and fast, in order to escape.

Habakkuk, as a whole, is largely patterned after Jonah's prayers (both Jonah's song of salvation and his complaint about Nineveh), as well as Jonah's actions amid those prayers. As Jonah longs for the destruction of Nineveh and positions himself to see that destruction played out before his eyes, so Habakkuk longs for the destruction of the gentiles and positions himself to see the vision of it from God (P28). Indeed, the vision he sees of the gentiles drowning at sea under the pummeling of God's wrath resembles Jonah's report of his own drowning at sea under the weight of God's rejection (P27). The implication of the parallel is that while God certainly will answer Habakkuk's prayer by pouring out judgment upon the gentiles, he will delight much more in the answer found in Jonah's prayer—that the gentiles obtain mercy by the death of his anointed one, on whom God pours out the very judgment intended for them.

Habakkuk himself finds this same desire for mercy well up within him, as he prays over the vision he has just seen. In a moving development, Habakkuk turns from longing for their destruction to reverent trembling at the sight of God's wrath upon the gentiles. He begs God to remember mercy, even as he sees the gentiles themselves trembling from their encampments (P29). Within the context of Joel–Habakkuk, Habakkuk's final prayer offers a resolution to the unresolved, final prayer of Jonah.

The foregoing analysis of Jonah's interaction with the rest of Joel–Habakkuk has proceeded one book at a time. This obscures the fact that, often, particular points of coherence between Jonah and a given book on one side of the chiasm are replicated by similar points of coherence between Jonah and another book on the other side of the chiasm. Thus, Jonah often functions as the turning point, marking a pivotal development for these connections across the span of Joel–Habakkuk.[26] The most significant pivoted matches are displayed in Table 3.2 to showcase the role of Jonah as the center-point for the coherence of Joel–Habakkuk.[27] In an effort to clarify the collective impact of these pivoted matches across Joel–Habakkuk, they have also been grouped together (in Table 3.2) under the following three broad themes:

1. God's desire to show mercy to both Israel and the gentiles.

2. God's selection of an individual—distinct from Israel and the gentiles—whose substitutionary dying and rising brings good news of salvation from judgment for both Israel and the gentiles.

3. The need for Israel and the gentiles to see God's judgment for what it is—namely, terrifying—so as to embrace God's mercy with a repentant heart, and to gladly proclaim that mercy to all.

Table 3.2: Points of coherence across Joel–Habakkuk where Jonah functions as the pivotal center.

	Joel	Obadiah	Jonah	Nahum	Habakkuk
Theme 1	he *is . . . slow to anger and abounding in* x comfort-himself compassion		you *are . . . slow to anger and abounding in* x comfort-himself compassion	YHWH *is slow to anger and great in* x Comforter/ comforters	compassion

---

26. For a similar discussion of *development* via repetition across a chiastic structure, see Quinn's analysis of Psalms 15–24 in this volume.

27. For an expanded version of this table, which correlates the various points of coherence to the pileup displays from which they originate, see Petrovich, "Toward," 297–98. For the formatting scheme of the present table, see note 17 (minus the sequential tagging of parallels via superscripted numbers).

	Joel	Obadiah	Jonah	Nahum	Habakkuk
Theme 2	cast lots	cast lots	cause **lots** to fall	cast lots	
	consider innocent		innocent	consider-innocent	
	dealings/dealt	dealt	dealt/dealings	deal	deal
	and he answered		*and he answered*		*and he answered*
	sea		sea	sea	sea
		distress	distress	distress	distress
		go-up	go-up	went-up	going-up
		saved-ones	salvation	preserved-one	save/salvation
Theme 3	great darkness/clouds		great storm	great storm/clouds/darkness	
	spend-the-night		laid-down/fast-asleep	laid-down/slumbered	
	go		go		go
	proclaim		proclaim		proclaim
	violence	violence	violence		violence
		cover (in shame)	covered (in sackcloth)		cover (in shame)
		Edom	Nineveh	Nineveh	
		cut-off	overthrown	cut-off	
		standing + stand	sat + sat		stand + station-myself
		see	see	see	see
	glad/rejoice	glad	glad		rejoice

Although the focus of the analysis has been on Joel–Habakkuk, that unit is merely a sub-unit within the larger textual hierarchy of the LXX Twelve. Ideally, an exhaustive search should have been made for all points of coherence across the entire textual hierarchy of the LXX Twelve, so as to establish boundaries and coherence for all the units, but time constraints did not allow for it. In lieu of this, and based on early research, a proposal is offered in Figure 3.8 as to the complete hierarchy of textual units for the LXX Twelve.[28]

---

28. For sample points of coherence (e.g., *bookends, seams, parallel openings, parallel closings*) for all units other than Joel–Habakkuk, see Petrovich, "Toward," 63–82. For a

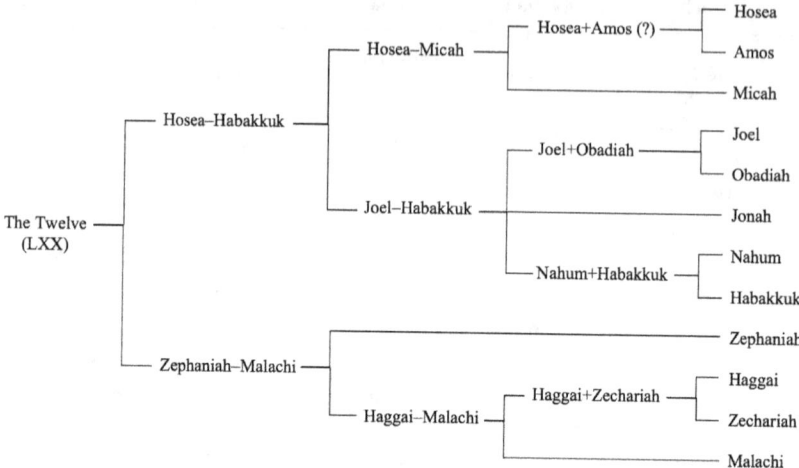

Figure 3.8: Proposal for the textual hierarchy of the LXX Twelve Prophets.

The LXX Shaping of the Twelve as the Original

Having demonstrated the strong coherence of the unique unit, LXX Joel–Habakkuk, it is highly likely that the LXX arrangement represents the originally authored shaping of the Twelve.[29] Considering that Jonah is central to the coherence of Joel–Habakkuk, a plausible explanation for the rise of the other variant shapings (MT and 4QXII[a]) becomes immediately evident. Since Joel–Habakkuk, with Jonah at its core, trumpets the call to proclaim mercy to the gentiles through repentance and faith in the substitutionary suffering of God's anointed servant, it is entirely possible that this message was not well received by many of the communities in Israel to whom the prophets had delivered the first edition of the Tanak, the Hebrew Bible, a few centuries prior to the coming of Jesus. After all, those pre-Christian centuries represent the textually

---

special set of *pointing forward* links between Hosea–Micah (Mic 7:14–20) and Joel–Habakkuk, further highlighting the centrality of Jonah, see Petrovich, "Toward," 168–71. In that regard, see Wendland's chapter in this volume on Mic 7:14–20, and especially his concluding remarks on the present-day recitation of Mic 7:18–20 alongside Jonah during Yom Kippur.

29. Contra Shepherd, who claims that the LXX order "does not show sufficient signs of original authorial/compositional intent" (Shepherd, *Commentary*, 20).

volatile period that led to the divergence of variant textual streams, most especially the MT and LXX traditions.[30]

As the manuscript traditions testify, all the communities in Israel made adjustments at times to the original text of the Tanak, based on how they understood its message. As such, it is well within reason to believe that certain communities adjusted the arrangement of the books of the Twelve in a way that would mute the voice of Jonah—a voice originally amplified within the context of LXX Joel–Habakkuk.[31] The MT arrangement appears to sideline Jonah from its prominent, central position in Joel–Habakkuk. In the MT, Jonah is attached to the end of Amos+Obadiah+Jonah, as part of the unsymmetrical combination of Hosea+Joel, Amos+Obadiah+Jonah, and Micah+Nahum+Habakkuk. The 4QXII[a] arrangement is even less considerate, placing Jonah at the end of the Twelve—at the farthest possible distance from its pivotal position in Joel–Habakkuk.

One does not need to read far into the Gospels or the Acts of the Apostles to see that, in those early centuries after the Tanak had been received and appropriated by these various communities, the thought of God's mercy being extended to the gentiles was distasteful, to say the least (even for the early followers of Jesus in the first several decades of the church). Add to this the idea of a suffering Messiah, or servant of YHWH, and Jonah (especially in the context of Joel–Habakkuk) clearly does not represent a message that would have been heartily embraced by the first wide readership of the Tanak. At the same time, the message of Jonah looms large in the thoughts of Jesus and the authors of the Gospels. Not only do these authors model the narratives of Jesus on the sea of Galilee after Jonah's sailor-story, but they also record teachings from Jesus showing his understanding of Jonah as a message of the substitutionary sacrifice of the Messiah, as shown in Table 3.3.

---

30. As Sailhamer points out regarding the pre-Christian era, "there was not one but at least two (or multiple) versions of the Tanak within ancient Judaism"; furthermore, he suggests that "the line that runs through and divides the early versions of the Tanak is the same line that separates John the Baptist from the religious leaders of his day" (Sailhamer, "Biblical Theology," 34, 37).

31. This would challenge the prevailing notion that "a movement from Septuagint to Masoretic Text admits no obvious explanation" (Seitz, *Prophecy and Hermeneutics*, 204).

Table 3.3: Jesus sees Jonah as foreshadowing the Messiah's suffering (and the repentance that should follow).

Matthew	Luke
[12:39] . . . a sign will not be given to (this evil and adulterous generation) except the sign of Jonah the prophet; [12:40] for just as Jonah was in the belly of the fish three days and three nights, so the Son of Man will be in the heart of the earth three days and three nights. [12:41] Ninevite men will stand up at the judgment with this generation, and they will condemn it, for they repented at the preaching of Jonah; and behold, a thing greater than Jonah is here.	[11:29] . . . a sign will not be given to (this generation) except the sign of Jonah; [11:30] for just as Jonah became a sign to the Ninevites, so also the Son of Man will be (a sign) to this generation.

Conclusion

This study has attempted to validate the theory that the Hebrew Bible (and every grouping of books within it) was authored in the same manner that every individual biblical book was authored—by actively shaping existing texts into a coherent whole. As such, a grouping of books would show the same depth of coherence that every individual book shows—namely, pileups of patterned repetition that clarify the boundaries between units at every level throughout the textual hierarchy. Additionally, as with an individual book, if variant arrangements of its constituent units are attested, the arrangement that demonstrates the strongest overall coherence for the entire text, while also explaining the rise of secondary arrangements, would prove to be the originally authored arrangement.

Choosing the books of the Twelve Prophets as a test-case, this study has shown that the LXX shaping of the Twelve is most likely the originally authored shaping, due to the incredible depth of coherence of the five-book sub-group, LXX Joel+Obadiah+Jonah+Nahum+Habakkuk—a unique unit that distinguishes the LXX shaping as having the strongest overall coherence. Perhaps most surprisingly, Jonah—which is often considered to be disruptive to the coherence of that sub-group—was found to play a pivotal role in its coherence. Indeed, both the MT and 4QXII[a] shapings of the Twelve appear to have arisen as a direct reaction to the semantics of that five-book sub-group.

Two areas where this theory could be further tested and refined would be in Psalms studies and studies of the Ketuvim. Both these corpora involve variously authored pieces of text that appear to have been actively shaped into a single, coherent, final text. The Psalms, while possessing a more-or-less stable arrangement in the manuscript tradition—at least between the MT and the LXX—nevertheless finds (possibly) competing arrangements among the DSS.[32] Applying the methodology of this study, one could generate a Hebrew retroversion of the LXX Psalter, and then, after loading it into one's Bible software package (where theoretically the MT and DSS texts also reside), an exhaustive search could be made for pileups of parallels across the entirety of each text. The goal would be to clarify boundaries and coherence for all units throughout the textual hierarchy of each arrangement and to assess which arrangement has the strongest overall coherence (from which secondary arrangements arose).[33]

The Ketuvim, like the Twelve, evidence multiple arrangements in the manuscript traditions. At the same time, the sheer number of arrangements attested (more than seventy) would make a comparison of all the textual hierarchies quite the undertaking. Helpful clues to the most likely original textual hierarchy could be found by comparing the Ketuvim with the higher-level grouping to which it is adjoined, namely, the Prophets (the closing unit of which is the Twelve).[34]

---

32. See discussions in this volume by Pavan, Ho, and also Ayars, regarding the Psalter at Qumran.

33. For a foundational analysis of the textual hierarchy of the MT Psalter, see Ho, *Design*. While the textual hierarchy of the LXX Psalter is likely to be quite similar to that of the MT, a separate analysis of the former could yield interesting insights regarding the boundaries of sub-collections that have proved difficult to pin down.

34. After this study was originally completed in 2015, the present writer stumbled on a 2013 monograph by Stone, in which he suggests that the Ketuvim's Megilloth section (Ruth+Song+Ecclesiastes+Lamentations+Esther) seems to demonstrate a five-book chiastic structure. See Stone, *Compilational History*, 204–7. This is intriguingly similar to the structure of Joel+Obadiah+Jonah+Nahum+Habakkuk detailed in this essay. Could it be that the original shaping of the Ketuvim was intended to parallel the original (LXX) shaping of the Twelve? Consider how both begin with a three-book block (Hosea+Amos+Micah vis-à-vis Psalms+Proverbs+Job) and conclude with a four-book block (Zephaniah+Haggai+Zechariah+Malachi vis-à-vis Daniel+Ezra+Nehemiah+Chronicles), again with intriguing similarities. This particular arrangement of the Ketuvim is attested in such manuscripts as Taschereau 33 and Peyron 102, while the general block-structure is present in numerous other arrangements. Beckwith, *Old Testament Canon*, 452–64.

For those wishing to further explore this theory of *biblical authorship above the book level*, here are a few highlights from this study that could serve as guiding principles for future research:

- Allow the LXX to fully speak, not merely consulting it for a single verse or variant. Consider producing an LXX Hebrew retroversion for the entire text under analysis.

- Look for all points of coherence, not just rarely occurring words. Some of the most critical connections in Joel–Habakkuk involve cases where several common words all occur in close proximity, the combination of which is rare.

- Always think in terms of the complete hierarchy of textual units, not just the units that are immediately adjacent to one another. Structured parallelism can bind units that are not adjacent.

At a more fundamental level, it is hoped that this study will encourage a greater amount of reading and reflection *above the book level* for all those who open and read the book of the Tanak.

Bibliography

Albertz, Rainer, et al., eds. *Perspectives on the Formation of the Book of the Twelve: Methodological Foundations, Redactional Processes, Historical Insights*. BZAW 433. Berlin; Boston: de Gruyter, 2012.

Beckwith, Roger T. *The Old Testament Canon of the New Testament Church: And Its Background in Early Judaism*. Eugene, OR: Wipf & Stock, 1985.

Dempster, Stephen G. *Dominion and Dynasty: A Theology of the Hebrew Bible*. NSBT 15. Downers Grove, IL: InterVarsity, 2003.

DiPede, Elena, and Donatella Scaiola, eds. *The Book of the Twelve—One Book or Many? Metz Conference Proceedings, November 5–7, 2015*. FAT II 91. Tübingen: Mohr Siebeck, 2016.

Dorsey, David A. *The Literary Structure of the Old Testament: A Commentary on Genesis–Malachi*. Grand Rapids, MI: Baker, 1999.

Fokkelman, J. P. "Genesis." In *The Literary Guide to the Bible*, edited by Robert Alter and Frank Kermode, 36–55. Cambridge, MA: Belknap, 1987.

Ho, Peter C. W. *The Design of the Psalter: A Macrostructural Analysis*. Eugene, OR: Pickwick, 2019.

House, Paul R. *The Unity of the Twelve*. JSOTSup 97. BLS 27. Sheffield: Almond, 1990.

Jones, Barry Alan. *The Formation of the Book of the Twelve: A Study in Text and Canon*. SBLDS 149. Atlanta, GA: Scholars, 1995.

LeCureux, Jason T. *The Thematic Unity of the Book of the Twelve*. HBM 41. Sheffield: Sheffield Phoenix, 2012.

Lee, Andrew Yueking. "The Canonical Unity of the Scroll of the Minor Prophets." PhD diss., Baylor University, 1985.

Nogalski, James D., and Marvin A. Sweeney, eds. *Reading and Hearing the Book of the Twelve*. SBL Symposium Series 15. Atlanta, GA: SBL, 2000.

Petrovich, Craig S. "Toward the Originally Authored Book of the Twelve: Testing the Coherence of the Variant Shapings of the Twelve Prophets." MA thesis, Biola University, 2015.

Redditt, Paul L., and Aaron Schart, eds. *Thematic Threads in the Book of the Twelve*. BZAW 325. Berlin; Boston: de Gruyter, 2003.

Sailhamer, John H. "Biblical Theology and the Composition of the Hebrew Bible." In *Biblical Theology: Retrospect and Prospect*, edited by Scott J. Hafemann, 25–37. Downers Grove, IL: InterVarsity, 2002.

———. *The Meaning of the Pentateuch: Revelation, Composition and Interpretation*. Downers Grove, IL: IVP Academic, 2009.

Schneider, Dale A. "The Unity of the Book of the Twelve." PhD diss., Yale University, 1979.

Seitz, Christopher R. *Prophecy and Hermeneutics: Toward a New Introduction to the Prophets*. STI. Grand Rapids, MI: Baker Academic, 2007.

Shepherd, Michael B. *A Commentary on the Book of the Twelve: The Minor Prophets*. Grand Rapids, MI: Kregel Academic, 2018.

Stone, Timothy J. *The Compilational History of the Megilloth: Canon, Contoured Intertextuality and Meaning in the Writings*. Tübingen: Mohr Siebeck, 2013.

Tiemeyer, Lena-Sofia, and Jakob Wöhrle, eds. *The Book of the Twelve: Composition, Reception, and Interpretation*. VTSup 184. Leiden; Boston: Brill, 2020.

Tov, Emanuel. *Textual Criticism of the Hebrew Bible*. 3rd ed. Minneapolis: Fortress, 2012.

Wenzel, Heiko, ed. *The Book of the Twelve: An Anthology of Prophetic Books or the Result of Complex Redactional Processes?* Osnabrücker Studien Zur Jüdischen Und Christlichen Bibel 4. Göttingen: Vandenhoeck & Ruprecht, 2018.

CHAPTER 4

Hope for the Ideal David and Temple

Eschatology as a Hermeneutical Frame for Interpreting the Shape of the Psalter

MATT AYARS

SCHOLARS READILY ACCEPT THAT there is an intentional editorial design to the macrostructure of the "book"[1] of Psalms. What is not as readily accepted or agreed upon is the organizing principle to the shape of the Psalms as a whole, or the scope and level of editorial input on the final form of the Psalter.[2] On the minimalistic end of the spectrum, some posit that the Psalter should be viewed merely as a loose but closed canon of hymns brought together through antiquity with minimal involvement from an editor.[3] On the other end of the spectrum, cases have been made for elaborate and highly sophisticated editorial programs that account for every detail of the Psalter, from superscriptions to syllable counting.[4]

---

1. I have "book" in quotation to acknowledge that there is still a lack of consensus on the precise definition of a "book" as an "anthology" or "collection."

2. See deClaissé-Walford, *Shape*.

3. For a detailed exposition of this view see Willgren, *Formation*. Also see this volume's introduction by Pavan for an in-depth review of the state of the field on this matter.

4. See Ho, *Design*, for an overview of the leading theories in this camp.

Most theories build their case on *internal evidence*, as they should. At the same time, as Brevard Childs pointed out forty-three years ago,[5] too few account for the hermeneutical frame of the various Jewish communities during the time that the final form of the Psalter was coming together or soon thereafter. How the Jewish community in late BC and early AD were interpreting the Psalms, it seems, should reflect the mindset of the editors of the final form of the Psalter.

Thankfully, history has given us a host of robust witnesses of psalms interpretation from the time of the finalization of the Psalter, including the Dead Sea Scrolls, the New Testament, the ancient translations, as well as various rabbinic traditions. As we will see in the sections below, all of these witness to a "future-predictive"[6] eschatological hermeneutical frame for the Psalter, which is explained by the historical context of the text-canonizing community. Evidence from history reveals that the Psalter reached its final form in a time marked by heightened anticipation of the final fulfillment of God's promises for the final vindication of his people, the restoration of the temple, the Davidic monarchy, and Hebrew hegemony. What better place to live in and live out that hope than in the prayers and hymns of David himself and the temple singers?

One of the numerous contemporary theories on the editorial design of the Psalter stands out in taking this witness from antiquity into account. In 1997, David Mitchell argued for the eschatological program of the arrangement of the Psalter in his *The Message of the Psalter: An Eschatological Programme in the Books of Psalms*. While making a strong case for an eschatological program, Mitchell limited his scope of study to the Songs of Ascent and the Songs of Asaph. This chapter aims to zoom out to consider the broader internal and external evidence for a future-predictive eschatological program behind the editing of the Psalter. I will also consider the feasibility that the editorial design of the Psalter presents to readers the book of Psalms as an instructional book of prayer and worship for the faithful community while awaiting the fulfillment of God's promises for a future David and temple. In closing, I will consider areas needing development in relation to the feasibility of an eschatological program to the editorial design of the Psalter.

---

5. Childs, *Introduction*, 515–17.
6. This is Mitchell's term.

Internal Evidence

The Psalter exhibits considerable internal evidence for an eschatological motif behind the editorial design of the book, particularly in support of hope for an ideal David and temple. Because there is not enough room here for a high-resolution account of the evidence, we will look broadly at the following as the primary internal evidence: (1) Psalms 1–2 as an introduction, (2) the five-book division and Davidic authorship, (3) superscriptions, (4) thematic shifts across psalm groupings, and (5) the placement of the pilgrimage festival psalms/ingathering collections in Book 5. Each of these is not to be taken in isolation, but together, one informing the other, to bring together a comprehensive and possibly explanatory image of the eschatological editorial program.

Psalms 1–2 as the Introduction to the Psalter

That Psalms 1–2 work together to introduce the book of Psalms has long been recognized and affirmed by interpreters.[7] One part of the support for such a view is the consensus that the first two psalms of the collection are pregnant with the major themes of the Psalter as a whole. Those themes are generally recognized as: (1) a contrast between the way of the wicked and the way of the righteous; and (2) the two-pronged key to blessing as (a) reverence and love for God (and his anointed one), and (b) the Torah.

As the supreme reign of God is the basis for these themes, these integrated concepts naturally project the anticipation of the establishment of God's eternal reign through his chosen one who will vindicate the righteous and punish the wicked, thereby demonstrating his covenant faithfulness by redeeming his purposes for creation. Read eschatologically, Psalms 1–2 together declare that the Torah is dependable for generating righteousness and that God will be faithful in vindicating the righteous among sinners through his Messiah.

Psalm 1 explicitly references final judgment (vv. 5–6), and Psalm 2 implies it (vv. 9 and 12). In the end, the ones who delight in the instruction of God will stand in God's assembly while the wicked, sinners, and mockers will fall (a vision that is fulfilled in Psalms 146–150). But who are those mockers? Psalm 2 answers that question. They are those who

---

7. For a dissenting view, see Willgren, *Formation*, 3–20.

conspire against YHWH and his anointed. Furthermore, how will those mockers fall? Again, Psalm 2 responds that the Messiah will mete out judgment. God's word stands, and so does his king, and those promises will be fulfilled at the end of time—and at the end of this book of Psalms (in Psalms 146–150).

Five Book Structure and Davidic Authorship

Psalm 1's emphasis on the Torah, together with the five-part structure to the Psalter, clearly implies that the editors intend for the Psalter to be understood as a sort of Torah. The Midrash on the Psalms observes the correlation between the five books of Psalms and the five books of Moses. As such, the view of the Midrash is that David is a second Moses. In commenting on Psalm 1, it says,

> But what man? He who is foremost among the Prophets; he who is foremost among kings. The foremost among Prophets—he is Moses, of whom it is said, And Moses went up unto God (Ex. 19:3); the foremost among kings—he is David. You find that whatever Moses did, David did. As Moses led Israel out of Egypt, so David led Israel out of servitude to Goliath. As Moses fought the battles of the LORD against Sihon and Og, so David fought the battles of the LORD in all the regions around him.... As Moses became king in Israel and in Judah ... so David became king in Israel and in Judah. As Moses divided the Red Sea for Israel, so David divided the rivers of Aram for Israel.... As Moses built an altar, so David built an altar. As the one brought offerings, so the other brought offerings. As Moses gave give books of Laws to Israel, so David gave five Books of Psalms to Israel.[8]

While not explicitly stated, this interpretation is likely drawing a connection to Deuteronomy 18:15–19's prediction of a future Moses by depicting David as a prophet in the likeness of Moses. If this is the case, then the voice of David that comes through the Psalter naturally points forward to a future, ideal David considering the fall of the Davidic kingdom in the rearview of the Psalter's redactors. This view fits with 4Q175 from the DSS, which "represent respectively the *Yahad's* expectations

---

8. Braude, *Midrash*, 4–5.

for the coming of a prophet like Moses, a royal scion of David to lead in war, and a proper high priest."⁹

But what kind of instruction do the psalms offer? In the Psalter, David has left the worshiping community an instructional manual on prayer and praise. How should we worship? The answer is the collection of Psalms. David, then, is presented as the prophetic worship leader of Israel.

Nevertheless, what does this have to do with eschatology? The Torah lays out laws for *temple worship*. A problem arises when there is no temple, a reality that the Psalms recognize through their reference to Babylonian exile (Ps 137:1–9). The destruction of the temple presents the need for instruction beyond that of the laws of Moses. The community needs instruction on worship without a temple, and the Psalter provides just that. The Psalter, then, can be received as an instructional manual on how to pray and worship without a temple while waiting for the fulfillment of God's promises for the ideal temple and the Messiah. With this frame, the correspondence of the five books of Psalms with the five books of the Pentateuch, then, is inherently eschatological, as it points readers to an anticipation of a future David and temple.

Superscriptions

The pendulum is constantly swinging regarding the scholarly view of the importance of the superscriptions in the Psalms. The current view is that they are to be considered a part of the final, canonical text and are therefore not to be disregarded. As such, the superscriptions undoubtedly indicate the intentional editorial design of the Psalter at the very least at a minimal level. The concentration of Davidic psalms in Book I of the Psalter alone demonstrates this. Furthermore, the Sons of Korah as the inaugural psalms of Book II, Moses as the first psalm of Book IV (Ps 90), and the clustering of the Songs of Asaph and the Songs of Ascent (Pss 120–134) are enough to demonstrate that there is at the very least minimal editorial intent behind the organization of superscriptions. But what is the program behind the organization?

The superscriptions indicate that the psalms are not strictly arranged chronologically. Moses in Psalm 90 and David in Psalms 3 and 103 alone make this evident. Taken together with other variables (five-part structure, thematic shifts, etc.), however, deClaissé-Walford

---

9. Wise et al., *Dead Sea Scrolls*, 258.

makes a strong case that each of the five books corresponds to an era of Israelite history[10] as follows:

- Book I: United Monarchy under David
- Book II: United Monarchy under Solomon
- Book III: Divided Monarchy
- Book IV: Exile
- Book V: Return from Exile.

While not without its weaknesses, the strengths of deClaissé-Walford's theory are hard to ignore. The argument from superscriptions and attributions at the seams of each book has considerable explanatory power. The Songs of Korah (temple singers) are introduced at the start of Book II, which would correspond to Solomon's temple era. There are no Korah songs in Book I (united monarchy under David) because David is not the temple builder. Furthermore, the Song of Moses, as the introductory psalm of Book IV (exilic period), is a callback to a time in which there was no king. In exile, God's people are taken back to the time of wilderness-wandering where God alone was King. This also explains the YHWH enthronement psalms of Book IV. During the time when there was no human king, YHWH was recognized as King.

The placement of Psalm 89 at the end of Book III strongly supports the theory, as the psalm asks God when his promise to David for an heir of the eternal throne will be fulfilled. This is an appropriate question heading into exile, which is the suggested corresponding era of Book IV.

Book V, then, inaugurates the crescendo-like call to praise, which would make sense considering a return to Jerusalem and the rebuilding of the temple. It also explains the re-introduction of Davidic psalms with Psalms 108–110. The reappearance of David as the worship leader is an answer to the concerns of Psalm 89.

One could argue that this way of interpreting the interplay of the superscriptions and the five-part structure could certainly be future-predictive oriented. If each book corresponds to an era of Israelite history beginning with the united monarchy, then the book as a whole would undoubtedly point the reader to the future and cultivate hope for the coming of an ideal temple and David.

---

10. deClaissé-Walford, "Canonical," 21–38.

Thematic Shifts Across Psalm Groupings/Collections

We noted in the previous section that there is a notable shift from lament to praise across the Psalter with a climax of praise in Book V, which certainly indicates an intentional editorial design. For one, an ending doxology is the convention across the Psalter as each book ends with a doxology. It is appropriate, then, that the book as a whole would end in a grand, final doxology. Furthermore, it is not likely that the last *five* psalms of the Psalter being *hallelujah* psalms is merely coincidental. This five-part final doxology can be interpreted as a psalm of praise for each of the five books of the Psalter. In sum, just as the Psalter has a multi-part introduction (Pss 1–2), it has a multi-part conclusion (Pss 146–150). The doxology-finale is faithful to Psalm 2's appeal to love and revere God. The one who is faithful to the end of the Psalter is the one who faithfully praises the God of Israel and therefore, the one who will be blessed (more on the final doxology/small Hallel below).

But where is the future-predictive or eschatological dimension in the thematic shift from lament to praise? It is two-fold. First, it is found in the sense of realized eschatology. The one who faithfully prays and praises in the face of one's enemies will be led in this life to a life of worship because of the faithfulness of God to redeem. Second, there is also the sense of unrealized eschatology. While one can be blessed now, there is a future blessing in which God will vindicate his chosen people from all their adversaries and there will be none who conspire against him or his people. The final judgment will yield the result that all who have breath will praise YHWH because those who do not will be dealt with.

Ingathering Festival Collections in Book V

We have already noted that chronology alone does not explain the ordering of the superscriptions and that there is a thematic layer to the arrangement. This comes through with the placement of the ingathering festival psalms in Book V.[11] Locating these collections in Book V indicates the anticipation of a future exodus. Knowing that the Psalter reached its final form during a time of Jewish oppression by gentile nations, and as external evidence demonstrates (more below), it can be inferred there was an expectation among the Jewish community that there would be another

---

11. The Egyptian Hallel (Pss 113–118), the Shavuoth psalm (Ps 119), and the Sukkoth psalms (Pss 120–134).

exodus-like event. God's promises for an eternal kingdom and Jewish hegemony had not yet been fulfilled at the time the Psalter came to its final form. What does that tell us about how Israel's great historic deliverance was celebrated? These psalms being placed in the last book of the Psalter likely indicates that they point to a future hope. Celebrating the exodus in the psalms is not merely a remembrance of a historical event but the anticipation and future prediction of final redemption.

Mitchell makes a strong case for reading the Songs of Asaph and the Songs of Ascent as collections that anticipate an eschatological ingathering of the people of God. Drawing on Ezekiel 34–48, Zechariah 9–14, and Joel 3–4, he writes:

> Although they differ in detail, there is substantial agreement in their broad picture. YHWH will gather scattered Israel to the land promised to their forefathers. Thereafter an alliance of hostile nations will gather to attack them. YHWH will destroy the invaders and save Israel. Then Israel will worship YHWH on Zion, together with the survivors of the nations. The same programme, either in eschatological or generally future time, is discernible also in Zephaniah, Micah, Isaiah and Jeremiah. If to these texts is added Daniel, where a similar programme is also found, and other texts that seem to contain particular aspects of it, then it seems plausible to suggest that some sort of eschatological programme, with motifs similar to those identified above, was widely recognized in biblical times and is an important aspect of Old Testament eschatology.[12]

Altogether, the internal evidence that there is an intentional editorial design to the final form of the Psalter is irrefutable. The internal evidence that the design was informed by an anticipation of God's fulfillment of his promises for an ideal David and temple is strong, but not irrefutable on its own. When taken together with the external evidence from the time of the finalization of the Psalter, however, this reading is heartily strengthened.

The Ideal David and Ideal Zion

But what of the evidence for the anticipation of an ideal David and Zion as an organizing theme to the macrostructural design of the Psalter? Some of the internal and external evidence for an eschatological

12. Mitchell, *Message*, 165.

reading covered above is naturally in support of this theme, especially the ancient community's interpretation of the prophetic role of David as the psalmist (the DSS in particular). The central role of David in the Psalter, together with the placement of Psalm 89 and Psalm 90, and the reappearance of Davidic psalms in Books III–V, naturally implies the ideal David as the worship leader of the people of God.

Furthermore, the very presence of royal psalms (e.g., Pss 2, 45, 72, 89, 110, etc.) in a collection that was compiled during a time of no king implies the anticipation of a Messiah. Craig Broyles writes:

> The final collection and editing of the book of Psalms, or the Psalter, was done in the postexilic period when Judah had no Davidic monarchy under the Persian empire. Why then were these royal psalms retained? It is doubtful the editors kept them simply as historical artifacts in a collection of liturgical and meditative songs and prayers. The most likely explanation is that they retained value because even before the Common Era they bore the hope of a new David. This transfer of referent—from the past Davidic kings to a future Davidic "Messiah"—was probably engendered by the Hebrew prophets. Prophecies contained in Isaiah (9:6–7; 11:1–5), Micah (5:2–5a), Jeremiah (23:5–6), Ezekiel (34:23–24; 37:24–28), and Zechariah (9:9–10) took up the language of the royal psalms and of the Davidic court and promised a new David, in view of the repeated failures of David's sons.[13]

It is also worth highlighting the strategic placement of royal psalms in the Psalter, namely, Psalms 2, 72, and 89. The placement of these psalms at the seams of the books creates a messianic frame to the content between the bookends. The anointed one is the center focus heading into and out of Books I–III. Childs comments on Psalm 2:

> One wonders why this psalm was placed in such a prominent place unless it was to emphasize the kingship of God as a major theme of the whole Psalter. Certainly the original mythopoetic setting of the older adoption formula in v. 7, "you are my son, today I have begotten you," has long since been forgotten (cf. von Rad). Rather, the weight of the psalm falls on God's claim of the whole earth as his possession, and the warning of his coming wrath against the presumption of earthly rulers. In other words, the psalm has been given an eschatological ring, both by its position in the Psalter and by the attachment of new meaning

---

13. Broyles, "Redeeming," 24.

to the older vocabulary through the influence of the prophetic message (cf. Jer 23:5; Ezek 34:23). Indeed, at the time of the final redaction, when the institution of kingship had long since been destroyed, what earthly king would have come to mind other than God's Messiah? (cf. Westermann, "Sammlung," 342).[14]

He goes on to comment more broadly on the royal psalms:

> The eschatological dimension of the royal psalms emerges in even clearer form in Pss. 89 and 132 where the prophetic promise to Nathan is actually cited. To be sure, the psalmist has developed this tradition along different lines from the prophet, but increasingly the prophetic model poured its content into the idiom of the psalmist.

In sum, although the royal psalms arose originally in a peculiar historical setting of ancient Israel that had received its form from a common mythopoetic milieu, they were treasured in the Psalter for a different reason, namely as a witness to the messianic hope, which looked for the consummation of God's kingship through his Anointed One.[15]

The Dead Sea Scrolls' placement of David's Last Words and David's Compositions further strengthens this view. For the DSS, David both begins and ends the Psalter, and the prophetic nature of his writing is highlighted.

But what about the theme of the establishment of the ideal Zion? There is a concentrated focus on Zion in the Songs of Ascent (Pss 120–134), which is explained by the fact that the Songs of Ascent (SOA) are sung in commemoration of Sukkot, a festival of the ingathering of God's people to Jerusalem. There is a movement towards Zion with the celebration of the festival. Even with the presence of Zion in the SOA, there are still references to a future deliverance from the enemies of God, meaning that while Zion is in view, the final judgment and the ideal, final Zion has yet to be consummated. Consider the following:

- Ps 120:3–7. What shall be given to you, and what more shall be done to you, you deceitful tongue? A warrior's sharp arrows, with glowing coals of the broom tree! Woe to me, that I sojourn in Meshech, that I dwell among the tents of Kedar! Too long have I had my dwelling among those who hate peace. I am for peace, but when I speak, they are for war!

14. Childs, *Introduction*, 516.
15. Childs, *Introduction*, 517.

- Ps 121:7. The LORD will keep you from all evil; he will keep your life.
- Ps 123:3–4. Have mercy upon us, O LORD, have mercy upon us, for we have had more than enough of contempt. Our soul has had more than enough of the scorn of those who are at ease, of the contempt of the proud.
- Ps 125:5. But those who turn aside to their crooked ways the LORD will lead away with evildoers!
- Ps 129:5. May all who hate Zion be put to shame and turned backward!
- Ps 132:18. His enemies I will clothe with shame, but on him his crown will shine.

This not-yet ideal Zion is referenced then in Psalm 137 from an exilic perspective:

- Ps 137:1. By the waters of Babylon, there we sat down and wept, when we remembered Zion.
- Ps 137:3. For there our captors required of us songs, and our tormentors, mirth, saying, "Sing us one of the songs of Zion!"

The following reference to Zion after Psalm 137 is Psalm 146:10, where the reader finally encounters the ideal Zion, "The LORD will reign forever, your God, O Zion, to all generations. Praise the LORD!" "Zion" appears two more times in Psalms 147:12 and 149:2. Together with these are references to Jerusalem in the final, five-psalm doxology that imply a restored, ideal Zion:

- Ps 147:2. The LORD builds up Jerusalem; he gathers the outcasts of Israel.
- Ps 147:12–14. Praise the LORD, O Jerusalem! Praise your God, O Zion! For he strengthens the bars of your gates; he blessed your children within you. He makes peace in your borders; he fills you with the finest of the wheat.

Interwoven within these references is Psalm 148, which is a call for all of creation to praise YHWH. Such a call is grounded in the vision of the establishment of the ideal Zion. Psalm 149 is also a call to praise, but this time to the "children of Zion" (Ps 149:2) alongside a commission for God's people to establish final peace through executing judgment on the wicked:

> Let the godly exult in glory; let them sing for joy on their beds. Let the high praises of God be in their throats and two-edged swords in their hands, to execute vengeance on the nations and punishment on the peoples, to bind their kings with chains and their nobles with fetters of iron, to execute on them the judgment written! This is the honor for all his godly ones. Praise the LORD! (Ps 149:5–9)

Psalm 149, one could argue, parallels the theme of Psalm 2, specifically with reference to binding with chains. Psalm 149 presents a vision for the fulfillment of that which is promised in Psalm 2.

The final Psalm 150 is the famous universal call to praise. On the heels of Psalm 149, Psalm 150 is the vision of the fulfillment of the promises of Psalms 1–2 together. Rather than some using breath to conspire in vain and rage against the LORD, Psalm 150 presents the reader with a scene in which everything that has breath praises the LORD. With Psalm 150, God's promises have been fulfilled. His sanctuary has been established and all of the creation praises him. There are no more conspiracies, no more rebels, sinners, or mockers. Within the context of the entire Psalter, it seems obvious how natural an eschatological reading of Psalm 150 is. Throughout the Psalter, we have faced the enemies of YHWH and his people. We have encountered lament, injustice, strife, struggle, wickedness, conspiring against God and his people, and an attempt to thwart the establishment of Zion and God's anointed. By the time we arrive at the end of the Psalter, judgment has been executed, God reigns, and his people alone remain in his presence within exuberant worship of their covenant King for his faithfulness to fulfill his promises.

External Evidence

History firmly attests that the Jewish communities in and around Palestine during the time that the Psalter reached its final form were anticipating the arrival of an ideal David who would deliver Israel from Gentile oppression and rebuild the temple. As we will explore broadly in the following sections, this contextual reality comes through in the New Testament, the Dead Sea Scrolls, the ancient translations (LXX, Targums, and Peshitta), and the Midrash on the Psalms.

The New Testament

The New Testament alludes to the book of Psalms more than four hundred times. Seventy of those four hundred-plus allusions are direct quotes from the Psalter. The majority of the seventy quotes are supportive of future-predictive fulfillment in the person of Jesus. To list a few:

- I am not speaking of all of you; I know whom I have chosen. But the Scripture will be fulfilled, "He who ate my bread has lifted his heel against me." (John 13:18 quoting Ps 41:9)

- But the word that is written in their Law must be fulfilled: "They hated me without a cause." (John 15:25 quoting Ps 69:4)

- So they said to one another, "Let us not tear it, but cast lots for it to see whose it shall be." This was to fulfill the Scripture which says, "They divided my garments among them, and for my clothing they cast lots." So the soldiers did these things. (John 19:24 quoting Ps 22:18)

- For these things took place that the Scripture might be fulfilled: "Not one of his bones will be broken." (John 19:36 quoting Ps 34:20)

- His disciples remembered that it was written, "Zeal for your house will consume me." (John 2:17 quoting Ps 69:9)

- Who said by the Holy Spirit through your servant David our forefather, "Why do the nations rage, and the peoples plot foolish things? The kings of the earth stood together, and the rulers assembled together, against the Lord and against his Christ." (Acts 4:25–26 quoting Ps 2:1–2)

Each of these examples (among others) is a clear demonstration that the Jewish community out of which the New Testament tradition emerged was reading the psalms eschatologically.

Examples from the New Testament extend beyond direct citation from the Psalms. For example:

New Testament Reference	Psalms Reference
Matt 2:11—As they came into the house and saw the child with Mary his mother, they bowed down and worshiped him.	**Ps 72:10-11, 15**—The Kings of Tarshish and the coastlands will offer gifts; the kings of Sheba and Seba will bring tribute. All the kings will bow down to him; all the nations will serve him . . . May he live! May they offer him gold from Sheba. May they continually pray for him. May they pronounce blessings on him all day long.
Matt 3:17—And a voice from heaven said, "This is my one dear Son; in him I take great delight."	**Ps 2:7**—The king says, "I will announce the Lord's decree. He said to me: 'You are my son. This very day I have become your father.'"
Matt 4:6—And said to him, "If you are the Son of God, throw yourself down. For it is written, 'He will command his angels concerning you' and 'with their hands they will lift you up, so that you will not strike your foot against a stone.'"	**Ps 91:11-12**—For he will order his angels to protect you in all you do. They will lift you up in their hands, so you will not slip and fall on a stone.
Matt 7:23—Then I will declare to them, "I never knew you. Go away from me, you lawbreakers!"	**Ps 6:8**—Turn back from me, all you who behave wickedly, for the Lord has heard the sound of my weeping!
Matt 13:35—This fulfilled what was spoken by the prophet: "I will open my mouth in parables, I will announce what has been hidden from the foundation of the world."	**Ps 78:2**—I will open my mouth in a parable; I will utter dark sayings from of old.
Matt 16:27—For the Son of Man will come with his angels in the glory of his Father, and then he will reward each person according to what he has done.	**Ps 62:12**—And you, O Lord, demonstrate loyal love. For you repay men for what they do.
Matt 21:42[16]—Jesus said to them, "Have you never read in the scriptures: 'The stone the builders rejected has become the cornerstone. This is from the Lord, and it is marvelous in our eyes.'?"	**Ps 118:22-23**—The stone that the builders discarded has become the cornerstone. This is the Lord's work. We consider it amazing!

Mitchell sums up the New Testament use of Psalms saying:

> The New Testament writers also regard the Psalms as future-predictive. David is described as a prophet, through whom the

---

16. Cf. Luke 20:17.

Holy Spirit spoke (Mt. 22:43; Mk 12:36; Acts 2:30; 4:25). Those psalms ascribed to him are reckoned to foretell messianic events after their date of composition (Mt. 22:43–45; Acts 2:25, 31; 4:11). The New Testament as a whole cites passages from the Psalms more than 70 times, more than any other Old Testament book, to endorse Christian messianic claims. A few examples may be given from the gospels alone. Ps. 91:11–12 is taken as referring to Messiah's deliverance from evil (Mt. 4:6; Lk. 4:11). Ps. 118:22, 23 is regarded as foretelling his rejection by the leaders of Israel (Mt. 21:42; Mk 12:10; Lk. 20:17), while 118:25, 26 is associated with his entry to Jerusalem (Mt. 21:9; 23:39; Mk 11:9; Lk. 13:35; 19:38; Jn 12:13). Ps. 22:1, 18 is held to foretell his suffering (Mt. 27:35 [some mss]; 27:46; Mk 15:34; Jn 19:24). Psalm 110 is referred to him as well, presumably in his role as conquering king (Mt. 22:41–46; Mk 12:36; Lk. 20:42–43).[17]

Mitchell's reference to the triumphal entry is worth highlighting because it is representative of the *crowd's* future-predictive orientation to the Psalter. At this moment, there is a convergence of the celebration of the Passover, the singing of the last psalm of the Egyptian Hallel (Ps 118), and the public entry of the one thought to be the second Moses coming to Jerusalem. It is no far-reached speculation to posit that the crowds were expecting Jesus to be their second Moses to bring about the second exodus in the form of deliverance from the Roman Empire.

The New Testament is an extant representation of Palestinian Judaism's hermeneutical frame for the Psalter around the time of the finalization of the Psalter. It demonstrates a strong future-predictive eschatological bent, namely, the anticipation of an ideal David who would rebuild the temple. They saw in Jesus the fulfillment of what the Psalms predicted because the worshiping community looked to the five books of David for an indication of what to expect.

The Dead Sea Scrolls

The Dead Sea Scrolls are replete with references and orientation to the last days, the anticipation of the Messiah, and the rebuilding of the temple. An exhaustive list of scrolls having a single eschatological focus is too long to include here; here are a few examples:

- The Damascus Document (4Q266–272)

17. Mitchell, *Message*, 27.

- Charter for Israel in the Last Days (1QSa [1Q28ᵃ], 4Q249ᵃ⁻ⁱ)
- Priestly Blessings for the Last Days ([1QSb], 1Q28b)
- The War Scroll (1QM, 4Q491–496)
- The Last Words of Judah (3Q7)
- The War of the Messiah (4Q285, 11Q14)
- A Last Days Commentary on Select Verses (4Q174 and 4Q177)
- A Collection of Messianic Proof Texts (4Q175)
- The Ages of the World (4Q180–181).

These, together with the calendar texts from Qumran, attest to the community's eschatological preoccupation. They were also preoccupied with psalms, for "among all the books of the Bible, the Psalms are the most numerous in the Dead Sea Scrolls, which indicates their immense popularity at Qumran."[18] It is impossible to cover all forty DSS manuscripts and scrolls comprising psalms here, so we will consider eschatological readings from 4Q174, 4Q177, 11Q13, and 4Q88.

4Q174 and 4Q177 (Eschatological Commentary)

These two scrolls contain eschatological commentary on select Old Testament verses, mainly from Ezekiel, Isaiah, and Psalms. The typical formula is for the scroll to cite the verse, then give an eschatological interpretation of that verse using the phrase, "The meaning is . . ."

---

18. Abegg et al., *Dead Sea Scrolls*, 505.

4Q174

Psalm	Interpretation
1:1a—Happy is the man who does not walk in the council of the wicked	The meaning is, [th]ey[19] are those who turn aside from the path of [the wicked], as it is written in the book of Isaiah the prophet in reference to the Last Days, "And it came to pass, while His hand was strong upon me, [that He warned me not to walk in the way of] this people" (Isa. 8:11). These are they about whom it is written in the book of Ezekiel the prophet, namely, "They shall ne[ver again defile themselves with] their idols" (Ezek. 37:23). They are the Sons of Zadok, and the m[e]n of the[i]r council who pu[rsue righ]teousness and follow them to join the *Yahad*.[20]
2:1—Why do the nations rage, and the peoples conspire in vain? The kings of the earth take a stand together against YHWH and his anointed?	[... The m]eaning [is that the na]tions [shall set themselves] and con[spire vainly against] the chosen of Israel in the Last Days.[21]
5:2–3a—Hear my words, Lord; consider my groaning. Pay attention to the sound of my pleading, my King and My God, for to you I pray. YHWH in the morning your hear my voice	[... The] meaning concerns the Last D[ays...][22]
13:4—Lest my enemy say, "I prevailed over him"; my foes for I am shaken.	[This refers to the Last] Days, when [the ...] will gather together against [them ...] [...] with the righteous and the wicked, the fool and the simple[ton ...] of the men who have served God [...] [...] who have circumcised themselves spiritually in the last generation [...] and all that is theirs is unclean [...][23]

19. Brackets surround lost or damaged areas in the scroll.
20. Wise et al., *Dead Sea Scrolls*, 257.
21. Wise et al., *Dead Sea Scrolls*, 257.
22. Wise et al., *Dead Sea Scrolls*, 257–58.
23. Wise et al., *Dead Sea Scrolls*, 266.

4Q177

11:1-2—To the choirmaster; of David. In YHWH I take refuge. How can you say to my soul, "Flee like a bird to your mountain, for behold, the wicked bend the bow; they have fitted their arrow to the string to shoot in the dark at the upright of heart	[This means that] the men of [the *Yahad*] shall flee [...] [... like] a bird from its place and be exiled [from their land][24]
12:1—To the choirmaster; according to the *shiminith*. A song of David	for them the eighth season [...] [...] there is no peace, for they [...][25]
13:1-2—Until when, YHWH? Will you forget me forever? Until when will you hide your face from me? Until when must I put counsel in my soul and have sorrow in my heart daily? Until when will my enemy exult over me?	This refers to the inner endurance of the men of [...] in the Last Days, for [...] to test them and to purify them. [...] them in the spirit and pure and refined [...][26]
12:6 YHWH's discourse is pure, like silver refined in an earthen furnace, refined seven times.	This refers to the inner endurance of the men of [...] in the Last Days, for [...] to test them and to purify them. [...] them in the spirit and pure and refined [...][27]

11Q13 (The Melchizedek Document)

11Q13 is a collection of interpretations of Scripture predicting a final jubilee in which sin will be atoned for and Melchizedek will bring righteousness to the world with the defeat of Belial/Satan. 11Q13 interprets Psalm 7:7-8 and 82:1-2 eschatologically within this frame.

> For this is the time decreed for "the year of Melchiz[edek]'s favor" (Isa. 61:2, modified) and for [his] hos[ts, together] with the holy ones of God, for a kingdom of judgment, just as it is written concerning him in the Songs of David, "A godlike being has taken his place in the coun[cil of God;] in the midst of the divine beings he holds judgment" (Ps. 82:1). Scripture also s[ays] about him, "Over [it] take your seat in the highest heaven; A divine being will judge the peoples" (Ps. 7:7-8). Concerning what scripture s[ays, "How long will y]ou judge unjustly, and

---

24. Wise et al., *Dead Sea Scrolls*, 265.
25. Wise et al., *Dead Sea Scrolls*, 265.
26. Wise et al., *Dead Sea Scrolls*, 265-66.
27. Wise et al., *Dead Sea Scrolls*, 265.

sh[ow] partiality to the wick[e]d? [S]el[ah" (Ps. 82:2),] the interpretation applies to Belial and the spirits predestined to him, becau[se all of them have rebe]lled, turn[ing] from God's precepts [and so becoming utterly wicked]. Therefore Melchizedek will thoroughly prosecute the vengeance required by Go[d's] statutes. [In that day he will de]liv[er them from the power] of Belial, and from the power of all the sp[irits predestined to him.] 14Allied with him will be all the ["righteous] divine beings" (Isa. 61:3). [Th]is is that wh[ich ... al]l the divine beings.[28]

4Q88 (Apocryphal Psalms)

4Q88 contains three psalms from the canonical Psalter (Pss 22, 107, and 103) and three apocryphal psalms. These three apocryphal psalms are: (1) the Apostrophe to Zion, (2) the Eschatological Hymn, and (3) the Apostrophe to Judah.

The Apostrophe to Zion has strong eschatological overtones. As Abegg, Flint, and Ulrich write, "the Apostrophe to Zion focuses on Jerusalem, in this case invoking blessing on her, affirming the defeat of her enemies, and looking forward to her salvation and everlasting righteousness."[29] It reads:

> I remember you for a blessing, O Zion, with all my might do I love you. May your memory be blessed forever! Great is your hope, O Zion: peace and the victory you await shall come. Age to age shall you be indwelled, generations of the pious will adorn you: they who long for the day of your victory, to rejoice in your bounteous glory. At your glorious bosom they will suckle, in your majestic streets rattle their bangles. The faithful acts of your prophets shall you recall, being glorified by the works of your pious. Purge wrongdoing from your midst, lying and iniquity be cut off from you. Your children shall rejoice within you, your loved ones join themselves to you. How they have hoped for your victory! How your blameless have mourned you! Hope for you shall not perish, O Zion, nor shall your prospect be forgotten. Who, being righteous, has ever perished? Who has escaped in his sin? Man is tested as to his way, each rewarded according to his works. All around your enemies are cut off, O Zion, all who hate you are scattered. How sweet is the waft of your praise, O Zion, over all the earth! Again and

---

28. Wise et al., *Dead Sea Scrolls*, 592.
29. Abegg et al., *Dead Sea Scrolls Bible*, 576.

again shall I remember you for blessing; I will bless you with all my heart. May you lay hold of righteousness everlasting, may you receive the blessings of the Glorified. Embrace the vision spoken of you, O Zion, the dreams of prophets sought for you! Grow high, spread wide, O Zion; praise the Most High, your redeemer—while my soul rejoices in your glory.[30]

As is evident in the title, the Eschatological Hymn is focused on final judgment and the establishment of peace on the earth:

Then shall they extol the name of the Lord, [fo]r He comes to judge every wo[r]k, to make an end of the wicked from upon the earth: Evil [men] shall no more be found. The heavens [shall give] their dew, no ev[il within] their [boun]ds; the earth [offer up] fruits in season, its [pro]duce never short; fruit trees, their cr[op] in their vineyards, their [spring]s never failing. The poor shall eat, they who [fe]ar the Lord, be satisfied.[31]

The Apostrophe to Judah is likewise focused on the final establishment of YHWH's eternal reign:

So, let heaven and earth praise as one, let all the twilight stars give praise! Rejoice, O Judah, rejoice, rejoice and be very glad! Make your pilgrimages, fulfill your vows for Belial is nowhere to be found. Lift your hand on high, fortify your right hand: behold, enemies have perished, all who work evil been scattered. For You, O Lord, are etern[al,] Your glory enduring foreve[r and ev]er.[32]

Each of the apocryphal psalms in 4Q88 is future-predictive. The only other apocryphal psalms at Qumran are exorcism psalms and worship hymns, which can also be interpreted eschatologically. The exorcism psalms are to be read in association with David as the sweet psalmist, prophet, chosen one, and exorcist,[33] and the worship hymns as a celebration of the final establishment of the ideal Zion and the vindication of the chosen people.

---

30. Wise et al., *Dead Sea Scrolls*, 575–76.
31. Wise et al., *Dead Sea Scrolls*, 224.
32. Wise et al., *Dead Sea Scrolls*, 224.
33. See 1 Sam 16:14–23.

Ancient Translations

The Septuagint, the Targum of Psalms, and the Peshitta—all of which endorse the arrangement of the biblical Psalter—also demonstrate an eschatological reading of the psalms. Barton comments on the Septuagint that "the thrust of the whole collection is strongly eschatological."[34] When there are interpretive options available, the LXX tends to lean to a future-predictive reading, especially in the translation of superscriptions. For example, translators opt for Εἰς τὸ τέλος for למנצח.[35]

The Targum is even more forward than the LXX in its eschatological orientation in that it inserts interpretive comments in the headings. David Stec comments on prophecy in the psalms writing:

> TgPss takes an interest in prophecy. In particular, the "spirit of prophecy" is a means of revelation associated with David (14:1; 49:16; 51:13, 14; and probably also 22:27; 45:3), the sons of Korah (45:1[mss]; 46:1), Asaph (77:3; 79:1), and the prophets (68:34). Moreover, David is said to have sung a psalm in prophecy (18:1), to have spoken in prophecy (103:1), and to have prophesied (49:17), and Solomon is said to have spoken in prophecy (72:1). Psalm 98 is described as a psalm of prophecy (98:1).[36]

The Peshitta also offers an eschatological expansion to superscriptions. Mitchell gives us the following examples, which are translations from Kirkpatrick:[37]

- Psalm 22. Spoken by David when his pursuers were taunting him, and a prophecy of all the suffering of the Messiah.
- Psalm 45. Prophesied about Messiah our Lord: and about the raising up of the church.
- Psalm 72. A Psalm of David, when he had made Solomon king, and a prophecy concerning the advent of the Messiah and the calling of the gentiles.
- Psalm 110. Prophesied about the dispensing of the deliverances of the Messiah: and knowledge for us also about the separation of nature.

---

34. Barton, *Oracles*, 22.
35. See Mitchell, *Message*, 20, for more examples.
36. Stec, *Targum*, 5.
37. Kirkpatrick, *Psalms*.

These examples from the ancient translations demonstrate that, at the very least, there was a tradition of future-predictive readings of individual psalms.

Midrash Tehillim

The future-predictive, eschatological orientation for interpreting the Psalter is just one of many hermeneutical frames in the Midrash on the Psalms. One of the most robust supports for an eschatological reading of the Psalms is the central role of David in the Psalter. Beginning with Psalm 1, David is front and center for the Midrash Tehillim. The Midrash identifies David as the אשרי האיש of Psalm 1. It says,

> These words are to be considered in the light of what Scripture says elsewhere: He that diligently seeketh good, procureth favor (Prov. 11:27). *Who was such a person? David, king of Israel* . . .[38]

It goes on to comment that David, as the blessed man of Psalm 1:1, does not sit in the seat of scoffers; rather "King David entered and sat in the presence of YHWH" (2 Sam 7:18). This interpretation is further supported in Psalm 2, where we find the Messiah taking his seat on the throne in the audience of those conspiring against him. The Midrash offers an eschatological interpretation of this enthronement, saying, "Yet even in the time-to-come, Gog and Magog will set themselves against the Lord and His anointed, only to fall down. David, foreseeing this, said: 'Why do the heathen rage?'"[39] Moreover, "And in the time to come Gog and Magog will fall before the children of Israel. Foreseeing their fall David cried out: 'Why do the heathen rage?'"[40]

The vision the Midrash offers of these two introductory Psalms is that of a future-predictive David, the blessed man who is likewise the Messiah who sits at the right hand of judgment. This reading of Psalms 1–2 has David and the temple in center focus.

---

38. Braude, *Midrash*, 3 (emphasis added).
39. Braude, *Midrash*, 35.
40. Braude, *Midrash*, 36.

Intentionally Designed Collections

While there is ample external evidence for a future-predictive reading of individual psalms, what about the arrangement of psalms into collections? The ancient translations endorse the canonical Psalter. The Dead Sea Scrolls endorse the arrangement of Psalms 1–89,[41] but deviate from the canonical Psalter after that. While nearly all the biblical psalms from Books III–V are accounted for (126 of the 150 total psalms are accounted for in the DSS), they appear with a very different arrangement along with additional apocryphal psalms mentioned above. Abegg, Flint, and Ulrich note, "The remaining twenty-four Psalms were most likely included but have since been lost due to deterioration and damage. Of Psalms 1 through 89, nineteen no longer survive, but of Psalms 90 to 150 only five are not represented, since the beginnings of scrolls are usually on the outside and are thus more prone to deterioration."[42]

11QPs[a] comprises the most prominent arrangement (also represented in 4QPs[e] and 11QPs[b]) of psalms following Psalm 89, which is as follows:

Exorcism Psalm 1	Psalms 113–118 (Egyptian Hallel)	Psalm 145	Psalm 155
Exorcism Psalm 2	Psalm 104	Psalm 139	Psalms 142–143
Exorcism Psalm 3	Psalm 147	Psalms 137–138	Psalms 149–150
Psalm 91	Psalm 105	Sirach 51	Hymn to the Creator
Psalm 92	Psalm 146	Apostrophe to Zion	David's Last Words
Psalm 94–100	Psalm 148	Psalm 93	David's Compositions
Psalms 101–103	Psalms 120–132	Psalm 141	Psalm 140
Psalm 112	Psalm 119	Psalm 133	Psalm 134
Psalms 109–110	Psalms 135–136	Psalm 144	Psalm 151A

---

41. The only deviation from the canonical Psalter here is in QPs[a] and QPs[q], which both have Psalm 33 following Psalm 31, also, in QPs[a] Psalm 71 follows Psalm 38.

42. Abegg et al., *Dead Sea Scrolls*, 506.

An in-depth analysis of this arrangement is beyond the scope of this chapter, however, we can make some broad observations. While the arrangement of psalms in the various collections at Qumran affirms and differs from the canonical Psalter, there is a clear understanding of Davidic authorship of the various collections and arrangements. David's authorship is understood to be divinely inspired and "composed *through prophecy* given him by the Most High,"[43] which indicates a prophetic frame to the collection. Furthermore, Qumran witnesses the grouping of apocryphal psalms, Davidic psalms, and exorcism psalms, which indicates an intentional design to the arrangements, even if the arrangement diverges from the canonical Psalter. All these support the view that the community at Qumran would have seen the canonical Psalter as intentionally ordered.

The Qumran community's preoccupation with the Psalms and eschatology cannot be ignored. The size of the collection of psalms at Qumran, the eschatological focus of the apocryphal psalms at Qumran, and Qumran's view of David as the prophetic psalmist together make the reality that the Qumran community read the psalms eschatologically irrefutable.

Need for Further Exploration: Integration with Other Theories

While the evidence for a future-predictive eschatological program behind the editorial design of the Psalter is quite strong, other elements of the collection indicate that eschatology is not the only program at work. For example, how does the Elohistic Psalter (Pss 42–83) fit into this program? The very presence of the Elohistic Psalter suggests that there are certainly *other* contributing factors to the editorial design apart from the future-predictive. What is the role of the Elohistic Psalter, and why does it stand where it does in the broader collection? The same goes for exorcism psalms among the DSS and theories related to synagogue reading cycles. Peter Ho's *The Design of the Psalter* is an excellent foray into an exploration of the integration of the layers of variables potentially at play in the editorial design of the Psalter.

---

43. Wise et al., *Dead Sea Scrolls*, 576 (emphasis added).

Conclusion

There is strong internal and external evidence for eschatology as an organizing feature behind the shape of the book of Psalms. More specifically, the evidence points towards the anticipation of the establishment of the final Temple/Zion and the Messiah from the line of David.

My view is that hope for the restoration of the temple, the Davidic king, and Hebrew hegemony are some of the main controlling factors in the macrostructure of the Psalter. At the same time, internal and external evidence also suggest that eschatology is not the *only program* at play. More detailed examination of the evidence both for and against the eschatological program behind the editorial design of the Psalter is beyond the scope of this study. In consideration of the sampling of evidence presented here, I agree with the following quote from Brevard Childs and therefore find it to be a fitting closing declaration:

> However one explains it, the final form of the Psalter is highly eschatological in nature. It looks toward to the future and passionately yearns for its arrival. Even when the psalmist turns briefly to reflect on the past in praise of the "great things which Yahweh has done," invariably the movement shifts and again the hope of salvation is projected into the future (Ps. 126:6). The perspective of Israel's worship in the Psalter is eschatologically oriented. As a result, the Psalter in its canonical form, far from being different in kind from the prophetic message, joins with the prophets in announcing God's coming kingship. When the New Testament heard in the psalms eschatological notes, its writers were standing in the context of the Jewish canon in which the community of faith worshipped and waited.[44]

Bibliography

Abegg, Martin G., Jr., et al. *The Dead Sea Scrolls Bible: The Oldest Known Bible Translated for the First Time into English.* New York: HarperOne, 1999.

Alexander, J. A. *The Psalms.* 3 vols. New York: Scribner's Sons, 1865.

Arens, A. *Die Psalmen im Gottesdienst des Alten Bundes.* Trier: Paulinus, 1968.

Barbiero, Gianni. *Das erste Psalmenbuch als Einheit: Eine synchrone Analyse von Psalm 1–41.* ÖBS 16. Frankfurt: Lang, 1999.

Braude, W. G. *The Midrash on the Psalms.* YJS 13. 2 vols. New Haven: Yale University Press, 1959.

---

44. Childs, *Introduction*, 518.

Broyles, Craig C. "The Redeeming King: Psalm 72's Contribution to the Messianic Ideal." In *Eschatology, Messianism, and the Dead Sea Scrolls*, edited by Craig A. Evans and Peter W. Flint, 23–40. Studies in the Dead Sea Scrolls and Related Literature. Grand Rapids: Eerdmans, 1997.

Childs, Brevard S. *Introduction to the Old Testament as Scripture*. Philadelphia: Fortress, 1979.

Collins, John J. "The Expectation of the End in the Dead Sea Scrolls." In *Eschatology, Messianism, and the Dead Sea Scrolls*, edited by Craig A. Evans and Peter W. Flint, 74–90. Studies in the Dead Sea Scrolls and Related Literature. Grand Rapids: Eerdmans, 1997.

deClaissé-Walford, Nancy L, ed. *The Shape and Shaping of the Book of Psalms: The Current State of Scholarship*, SBLAIL 20. Atlanta: SBL, 2014.

Ho, Peter C. W. *The Design of the Psalter: A Macrostructural Analysis*. Eugene, OR: Pickwick, 2019.

Mitchell, David C. *The Message of the Psalter: An Eschatological Programme in the Book of Psalms*. JSOTSup 252. Sheffield: Sheffield Academic, 1997.

Stec, David M. *The Targum of Psalms: Translated, with a Critical Introduction, Apparatus, and Notes*. Edited by Kevin Cathcart et al. Aramaic Bible 16. Collegeville, MN: Liturgical, 2004.

Willgren, David. *The Formation of the "Book" of Psalms: Reconsidering the Transmission and Canonization of Psalmody in Light of Material Culture and the Poetics of Anthologies*. FAT II 88. Tübingen: Mohr Siebeck, 2016.

Wilson, Gerald H. *The Editing of the Hebrew Psalter*. SBLDS 76. Atlanta: Scholars, 1985.

———. "The Qumran Psalms Scroll (11QPS^a) and the Canonical Psalter." *CBQ* 59 (1997) 448–64.

Wise, Michael O., et al. *The Dead Sea Scrolls: A New Translation*. New York: HarperOne, 2005.

Zenger, Erich. "Der Psalter als Buch." In *Der Psalter in Judentum und Christentum*, edited by Erich Zenger and Norbert Lohfink, 1–58. HBS 18. Frieburg: Herder, 1988.

CHAPTER 5

A Methodology for the Cohesion of the Psalms

Psalms 15, 19, and 24 as a Test Case

CARISSA M. QUINN

THE BOOK OF PSALMS is a treasured collection of prayer, a source of song for communal worship, and a consistent component of church liturgy.[1] Many readers approach the psalms as individual poems for reflection, meditation, and encouragement through the various seasons of life. This is certainly valuable, and yet there is another layer to reading the book of Psalms, with which many are less acquainted—that is, reading the Psalter as a collection of individual psalms that have been arranged to tell an overarching story.

Various scholars who study the shape of the Psalter as a whole have observed that it has a narrative-like movement from beginning to end.[2]

---

1. Much of the content of this article is adapted from my book-length publication, Quinn, *Arrival*, used with permission from Lexham Press.

2. Observing the arrangement of and correlation between psalms is an ancient method, attested by early Jewish and Christian interpreters as well as pre-critical scholars. For example, the church fathers regarded the order and number as significant (e.g., Origen, *Selecta in Psalmos*, xi, xiii, 107, 352–54, 370–71; Augustine, *Enarrationes* §3; Jerome, *Commentarioli in Psalmos*, Ps 1); rabbinic interpreters gave attention to repeated words, cohesion between neighboring psalms, and how the five-part shape of the psalms mirrors the Torah (e.g., bar. *Ber.* 10a, Midr. Psalms 1:2, 3:2, 111:1; and Kid. 33a); and later Reformers gave attention to the introduction and distinct collections

Broadly speaking, the story begins with a two-part introduction setting out a thriving way of life grounded in YHWH's instruction (Ps 1) and God's faithfulness to his anointed king (Ps 2). These introductory psalms are closely connected by repeated words, and together depict a Torah-obedient king who will reign over the nations' kings. Books I (Pss 1–41) and II (Pss 42–72) are associated with David's life, kingship, and suffering at the hands of his enemies. Book III (Pss 73–89) seems to follow the Davidic kingship toward exile and the destruction of the city and temple. The ending of Book III poses a challenge to the vision set out in the introduction of YHWH's anointed ruling over the nations. Book IV responds to this challenge by beginning with "A prayer of Moses," recalling a time when there was no human king, but YHWH himself reigned over the people of Israel. Book V ends the collection with renewed hope in the Davidic king and praise of YHWH, who reigns over all. The story the Psalter tells seems in many ways like a microcosm of the biblical story.

And yet, to speak of the Psalter as a story brings up some important questions. For example, how do *poetic* texts *narrate stories*? What kind of coherent story should we expect from seemingly independent psalms? How closely related are individual psalms? And what literary cues and conventions help us to interpret them within their literary context? While there is insufficient space in this article to comprehensively answer these questions, I think an analysis of cohesion between individual psalms within a group can provide some insight.

The inquiry into the shape and story of the Psalter relies on whether its individual psalms exhibit cohesion, both between psalms and within groups (the micro-level) and across the entire Psalter (the macro-level). Much like fractal art,[3] the Psalter seems to exhibit self-similarity—in other words, its macro-level structural devices and patterns are similar to those used on the micro-levels. Therefore, analysis at the level of the collection can shape our expectations about macro-level features. In addition, understanding the meaning of smaller sub-plots contributes to the larger discussion of the plot of the whole.

(e.g., Calvin, *Book of Psalms*, 1; Luther, *Luthers Werke*, 4:3–4).

It was G. H. Wilson's seminal work on editorial markers in the Psalter in 1985 that created the impetus for a robust renewal of interest in the shape of the Psalter (Wilson, *Editing*), although the modern emergence of this interpretive method is represented by the following: Childs, *Introduction*; Zimmerli, "Zwillingspsalmen," 105–13; Westermann, *Praise and Lament*; Barth, "Concatenatio," 30–40.

3. Fractals are patterns that repeat at different scales. These patterns can be found in nature and also expressed in art by iterating a pattern at increasingly finer scales.

In this article, I seek to identify various correlations between individual psalms in a group and assess the cohesion created by those correlations. I also seek to discover what potential shape and message might result from that cohesion. The methodology I will set forth has the potential to help us understand the shape of the whole Psalter, as well as help us quantify correlations among other anthologies, like the Book of the Twelve or Proverbs. Because Psalms 15–24 has been recognized as a highly structured collection by various scholars, the psalms within will provide a helpful test case for discerning cohesion and structure.

A Methodology for Discerning Cohesion Between Psalms

The disciplined practice of noticing correlations between psalms can be termed "editorial criticism" because it looks for evidence of the editorial hands which shaped the Psalter. I will use the words *design*, *shape*, and *link* to indicate this shaping process.[4] If there is evidence of design, then individual psalms may be interpreted within their literary context rather than solely as isolated units or within the settings in which they originated and were used.

Upon reading through Psalms 15–24, we are likely to notice a variety of correlations between individual psalms. But how do we know whether correlations are invitations to read two psalms together, or whether correlations are merely coincidental? This question deserves a thoughtful answer, since reading psalms as linked together can influence how we perceive their meaning. While there are correlations where the intentionality of a link is highly plausible (e.g., direct quotations or unique superscripts), others are not so easy to discern. What can keep interpreters from either missing intentional links or seeing more than is there?

Simply put, when we compare two psalms, we can observe repeated elements (lexemes, themes, structures, etc.), determine the rarity of these repetitions, and notice how many rare correlations, or links, occur

---

4. I will use the term "editor" loosely to refer to a person or group who arranged and recomposed (edited) psalms into their present, synchronic arrangement. I will not distinguish between an editor and an author, for primarily two reasons: First, it is nearly impossible to distinguish between these differing hands; and second, it is possible that editors authored new material, and that authors composed new psalms in relation to others. Rather than distinguishing between an original author and subsequent editors, I will refer to the group responsible for the present composition as editor(s).

between the psalms. This process can be carried out in various ways. A person may read closely and make note of what seems like an abundance of unique repetitions. This is perhaps the most accessible practice of noticing links between psalms. For more precision, one might use Bible softwares or concordances to identify whether a repetition is rare—in other words, whether a repetition occurs within the psalm pair at a higher rate than its average within the broader literary context (i.e., the collection, book, or entire Psalter).[5] For even greater confidence, one could quantify whether the intentionality of a link is beyond reasonable doubt by calculating the plausibility of intentionality through a hypothesis test. To my mind, each of these practices has its place. In this article, I will elaborate on the third way since, as far as I am aware, no such calculation has been used to analyze correlations between psalms. Nonetheless, my hope is that my methodological explorations and conclusions will benefit the interpreter, whichever of these three paths they choose.

Linking Criteria

Several strategies for coordinating psalms across the entire Psalter have been identified by Gerald Wilson in his analysis of common ancient Near Eastern editorial devices.[6] Others, notably David Howard and Michael Snearly, have applied these criteria to the level of the collection and book.[7] Building on common ancient Near Eastern editorial strategies as well as an understanding of Hebrew parallelism, I propose observing the following criteria for discerning links between psalms:

1. **Lexical links:** The repetition of any morphological form of a particular root. I do not include conjunctions, prepositions, particles, negative adverbs, or pronouns, since these are often incidental.[8]

---

5. See Quinn, *Arrival*, where I have performed such an analysis of Psalms 15–24.

6. Wilson compares the Mesopotamian Hymnic Incipits, the Sumerian Temple Hymns, and the Qumran Psalms scrolls with the Masoretic Psalter and finds the following tacit editorial groupings in the latter: genre, deity addressed, concatenation, lack of superscription, and thematic correspondence. Wilson, *Editing*, 121–98.

7. Howard focuses on keyword links, thematic connections, and genre similarities. Snearly adds to this distant parallelism and common superscripts. See Howard, *Structure*; Snearly, "Return."

8. Anytime I refer to a lexeme or root, I mean a *non-incidental* lexeme or root, unless otherwise indicated.

2. **Morphological links:** The repetition of a root in the same morphological form, including part of speech, gender, number, and conjugation (if a verb).

3. **Phrasal links:** The repetition of at least two lexemes used within the same clause. Phrasal links may include conjunctions, prepositions, particles, negative adverbs, and pronouns when they are used to construct a recognizably corresponding phrase.

4. **Thematic links:** The repetition of essential content or subject matter within a psalm. This may include repetition of the same idea or an allusion to the same passage.

5. **Structural/Genre links:** The correspondence in structure on the level of the whole psalm. Often these correspond with modern, form-critical categories (e.g., lament, praise, thanksgiving), but at other times they do not (e.g., a chiastic structure).

6. **Superscript links:** The correspondence of superscripts. Corresponding superscript elements include the same designation of an associated figure (e.g., David), psalm type (e.g., מזמור), and/or the same root.

Noticing every repetition of each of these kinds is the first step to discerning cohesion between psalms.

The Rarity of Repeated Elements

The second task in understanding whether two psalms are highly cohesive is to determine the rarity of each repeated element, whether it is a lexeme, phrase, theme, etc. Rarity is important for identifying cohesion. If a common word is repeated in two psalms, it's very possible that the repetition is coincidental, rather than functioning to link the two psalms. But when an extremely rare word is used in two psalms, it creates more cohesion and suggests that the two texts should be read together.

Determining the Rate of Occurrence

Rather than assuming that every repetition is significant, we can analyze the *strength* of each repetition by comparing the rate of the repetition in a psalm pair with its average rate in the collection.[9] Here's an example: Let's say you notice that Psalms 15 and 19 both use the lexeme *blameless* תמם (Pss 15:2; 19:8[7], 14[13]).[10] The lexeme also occurs in other psalms in the collection of Psalms 15–24. The goal is to understand whether *blameless* occurs at a higher rate in the psalm pair than in the collection. Within Psalms 15 and 19, *blameless* occurs three times; there are 153 lexemes within Psalms 15 and 19 together, so the rate of occurrence of *blameless* is 3/153, or on average, once every 51 words. Now we can compare this to its average rate in the collection: *blameless* occurs eight times, and there are 1130 lexemes in total, so the average rate of occurrence is 8/1130, or once every 141.25 words. So, the lexeme *blameless* occurs at a rate almost three times as high in the psalm pair than in the collection. It is plausible that this is an example of an intentional link, but just *how* plausible?

Determining the Significance of a Repetition

We can apply even stricter criteria to assess whether a repetition is plausibly intentional by using a hypothesis test (or *z*-test) to analyze statistical significance. *Statistical significance* means that a relationship between two or more items is caused by something other than chance or coincidence. In our case, we want to understand whether the rate of occurrence of a repetition in a psalm pair is so rare that it is not likely to be coincidental.

The test is called a hypothesis test because we are testing a hypothesis for a model of how the world (in this case, a text) typically works. We are treating the potential linking elements of Psalms 15–24 as a random

---

9. In the Psalms, I find it most compelling to use the collection or distinct psalm-group as the comparative reference, rather than the book or the Psalter, for two reasons. First, if editors intend for their audience to notice links, the more proximate those links are, the more likely they will be noticed. Second, it is likely that many collections existed on their own before being situated in the Psalter, so it is more conservative to expect links within collections than more broadly. Certainly, more editorial shaping took place as collections were arranged into the Psalter, so looking at the rarity of repetitions on the book or macro-structural level is also helpful, especially when there is a cluster of links. Using the collection as the literary context requires first determining the boundaries of the collection. Psalms 15–24 are demarcated by their unique entrance liturgy form in Psalms 15 and 24.

10. By lexeme, I am referring to any morphological form of the tri-consonantal root, the latter of which I include in Hebrew, following an English translation of the root. After the introduction of the Hebrew root in a paragraph, I often will use only the English. N.B., all verse numbers refer to Masoretic numbering.

sample. We begin with the *null* hypothesis (H_0)—*null*, meaning that nothing has changed from what is typically expected if we were to compare two unrelated texts. We adopt the null hypothesis until we can test it. Our null hypothesis (H_0) is that the rate of occurrence of a particular element in a psalm pair is equal to its average within the collection. In order to reject the null hypothesis, we must pile up enough evidence. Until we become convinced, we accept the null's assertion that nothing is unusual or different and that the rate is close enough to the average to be coincidental. Our alternate hypothesis (H_A) is that the rate of occurrence of a particular element in a psalm pair is higher than its average in the collection. But we would expect some fluctuation around the average rate, so *how high* of a rate would convince us that a repetition is actually different from the average, and not coincidental?

A hypothesis test can help us understand when an event (in this case a rate of occurrence) would happen only 5 percent (or less) of the time by chance. When we see a variety of repetitions that would occur only 5 percent of the time by chance, it challenges the null hypothesis by causing us to ask, "Aren't these data surprising in light of the null hypothesis we've adopted?" And, "If these psalms are not intentionally linked, isn't it remarkable that we have such strong correlations?" With a hypothesis test, we can quantify how surprising the evidence is if the null hypothesis were true. While we cannot have complete certainty of intentionality, when we find evidence of statistically significant links, we can judge the null hypothesis to be insufficient beyond reasonable doubt, and links to be plausibly intentional.

We can perform what's called a one-sided *z*-test—one-sided because we are only interested in when the values occur at a higher-than-average rate, rather than higher *or* lower.[11] A *z*-score is the number of standard deviations above the average, which helps us understand how plausible it is that a repetition is coincidental. So, we will subtract the average proportion (p_0) from the true proportion ($\hat{p}$), and divide it by the standard deviation (σ), using the formula $z = (\hat{p} - p_0)/\sigma$. We will calculate the standard deviation (σ) in terms of the average proportion (p_0) as shown in the denominator of the formula below. According to a normal distribution table, when *z* is equal to or greater than 1.65, this tells us that there is only a 5 percent chance or less that the repetition is

---

11. A lower-than-average rate could indicate intentional *omission*, for example, if a theme is used in every psalm but one in a collection. The scope of this paper does not explore this data, but it could be worth examining in future research.

coincidental.[12] With a value so small, we can reject the null hypothesis that the repetition is merely coincidental.

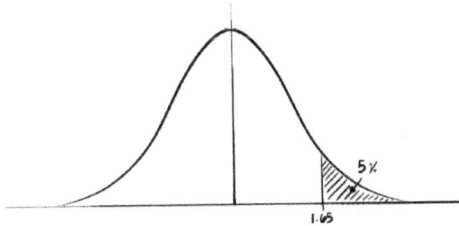

Figure 5.1: One-sided *z*-test for calculating rarity.

- H$_0$ (the null hypothesis) is that the rate of occurrence of a particular element in a psalm pair ($\hat{p}$) is equal to its average within the collection (p_0).
- H$_A$ (the alternative hypothesis) is that the rate of occurrence of a particular element in a psalm pair ($\hat{p}$) is higher than its average in the collection (p_0).

$$z_{.05} = \frac{\hat{p} - p_0}{\sqrt{\frac{p_0(1 - p_0)}{n}}}$$

- $\hat{p}$ is the rate of occurrence of a particular element (e.g., a lexeme) in a psalm pair.
- p_0 is the average rate of occurrence of that same element in the collection.
- n is sample size.
- If $z \geq 1.65$, we can reject the null hypothesis.[13]
- If $z < 1.65$, we fail to reject the null hypothesis.

Let's consider again the repeated lexeme *blameless* תמם in Psalms 15 and 19. The rate of occurrence in the psalm pair was almost three

---

12. See ztable.net for an example table. Refer to the positive *z*-score table. Subtract the table value from 1 to find the area on the right of the *z*-score.

13. Though this language of rejecting a hypothesis may sound odd, it is important, since we cannot prove causation with a hypothesis test. We can only conclude that there is enough evidence to believe something is definitely false (in this case, the coincidental nature of a repetition).

times as high as compared to in the collection of Psalms 15–24, but the question is, *does it occur at a high enough rate to be considered significant (i.e., intentional)*? Our $\hat{p}$ (true) and p_0 (average) values are the rates of occurrence, which we have already determined: In this case, $\hat{p}$ is the rate of occurrence of *blameless* in the psalm pair, 3/153, and p_0 is the rate of occurrence in the collection, 8/1130. Finally, n is the sample size, or all of the possible places where the repeated element could occur. Because we are looking at a lexeme, n is the number of non-incidental lexemes in Psalms 15 and 19, combined: 153.[14] Below is the formula with the values plugged in:

$$z_{.05} = \frac{(3/153) - (8/1130)}{\sqrt{\frac{(8/1130)[1 - (8/1130)]}{153}}}$$

Our *z*-score comes up to 1.85, which is greater than 1.65. If we consult a normal distribution table for a *z*-score of 1.85,[15] the corresponding value of .0322 says that given the true proportion of the rate of occurrence of *blameless* in the collection of 8/1130, an observed proportion of 3/153 (or larger) would occur only 322 times in 10,000. In other words, this rate of occurrence would occur only 3.22 percent of the time. With a value so small, we can reject H_0. Put differently, there is reasonable statistical evidence to suggest that the repeated lexeme *blameless* is an intentional link between these psalms.

Parallel Psalms

Now, while the presence of one significant repetition may have bearing on interpretation, I am interested in cases where two psalms contain a high number of these significant links in comparison to their surrounding psalms. In such cases, I conclude that two psalms are 'parallel' and can be read together. This designation as parallel is founded on the idea that Hebrew parallelism can exist on various levels of the text, including between entire psalms.[16]

---

14. By "non-incidental," I mean lexical roots other than conjunctions, prepositions, particles, negative adverbs, or pronouns. If we were looking at a genre, theme, or superscript, the *n* value would be the number of psalms in the pair (two), since that is the number of possible places it could occur.

15. See note 12.

16. I have performed this analysis on the level of the collection, but such analysis

I have performed a hypothesis test for every repeated element (lexemes, morphological forms of roots, phrases, themes, structures/genres, and superscripts) within every possible psalm pair in the collection (Psalms 15 and 16; 15 and 17; 15 and 18, and so on). I give attention to the *number* of significant repetitions between each psalm pair (i.e., those with a z-score greater than 1.65); I also pay attention to the *strength* of those repetitions—the higher the z-score, the more significant (or rare) the repetition. By adding all of the significant z-scores together within one category (e.g., lexical), I can find what I call the *strength*, or *degree, of significance* for a particular element type in the psalm pair.

For example, when I pair Psalm 15 with each of the other psalms in the collection, I find that it shares the greatest number of significant words with Psalm 22—*eight* words in total. It also shares *seven* significant words with Psalm 24. The question is whether these seven shared words are stronger links than the eight shared words of Psalms 15 and 22. When I calculate the strength of these repetitions (the z-scores) and add these values together for each psalm pair, I find that the degree of lexical significance between Psalms 15 and 22 is 17.85, whereas the degree of lexical significance between Psalms 15 and 24 is 26.84—much higher. This is because some of the repetitions between Psalms 15 and 24 are extremely rare (e.g., *to swear* שבע only occurs in these two psalms within the collection) or occur at high rates in the two psalms (*to lift up* נשא occurs seven of eight times). Below are the numbers and overall degrees of lexical significance that Psalm 15 shares with each psalm in the collection:

---

could also be performed on the level of the book or entire Psalter. Psalms likely have close relationships to nearby psalms as well as more distant psalms. Different levels of analysis may reveal different layers of structure and cohesion. See the following works, which suggests that parallelism can exist on various levels of the text: Alter, *Biblical Narrative*, 55–78, 111–42; *Biblical Poetry*, 1–28; Berlin, *Dynamics*, 3; Fokkelman, *Remaining 65 Psalms*, 61–157; Weber, *Psalmen 1 bis 72*, 99.

Psalm pair	Number of Significant Lexemes	Degree of Lexical Significance
15 and 16	3	8.53
15 and 17	5	13.56
15 and 18	3	5.64
15 and 19	5	15.43
15 and 20	1	3.28
15 and 21	5	11.18
15 and 22	8	17.85
15 and 23	3	11.54
15 and 24	7	26.84[17]

Table 5.1: Psalm 15: Strengths of lexical significance.

Before drawing conclusions about which psalms Psalm 15 is most closely connected to, I analyze the overall degree of significance for every other type of linking criteria: morphological forms of roots, phrases, themes, structures/genres, and superscripts. These are the results per link type:[18]

17. The highest degrees of significance per category are in bold in each figure.

18. Notes: (1) For genre, theme, and superscript, the rate is calculated according to the number of psalms ($n = 2$) rather than according to word count, since that is the number of possible places it could occur. (2) The superscript value in the table is 0.00 because it did not show any statistically significant connections. For example, the repetition of לדוד occurs often enough in the collection that its occurrence in any given psalm is not statistically significant. (3) The values for Structures and Themes are identical, because Psalms 15 and 19 share a theme and a structure that occurs in only one other place in the collection (speech, and the similar Righteousness-Result structure), and Psalms 15 and 24 share these same themes and structures, plus the theme of entering YHWH's dwelling and the entrance liturgy structure (see Table 5.5).

Psalm pair	Lexemes	Morphologies	Phrases	Structures	Themes	Superscripts
15 and 16	8.53	4.10	6.68	0.00	0.00	0.00
15 and 17	13.56	6.66	1.97	0.00	0.00	0.00
15 and 18	5.64	2.65	0.00	0.00	0.00	0.00
15 and 19	15.43	3.33	0.00	2.16	2.16	0.00
15 and 20	3.28	8.21	0.00	0.00	0.00	0.00
15 and 21	11.18	7.46	2.30	0.00	0.00	0.00
15 and 22	17.85	9.30	2.37	0.00	0.00	0.00
15 and 23	11.54	5.05	0.00	0.00	0.00	0.00
15 and 24	26.84	15.11	12.02	4.99	4.99	0.00

Table 5.2: Psalm 15: Degrees of statistical significance per link type.

At this point, I notice that Psalms 15 and 24 have the highest degree of statistical significance in every category.

What we cannot do yet is compare across categories—as in from lexemes to structures/genres to phrases. Just because the degree of lexical significance between Psalms 15 and 24 is represented by a number twice as high as the degree of thematic significance, this does not mean that the thematic connections are only half as strong. Until we scale the columns, comparisons can only be made *within* each criterion (or column), rather than across them. To scale the columns, I calculate the statistical significance per link type for every possible psalm pair within the collection. In other words, I create the above chart for every psalm in the collection, not just Psalm 15. Once I am able to see which number within its own category, or column, is highest across all the charts, I can scale the entire category to that number. The result is that the highest degree of lexical significance would be represented by the number 1.00, and the other degrees of lexical significance would be less than 1.00. For example, Psalms 15 and 24 actually have the highest degree of lexical significance of any other possible psalm pair in the entire collection, at 26.84, so I scale each degree of lexical significance to this number by dividing by it. The result is that Psalms 15 and 24 have a scaled degree of lexical significance of 1.00, and every other psalm pair has a scaled lexical degree of less than 1.00. See the scaled chart for Psalm 15 paired with every other psalm in the collection:[19]

Psalm pair	Lexemes	Morphologies	Phrases	Structures	Themes	Total Degree
15 and 16	0.32	0.27	0.56	0.00	0.00	*1.15*
15 and 17	0.51	0.44	0.16	0.00	0.00	*1.11*
15 and 18	0.21	0.18	0.00	0.00	0.00	*0.39*
15 and 19	0.57	0.22	0.00	0.43	0.18	*1.40*
15 and 20	0.12	0.54	0.00	0.00	0.00	*0.66*
15 and 21	0.42	0.49	0.19	0.00	0.00	*1.10*
15 and 22	0.67	0.62	0.20	0.00	0.00	*1.47*
15 and 23	0.43	0.33	0.00	0.00	0.00	*0.76*
15 and 24	1.00	1.00	1.00	1.00	0.43	*4.43*

Table 5.3: Psalm 15: Total degrees of statistical significance.

Notice that Psalms 15 and 24 have the highest degrees of significance in almost every category (represented by 1.00).[20] I have added a column titled "Total Degree" that adds the degrees of significance per category across each row. The column's total degrees of significance show that Psalm 15 is most closely connected to Psalm 24. Because of this, I view these two psalms as parallel, and meant to be read together.

The connections between Psalms 15 and 24 might be intuited, but now there is strong statistical evidence to suggest that impression is founded. What is also interesting from the figure above is that Psalm 15 shows some strong connections with Psalms 19 and 22—connections that are perhaps not as quickly discerned upon reading. Repeating the same process and chart for Psalms 19 and 22 reveals that Psalm 22 is not reciprocally connected to Psalm 15, but that Psalm 19 is. In fact, Psalms 15, 19, and 24 seem to have a unique relationship: Psalm 19 is most closely connected first with Psalm 24, followed by Psalm 15; and Psalm 24 is most

19. I have removed the superscript category on this chart since superscripts did not prove to be statistically significant anywhere across the collection.

20. The 0.43 value in the Themes column signifies that when every psalm within the entire collection is paired, there is another psalm pair (Psalms 20 and 21) that has a higher overall degree of significance.

closely connected to Psalm 15, then to Psalm 19. Together, the three function as a frame for the collection, as shown in Figure 5.2.

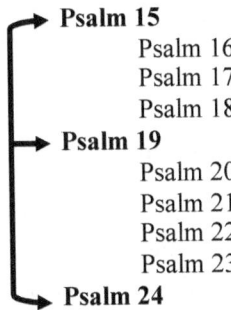
- Psalm 15
- Psalm 16
- Psalm 17
- Psalm 18
- Psalm 19
- Psalm 20
- Psalm 21
- Psalm 22
- Psalm 23
- Psalm 24

Figure 5.2: The Frame.

Because of their cohesion, I view these *three* psalms as parallel to one another and intended to be read together. The remainder of this article will comprise such a reading.

Reading Psalms 15, 19, and 24 as Parallel Texts

As I mentioned above, many scholars have recognized that parallelism exists on various levels of the text, including between entire psalms. Hebrew parallelism is not defined by static repetition, but modification, or dynamic movement, from the first element to the second, such as heightening, intensification, specification, etc. My goal in reading Psalms 15, 19, and 24 as parallel texts is to discern how, in their present arrangement, each latter psalm echoes and modifies elements of the former, giving careful attention to how those significant, correlated elements are used differently in the latter psalm. This difference in use contributes to a perceived development in the storyline of the whole. This analysis of development, or progression of the plotline, is one of the primary ways this study goes beyond previous editorial-critical studies, and could be practiced whether someone uses a hypothesis test or simply performs a close reading.

In what follows, I draw conclusions about the meaning of Psalms 15, 19, and 24 based on the statistically significant elements they share. Throughout, I use the word "significant" in a technical sense to denote not just that a connection is meaningful, but that it is mathematically significant according to the z-test referenced above. Of course, there are many more correspondences between these psalms, but I focus here on only the statistically significant connections, since these are the ones that have the highest plausibility of intentionality.

Significant Links among Psalms 15, 19, and 24

When paired together, Psalms 15 and 24 are more closely connected by statistically significant elements than when paired with any other psalm in the collection.[21] Both psalms begin with twin questions about who may ascend YHWH's holy mountain (Pss 15:1; 24:3). The lexemes *holy* קדש and *mountain* הר are lexically and morphologically significant (only found here in the collection), and when paired with the interrogative, *who* מי, they become significant phrases only matched by one another. These opening phrases frame the entire collection with the significant theme of entering YHWH's presence. These psalms also share additional significant lexemes (*innocent* נקה, *swear* שבע, *lift up* נשא, *glory* כבד, and *ever* עולם); morphological forms of roots (*he swears* נשבע, and *he lifts up* נשא), the phrase *he does not lift up* לא־נשא, themes (*speech* and *entering YHWH's dwelling*), and an overarching structure (question-answer-result). These significant elements create a noticeably strong cohesion between Psalms 15 and 24.

It may be surprising to find that Psalm 19 is also most closely connected to Psalms 15 and 24. Psalms 15 and 19 share significant lexemes (*tent* אהל, *blameless* תמם, *do/work* עשה, *innocent* נקה, and *truth* אמן); the same morphological form of *truth* אמת; the theme of *speech*; structural/genre similarities. Psalms 19 and 24 are even more closely united, sharing the following significant elements: lexemes (*world* תבל, *clean/innocent* נקה, *glory* כבד, *mighty* גבר, and *result/Jacob* עקב); morphological forms (*world* תבל and *mighty one* גבור); themes (*creation* and *speech*); structural correspondences. These connections create a strong cohesion among these three psalms.

Remember that parallelism does not involve simply static repetition but a dynamic movement. Therefore, we can ask how, in their present arrangement, the correspondences between Psalms 15 and 19 exhibit dynamic movement and also how the same occurs in Psalm 24.

---

21. See the appendices in Quinn, *Arrival*, for a list of all repeated elements identified.

In other words, when we consider the present shape of the collection of Psalms 15–24, how does Psalm 19 carry the message of Psalm 15 forward through repetition and difference? And how does Psalm 24 further develop the message, or storyline, as it has taken shape in Psalms 15 and 19? This dynamic reuse and the resulting development of the storyline is the focus of what follows.

Structural Correspondence among Psalms 15, 19, and 24

Psalms 15, 19, and 24 share structural correspondences that are statistically significant within the collection. In terms of modern form-critical genres, Psalms 15 and 24 can be designated as entrance liturgies by their question-answer-result structure—the only two of their kind in the entire Psalter. Psalm 19 is often designated in form-critical categories as a wisdom or Torah psalm.[22] Although wisdom psalms do not have a defined structure, the correspondences between the three psalms are striking.[23]

To see the correspondences that Psalms 15 and 24 share with 19, we must begin by comparing Psalms 15 and 24, as in Table 5.4 (verse numbers are in parenthesis):

---

22. My methodology recognizes as links those genres that also have corresponding structures. To my mind, "wisdom" or "Torah" are better suited for and analyzed within the "theme" category rather than "structure/genre."

23. This is especially true when compared to the other psalms in the collection, which are songs of trust (Pss 16 and 23), laments (Pss 17 and 22), thanksgiving (Ps 18), and communal petition and praise (Pss 20 and 21).

Ps 15	Ps 24
	Creation (1–2)
Righteousness	Righteousness (3–6)
1. Question (1) 2. Answer (2–5b) 3. Result (5c)	1. Question 2. Answer 3. Result • +1 Community
	Arrival (7–10)

Table 5.4: Structural correspondences between Psalms 15 and 24.

Both Psalms 15 and 24 have three parts (Ps 15:1, 2–5b, 5c; Ps 24:1–3, 3–6, 7–10). The question-answer-result structure comprises the entirety of Psalm 15; the central concern is the righteousness required to enter YHWH's presence. In Psalm 24, the question-answer-result structure contains the added element of the community, creating a 'three-plus-one' structure in that part.[24] It is also preceded by creation imagery and followed by the arrival of YHWH among the community of his people.

When we compare these two psalms with Psalm 19, we can see how the latter bridges the content of Psalms 15 and 24:

---

24. The 'three-plus-one' or 'three . . . and for four' structure is a common literary device in the Hebrew Scriptures. For extensive treatments, see Zakovitch, *"For Three"*; Paul, *Amos*, 27–30; Talmon, "Topped"; Golani, "Three."

Ps 15	Ps 19	Ps 24
	Creation (2–7)	Creation (1–2)
Righteousness 1. Question (1) 2. Answer (2–5b) 3. Result (5c)	Torah Righteousness (8–11) *3+1 structure* **Human Righteousness** (12–15)	Righteousness (3–6) 1. Question 2. Answer 3. Result *+1* Community
		Arrival (7–10)

Table 5.5: Structural correspondences between Psalms 15, 19, and 24.

Like Psalms 15 and 24, Psalm 19 also has three parts (vv. 2–7[1–6], 8–11[7–10], 12–15[11–14]), and also focuses on righteousness and the result of such righteousness for the human (underlined in the Table). Psalm 19 differs from both Psalms 15 and 24 by including two parts focused on righteousness—human righteousness and Torah righteousness—binding those ideas closely together. The structure of Psalm 19 bridges the content of Psalms 15 and 24 in that its first part focuses on creation, just as Psalm 24 does. Like Psalm 24, Psalm 19 also has a 'three-plus-one' structural element (Pss 19:8–11[7–10]; 24:3–6).[25]

There are certainly structural similarities between these three psalms, and yet the differences between them carry the narrative strand forward. The focus on creation in Psalms 19 and 24 creates a sense of spatial expansion: The setting of Psalm 15 is the holy mountain in Jerusalem (v. 1); in Psalm 19, the revelation of YHWH goes out into all creation (vv. 2–7[1–6]); in Psalm 24, all of creation is under YHWH's dominion (vv. 1–2). In addition to spatial expansion, there is an expansion to the community in Psalm 24: The focus of Psalms 15 and 19 is on the righteous individual, but in Psalm 24:6, all "those who seek YHWH" are present for his arrival. Finally, and most significantly, the entire collection closes with the climactic arrival of YHWH as king of the world (Ps 24:7–10),

---

25. All three psalms also contain an ABA'B' structure, not represented in the chart (Pss 15:2, 3, 4a-b, 4c-5b; 19:2–4, 5–7, 8–11, 12–15; 24:7, 8, 9, 10). In Psalm 19, this structure is a second overlaying structure to its three-part structure, which is not uncommon. See Quinn, *Arrival*.

which is unparalleled in the structures of Psalms 15 and 19. YHWH's arrival provides resolution to the initial question of the collection: Who may access YHWH's presence (Ps 15:1)? A comparison of psalm structures reveals some meaningful ways that Psalms 19 and 24 push the story forward. Let us now look at some additional ways that Psalm 19 develops the story, before exploring how Psalm 24 does the same.

Psalms 15 and 19: Correlation and Development

In its present position in the collection, Psalm 19's correlations with Psalm 15 have the effect of developing the storyline. An exploration of statistically significant correlations between the two psalms can shed light on which are most likely intentional and, therefore, most important to pay attention to when it comes to discerning the meaning of the relationship.

Psalm 15 is all about defining the perfectly righteous one who may access YHWH's presence. The description of the righteous worshiper alternates in an ABA'B' forward symmetry, describing the things they do (vv. 2, 4a–b) and do not do (vv. 3, 4c–5b). Righteousness permeates the whole person, with special emphasis given to their speech—they speak the truth in their heart (v. 2c), do not slander (v. 3a) or lift up reproach against a close one (v. 3c), and swear oaths without changing (4c). The description of the righteous worshiper may leave readers with the question: How could one attain such perfection? Significant correlations with Psalm 19—especially the theme of *speech* and lexemes related to *righteousness*—provide an answer to this question.

Speech is a major theme only in Psalms 15, 19, and 24 across the collection, making it significant. In Psalm 15, the speech is that of the righteous worshiper. In Psalm 19, speech is that of creation and the Torah. This difference provides a clue to how one becomes the righteous worshiper. After the title, Psalm 19 consists of three parts: The first focuses on the communication of creation (vv. 2–7[1–6]); the second focuses on the communication and character of the Torah (vv. 8–11[7–10]); the third focuses on the servant's prayer that his speech and character would be blameless (vv. 12–15[11–14]). The progression is meaningful—the psalmist's prayer in part three expresses a desire that the quality of his speech and character would correspond to what parts one and two of the psalm were all about: the speech of creation and the speech of YHWH's Torah. This, along with the shift in focus from the *righteous one's speech* in Psalm 15 to *creation* and *the Torah's speech* in Psalm 19, implies that in order to become the righteous worshiper of Psalm 15, one has resources in YHWH's created order and in his Torah. Significant lexemes shared by Psalms 15 and 19 further the point: Psalm 15 uses the lexemes *blameless* תמם and *truth* אמת to describe the righteous worshiper,[26] but Psalm 19 reuses them to describe the Torah. The effect again is that the Torah is one of the resources a person has for becoming the righteous one of Psalm 15, who may enter YHWH's presence.

But what if a person is *not* righteous? Have they lost the privilege of entering YHWH's presence? Corresponding significant lexemes can also shed light on the developing storyline here. In Psalm 15, the worshiper is described as *innocent* נקה and *blameless* תמם. The use of these lexemes in the psalmist's prayer in Psalm 19 (vv. 13–14[12–13]) sheds light on how one who is not innocent may become so: The psalmist prays for YHWH to search out hidden sins and *acquit* him (נקה), and that this (along with keeping from sin), will make him *blameless* and *innocent*. It seems that the depiction is that one may become the *blameless one* of Psalm 15 through the forgiveness of sin by YHWH. This is a significant development since Psalm 15 pictures only a perfectly righteous human being able to enter YHWH's presence.

The lexeme *tent* אהל is another significant link between Psalms 15 and 19 that further elaborates how relentless YHWH is in his forgiveness and deliverance of his people. In Psalm 19, it's the sun that dwells in a *tent* (v. 5[4]); *tent* is a significant lexeme only used of God's dwelling in the psalm group (Ps 15:1), implying an analogy between God and the sun. Internal coherence within Psalm 19 further supports this conclusion. Within Psalm 19, YHWH's activity is united with that of the sun thematically and through the lexeme *hidden* סתר : Just as the sun actively goes from extremity to extremity, and "nothing is *hidden* from its heat" (vv. 5–7[4–6]), YHWH actively discerns all parts of a human heart, including the *hidden* errors (vv. 13–14[12–13]). This analogy depicts YHWH as relentless in delivering his people from sin to present them as blameless and innocent before him (v. 14[13]).

To summarize, Psalm 15 opens the collection with the desire to dwell in YHWH's presence, and describes the righteousness required to ascend to his dwelling place. When we reach Psalm 19, we find, again, the theme of Torah righteousness along with the new theme of creation. Analysis of

---

26. *Truth* is also a significant morphological link, occurring in only two places in the whole collection as אמת.

significant elements in Psalm 19 reveals that to dwell in YHWH's presence as the righteous one of Psalm 15, one has resources in the created order, in God's instruction, and in his relentless forgiveness.

Correlation and Development in Psalm 24

At the close of the collection, Psalm 24 echoes and develops the content of Psalms 15 and 19. Psalm 24, like Psalm 19, opens with all creation in view (vv. 1–2). Like Psalm 15, Psalm 24 returns to the question of who may ascend. The question has been thoroughly explored in Psalms 15 and 19; Psalm 24 provides only a brief summary, using significant repeated lexemes to describe the righteous one. Like Psalm 15, both the speech and action of the worshiper are the focus, using the lexically and morphologically significant elements *swear* שׁבע and *lift up* נשׂא. The lexeme *lift up* occurs as part of a significant phrase in both psalms to describe righteous action (*not lift up* לא־נשׂא Pss 15:3; 24:4).

The significant lexeme, *innocent/clean* נקה, also creates a correlation, recalling the forgiveness offered in Psalm 19. Psalm 15 had defined the righteous one as *blameless* תמם; Psalm 19 had said YHWH, through forgiveness and Torah, would make the worshiper *blameless* and *innocent*, and now in Psalm 24, this worshiper stands with *innocent/clean* hands before the gate of YHWH.

In addition to its close correspondences, Psalm 24 also introduces new themes to the storyline—namely, *community* and *the arrival of YHWH the warrior*. These themes both develop the storyline and also bear continuity with Psalms 15 and 19 through the use of significant corresponding vocabulary. The theme of *community* in Psalm 24 is an additional structural element in comparison to Psalms 15 and 19 (refer to Table 5.5 above). In Psalm 24, we find God's people, called the "seekers of YHWH" and "Jacob," present just before the arrival of YHWH at his holy temple (Ps 24:6). It is fitting that the significant lexical root of *Jacob*, עקב, is the same root used in Psalm 19:12 to speak of the *result* or *reward* of keeping the Torah.[27] The correlation has the effect of identifying this community called *Jacob*, who is present at the arrival of King YHWH, as a Torah-keeping community.

---

27. It is likely that this root also recalls the use of *Jacob* in Psalm 22, where all of Israel and the nations gather to feast with YHWH after the human king is delivered from death by the glorious King YHWH.

The arrival of YHWH as the glorious king in Psalm 24:7–10 is the climax of the plot in the collection and uses significant lexemes introduced earlier, especially in Psalm 19. In this culminating section of Psalm 24, YHWH is called the *mighty one* גבור and the king of *glory* כבד multiple times. The description of YHWH as the king of *glory* recalls how, in Psalm 19, the skies are declaring the *glory* of God (v. 2[1]). There, the sun is the primary example of this glory, in its persistent, consistent activity, which goes out into the whole earth (vv. 5–7[4–6]). The description of YHWH as the *mighty one* in Psalm 24 is, in fact, the same word used in Psalm 19 of the sun—this is the only other time the word is used in the collection, and it is both lexically and morphologically significant. Recall how within Psalm 19 itself, YHWH is set in analogy to the sun, as one who actively delivers his people from sin to present them as blameless and innocent before him. So, when Psalm 24 calls YHWH the king of *glory*, and the *mighty one*, it portrays YHWH as a persistent, active, and engaged deliverer of his people. Psalm 19 calls YHWH a *rock* צור and *redeemer* to summarize YHWH's delivering work of the psalmist from internal sin (v. 15[14]). It is worth noting that the identification of YHWH as a *rock* likely recalls the same significant word used of YHWH throughout the previous Psalm 18, where YHWH is depicted as a warrior who delivers his king in battle (vv. 3[2], 32[31], 47[46]). While connections with Psalm 18 are not the focus of the present study, those connections are interesting to note in relation to the depiction of YHWH as a *glorious mighty one*. The result is that the description of YHWH as a *mighty one*, by analogy to the *glorious* sun in Psalms 19 and 24, refers to his persistent, perpetual rescue of his people from both internal and external threat.

The storyline of Psalms 15–24 ends with this mighty, delivering king arriving to claim all of creation as his kingdom and invite all those who seek his face into his presence on his holy mountain (Ps 24:6). The collection closes by recalling the promise in Psalm 15 that the righteous worshiper would dwell in YHWH's presence *eternally* עולם (Ps 15:5c): The *eternal* doors are lifted up (24:7, 9), so that YHWH and all those who seek him would dwell together in his holy space.

Conclusions and Future Potential

Through analysis of statistically significant repeated elements in Psalms 15, 19, and 24, I am convinced that these psalms are intentionally linked and should be read in conversation with one another. While a reader may certainly compare texts through close reading and observation, the benefit of mathematical analysis is that we can give attention to those shared elements that are most plausibly intentional. An exploration of those elements suggests that, taken together, these three psalms frame the collection with the goal of entering into YHWH's presence and dwelling with him forever. These psalms reveal not only that the righteous may do so, but that God is an active participant in delivering his people and making them blameless before him. The story ends with this delivering, cosmic king arriving on his holy mountain and dwelling with all those who seek his presence, forever.

These three psalms have provided a helpful case study for demonstrating the payoff of using this method. This method has the potential to discern the significant connections and message of entire psalm groups (e.g., Psalms 15–24) and books of the Psalter (e.g., Psalms 1–41), by carrying out the same methodology for each potential psalm pair. Applying this method to psalm groups has the potential to reveal a tightly structured overarching shape. In the case of Psalms 15–24, this group forms a chiastic structure, with Psalms 18–21 closely united at the center to portray a Torah-obedient king, and a movement toward YHWH's cosmic kingdom in the latter half of the chiasm. Once the structure of individual collections is established, individual psalms may be compared across collections to see which psalms are most closely linked together and what kinds of overarching structures emerge. The same can be done at the level of the entire Psalter, especially giving attention to those psalms that occur at structurally prominent positions: at the seams and centers of collections.

This method could also shed light on intentional correlations and therefore the overarching shape and message of anthologies like the Book of the Twelve or Proverbs. Each book or proverb could be treated as a discrete unit and its literary elements (lexemes, themes, etc.) compared mathematically to every other book or proverb, to see what significant correlations occur and where. Mathematical comparison could take the form of an analysis of rarity or statistical significance. The result could be an overarching shape (on the level of the whole or within sub-collections) or could simply be the identification of literary elements that are likely intentional links between literary units. Comparing the literary units which contain the intentional links (especially where there is a cluster of links) to discern what developments occur between the units could help scholars understand whether and how these anthologies also show any sense of narrativity, as the Psalter does.

Bibliography

Alter, Robert. *The Art of Biblical Narrative*. 2nd ed. New York: Basic, 2011.
———. *The Art of Biblical Poetry*. 2nd ed. New York: Basic, 2011.
Augustine. *Enarrationes in Psalmos*. Edited by E. Dekkers and J. Fraipont. CCSL 38. Steenbrugge: Brepols, 1990.
Barth, Christoph. "Concatenatio im ersten Buch des Psalters." In *Wort and Wirklichkeit: Studien zur Afrikanistik und Orientalistik,* edited by Brigitta Benzing et al., 30–40. Meisenheim am Glan: Hain, 1976.
Berlin, Adele. *The Dynamics of Biblical Parallelism*. Rev. ed. Grand Rapids: Eerdmans, 2008.
Calvin, John. *Commentary on the Book of Psalms*. Translated by James Anderson. 5 vols. Edinburgh: Calvin Translation Society, 1557.
Childs, Brevard S. *Introduction to the Old Testament as Scripture*. Philadelphia: Fortress, 1979.
Fokkelman, J. P. *The Remaining 65 Psalms*. Vol. 3 of *Major Poems of the Hebrew Bible: At the Interface of Prosody and Structural Analysis*. SSN 43. Assen: Royal Van Gorcum, 2003.
Golani, Shira J. "Three Oppressors and Four Saviors—The Three-Four Pattern and the List of Saviors in 1 Sam 12,9–11." *ZAW* 127.2 (2015) 294–303.
Howard, David M., Jr. *The Structure of Psalms 93–100*. BJSUCSD 5. Winona Lake: Eisenbrauns, 1997.
Jerome. *Commentarioli in Psalmos*. Edited by P. de Lagarde et al. CCSL 72. Turnhout: Brepols, 1959.
Luther, Martin. *Luthers Werke*. 63 vols. Weimar: Böhlau, 1883–1987.
Origen. *Selecta in Psalmos*. Ed. Lommatzsch.
Paul, Shalom M. *A Commentary on the Book of Amos*. Hermeneia. Minneapolis: Augsburg Fortress, 1991.
Quinn, Carissa. *The Arrival of the King*. Bellingham: Lexham, 2024 (*forthcoming*).
Snearly, Michael K. "The Return of the King: Book V as a Witness to Messianic Hope in the Psalter." In *The Psalms: Language for All Seasons of the Soul*, edited by A. J. Schmutzer and D. M. Howard Jr., 209–17. Chicago: Moody, 2013.
Talmon, Shemaryahu. "The Topped Triad in the Hebrew Bible and the Ascending Numerical Pattern." In *Literary Motifs and Patters in the Hebrew Bible: Collected Studies*, 77–124. University Park: Penn State University Press, 2021.
Weber, Beat. *Die Psalmen 1 bis 72*. Vol. 1 of *Werkbuch Psalmen*. Stuttgart: Kohlhammer, 2001.
Westermann, Claus. *Praise and Lament in the Psalms*. Translated by Keith R. Crim and Richard N. Soulen. Atlanta: John Knox, 1981.

Wilson, Gerald H. *The Editing of the Hebrew Psalter*. SBLDS 76. Chico: Scholars, 1985.
Zakovitch, Yair. *"For Three . . . and for Four": The Pattern of the Numerical Sequence Three-Four in the Bible*. 2 vols. Hebrew. Jerusalem: Makor, 1979.
Zimmerli, W. "Zwillingspsalmen." In *Wort, Lied, und Gottesspruch: Beiträge zu Psalmen und Propheten*, edited by Josef Schreiner, 105–13. Würzburg: Echter, 1972.

PART 2
Thematic Approaches

CHAPTER 6

The Conceptualization of the Eternal Covenant in the Book of the Twelve in Dialogue with the Understanding of the Covenant in the Book of Psalms

MARVIN A. SWEENEY

THE CONCEPTUALIZATION OF THE covenant between YHWH and Israel/Judah throughout the Hebrew Bible is subject to serious reflection and diversity of viewpoints.[1] With regard to the Pentateuch, Genesis 17, Exodus 31:12–18, Leviticus 24:5–9, Numbers 18:12–18, and Numbers 25:6–15 display different aspects of an eternal, unconditional covenant (see also Gen 9), whereas Deuteronomy 28–30 presents a conditional understanding of a covenant that takes account of its unconditional aspects once Israel repents and returns to YHWH after having violated the stipulations of the book.[2] The Former Prophets likewise posit an eternal, unconditional covenant for the House of David in 2 Samuel 7 and 23:1–7, whereas 1 Kings 2:1–4, 8:25–26, and 9:1–9 posit a conditional covenant with the House of David that presupposes royal observance

---

1. Sweeney, "Eternal Covenant," 1–19. See also Mason, *Eternal Covenant.*
2. Sweeney, "Eternal Covenant," 4–10. See also Shechter, *Land.*

of YHWH's commands.³ The Latter Prophets also present evidence of such reflection and rethinking.⁴ Isaiah 55 redefines the eternal covenant between YHWH and the House of David to include all Israel as well as the Davidic dynasty,⁵ and Jeremiah 33:14–26, which is absent in the Septuagint form of the book, expands the eternal covenant with the House of David to include the city of Jerusalem and the Levitical priesthood as well.⁶ Ezekiel affirms the notion of an eternal covenant for both Jerusalem in Ezekiel 16:59–63 and Israel at large in Ezekiel 37:26. Ezekiel does not envision any supplanting of the role of the House of David as indicated by the references to the Davidic King in Ezekiel 37:24, although the book frequently refers to the King as Prince.⁷

All of these examples display a necessary willingness to rethink early notions of an unconditional eternal covenant in relation to the realities of the historical experiences of Israel and Judah, who are subjugated by major ancient Near Eastern superpowers such as Assyria, Babylonia, and Persia, and whose Davidic dynasty is ultimately compromised and removed from power by those nations. Such willingness is also evident in the Book of the Twelve Prophets and the Book of Psalms. In the case of the Book of the Twelve, the eternal covenant is never mentioned, but the so-called "bookends" in Hosea and Malachi put forward an understanding of covenant that envisions disruption and restoration—Hosea does this through the metaphorical depiction of marriage between the groom, YHWH, and the bride, Israel; Malachi recounts YHWH's hatred for divorce with the understanding that the metaphorical marriage between YHWH and Israel will nevertheless continue.⁸ In the case of Psalms, Psalm 105:10–11 refers to YHWH's covenant with Jacob, that is, Israel (see also 1 Chron 16:17), although other psalms, such as Psalms 89 and 132, present a variety of viewpoints concerning the nature of the covenant in relation to the House of David or Jerusalem.⁹

This essay, therefore, examines the conceptualization of the covenant in the Book of the Twelve Prophets and the Book of Psalms. Although both the Twelve and the Psalms display a diversity of viewpoints

3. Sweeney, "Eternal Covenant," 10–13. See also Nelson, *Double*, 99–118.
4. Sweeney, "Eternal Covenant," 13–17.
5. See also Sweeney, "Davidic Covenant in Isaiah," 41–61; *Isaiah 40–66*, 235–48.
6. See also Goldman, *Prophétie*, 9–64; Sweeney, "Books of Jeremiah," 167–81.
7. For discussion of Ezekiel 37:15–28, see Sweeney, "Royal Oracle," 239–53.
8. Sweeney "Eternal Covenant," 16–17.
9. Sweeney, "Eternal Covenant," 17.

within their respective purviews, both ultimately affirm an unconditional covenant between YHWH and Israel (or Jerusalem) / Judah. Such an affirmation stands in agreement with the conceptualization of the covenant in the Pentateuch, the Former Prophets, and the Latter Prophets, although the variety of viewpoints expressed within each major element of the Hebrew Bible points to a serious process of reflection and reconceptualization of the covenant in relation to the realities of Israel and Judah's historical experiences.

I. Eternal Covenant in the Book of the Twelve

The Book of the Twelve Prophets constitutes a single prophetic book in Jewish tradition that includes twelve discrete prophetic compositions, whereas the Minor Prophets in the Christian traditions constitute twelve discrete books that are considered collectively as the Dodekapropheton.[10] At least two major forms of the Twelve Prophets or Minor Prophets are extant. The Masoretic Hebrew version of the Book of the Twelve, which constitutes the biblical book as part of the Latter Prophets in Judaism, also constitutes a witness to the Minor Prophets as part of the Christian Old Testament. The Masoretic version presents the order of the Twelve as Hosea, Joel, Amos, Obadiah, Jonah, Micah, Nahum, Habakkuk, Zephaniah, Haggai, Zechariah, and Malachi, which emphasizes the role of Jerusalem in the pattern of judgment and restoration in the sequence of the Twelve. The Septuagint version of the book presents the order as Hosea, Amos, Micah, Joel, Obadiah, Jonah, Nahum, Habakkuk, Zephaniah, Haggai, Zechariah, and Malachi, which emphasizes the experience of the northern kingdom of Israel in the first three books as a model for the experience of Judah in the subsequent nine books of the sequence. A third order is evident in 4QXII, one of the major Twelve Prophets scrolls at Qumran, which clearly portrays Jonah following Malachi, but no complete copy of this sequence has survived, nor does it constitute sacred scripture for any movement, Jewish or Christian, in the modern world.

Despite their differences, both the Masoretic Hebrew and the Septuagint Greek versions of the Book of the Twelve Prophets begin the sequence with Hosea and conclude it with Malachi. This observation is important theologically because it points to the understanding of

---

10. For discussion, see Sweeney, *Twelve Prophets*, xv-xlii; "Sequence," 175–88; "Synchronic," 21–33; "Minor Prophets," 238–41; "Book of the XII," 267–78.

covenant among the parties that assembled the books and arranged them in their respective contexts, that is, the rabbinic tradition in the case of the Masoretic Hebrew text and the Alexandrian Jewish tradition in the case of the Septuagint Greek version. Although proto-Masoretic Hebrew copies of the book appear among the Judean wilderness scrolls, and a Greek version of the Book of the Twelve appears as well, all versions of the Book of the Twelve, apart from 4QXII, follow the Masoretic Hebrew sequence. No Judean Wilderness scroll represents a Hebrew *Vorlage* for the Septuagint Greek sequence, although Talmudic tradition appears to be aware of at least the arrangement of the first three books (b. B. Bat 14b). As noted above, the phrase, "eternal covenant" (*bĕrît 'ôlām*, or Greek, *diathēkēn aiōnion*), does not appear in the Book of the Twelve in either its Hebrew or Greek versions. Nevertheless, the use of the marriage metaphor to portray the covenant relationship between YHWH and Israel/Judah contextualizes the understanding of the covenant as an eternal covenant that is threatened at the outset in Hosea by the portrayal of Israel's abandoning of YHWH for other gods (Hos 1–3). The covenant is nevertheless affirmed at the end in Malachi in which YHWH expresses hatred, that is, disapproval or rejection of divorce, which illustrates YHWH's commitment to maintain the covenant forever despite allegations of wrongdoing done by Israel and Judah (Mal 2:16).

Hosea's account of Israel's alleged violation of its covenant with YHWH appears in Hosea 1–3, which opens both the Book of Hosea and the Book of the Twelve in both the Masoretic Hebrew and Septuagint Greek versions of the Twelve.[11] Following the superscription to Hosea in Hosea 1:1, which places the prophet in the late-eighth-century reigns of Uzziah, Jotham, Ahaz, and Hezekiah of Judah, and Jeroboam ben Joash of Israel, Hosea 1:2–9 presents YHWH's instructions to Hosea to marry Gomer, described as "a woman of harlotry," and have children with her. YHWH's instruction is intended to have Hosea engage in a prophetic sign act in which his marriage represents YHWH's relationship with Israel, with Hosea playing the role of YHWH, the husband, and Gomer playing the role of Israel, the allegedly wayward wife. From the sequence of the names of the children—the first son, Jezreel, a reference to the Jezreel Valley; the daughter, Lo-Ruḥamah, "No Mercy"; the second son, Lo-Ammi, "Not My People"—it is clear that the book points to the Jehu dynasty, beginning with King Jehu (842–815 BCE)

---

11. For commentary on Hosea, see Sweeney, *Twelve*, 1:1–144. See also Baumann, *Love and Violence*, 7–81, 85–104.

and culminating in the reigns of Jeroboam ben Joash (786–746 BCE) and Zechariah ben Jeroboam (746 BCE). Jehu founded the dynasty in 842 BCE by assassinating the previous Omride King, Jehoram ben Ahab (849–842 BCE) and his vassal, King Ahaziah ben Jehoram of Judah (842 BCE) in Jezreel while Jehoram was recovering from wounds suffered in battle at Ramot Gilead while defending Israel from Aramaean attack. The name of Hosea's first son with Gomer, Jezreel, symbolizes Jehu's overthrow of the ruling Omride dynasty.

Jehu's submission to Shalmanezer III, King of Assyria, was apparently the basis for Hosea's charges that Israel under the Jehu dynasty had abandoned YHWH for other gods, depicted metaphorically as adulterous lovers. As a result of its alleged betrayal of YHWH, Israel would receive "no mercy" from YHWH, as indicated in the name of Hosea's daughter with Gomer, and Israel would no longer be YHWH's people, as indicated in the name of Hosea's second son with Gomer. Jehu's submission to Shalmanezer III is depicted pictorially and in writing in the Black Obelisk of Shalmanezer III (858–824 BCE), a stele carved from black limestone and displayed in a public area in ancient Nimrud.[12] The continuing submission of the ruling House of Jehu to Assyria is also evident in the Tell Rimah Inscription of Adad-Nirari III, King of Assyria (811–783 BCE), which names Jehoash ben Jehoahaz, King of Israel (801–786 BCE) and grandson of Jehu, as one of his many vassals.[13] The reason for the relationship between the House of Jehu and the Assyrian empire was to gain protection from the Aramaeans, who were continually threatening Israel by attacking the Trans-Jordanian region in order to invade the Jezreel Valley and subjugate Israel. King Ahab ben Omri of Israel (869–850 BCE) had been killed by the Arameans at Ramot Gilead, and his son, Jehoram, was later wounded there, only to be assassinated by Jehu because of Israel's failure to defeat the Aramaeans. In Hosea's view, such an alliance was forbidden, particularly since it entailed engaging in trade with both Assyria and its ally, Egypt (Israel's traditional enemy from the Exodus tradition), in olive oil and other commodities (Hos 12:2). Hosea rejected the view that Assyria could save Israel as opposed to its own G-d, YHWH (Hos 14:2–9). Such an alliance would also entail recognition of Assyrian gods as indicated in Hosea and in the ratification ceremonies of Assyrian vassal

---

12. Pritchard, *ANEP*, 351, 355.
13. Page, "Stela of Adad Nirari," 139–53.

treaties, which called for the signatories to pass between the severed bodies of animals sacrificed to their respective gods.

Hosea's concern with Israel's relationship with foreign gods is evident in Hosea 2, in which Hosea 2:1–2 cites elements of the ancestral covenant between YHWH and Israel that refer to YHWH's promises to Jacob (also known as Israel), the eponymous ancestor of Israel, to make the nation as numerous as "the sands of the sea" (Gen 32:13[12]; cf. Gen 22:17, in which YHWH makes the same promise to Abraham). It continues in Hosea 2:3–25, in which Hosea accuses Gomer of committing adultery with other lovers, although the metaphorical imagery gives way in Hosea 2:11 as it becomes evident that YHWH is the aggrieved husband, and that Israel is the wayward bride. In the closing segment of Hosea 2:16–25, YHWH announces his intention to take back his bride, Israel, and thereby to restore the marriage relationship that had been disrupted by Israel's alleged adultery. Hosea 2:21 includes YHWH's statement, "and I will espouse you to myself forever," which constitutes YHWH's pledge to maintain the covenant with Israel forever.

Various concerns that are in some way connected with the concept of covenant appear among the subsequent prophetic compositions of the Book of the Twelve.[14] Joel portrays YHWH's defense of Jerusalem; Amos portrays YHWH's dissatisfaction with northern Israel's treatment of its vassal, southern Judah; Obadiah condemns Edom for its role in Jerusalem's subjugation; Micah decries the policies of the Israelite and Judean kings who made him a refugee; Jonah portrays the northern prophet's futile attempts to escape his task of calling Assyria to repentance, which will later result in Israel's destruction; Nahum celebrates YHWH's defeat of Nineveh; Habakkuk questions YHWH's role in subjugating Judah to Babylon; Zephaniah calls for Judah to repent on the Day of YHWH; Haggai anticipates the building of the Second Temple and Zerubbabel's never-realized role as the next King of Judah; and Zechariah looks forward to a Davidic monarch who will subdue Jerusalem's oppressors, likely the Persian empire, once the Temple is rebuilt. Nevertheless, only Hosea and Malachi are directly concerned with the concept of covenant per se, particularly as it is metaphorically expressed as a marriage between YHWH and Israel/Judah.

Malachi portrays YHWH's rejection of divorce in the context of the metaphorical marriage between YHWH and Israel/Judah, which entails

---

14. For commentary on each of the Twelve Prophets mentioned here, see Sweeney, *Twelve*, ad loc.

YHWH's never-ending commitment to the covenant.[15] The composition is identified in its superscription as "a pronouncement, the word of YHWH to Israel, by the hand of Malachi." Although Malachi (*mal'ākî*), now functions as a personal name in Hebrew, the term means, "my messenger, angel," which may refer to a messenger or angel who speaks on behalf of YHWH, perhaps based on the portrayal of YHWH's messenger who will lead Israel through the wilderness in Exodus 23:20, 33:2, and Numbers 20:16. Interpreters have raised questions concerning the formal character of the book, insofar as its identification as a *maśśā'* ("pronouncement") may identify as the third pronouncement in Zechariah that follows other such pronouncements in Zechariah 9–11 and 12–14.

The literary form of Malachi appears as a parenetic address to the priests and people of Persian period Judah, apparently in the period leading up to the reforms of Nehemiah and Ezra, which is designed to persuade them to provide proper reverence for YHWH. Following the superscription in Malachi 1:1, the body of the book presents a succession of six disputation speeches that call upon the audience to properly observe YHWH's expectations. They include Malachi 1:2–5, which argues that YHWH loves the people; Malachi 1:6–2:9, which argues that the priesthood must honor YHWH with proper offerings at the Temple altar; Malachi 2:10–16, which argues that the people must sanctify themselves with proper marriage practices; Malachi 2:17–3:7, which argues that YHWH's messenger will come to establish proper practices of YHWH's justice; Malachi 3:6–12, which argues that proper Temple tithes will bring YHWH's blessing; Malachi 3:13–24, which calls on the people to observe YHWH's Torah.

The understanding of the covenant is key here. Malachi concludes with exhortations in Malachi 3:22 to remember the Torah, that is, the "Instruction" of Moses that YHWH commanded at Mt. Horeb, the alternative name of Mt. Sinai in Deuteronomy. This is followed by YHWH's pledge in Malachi 3:23–24 to send Elijah the prophet prior to the coming Day of YHWH to restore the hearts of fathers for their sons and sons for their fathers to avoid the destruction of the entire land. Altogether, Malachi appears designed to anticipate the reforms of Ezra and possibly Nehemiah before him.

The third disputation in Malachi 2:10–16 argues that the people have profaned the covenant of their ancestors by defiling the marriages

---

15. For commentary on Malachi, see Sweeney, *Twelve*, 2:713–52. See also Pfeiffer, "Die Disputationsworte," 546–88; Jacobs, *Haggai*, 127–336.

of their youth due to marriages with foreign women who worshiped foreign gods. Such a statement entails divorcing or abandoning marriages with Jewish women for marriages or relationships with foreign women who would not be able to raise their children in the traditions of Judaism. The disputation concludes in Malachi 2:16 with YHWH's assertion, "I hate divorce" (šalaḥ, literally, "sending away [a wife]"), and further assertions that such divorce results in "violence that covers over his garment," that it results in trouble, and that "you should be observant in your spirit so that you do not betray," the covenant with YHWH. Throughout this disputation, it is clear that marriage and divorce are employed as metaphors for observing or abandoning YHWH's covenant with Israel/Judah. By asserting that YHWH hates divorce, Malachi 2:10–16 calls its audience to a continuing adherence to the covenant with YHWH so as not to follow other gods due to marriage with foreign women who would worship such deities.

The focus on the metaphorical portrayal of the covenant with YHWH as a marriage relationship in Malachi coincides with the analogous use of the metaphor in Hosea. In both cases, YHWH calls upon the men to restore their marriages—for Hosea to reconcile with Gomer and thereby bring her back both to her husband and to YHWH, and for the men in Malachi to return to the marriages of their youth and thereby to abandon the foreign wives that they have subsequently married. In both cases, the metaphorical marriage relationship with YHWH is at stake, and the concern with Jews married to foreign women is an important feature of the covenant reforms enacted by Nehemiah and Ezra. One may observe that neither Nehemiah nor Ezra ever disputed the role of conversion to Judaism, such as that portrayed in the Book of Ruth. Indeed, they appear to know something of Deuteronomy, which includes an instruction in Deuteronomy 21:10–14 as to how a foreign woman might become a part of Israel and therefore a convert to Judaism.

It is doubtful that either Hosea or Malachi were composed to serve as the so-called "bookends" of the Book of the Twelve. There is no clear evidence of intentional modeling of the one or the other; both appear to have their own distinctive forms, settings, and concerns that gravitate around the integrity and continuity of the covenant between Israel/Judah and YHWH.[16] Rather, they appear to have been selected by the compilers

---

16. Contra Nogalski, *Twelve*; *Literary*; *Redactional*; Wöhrle, *Sammlungen*; *Der Abschluss*, who argue that motifs, such as the Day of YHWH, indicate evidence of a comprehensive redaction of the Book of the Twelve despite that fact that these motifs do

of the Book of the Twelve for their respective roles as the introductory and closing prophetic compositions in both the Masoretic Hebrew and Septuagint Greek forms of the Book of the Twelve Prophets. Even so, the two models differ. Hosea envisions a model in which the bride, whether Gomer or Israel, repents and remains with her husband, whether Hosea or YHWH. Malachi envisions a model in which the husband(s) repent, divorce their foreign wives, and return to the Jewish wives of their youth. Such a model reinforces the conclusion that Hosea and Malachi were not composed to serve as "bookends" for the Book of the Twelve; rather, they are discrete compositions that were put in their places by the compilers of the Book of the Twelve. Nevertheless, the Book of the Twelve Prophets envisions a covenant that might be profaned, but nevertheless can be re-sanctified. The Book appears to respond to the Book of Isaiah, which in Isaiah 55, expands the Davidic covenant to include all Israel, by asserting that a Davidic monarch will act on YHWH's behalf to ensure Zion's sanctity as a place where nations may come together in peace and independence from foreign oppression. Although portions of the Book of the Twelve employ hymnic elements or entire psalms, especially in the hymnic element of Amos, Jonah 2, Nahum 1, and Habakkuk 3,[17] there is no clearly deliberate reference to the Book of Psalms.

II. Eternal Covenant in the Book of Psalms

The Book of Psalms is a compilation of 150 hymnic compositions in the Masoretic Hebrew version of the book that would have served as the hymn book for the Jerusalem Temple.[18] The Septuagint version of the book includes 151 psalms, although they are grouped so that they number 150. The Syriac Peshiṭta includes 155 psalms. The Masoretic Book of Psalms comprises five distinct books— Psalms 1–41, 42–72, 73–89, 90–106, and 107–150—each with their own hymnic conclusion. Interpreters have suggested various bases for the organization of the psalms into five books, such as a process of continued growth of the book over time from one to five books or an attempt to correlate the five books of psalms with the five books of the Torah, but so far, no

---

not appear consistently throughout the entire book. For discussion, see esp. Sweeney, "Minor Prophets"; "Book of the XII."

17. For discussions of the hymnic elements in Amos, Jonah, Nahum, and Habakkuk, see Sweeney, *Twelve*, ad loc.

18. Sweeney, *Tanak*, 375–97.

satisfactory theory for its organization has yet gained widespread acceptance. But an overview of the individual psalms within the book that take up concern with the *bĕrît*, "covenant" (i.e., Psalms 25, 44, 50, 74, 78, 89, 103, 105, 106, 111, and 132), indicate that those concerned with an eternal, unconditional covenant (i.e., Psalms 103, 105, and 111) appear in Book IV (and V) of the Psalms (Pss 90–106), whereas the other psalms that posit conditions for the covenant appear in Books I, II, III, and V. A survey of the psalms concerned with the *bĕrît*, "covenant," will illumine their distinctive concerns.

Psalm 25 (Book I) is a congregational complaint, attributed to David and formulated as an acrostic, which appeals to YHWH for deliverance from enemies.[19] Following the superscription in verse 1a, it includes an affirmation of confidence in YHWH in verses 1b–3, a petition in verses 4–7, hymnic praise in verses 8–11, an exhortation in verses 12–15, and another petition in verses 16–22. In its appeal for divine support against enemies, the hymnic praise in verses 8–11 and the exhortation in verses 12–15 take up concerns with YHWH's covenant. Psalm 25:10 emphasizes that YHWH's paths express fidelity and truth (*ḥesed we'ĕmet*), for "those who keep his covenant and his testimonies." Psalm 25:14 asserts that YHWH's "secret counsel" (*sôd*) is available to those who fear or revere (*lîrē'āyw*) YHWH, specified as those to whom YHWH makes known his covenant. The psalm does not refer to an eternal covenant, although such an understanding might be inferred from its connection with YHWH and YHWH's fidelity and truth. Nevertheless, the emphasis on those who keep YHWH's covenant and testimonies and those who revere YHWH suggests that the covenant is conditioned on one's observance of the covenant and its requirements.

Psalm 44 (Book II) is a communal complaint, which is identified as a *maśkîl*, "a didactic song."[20] Psalm 44 is part of the Songs of Korah and also part of the Elohistic collection in Psalms 42–83, which may have originated in northern Israel.[21] The psalm is once again concerned with deliverance from enemies, although it stresses that G-d hides the divine face in verse 25.[22] Following the superscription in verse 1, the psalm comprises a hymnic remembrance in verses 2–9, a complaint in verses 10–17, a protestation of innocence in verses 18–23, and a petition in

---

19. Gerstenberger, *Psalms, Part 1*, 119–21.
20. Gerstenberger, *Psalms, Part 1*, 182–86.
21. Rendsburg, *Linguistic*, 51–60.
22. Balentine, *Hidden*.

verses 24–27. The one reference to the covenant appears at the beginning of the protestation of innocence in verse 18, in which the psalmists protest that they suffer despite the fact that they have not forgotten G-d and did not betray (*wĕlō' šiqqarnû*, "and we did not make false"), G-d's covenant. Verse 18 indicates a conditional understanding of covenant in which the people might be punished for forgetting G-d or violating the divine covenant, although such punishment is envisioned in cases of wrongdoing by David's sons in 2 Samuel 7. Indeed, verse 27 appeals to G-d's fidelity (*ḥesed*), in calling for deliverance.

Psalm 50 (Book II), identified as "a song of Asaph" in verse 1, constitutes a communal instruction or sermon that critiques those who observe the covenant superficially while otherwise acting in ways that are contrary to G-d's expectations.[23] The psalm comprises the superscription in the first two Hebrew words of verse 1, an introduction in verses 1–6, and divine discourse or instruction in verses 7–23. It refers to the covenant twice. The first reference in verse 5 simply refers to those who have made a covenant with G-d concerning the presentation of the sacrifice, that is, the *zebaḥ*, which likely refers to the *zebaḥ šĕlāmîm* (Lev 3), which is eaten at the Temple by the people. The second reference in verse 16 upbraids those who are wicked even as they recite G-d's statutes and pronounce his covenant (*watiśśā' bĕrîtî 'ălê-pîkā*, "and you raise my covenant upon your mouth"). The psalm clearly envisions punishment for the violation of the covenant as portrayed here, although again there is no clear indication that the covenant will be ended.

Psalm 74 (Book III), identified as a *maśkîl*, "didactic song," of Asaph in verse 1, is another Elohistic psalm that perhaps originated in northern Israel. It is a communal complaint that calls upon G-d to observe the covenant and rise up against enemies that have burned the divine sanctuary, although it appears to presuppose Mt. Zion in verse 2, rather than a northern sanctuary.[24] The psalm comprises the superscription in verse 1, an initial complaint, petition, and hymn in verses 1b–2, a complaint in verses 3–9, a plaintive petition in verses 10–11, a hymn in verses 12–17, and a petition in verses 18–23. The reference to the covenant appears in verse 20 in which the psalmist calls upon G-d to "look to the covenant" (*habîṭ labbĕrît*), as part of the main petition, because the land is full of violence as enemies rampage about, in order to motivate G-d, called YHWH in verse

---

23. Gerstenberger, *Psalms, Part 1*, 207–15.
24. Gerstenberger, *Psalms, Part 2*, 77–81.

18, to rise up to end the shame suffered by G-d and the vulnerable people. The petition does not presume wrongdoing on the part of the people, but it does presume divine fidelity to the covenant by the G-d who acts as creator of the world and redeemer of the people.

Psalm 78 (Book III), also identified as a *maśkîl* of Asaph in verse 1, is yet another example of an Elohistic psalm from Psalms 42–83.[25] The psalm comprises the superscription in verse 1a, an introduction in verses 1b–4, an exhortation in verses 5–8, lessons from Scripture based on the Ephraimites, the Exodus and wilderness, Egypt, and Shiloh in verses 9–64, and the decision of the past in verses 65–72. The lengthy rehearsal of early Israelite history is designed to charge Ephraim, the primary tribe of northern Israel, with having tested G-d repeatedly and not upholding the covenant, with the result that G-d rejected Israel, and chose Judah, Mt. Zion, and David instead. References to covenant appear twice in the psalm. The first reference in verse 10 charges the Ephraimites with not observing the covenant of G-d (*lō' šāměrû běrît 'ĕlōhîm*), and refusing to walk in G-d's Torah. The second in verse 37 charges Israel with being unfaithful to the covenant (*wělō' ne'emnû bibrîtô*). Psalm 78 is very clear that failure to observe YHWH's covenant results in punishment, including rejection of Israel by YHWH, who chooses Judah in Israel's place.

Psalm 89 (Book III), a *maskîl* of Ethan the Ezrahite, is a communal complaint, which charges YHWH with having rejected the eternal covenant with David and calls upon YHWH to demonstrate divine fidelity to protect David and the people from the enemies that threaten them.[26] The psalm includes the superscription in verse 1, initial praise of YHWH in verses 2–3, the Davidic oracle in verses 4–5, a lengthy hymn to YHWH in verses 6–19, a retrospective on the David story in verses 20–38, a complaint in verses 39–46, a petition in verses 47–52, and the praise formula in verse 53. The psalm stresses from the beginning YHWH's eternal fidelity (*ḥasdê yhwh 'ôlām*, vv. 2–3), and YHWH's eternal covenant with David to establish his seed forever (v. 4). Again, in verse 29, YHWH states, "Forever I will observe for him my fidelity, and my covenant is secure for him" (*ne'ĕmenet lô*). Verse 30 continues with YHWH's assertion that "I will set for ever his seed and his throne like the days of heaven," but YHWH continues in verses 31–33 by stating that "If his sons abandon my Torah and in my laws they do not walk; if

---

25. Gerstenberger, *Psalms, Part 2*, 92–100.
26. Gerstenberger, *Psalms, Part 2*, 147–57.

my statutes they profane and my commands they do not observe, then I will punish with the rod their rebellion and with plagues their iniquity." But in verse 34, YHWH states, "But my fidelity I will not break (*lō'-'āpîr*) from him, and I will not betray (*wělō'-'ăšaqqēr*) my faithfulness," and in verse 35 YHWH states, "I will not profane my covenant, and what comes out of my mouth I will not change," before repeating the divine promise to David in verse 37, "his seed forever shall be." Overall, Psalm 89 presumes the eternity of the divine covenant with the House of David, and it calls upon YHWH to observe that commitment at a time when YHWH has hidden the divine face.[27]

Psalm 103 (Book IV), identified as a Song of David in verse 1, is a communal hymn in praise of YHWH.[28] It comprises the superscription in verse 1a, a summons to praise in verses 1b–2, a promissory hymn in verses 3–5, a penitential hymn in verses 6–14, a sapiential hymn in verses 15–18, and a glorifying hymn in verses 19–22. With a brief review of history in the time of Moses, the psalm asserts in verses 17–18 that YHWH's fidelity (*ḥesed*), is for all eternity to all who revere YHWH, and that YHWH's righteousness is for those who observe YHWH's covenant and those who remember to do YHWH's commissions. Such assertions presume the eternity of YHWH's covenant, although they hold out for punishment—or negligence—for those who do not observe the covenant.

Psalm 105 (Book IV) lacks a superscription, although it is identified as a hymn or instruction.[29] In a review of history that extends from YHWH's promises to the ancestors through to the Exodus and the promise of land, the psalm reaffirms YHWH's covenant. It includes a summons to worship in verses 1–6, praise of YHWH's acts in history in verses 7–45b, and a summons to praise in verse 45c. The conceptualization of the covenant as the eternal promise of the land of Canaan to the ancestors of Israel, Abraham, Isaac, and Jacob, appears in verses 7–11, where it is labeled unequivocally as an "eternal covenant" (*běrît 'ôlām*), that is, a covenant that cannot be broken, in verse 10. The same statements are repeated in 1 Chronicles 16:8–22, which is drawn from Psalm 105:1–15.

Psalm 106 (Book IV) is a communal confession of guilt and hymnic instruction concerning issues in the relationship between YHWH and Israel.[30] It recounts Israel's rebellions against YHWH from the time

27. Balentine, *Hidden God*.
28. Gerstenberger, *Psalms, Part 2*, 215–21.
29. Gerstenberger, *Psalms, Part 2*, 230–36.
30. Gerstenberger, *Psalms, Part 2*, 236–45.

of the Exodus from Egypt through to the pre-monarchic period in the land of Israel, together with YHWH's benevolence toward the people despite their rebellions. The psalm comprises an introduction in verses 1–7c, accounts of Israel's failures and deliverances in verses 7d–39, a summary in verses 40–46, a petition and vow in verse 47, and a blessing and communal response in verse 48. Verse 1 calls upon the people to give thanks to YHWH because his fidelity (*ḥesed*), is forever, and verse 45 reiterates that YHWH remembered for them (the people) his covenant and relented according to the multitude of his fidelities. The reference to YHWH's covenant in verse 45 does not specify that the covenant is eternal, but the opening statement in verse 1 concerning YHWH's eternal fidelity confirms that it is.

Psalm 111 (Book V) is an acrostic hymn that includes a summons to praise in verse 1a, thanksgiving in verse 1bc, hymnic affirmation in verses 2–9, and praise of wisdom in verse 10.[31] The understanding of the covenant is that it is clearly eternal, insofar as verse 5 repeats the motif from Psalms 105 and 106 that YHWH remembers his covenant forever and verse 9 asserts that YHWH commanded forever his covenant. Other statements, such as "and his righteousness stands for eternity" in verse 3, "all his appointments are secure, set forever and ever" in verses 7–8, and "his praise stands for eternity" in verse 10, reinforce the notion of YHWH's eternal covenant with his people (verse 9).

Psalm 132 (Book V), a psalm of ascents, is a Zion psalm and royal hymn.[32] It comprises the superscription in verse 1a, a remembrance of David's vow in verses 1b–5, a description of the Ark's procession in verses 6–7, a communal prayer in verses 8–10, a divine oracle in verses 11–12, and another divine oracle in verses 13–18. The psalm presents a bifurcated understanding of covenant. YHWH's oracular oath to David in verses 11–12 asserts that YHWH has sworn to David truly, an oath that YHWH will not renounce (*lōʾ yāšûb mimennāh*, "he will not return from it")—that David's descendants will ascend to the throne only if they observe YHWH's covenant and testimony. If they observe the covenant and the testimony, they will sit upon the throne "forever" (*ădê-ʿad*). But the second oracle turns to Zion, the site of the Temple in Jerusalem, to assert that YHWH has chosen Zion as the divine resting place, once again, "forever" (*ădê-ʿad*). The result is that the Davidic

---

31. Gerstenberger, *Psalms, Part 2*, 270–74.
32. Cf. Gerstenberger, *Psalms, Part 2*, 362–70.

covenant is conditioned, but the covenant with Zion, or Jerusalem, is eternal and therefore unconditional.

This survey of the psalms concerned with covenant (*bĕrît*), shows continuous and progressive reflection and development of the concept throughout the five books of Psalms. Psalm 25 in Book I is somewhat ambiguous in that the covenant appears to be conditional and dependent upon observance by the people, and there is no clear indication that the covenant is permanent. Psalms 44 and 50 in Book II are also somewhat ambivalent in that they envision punishment for those who violate the covenant, but the appeals to YHWH's fidelity suggest that the covenant is permanent. Psalms 74, 78, and 89 in Book III presume wrongdoing on the part of Ephraim or northern Israel in Psalms 74 and 78 and by the people in Psalm 89, but the appeal to look to the covenant in Psalm 74, the choice of Zion in Psalm 78, and the covenant with David in Psalm 89 all presuppose a permanent covenant, especially with Judean sites and Davidic figures. Psalms 103, 105, and 106 in Book IV all presume an eternal covenant with Israel, even though they concede that some might not observe that covenant. Finally, Psalms 111 and 132 in Book V arrive at an understanding of covenant that is permanent in Psalm 111, although Psalm 132 envisions a conditional covenant with the House of David and a permanent covenant with Zion or Jerusalem. Such an understanding is consistent with the redefinitions of the Davidic covenant in Isaiah, especially Isaiah 55, which envisions an expansion of the eternal covenant with the House of David to include all of Israel,[33] and in Jeremiah, especially in Jeremiah 33:14–26, which envisions an expansion of the Davidic covenant to include Jerusalem and the Levitical priesthood.[34] But Psalms shows no clear reference to the Book of the Twelve, which throughout presumes that a Davidic monarch will or should act on YHWH's behalf.

Conclusion

This study demonstrates that there is a serious reflection on the concept of covenant (*bĕrît*), in both the Book of the Twelve Prophets and the Book of Psalms, although their respective approaches to the issue differ. The Book of the Twelve employs two prophetic compositions as the "bookends" for the book, that is, Hosea at the beginning and Malachi at the end, both

---

33. Sweeney, "Davidic Covenant in Isaiah"; *Isaiah 40–66*, 235–48.
34. Sweeney, "Books of Jeremiah."

of which employ the marriage metaphor to depict the continuity of the covenant relationship between YHWH and Israel. In Hosea, the marriage between Hosea and Gomer represents the relationship between YHWH and Israel, in which Gomer/Israel abandons Hosea/YHWH for other lovers, but eventually, the marriage is restored. In Malachi, Jewish men abandon their Jewish wives for gentile women, but are called upon to return to the Jewish wives of their youth to restore the covenant. The intervening compositions within the Twelve reflect upon a variety of issues relevant to the covenant, but Hosea and Malachi are the two compositions that reflect upon the concept of covenant per se.

In the Psalms, individual psalms in Books I–V illustrate a development in the concept of covenant. Psalm 25 in Book I shows an ambiguous understanding of covenant and Psalms 44 and 50 in Book II show an ambivalent understanding that may presume a permanent covenant despite violation by the people. Psalms 74, 78, and 89 in Book III charge Ephraim and northern Israel with violating the covenant as YHWH chooses Judah and the House of David for a permanent covenant. Psalms 103, 105, and 106 in Book IV assert an eternal covenant with Israel even as they concede violation, and Psalms 111 and 132 in Book V assert a permanent covenant in Psalm 111, although Psalm 132 then distinguishes between a conditional covenant with the Davidic House and an eternal covenant with Mt. Zion or Jerusalem as the site for YHWH's sanctuary.

Although there is no clear evidence of direct citation, either of the Book of Psalms by the Book of the Twelve or of the Book of the Twelve by the Book of Psalms, the two books are nevertheless in dialogue with each other, insofar as they are both part of the distinctive scriptural canons of Judaism and Christianity.[35] Both books show serious effort to reflect upon the concept of covenant, which is central for both Judaism and Christianity even as they differ from each other in their understandings of covenant. Consequently, both the Book of the Twelve and the Book of Psalms serve as resources for intertextual dialogue within the Jewish Tanak and the Christian Old Testament for theological reflection on the covenant in both traditions.

---

35. Sweeney, *Tanak*, 3–41.

Bibliography

Balentine, Samuel E. *The Hidden God: The Hiding of the Face of God in the Old Testament.* Oxford: Oxford University Press, 1983.

Baumann, Gerlinde. *Love and Violence: Marriage as Metaphor for the Relationship between YHWH and Israel in the Prophetic Books.* Collegeville, MN: Liturgical, 2003.

Gerstenberger, Erhard S. *Psalms, Part 1, with an Introduction to Cultic Poetry.* FOTL 14. Grand Rapids: Eerdmans, 1988.

———. *Psalms, Part 2 and Lamentations.* FOTL 15. Grand Rapids, 2001.

Goldman, Yohanan. *Prophétie et royauté au retour de l'exil.* OBO 118. Freiburg: Universitätsverlag; Göttingen: Vandenhoeck & Ruprecht, 1992.

Jacobs, Mignon R. *The Books of Haggai and Malachi.* NICOT. Grand Rapids: Eerdmans, 2017.

Mason, Steven D. *"Eternal Covenant" in the Pentateuch: The Contours of an Elusive Phrase.* LHBOTS 494. London: T&T Clark, 2008.

Nelson, Richard D. *The Double Redaction of the Deuteronomistic History.* JSOTSup 18. Sheffield: JSOT, 1981.

Nogalski, James D. *The Book of the Twelve: Hosea–Jonah.* Smyth and Helwys Bible Commentary. 2 vols. Macon: Smyth and Helwys, 2011.

———. *Literary Precursors to the Book of the Twelve.* BZAW 217. Berlin; Boston: de Gruyter, 1993.

———. *Redactional Processes in the Book of the Twelve.* BZAW 218. Berlin; Boston: de Gruyter, 1993.

Page, S. "A Stela of Adad Nirari III and Nergal Ereš from Tell al-Rimah." *Iraq* 30 (1968) 139–53.

Pfeiffer, E. "Die Disputationsworte im Buche Maleachi." *EvT* 12 (1959) 546–88.

Pritchard, James B. *The Ancient Near East in Pictures.* Princeton: Princeton University Press, 1969.

Rendsburg, Gary. *Linguistic Evidence for the Northern Origin of Selected Psalms.* SBLMS 43. Atlanta: Scholars, 1990.

Shechter, Jack. *The Land of Israel: Its Theological Dimensions. A Study of a Promise and of a Land's "Holiness."* Lanham, MD: University Press of America, 2010.

Sweeney, Marvin A. "Berit Olam, The Eternal Covenant: Is the Eternal Covenant Really Conditional?" *Conversations with the Biblical World* 33 (2019) 1–19.

———. *Isaiah 40–66.* FOTL 19. Grand Rapids: Eerdmans, 2016.

———. "Minor Prophets." *EBR* 19 (2021) 238–41.

———. "The Minor Prophets and the Book of the Twelve in Late-Eighteenth through Early-Twenty-First-Century Research." In *The Oxford Handbook of the Minor Prophets*, edited by Julia O'Brien, 267–78. Oxford: Oxford University Press, 2021.

———. "The Reconceptualization of the Davidic Covenant in the Books of Jeremiah." In *Reading Prophetic Books: Form and Intertextuality in Prophetic and Post-Biblical Literature*, 167–81. FAT 89. Tübingen: Mohr Siebeck 2014.

———. "The Reconceptualization of the Davidic Covenant in Isaiah." In *Studies in the Book of Isaiah: Festschrift W. A. M. Beuken*, edited by J. van Ruiten and M. Vervenne, 41–61. Leuven: Peeters and Leuven University Press, 1997. Republished in *Reading Prophetic Books: Form and Intertextuality in Prophetic and Post-Biblical Literature*, 94–113. FAT 89. Tübingen: Mohr Siebeck, 2014.

———. "The Royal Oracle in Ezekiel 37:15–28: Ezekiel's Reflection on Josiah's Reform." In *Israel's Prophets and Israel's Past: Essays on the Relationship of Prophetic Texts and Israelite History in Honor of John H. Hayes*, edited by B. E. Kelle and M. B. Moore, 239–53. LHBOTS 446. London: T&T Clark, 2006. Republished in *Reading Prophetic Books: Form and Intertextuality in Prophetic and Post-Biblical Literature*, 219–32. FAT 89. Tübingen: Mohr Siebeck 2014.

———. "Sequence and Interpretation in the Book of the Twelve." In *Form and Intertextuality in Prophetic and Apocalyptic Literature*, 175–88. FAT 45. Tübingen: Mohr Siebeck, 2005.

———. "Synchronic and Diachronic Concerns in Reading the Book of the Twelve Prophets." In *Perspectives on the Formation of the Book of the Twelve: Methodological Foundations, Redactional Processes, Historical Insights*, edited by Rainer Albertz et al., 21–33. BZAW 433. Berlin; Boston: de Gruyter, 2012.

———. *Tanak: A Theological and Critical Introduction to the Jewish Bible*. Minneapolis: Fortress, 2012.

———. *The Twelve Prophets*. Berit Olam. 2 vols. Collegeville, MN: Liturgical, 2000.

Wöhrle, Jakob. *Der Abschluss des Zwölfprophetenbuches: Buchübergreifende Redaktionsprozesses in den späten Sammlungen*. BZAW 389. Berlin; Boston: de Gruyter, 2008.

———. *Die frühen Sammlungen des Zwölfprophetenbuchs: Enstehung und Komposition*. BZAW 360. Berlin; Boston: de Gruyter, 2006.

CHAPTER 7

"Take Away from Me the Noise of Your Songs" (Amos 5:23)

The Divine Desire for Justice and Righteousness in the Book of Amos and the Book of Psalms

J. CLINTON MCCANN JR.

AMONG SEVERAL STINGING INDICTMENTS of Israelite or Judean worship in the prophetic canon, Amos 5:21–24 is perhaps the strongest, the most comprehensive, and the most severe (although it is rivaled by Isa 1:10–20). In the first-person address, God declares that "I hate, I despise" (v. 21) every aspect of and occasion for Israelite worship.[1] The language could not be stronger, and yet the NRSV does not make it strong enough. The translation "despise" could just as accurately be "reject"—that is, God finds Israelite worship to be totally unacceptable.

God's rejection of Israelite worship includes the range of sacrifices and offerings that were integral to the cult—"burnt offerings," "grain offerings," and "offerings of well-being" (v. 22). And God is not finished yet. It gets worse. The "songs" (שִׁיר) mentioned in v. 23 almost certainly would have been what we know as the psalms. The Hebrew noun translated "songs" occurs in the titles of over 20 percent of the individual psalms in the book of Psalms, beginning with Psalm 18 (see also a verbal form of the Hebrew root in the title of Psalm 7). Furthermore, the Hebrew root

---

1. Biblical quotations are from the NRSV, unless indicated otherwise.

underlying "melody" (v. 23) is the same Hebrew root that lies behind the English, "A Psalm," which occurs in the titles of over a third of the psalms in the book of Psalms, beginning with Psalm 3. Even the Psalms are unacceptable! God will not "look upon" (v. 22) or "listen to" (v. 23) anything that has to do with Israelite worship.

Given the divine displeasure, indeed total disgust, with Israelite worship that is expressed in the book of Amos, it would seem unlikely that the book of Amos and the book of Psalms would have anything in common. The book of Psalms, after all, was almost certainly compiled from the collection of Israelite songs and prayers that the book of Amos roundly criticizes and rejects. But, as it turns out, a comparison of the book of Amos and the book of Psalms reveals a congruent understanding of the divine will—that is, justice and righteousness on a world-encompassing scale.

Before exploring this congruence, it is necessary to say a word about methodological perspective. In short, my approach is canonical rather than historical. We simply cannot date with confidence the material in the book of Amos, for instance. While the book almost certainly originated in the mid-eighth century BCE, it was almost certainly redacted, perhaps several times, over two hundred or more years.[2] The dating of the material in the book of Psalms is even more elusive. So, we cannot safely conclude that the eighth-century prophets, Amos among them, were opposed to corporate worship in principle as earlier generations of commentators were inclined to suggest. Indeed, this is quite unthinkable, and we simply do not know enough to draw such historical conclusions.

What we can say, however, is that the book of Amos and the book of Psalms in their final forms are remarkably congruent in their portrayal of God's will. Or, if one prefers to think historically, we might say this: *If* Amos 5:21–24 is an eighth-century text, and *if* the prophet Amos had access to something like what would later become the book of Psalms that we have received, then he would have found no reason to oppose Israelite worship, per se. Rather, he would have found motivation within Israel's collection of songs to redirect Israelite liturgical practice so that it formed a community committed to the pursuit of the justice and righteousness that God willed. Amos 5:24 points in this direction, but there is more to be said.

---

2. For a brief summary of the scholarly consensus on the editorial history of the book of Amos, see Jeremias, *Book of Amos*, 5–9.

The Book of Amos

Regardless of what eighth-century Amos or the editors of the book of Amos thought about worship, it is clear what he or they thought about justice and righteousness. The key verse is 5:24, "But let justice roll down like waters, and righteousness like an ever-flowing stream." Other portions of chapter 5, along with the rest of the book, are also involved. While there are several ways to understand the editorial process that led to the final form of the book of Amos, and several ways to understand the structure of the final form itself, it is hard to escape the conclusion that chapter 5 lies at the very heart of the book.[3] Therefore, it will be our focal point.

Since it appears to be central, chapter 5 unsurprisingly contains most of the occurrences of the nouns "justice" and "righteousness" in the book of Amos. In addition to v. 24, the pair of words also occurs in v. 7 (see also 6:12), and the noun "justice" occurs alone in v. 15. The occurrence of the word pair in v. 7 is particularly interesting, not only because it anticipates v. 24, but also because it is followed immediately by the second of the three creation-oriented doxologies (vv. 8–9) that seem to have figured in the editorial history of the book (see also 4:13; 9:5–6). This location alone invites further attention.

The scope of this essay does not permit a consideration of the history of the scholarly discussion of these doxologies.[4] Suffice it to say that I will proceed not historically, but rather literarily and canonically—in short, I am interested in the effect of reading vv. 8–9 immediately after the mention of "justice" and "righteousness" in v. 7, however or whenever vv. 8–9 got placed in this position.

But first, consider the first and third doxologies in the book of Amos. Both occur immediately following divine warnings about the future, or more accurately, the non-future, of Israel. In 4:11–12, God is going to "do to you, O Israel" what he had previously done to Sodom and Gomorrah. And 9:2–4 announces that Israel will not be able to escape God's devouring presence. No matter where they might try to flee and hide, God "will command the sword, and it shall kill them" (9:4). But the doxology in 5:8–9 is placed differently. It follows the mention of

---

3. Jeremias, *Book of Amos*, 6–7.

4. A major study of the doxologies in the book of Amos is found in Crenshaw, *Hymnic*. Crenshaw includes an extensive history of the scholarly research on the doxologies, as well as analyses of each doxology. See also Jeremias, *Book of Amos*, 76–80.

"Those turning justice into wormwood, and righteousness they throw to the ground" (my translation). "Those turning" is a masculine plural participle that begins the verse (there is no "Ah" like the NRSV would lead one to believe), and "they throw" is a third-person plural perfect form. This grammatical pattern is continued in v. 10 with the two perfect forms translated "they hate" and "they abhor." It is very likely, therefore, that the doxology in vv. 8–9 has been inserted into an otherwise complete oracle of judgment (5:6–7, 10–11; or perhaps 5:6–7, 10–13).[5] But why here? And to what effect?

As I see it, the final form of chapter 5, especially vv. 6–13, suggests that justice and righteousness constitute something like what we might call an order of creation—that is, *God has built them into the very structure of the universe.* The God who put the stars in their place and who governs the heavens and the waters (v. 8) has so ordered creation such that justice and righteousness are necessary for the universe to operate the way that God intends. Whereas previous scholarship on 5:8–9 has concluded that these verses function as a "Doxology of Judgment,"[6] I prefer to understand it more as a *doxology of justice and righteousness.* Although she does not use this exact language, Ellen F. Davis comes closest to this understanding of 5:8–9. Noting the use of the root *hpk* in both 5:7 ("Those *turning* justice into wormwood") and 5:8 ("The one who . . . *turns* deep darkness into the morning"), Davis sees the doxology in 5:8–9 not only as hymnic support for the divine ability to bring judgment upon sinful Israel, but also an affirmation of what God wills for the universe. As she concludes, "Buried in the threat of destruction is a call to align with the power that undergirds both political history and creation itself."[7] This power is the God who wills justice and righteousness.

The verses immediately following the doxology in 5:8–9 demonstrate in detail what God's justice and righteousness involve—for starters, a legal system that operates with honesty and integrity so as not to victimize "the poor" (v. 11) and "the needy" (v. 12). Note that "the gate," which refers to the Israelite legal system, is mentioned three times (vv. 10, 12, 15). Justice and righteousness also demand that the legal system that God desires be accompanied by an economic system that would

---

5. *The Revised Common Lectionary* configures the text as Amos 5:6–7, 10–15 (the Old Testament Lesson for Proper 23 [28], Year B). See *The Revised Common Lectionary*, 53.

6. Crenshaw, *Hymnic*, 155–57.

7. Davis, *Scripture*, 130.

operate equitably and that would see to the well-being of everyone (v. 11; see also Amos 2:6–8; 6:1–7; 8:4–6). And if we keep reading on in chapter 5, we conclude that God also desires a liturgical system that facilitates the formation of an Israelite community characterized by such justice and righteousness (5:24). As we have seen, if worship instead serves to provide only a religious veneer to an unjust and oppressive *status quo*, it is simply unacceptable and to be rejected.

To be sure, God intends that justice and righteousness exist within Israel, but not only within Israel. The creation-oriented doxology in 5:8–9 itself suggests the expansiveness of God's concern for justice and righteousness, but there is more within the book of Amos to support this direction. Like the other prophetic books, the book of Amos contains so-called Oracles Against the Nations; Amos is the only prophetic book that begins with such material (1:3—2:16). And as it turns out, the Oracles Against the Nations in this case culminate as Oracles Against Judah (2:5–6) and Israel (2:6–16)! The effect is to suggest not only that God holds all nations accountable for their misdeeds, but also that the God of all nations and all creation wills the well-being of all nations. From God's perspective, the existence of justice and righteousness is an order of creation.

It is probably not coincidental that the very next passage, Amos 3:1–2, contains the phrase "all the families of the earth" (v. 2), echoing exactly the wording of Genesis 12:1–3, where Abram and his descendants are not only promised a blessing, but also commissioned to be a source of blessing for "all the families of the earth" (Gen 12:3). It is probably also not coincidental that the expansiveness of God's concern is communicated again very near the end of the book of Amos where it is suggested that Israel is not the only nation to benefit from God's saving work in the world (9:7–8). That is, other nations, including several of Israel's traditional enemies (Egypt, the Philistines, and the Arameans), have had exodus-experiences of their own. The two blocks of material (1:3—2:16 and 9:7–8) seem to form an envelope structure for the book, communicating that what is featured at the heart of the book of Amos—God's will for justice and righteousness—should be understood as world-encompassing. Indeed, as suggested above, justice and righteousness are built into the very structure of the universe as God intends it to operate.

The Book of Psalms

We began our consideration of Amos at the heart of the book, and we shall do the same with the book of Psalms. Since the publication of Gerald H. Wilson's *The Editing of the Hebrew Psalter* in 1985, a consensus has emerged that Book IV (Pss 90–106) represents "the editorial 'center'" of the book of Psalms.[8] Books I–III feature royal psalms at key points, including Psalm 2 as part of the paired introduction to the Psalter, and Psalms 72 and 89 at the conclusions of Books II and III respectively. The effect, according to Wilson, is to communicate the failure of the Davidic covenant, which was signaled by the destruction of Jerusalem in 587 BCE and the subsequent Babylonian exile. Psalm 89:1–37 rehearses at some length all the major elements of the Davidic covenant, but the psalm concludes with a royal lament as the imagined voice of an exiled Davidic descendant complains that he has been rejected (v. 38) and poignantly asks what has happened to the steadfast love promised to David (v. 49; see 2 Sam 7:15–17). As Wilson concludes, "The Davidic covenant introduced in Ps 2 has come to nothing and the combination of three books concludes with the anguished cry of the Davidic descendants [Ps 89:38–51]."[9]

The response to this crisis begins in Book IV. Psalm 90 is the only psalm attributed to Moses, who presided over the people before they had any of the things that were lost in 587—land, temple, and monarchy. Thus, the superscription of Psalm 90 already suggests that an ongoing relationship with God is still possible, even in the midst of devastating loss. Book IV remembers an era of Israelite history when there was no king over them but YHWH. This suggestion is reinforced by what is the most obvious structural feature of Book IV: the collection of enthronement psalms (Pss 93, 95–99; or as some scholars suggest, Pss 93–100). The enthronement collection affirms that not all is lost. While the earthly king may be gone, Israel still has a king, because YHWH reigns! This, according to Wilson, is the Psalter's "theological 'heart.'"[10]

In terms of the purposes of this essay, it is crucial to note that the Psalter's "theological 'heart'" features the fundamental importance of

---

8. Wilson, *Editing*, 215.

9. Wilson, *Editing*, 213. The recent work of Ho largely confirms Wilson's conclusion, while providing a much more detailed proposal for the shape of the Psalter. See Ho, *Design*, 334–38.

10. Wilson, "Use," 92.

justice and righteousness. Each of Psalms 96–99 contains the root *mlk* as either a noun ("King" in 96:10; 98:6; 99:4) or a verb ("is king" in 97:1; 99:1), and each contains the words "justice" and "righteousness" at least once. Psalms 96 and 98 are especially important in this regard. Both begin by inviting the singing of a new song (96:1; 98:1), and both conclude with very similar portrayals of an effusive, world-encompassing outpouring of praise that celebrates God's "justice" and "righteousness" (96:11–13; 98:7–9). In both cases, the celebration follows closely upon the explicit affirmation that YHWH is king (96:10; 98:6).

The NRSV and other standard English translations of 96:13 and 98:9 are misleading on two counts. First, they seem to suggest that God's coming is a future event. The NRSV's "for he is coming" in 96:13 and 98:9 is a translation that almost inevitably suggests to English readers that God has not yet arrived. Second, according to the NRSV, the purpose of God's coming is "to judge the earth." But different translations of 96:13 and 98:9 are possible. I suggest the following:

> ... before the LORD; for he has come,
> for he has come to establish justice on the earth.
> He will establish world-justice with righteousness,
> and (among) peoples with his faithfulness. (96:13)

> ... before the LORD, for he has come
> to establish justice on the earth.
> He will establish world-justice with righteousness
> and (among) peoples with equity. (98:9)

It is to be noted that the verb form that the NRSV and others translate as "is coming" is ambiguous. The form can be a masculine singular active participle of *bô*', but it can also be the third-person masculine singular perfect form of the verb. In my view, the latter is better. All creation is celebrating (96:11–12; 98:7–8) because God "has come."

Support for this construal is found in the often-noted relationship between the enthronement collection, especially Psalms 96 and 98, and the material in Isaiah 40–55.[11] Both the enthronement psalms and Isaiah 40–55 are responses to the rupture of exile. Like Psalms 96 and 98, Isaiah 42:10 invites the singing of a new song. Unlike Psalms 96 and 98, this invitation does not immediately follow an affirmation of YHWH's kingship,

---

11. See, for instance, Creach, "Shape."

however, Isaiah 52:7 makes this proclamation, which is described as "good news." Not coincidentally, it would seem, Psalm 96:2 uses the same Hebrew root (בשר), which the NRSV very weakly translates as "tell." More appropriately, the second portion of 96:2 could be translated, "proclaim the good news of his saving work from day to day." In Isaiah 40–55, the good news, including the good news that God reigns, is grounded in the message that God is still present with God's people. This message culminates in the opening passage of Isaiah 40–55, as the cities of Judah are invited to hear the "good tidings" (Isa 40:9—the same Hebrew root found in Ps 96:2 and Isa 52:7): "Behold your God" (my translation). The NRSV translation of the good news is, "Here is your God." In short, God is present, that is, God has already come, and we should understand Psalms 96:13 and 98:9 as affirmations that God "has come."

For what purpose has God come? As suggested in the above translations of Psalms 96:13 and 98:9, God "has come to establish justice . . . with righteousness." Just as the creation-oriented doxology in Amos 5:8–9 (along with the other two doxologies and other literary features of the book of Amos) suggests that the scope of God's desire for justice and righteousness is world-encompassing, so do the descriptions of a worldwide celebration of God's arrival in Psalms 96:11–12 and 98:7–8. Here, as in Amos, every element of creation praises God—heavens, earth, and seas. The book of Amos and the book of Psalms are congruent at this point.

Furthermore, there are other psalms that reinforce the crucial importance of justice and righteousness for the operation of the world as God desires. And there are other psalms that make clear that the Psalter's understanding of the nature of justice and righteousness is congruent with the understanding of the nature of justice and righteousness in the book of Amos. A vocabulary link between Psalms 96:10 and 82:5 invites attention to one of these psalms—Psalm 82. Anticipating the announcement that God "has come to establish justice . . . with righteousness," and thus that God is presently reigning (96:10a), the psalmist declares in Psalm 96:10b that "The world is firmly established; it shall never be moved." This affirmation alone reinforces the conclusion that justice and righteousness are essential for the operation of the world as God intends; in addition, this affirmation recalls Psalm 82:5, where clearly the world is not firmly established. Rather, "all the foundations of the earth are shaken." The verb, "moved," in 96:10 and the verb, "shaken," in 82:5 represent the same Hebrew root (מוט).

This is a worst-case scenario because the "foundations of the earth" are the mountains that hold up the domed firmament, which holds back the waters above. The mountains also anchor in place the dry land, which keeps at bay the waters below. When the mountains "are shaken," the world is threatened with a deluge from the waters above and from the waters below. In short, it is a de-creation: the ordered, life-supporting creation is completely undone. And as Psalm 82 makes abundantly clear, this threat to the world revolves around the issue of justice, the four-times-repeated keyword in the psalm (see "holds judgment" in v. 1; "judge" in v. 2; "Give justice" in v. 3; and "judge" in v. 8—all of these represent the same Hebrew root).

More specifically, the problem is the lack of justice, which is the result of the misadministration of the earth by "the gods" (v. 1), a reference to the Canaanite deities, or better perhaps, the hierarchical Canaanite system that benefited a small ruling elite ("the wicked" in v. 2) and consigned the large majority of folk to destitution and perpetual neediness (vv. 3–4). This is precisely the problem that is highlighted in the book of Amos. It is not coincidental that the victims of injustice are named with the same vocabulary in Psalm 82 and the book of Amos (see "weak" in Ps 82:3–4, and Amos 4:1; 5:11; 8:6 where the same Hebrew word is translated "poor"; see "lowly" in Ps 82:3, and Amos 8:4 [*Qere*] where the same Hebrew word is translated "poor"; see "needy" in Ps 82:4 and Amos 2:6; 4:1; 5:12; 8:4, 6).

In both the book of Amos and the Psalms, justice and righteousness begin with attention to and provision for the most vulnerable. The parallelism in Psalm 82:3 of "Give justice" and "maintain the right" is the same parallelism found in Amos 5:24. In both instances, what constitute the justice and righteousness that God desires are legal, economic, and liturgical systems that operate with integrity and that provide equitably for the well-being of everyone, beginning with the most vulnerable and the most victimized. This is why Psalm 82 ends with the one element that is most typical of the Psalter—a prayer. It is a prayer for justice. My translation of Psalm 82:8 is this:

> Arise, O God, establish justice on the earth;
> for you possess all the nations.

Note too that Psalm 82:8 is another reminder that God's desire for justice and righteousness is world-encompassing. When injustice threatens the world with de-creation (v. 5), what God desires is justice not just for Israel but rather for "all the nations" that belong to God. Again, the congruence with the perspective of the book of Amos is clear.

Some may object that the criticism of the Canaanite system in Psalm 82, culminating in vv. 6–7 where the Canaanite deities are deposed, seems to compromise God's desire for justice for "all the nations." What about the Canaanites? Furthermore, vv. 6–7 may even sound arrogantly offensive to some readers, that is, our God is better than your gods, so your gods have to go. But the point is not that God stands against Canaanites. Rather, the point is that God stands against *injustice*. Especially when the Psalms are read in conversation with the book of Amos, as we are doing, it is a reminder that the Israelite system, including Israelite worship, also becomes unacceptable to God.

This reminder is contained within the final form of the Psalter itself. The mention of a "prince" in Psalm 82:7, whether the Canaanite deities are addressed collectively as "O prince" (see the NRSV note) or whether the line is understood as part of a simile, is at least a subtle anticipation of Psalm 89 that calls attention to Judean royalty. Psalm 89, the royal psalm that concludes Book III of the Psalter, celebrates both God's sovereign claim on the whole world, a rule grounded in justice and righteousness (vv. 5–14, especially v. 14), and God's choice of the Davidic line (vv. 19–37), before concluding with a royal lament that communicates that the Davidic monarchy has fallen (see above). In short, the Davidic king has fallen "like any prince" (Ps 82:7). God will oppose, and even depose, God's own son (see Ps 2:7 where the king is referred to by the divine voice as "my son"; see 2 Sam 7:14) if and when that son fails to do the justice and righteousness that God wills. God does not stand against any particular people or nation. Rather, God stands against injustice wherever, whenever, and by whomever, it is perpetrated, including God's own people and God's own son! Again, the congruence with the book of Amos is evident at this point.

If Psalm 82 is an anticipation of the royal Psalm 89 that concludes Book III, as I have suggested, it is also a recollection of the royal Psalm 72 that concludes Book II. And Psalm 72 is another psalm that reinforces both the conclusions that justice and righteousness are essential for the operation of the world as God intends, and that the Psalter's understanding of the nature of justice and righteousness is congruent with that of the book of Amos. While both the book of Amos and the book of Psalms make clear that God was forced to oppose his own people and their leaders, Psalm 72 indicates that at least an attempt was made at some point to make the monarchy a faithful institution. Psalm 72 is a prayer for the king, who was introduced in Psalm 2. Despite the violent imagery in vv. 8–9 (that would depict a heartless conqueror), the prayer in Psalm 72 suggests that the king has a pivotal role in enacting God's will (of justice and righteousness) in the world.

This being the case, it is not surprising that the first request in Psalm 72 is that the king possess God's "justice" (the noun here is plural, so "acts of justice" might be an appropriate translation) and "righteousness" (v. 1). These two words become the keywords in vv. 1–7. The root underlying "justice" in v. 1 is repeated in vv. 2 and 4 (NRSV, "May he defend"); and the root underlying "righteousness" recurs in vv. 2, 3, and 7. As is the case in Psalm 82 and the book of Amos, the king's efforts are to be especially focused upon the "poor" (vv. 2, 4, 12; see Amos 8:4; Ps 82:3, NRSV "lowly"), "needy" (vv. 4, 12, 13, 13; see Amos 2:6; 4:1; 5:12; Ps 82:4), and the "weak" (v. 13; see NRSV "poor" in Amos 4:1; 5:11; 8:6; Ps 82:3, 4).

The king's pursuit of justice and righteousness ensures the proper functioning of creation. The mountains, rather than shaking like in Psalm 82:5, "bear *shalom* for the people" (my translation; see *shalom* in v. 7 as well, NRSV "peace"). In this context, since the mountains and hills were where the Judean farmers lived and worked, *shalom* means food! In short, the king is to provide what life requires, beginning with a sufficient supply of food. His work is a force of creation itself, and he is to be "like rain that falls on the mown grass" (v. 6). Justice and righteousness—the essence of the king's job—are essential for the world to operate as God intends.

The food-producing, creation-sustaining work of the king is in view again in v. 16 with the mention of an "abundance of grain," which will "wave on the tops of the mountains" (see v. 3). As v. 17 suggests, the king is to be commended for his work—the work of justice and righteousness (vv. 1–7)—that makes the life of his people possible.[12] And in the final analysis, the king's people are not just Israel and/or Judah. Ultimately, "all nations" are involved, and they are to be "blessed in [or, 'by'] him" (v. 17). As in Amos 3:1–2, the allusion is to Genesis 12:3. The justice and righteousness that God wills and that lead to blessing are to be world-encompassing. Having been blessed with the sustenance that makes life possible, the nations will "pronounce him [the king] happy." In psalmic terms, happiness derives from constantly attending to and

---

12. See Davis, *Scripture*, 11–12, 165; McCann, "Bread."

pursuing God's *Torah*—that is, God's "teaching" or God's "will" (see Ps 1:1–2, where NRSV translates *Torah* as "law"). Psalms 96 and 98, along with Psalms 82 and 72, have shown what God wills—justice and righteousness on a world-encompassing scale. Again, the congruence with the book of Amos is clear.

Although it may be coincidental, it is worth noting and not surprising that several of the final psalms return to language and themes found at the beginning of the Psalter and at its "editorial center," the enthronement collection (Pss 93–100; see above). For instance, Psalm 145 recalls the enthronement collection as it marks a sort of transition between the final collection of Davidic psalms (Pss 138–145) and the concluding collection of *hallelu-yah* psalms (Pss 146–150). It addresses God in v. 1 as "King." Plus, the root *mlk* occurs four more times in Psalm 145 (vv. 11, 12, 13, 13; NRSV "kingdom"); and all four of these occurrences are in the *kaf*, *lamed*, and *mem* lines of this alphabetic acrostic poem—they appear in lines that spell *mlk* backwards, perhaps a playful way of emphasizing that YHWH is king.

It's as if the highlighting of *mlk* anticipates Psalm 146, the final line of which features *mlk* in the first position as a verb ("will reign" in v. 10). Like the enthronement collection, Psalm 146 associates God's reign with both God's creative work (v. 6) and God's establishment of justice (v. 7). The theme of justice recurs in Psalm 149, which also contains the final occurrence of the root *mlk* in the Psalter. In Psalm 149:2, God is referred to as "King." Another reminder of the enthronement collection is the opening invitation of Psalm 149, "Sing to the LORD a new song" (v. 1; see Pss 96:1; 98:1). While the earthly king is not mentioned, Psalm 149 also clearly recalls Psalm 2 (vv. 6–9; compare Ps 2:8–9). But the international responsibility of the king in Psalm 2 seems to have been transferred to "the faithful" (vv. 1, 5) or "his [God's] faithful ones" (v. 9). As it turns out, the "glory for all his faithful ones" (v. 9b) is "to do among them [the kings and nobles of the nations and peoples in vv. 7–8] justice (as it is) written" (v. 9a, my translation).

If the Psalms themselves are any clue to "justice (as it is) written," and it seems that they are, then the faithful people of God have a pivotal role to play in enacting God's will in the world, as the king is said to have had in Psalm 2—enacting justice and righteousness on a world-encompassing scale. As suggested above, Ellen F. Davis hears in Amos 5:8–9 an implicit "call to align with the power that undergirds both political history and creation itself."[13] A similar call is implicit in Psalm 149 and the book of Psalms in its entirety—a call to align with the God who wills world-encompassing justice and righteousness in the way that Psalms 96, 98, 82, 72, and 146 portray.

Note that this call to align with God is sandwiched between Psalms 148 and 150, two psalms that invite a community of praise that is world-encompassing (see Ps 150:6, "Let everything that breathes praise the LORD!"), indeed universe-encompassing (see Ps 148:1, 7, "Praise the LORD from the heavens . . . Praise the LORD from the earth"). It is helpful at this point to think of praise not only as a liturgical activity, but also as "a mode of existence."[14] As they bring the book of Psalms to a close, Psalms 148–150 effectively invite participation in a universe-encompassing community of praise that is aligned with the God who wills the establishment of justice and righteousness as an order of creation. To such a conclusion, the prophet Amos, or at least the editors of the book of Amos, would offer an enthusiastic "Amen."

Aligning with God: Amos and the Psalms Today

In assessing the messages of the writing prophets, including the prophet Amos, Ellen F. Davis points out that the prophetic books put us in touch with the failures of ancient Israel. But, she adds, "Confronting those failures from the distant past may enable us to recognize our own, perhaps for the first time."[15] And Davis also observes that the situations we confront in the twenty-first century "at certain points bear striking resemblance to the situations"[16] addressed by Amos and the other individual prophets, along with the redactors of the prophetic books.

We can identify our own failures by way of the same categories that we used to analyze the failures that Amos identified in Israel. Our legal system, for instance, is regularly manipulated by the wealthy and powerful to their advantage at the expense of others. I live in St. Louis County, Missouri, about ten miles from another St. Louis County municipality, Ferguson, a place that has become virtually synonymous with a set of legal arrangements that regularly victimize low-income folk, especially

13. Davis, *Scripture*, 130.
14. Westermann, *Praise and Lament*, 160.
15. Davis, *Opening*, 222.
16. Davis, *Opening*, 221.

black and brown people. But Ferguson is not unique. As Leah Gunning Francis points out, "There Is a Ferguson Near You."[17]

Legal abuses often go hand-in-hand with economic abuses, as they did in ancient Israel. Amos and the other eighth-century prophets were particularly concerned with loss of land by small farmers. Israel's equitable distribution and possession of land (see Josh 13–21) were supposed to provide an alternative to the hierarchical systems of Egypt and Canaan. But Israel regressed as it became "like other nations" (1 Sam 8:5), and as its kings increasingly acted Pharaoh-like in their assertion of power, appropriation of land, and accumulation of wealth.[18] In the subsistence agrarian context of ancient Israel, loss of land meant the inability to grow food and the absence of a stable place to live. The result was extreme vulnerability in the form of poverty, including hunger, and perhaps homelessness.

Over 2,500 years later, these realities are still with us in our urbanized, suburbanized global village. These contemporary realities constitute the "striking resemblance" between then and now, and they highlight our own failures. Even in the United States of America, perhaps the richest country in the history of the world, the outrageous fact is that we are not adequately feeding all our children, and the unhoused population continues to increase. Much of the rest of the world is faring no better as about 10 percent of people in the world live in extreme poverty, and two million children die every year from severe malnutrition, even though there is currently sufficient food for all the world's population. Appropriately, indeed urgently, the first of the Sustainable Development Goals of the United Nations is the elimination of poverty.

The continuing existence of unjust legal systems and the persistence of life-diminishing and life-threatening poverty beg for the kind of response invited by the book of Amos and the book of Psalms. The purpose of worship is to glorify God by shaping communities of faith to pursue the justice and righteousness that God wills. But so often, worship today,

---

17. Francis, *Ferguson*, 123. This quote is the title of chapter 8 of her book (123–36). See also Francis, *Faith*. In addition to the manipulation of legal systems on local levels, there is the national disgrace of privatized prisons that profit from incarcerating more and more people. The victims are disproportionally young black and brown men in the school-to-prison pipeline. See Alexander, *New*.

18. See Davis, *Scripture*, 111–14, 120–30. First Sam 8:1–16 is framed as Samuel's warning to the elders of Israel about the "justice of the king" (vv. 9, 11, my translation; NRSV "ways of the king"). See also 1 Kgs 21:1–16, the story of the appropriation of Naboth's vineyard by King Ahab. See also Mic 2:1–5.

as it is in ancient Israel, is aimed at preserving an oppressive *status quo*, allowing the well-to-do to congratulate themselves for their prosperity and their piety. As we become increasingly aware that we participate in a global economy, it has become increasingly evident that, as Martin Luther King Jr. observed over sixty years ago, "Injustice anywhere is a threat to justice everywhere."[19] For God's sake, as well as for the sake of a livable future for the whole human family, it is essential that we heed the call of the book of Amos and the book of Psalms to align ourselves with the God who wills justice and righteousness on a world-encompassing scale.

Bibliography

Alexander, Michelle. *The New Jim Crow: Mass Incarceration in the Age of Colorblindedness*. New York: New, 2012.

Creach, Jerome F. D. "The Shape of Book Four of the Psalter and the Shape of Second Isaiah." *JSOT* 80 (1998) 63–76.

Crenshaw, James L. *Hymnic Affirmation of Divine Justice: The Doxologies of Amos and Related Texts in the Old Testament*. SBLDS 24. Missoula: Scholars, 1975.

Davis, Ellen F. *Opening Israel's Scriptures*. Oxford: Oxford University Press, 2019.

———. *Scripture, Culture, and Agriculture: An Agrarian Reading of the Bible*. Cambridge: Cambridge University Press, 2009.

Francis, Leah Gunning. *Faith After Ferguson: Resilient Leadership in Pursuit of Racial Justice*. St. Louis: Chalice, 2021.

———. *Ferguson and Faith: Sparking Leadership and Awakening Community*. St. Louis: Chalice, 2015.

Ho, Peter C. W. *The Design of the Psalter: A Macrostructural Analysis*. Eugene, OR: Pickwick, 2019.

Jeremias, Jörg. *The Book of Amos: A Commentary*. Translated by Douglas W. Stott. OTL. Louisville: Westminster John Knox, 1998.

McCann, J. Clinton, Jr. "Bread for the World: Toward an Agrarian Reading of the Psalter (or Reading the Christ 'Psalmologically')." *RevExp* 112.2 (2015) 303–10.

The Revised Common Lectionary: The Consultation on Common Texts. Nashville: Abingdon, 1992.

Washington, James M., ed. *A Testament of Hope: The Essential Writings and Speeches of Martin Luther King Jr*. San Francisco: HarperSanFrancisco, 1991.

Westermann, Claus. *Praise and Lament in the Psalms*. Translated by Keith R. Crim and Richard N. Soulen. Atlanta: John Knox, 1981.

Wilson, Gerald H. *The Editing of the Hebrew Psalter*. SBLDS 76. Chico: Scholars, 1985.

———. "The Use of Royal Psalms at the 'Seams' of the Hebrew Psalter." *JSOT* 35 (1986) 85–94.

---

19. Washington, *Essential*, 290. The quote is from King's "Letter from Birmingham City Jail." A few lines prior to this quote, King notes how "the eighth-century prophets left their little villages and carried their 'thus saith the Lord' far beyond the boundaries of their hometowns."

CHAPTER 8

Wrestling with the Absence of God

Theodicy as a Problem within the Psalter and Habakkuk

DAVID G. FIRTH

A SIMPLE READING OF Psalm 1 might suggest that Yahweh's presence is automatically experienced by the righteous. But this is quickly challenged by the psalms that follow. In particular, the issue of God's absence is raised by Psalms 9–14, a sub-collection bounded by the cited statement: "There is no God." Psalms 52–55 explore this further within a collection of *maskil* (משכיל) centered on David's experience and the Asaphic psalms, which also cite others who deny that Yahweh knows what they do. Each of these collections both problematizes and yet ultimately affirms the view of Psalm 1 while enriching our understanding of it. The material in Psalms can be effectively placed in dialogue with Habakkuk 3, itself a psalm, which explores the effect of God's presence and yet offers an alternative perspective on this. These contrasting approaches have points of overlap but also represent a wider understanding of how God's presence might be experienced within the canon.

Psalm 1 as an Orientation to God's Presence

It is now widely accepted that Psalms 1–2 form an introduction to the Psalter. Both are still to be read as distinct poems in their own right, but the combination of their placement at the entry to the Book of Psalms and numerous shared features marks them out as texts that are to be read in conjunction too.[1] One effect of their role as an introduction to the Psalter is that they become a key point of reference as we read the rest of the Psalter, with numerous psalms alluding to both. Indeed, as Wilson notes,[2] we find allusions to both, quite often at the "seams" of the Psalter, the points where we move between each of the Psalter's five books. Without exploring this evidence in detail, it seems clear that Psalms 1 and 2 are to be read both individually and contextually. Read individually, we treat them as distinct poems that are examined on their own, whilst a contextual reading considers them not only in light of each other but also through the dialogue that they generate with the wider Psalter.

This background is important to the process of reading Psalm 1. Read on its own, we can see it offering a relatively straightforward application of the "two ways" motif that is widely known across both Old and New Testaments and is particularly associated with the wisdom tradition. The poem itself problematizes this in subtle ways, though most of this process is left to the rest of the Psalter. Psalm 1 has a simpler goal, encouraging its readers to orient their lives such that they reflect Yahweh's תורה (instruction or law). The psalm recognizes a contrast between the individual who makes this commitment and the many who choose the alternative path,[3] an initial hint that this might not be a simple choice, but it is not a principal focus in the poem. Rather, it describes the life which is devoted to choosing Yahweh's way as one which is marked by flourishing (Ps 1:3, cf. Pss 52:8; 92:12–15[4]), contrasting this with the way of the wicked, whose life is, by contrast, ephemeral. Moreover, the psalm closes by pointing to the contrasting outcomes of these two ways—the way of the righteous is known by Yahweh, whereas the way of the wicked perishes. Exactly what having one's way known by Yahweh might mean is not detailed here, but at least one implication is that God remains close to the righteous. It is not stated that God destroys the wicked, but that their way finally perishes encourages the righteous to continue in their way even when the way of the majority might seem more positive.

1. See Botha, "Ideological"; "Intertextuality"; Cole, *Psalms 1–2*; Grant, *King as Exemplar*, 41–70.

2. Wilson, *Editing*, 204–8. Admittedly, at this point Wilson was convinced only of Psalm 1's role, but the basic point holds.

3. deClaissé-Walford et al., *Psalms*, 60.

4. For consistency, English versification is referred to throughout.

In making these points, it is notable that Psalm 1 is also structured as an alphabetic composition, with its first and last words commencing with the first and last words of the Hebrew alphabet.[5] Psalm 1 opens with a beatitude (אשרי), traditionally translated "blessed" or "happy," it finishes with תאבד ("perish"). This pattern is repeated in Psalm 112 apart from the הללו יה ("Praise the LORD") frame, which joins it to Psalms 111–118. Psalm 112, which is paired with Psalm 111, is not only an alphabetic composition but also the simplest acrostic in the Psalter, with one half-line for each letter of the alphabet, a pattern it shares with Psalm 111. Given the literary links it establishes with Psalm 1, it is not surprising that it explores various ways in which the blessed one experiences God's presence, noting that the righteous will never be made to stumble (מוט, v. 5—itself an allusion to Ps 15:6). Other psalms containing beatitudes also explore the motif of God's presence with the righteous. For example, Psalm 41 closes Book I with a beatitude that joins this poem to Psalm 1, while insisting that Yahweh delivers the righteous in the day of trouble (v. 2). Similarly, Psalm 146 opens the *Great Hallel* with which the Psalter closes (Pss 146–150) by proclaiming a beatitude on any whose help is the God of Jacob, because of how Yahweh cares for the needy (Ps 146:5–9). Similar examples can be explicated, but these suffice to demonstrate the presence of a strong seam within the Psalter, which emphasizes God's presence with those who choose his way, and they now all, in some way, dialogue with Psalm 1. These psalms all recognize ways in which these reassurances might be problematized but are more interested in encouraging a life of commitment to God's ways, a life which is lived in the confidence of God's presence. Psalm 1 is, as Brueggeman suggests, a psalm of orientation,[6] and such poems do not muddy the waters by pointing to complexities. These psalms insist that God is present and that his presence can be seen in his watching of the righteous and the end of the wicked.

---

5. See Ho, *Design*, 309–16. Ho also points out that when Psalms 1–2 are read together that they also form a combined alphabetic composition, though in a different style.

6. Brueggemann, *Message*, 38–39.

Questioning God's Presence

Psalms 9–14

Despite the reassurances that are scattered through the Psalter, there are also numerous examples where the basic orientation of Psalm 1 is problematized through the apparent flourishing of the wicked, making theodicy a central issue with which the psalms wrestle. This can happen implicitly because of the suffering described by many psalmists, but it can also be challenged explicitly in texts that note either the direct denial of God's involvement with his world or at least his relative indifference to it. It is these more explicit texts that we explore in this essay. If God's presence is open to challenge, can readers continue to trust in the outcomes suggested by Psalms 1–2?

Indeed, when we reach Psalm 3, we encounter numerous enemies and a poet citing the claim of foes who insist that "There is no salvation for him in God" (Ps 3:2). The poet here can still draw on the memory of God's presence, with this providing hope in the future (Ps 3:4–6), but the enemies' claim raises important questions about God's presence. Of course, the "many" who speak here might also be the many who walk in the way of the wicked in Psalm 1, but they are here able to voice something not evident in Psalm 1—that God's presence might be questioned. The theme of the many who speak finds a further echo in Psalm 4:6, which again cites opponents questioning God's presence, even though the psalmist remains confident of it (Ps 4:8).[7] Questioning of God's presence is thus voiced through adversaries, but this allows the topic to be raised for reflection. Each of Psalms 3–7 is a complaint, a prayer asking God to intervene in a situation where he is not self-evidently present, making this a topic that needs to be addressed.

Structurally, there is good reason to see Psalms 3–14 as a unit within the Psalter,[8] though when we do so we can note that it is compiled of two blocks of complaint psalms (Pss 3–7, 9–14) which pivot around Psalm 8, the only praise poem in the Psalter entirely addressed to God. Although these blocks of complaint psalms can be read within the larger block, there is also value in treating each of Psalms 3–7 and 9–14 on their own even if their contribution to the larger unit should be noted. For our

---

7. On the links between Psalms 3 and 4, see Schaefer, *Psalms*, 11–12; Auffret, "Sur," 332.
8. See Hartenstein, "Schaffe."

purposes, this is beneficial because it allows us to note that although the question of God's presence is *implicitly* challenged in Psalms 3–7, it is *explicitly* challenged in Psalms 9–14. On this theme, at least, we can read Psalms 9–14 as an intensification of Psalms 3–7.[9]

As evidence of this, we begin by noting that Psalms 9–14 as a collection is bounded by the claim that "there is no God." As with Psalms 3–7, this is voiced by adversaries, but the presence of speech like this within the Psalter indicates that there were those who were prepared (in some way) to make an assertion such as this, challenging the idea of God's presence by insisting that it could not be assumed. The motif does not occur in Psalm 9, but Psalms 9–10 also (more or less) form a single acrostic, with Psalm 10 commencing with the ל-colon and carrying through to the end of the alphabet. The Masoretic Psalter commences this section with one poem that is divided into two psalms.[10] Yet it also marks these two psalms as a text that is to be read both separately and as a unit. Read separately, we can note that the claim, "there is no God," is held back until Psalm 10, but the division of the poem into two psalms now places a greater emphasis on the appeal of Psalm 9:19–20, asking that Yahweh demonstrate the weakness of humans compared to him. It also means that Psalm 10 concludes with an observation on human limitation because humans cannot terrorize others when they encounter Yahweh. There are probably other reasons for the division of the one poem into two psalms,[11] so the question of the division of the poem is not solely about the question of divine presence and human limitation, though this seems to be a prominent one. But as noted, by retaining the acrostic form, the Masoretes signal the poem's unity. This is also signaled by the relatively unusual decision to end Psalm 9 with *selah*[12] and the absence of a title for Psalm 10. Within Books I and II, wherever a psalm is without a title, it can be shown to be closely linked to the preceding psalm. This is true of Psalms 1 and 2, while Psalm 33 provides an immediate response to the close of Psalm 32. Psalm 43, like Psalm 10, is a continuation of the preceding psalm, making this another instance of two psalms but only one poem. Psalm 71, the only other untitled psalm in Book II, also has

---

9. For further exploration of this, see Firth and Melton, "World without God," 101–5.

10. LXX keeps the poem as a single unit.

11. For example, Goldingay, *Psalms 1–41*, 169, points to the more national emphasis in Ps 9, contrasting this with Ps 10, which is more concerned with individuals.

12. Elsewhere only in Pss 24 and 46.

close links with Psalm 70, and indeed the two are treated as one psalm in some manuscripts.[13] Readers of Psalms 9–10 are thus encouraged by the Masoretes to employ two reading strategies, one that treats them as separate psalms and one that regards them as a single poem.

Reading Psalms 9–10 as a single poem means that the statement "there is no God" occurs at the two outer points of Psalms 9–14. We first find that the schemes (מזמה) of the wicked are built around the thought that "there is no God" (Ps 10:4). As becomes clear in Psalm 10:11, this statement is not about the actual absence of God but rather the belief that God will not act to intervene against the acts of the wicked. These thoughts are expressed through the idiom of speaking in one's heart in Psalm 10:6 and 10:11, and though the first of these does not state that there is no God, it assumes that God is not functionally present to act against the wicked or in favor of the righteous. This idiom recurs in Psalm 14:1 where fools (נבל) say in their heart "there is no God." In this case it is possible to read this statement as a more explicit statement of atheism, but it is more likely that we are again dealing with "practical atheism," the idea that God is not sufficiently involved in the world for his presence to make any real difference. If God is absent in this sense, then the wicked can act with freedom against the righteous, and this belief shapes their acts. In Psalm 14, the wicked from Psalm 10 can be described as "fool[s]," thus marking their confidence in their position as misplaced, but it is still an issue with which the community must wrestle. In Psalm 14 the alternative position is outlined by verse 4. The question here is terse, but the basic point is clear. As Botha has noted, that the fools "eat up my people" means that they are the ones with social power.[14] Nevertheless, from the perspective of the psalm, *might* does not, in this case, equal *right*. Rather, it demonstrates that these people are fools because they ignore the fundamental reality of Yahweh's presence with the righteous (v. 5). Hence, in verse 6, the poet addresses the fools directly, pointing out that they ignore the fact that Yahweh is the refuge of the poor. The psalm thus closes the sub-unit (Pss 9–14) by declaring once again that divine presence is something of which the poor and righteous can be confident. There will be

---

13. Vesco, *Le psautier*, 616, claims that Pss 70:2 and 71:13, 24 constitute a refrain that indicates that this is a single text, though it would be better to argue that these verses represent a repeating motif. Nevertheless, these verses do provide further evidence for believing that the Masoretes saw these two psalms as being joined in some way even if they were meant to be read individually.

14. Botha "Ironie," 22.

times when the powerful might seem to be free to act without regard to God, but God's presence is not to be denied because of this. The poor may well suffer for periods because of the practical atheism of wicked fools, but Psalm 14 insists that this is not how things must always be.

Psalms 52–55

A peculiarity of the Psalter is that it includes poems which are almost exact repeats of other psalms. One of the best-known examples of this is Psalms 14 and 53. But where earlier research tended to treat them simply as doublets, with the variances between them largely considered as text-critical problems for determining the form of the original poem,[15] more recent research has begun to probe the contribution each makes within its current location in the Psalter.[16] It is this latter approach which guides our reading here as it demonstrates that just as Psalm 14 is integrated into the sub-unit of Psalms 9–14, so also Psalm 53 is integrated into the sub-unit of Psalms 52–55. This sub-unit is part of the larger collection known as "The Prayers of David," which covers Psalms 51–72 (cf. Ps 72:20). Within the larger collection, Psalms 52–55 are marked as a distinct sub-unit by the fact that each is labelled as a *maskil*. Though the exact sense of this label is uncertain, one clear organizing principle in the Prayers of David is the use of terms like this. Hence, Psalms 56–60 are all labelled as a "miktam" (מכתם), a term that appears otherwise only in the title of Psalm 16. In this case, the compilers of the Psalter have used a formal mechanism for marking the connections between these psalms. These formal links are strengthened by the significant range of keywords shared between them.[17]

As a sub-unit, Psalms 52–55 can be further divided into two groups, Psalms 52–53 and 54–55. A common feature of the Prayers of David is that the titles refer to specific points in David's life found in the books of Samuel. In this sub-unit, Psalms 52 and 54 are tied to specific events, whereas Psalms 53 and 55 are not. One effect of this is to encourage readers to draw on the background of the previous psalm

---

15. For instance, Kraus, *Psalms 1–59*, 513, makes no comment on Ps 53, simply directing readers to his comments on Ps 14, while Seybold, *Die Psalmen*, 217–18, notes the differences but otherwise assumes no further comment is needed.

16. See, for example, Hossfeld and Zenger, *Psalms 51–100*, 36–39; Botha, "Psalm 53."

17. See Botha, "Psalm 55," 114–17.

when reading Psalms 53 and 55. When we do this, it is evident that the claim that there is no God, or those who act as if God is not present, is once again an issue here. As with Psalms 9–14, the issue of theodicy is again prominent, though Psalm 53 does play a different role within this sub-unit as compared to Psalms 9–14.

Psalm 52 opens this sub-unit with a psalm that is primarily addressed to an adversary, with God only addressed in the last verse. The adversary is identified in the title as Doeg the Edomite, linking the psalm to an event recorded in 1 Samuel 21:1–10. The psalm itself does not mention Doeg, but the content of the psalm is consistent with Doeg's presentation in Samuel. Nevertheless, the anonymity of the "mighty one" (הגבור) addressed in the psalm means that it is applicable to a wider range of adversaries than Doeg alone. In verses 1–5, the poet addresses the adversary, pointing to his boastful and abusive speech. Indeed, his speech is a major component of the complaint, though focusing on it is also a mechanism by which the poet here demonstrates the commitment to instructing sinners, that was vowed in Psalm 51:13.[18] This section of the psalm ends by noting that God would uproot the adversary from the land of the living. Verses 6–7 then provide a response from the righteous who laugh at their adversary because of his failure to make God his refuge, whereas the psalmist is likened to a green olive tree in the temple. Failing to make God one's refuge is broadly equivalent to the practical atheism expressed in Psalm 10, living in a manner that assumes God's presence would not affect one's experience. The community is to learn from the end of the mighty one that a life which ignores God is one that will ultimately see God act, though no timeframe for this is specified. That God will act against such a person recalls both Psalms 1 and 2—picking up on the word of assurance from Psalm 1:6, while also pointing to the closing beatitude of Psalm 2:12. The laughter of the righteous echoes God's response to rebellious nations in Psalm 2:4, while the mention of the righteous also points to the contrast between the righteous and the wicked in Psalm 1. Allusions to Psalm 1 become more pronounced in the comparison of the poet to an olive tree in the temple, associating the poet with the righteous in Psalm 1:3. By contrast, the language of refuge evokes Psalm 2. In this case, the mighty one has sought refuge in his own desire,[19] a desire that is also his destruction. In

---

18. deClaissé-Walford et al., *Psalms*, 459.

19. Many modern English versions render הוה as "destruction" (e.g., ESV). However, *DCH* lists four possible roots for the word, two of which are plausible, "destruction"

effect, the path the mighty one has taken could be broken down directly by God, but it is also possible that God has so ordered the world that such actions are intrinsically destructive to those who follow them. In either case, the psalm insists that the practical atheism of the adversary will fail, with echoes to Psalms 1–2 crucial to demonstrating this.

When Psalm 53 then reports the fool thinking that there is no God, it further characterizes the mighty one of Psalm 52 as a fool. That is, the adversary in Psalm 52 has lived as if there is no God, or at least that God's presence makes no discernible difference. Psalm 52 has several wisdom features, and the language of the fool here continues that. The "two ways" pattern hinted at in Psalm 52 is also present here, where the actions of the fools who deny God and practice iniquity are set in contrast to God seeking those who do good, here defined as seeking God (verses 1–2).[20] The deeds of the mighty one in Psalm 52 are here an example of those who do evil, destroying God's people and not calling upon him. The point of the rhetorical question in verse 4 is that these people should understand that God will not ultimately tolerate their abusive actions. The importance of this for the worshiping community is made explicit in verse 5b, a line not found in Psalm 14, which reminds them that God acts against those who encamp against them and that they have put such people to shame by their faithfulness precisely because God has rejected them. As with Psalm 14, a closing appeal looks for God to bring about the full restoration of his people, but the point remains that the failings of practical atheism are again laid bare. Nevertheless, circumstances continue, which means that at least some consider this a viable approach. God's presence can be recognized, but there remain situations where some still choose to act as if God's presence does not matter.

Although less developed, the problem of practical atheism continues in Psalm 54, introducing the second half of this sub-unit. We see it most clearly in the actions of the strangers who have risen against the poet, in that they do not set God before themselves. Accordingly, they continue the pattern of the fool in Psalm 53, providing another example of those who choose to live as if God is not present. In contrast, the poet here

---

or "desire." It is intrinsically unlikely that one would choose to take refuge in one's own destruction, but one's own desire is plausible, making this the more likely translation. Nevertheless, one should also allow that the poet might have intended for both senses to be present, so that the mighty one's desire is also his destruction.

20. Such people are prudent, with the word משכיל (v. 2) here linking the psalm's title to the righteous.

claims to have been helped by God (v. 4), making clear that even though some might deny it, God's presence can be known, and that the claim of God watching over the way of the righteous from Psalm 1 can be affirmed. Accordingly, the poet can also anticipate the point where God will put an end to the enemies, further confirming Psalm 1:6. Psalm 55 then extends this hope, ultimately reaching the conclusion that God will act against the enemies, allowing the psalmist to trust in God (Ps 55:23).

As with Psalms 9–14, Psalms 52–53 wrestles with the question of God's presence, and how the reassurances of Psalms 1–2 work out in practice. Once again, it allows that there are some who live as if God's presence does not matter and therefore assume that they can act against others without consequences. But this sub-unit also declares such an attitude to be both evil and foolish, and this is unlike Psalms 9–14, which introduces the motif of testimony (however briefly) in Psalm 54 to indicate that the claims of Psalms 1–2 can be substantiated. God's presence might not be recognized by all, but this sub-unit shows that there is enough evidence for the faithful to continue shaping their life around this pattern.

The Asaph Psalms

The issue of the perceived absence of God is also prominent in the Asaph psalms (Pss 50, 73–83). These texts point to one important shift in comparison to the others that we have considered in that the sense of divine absence is here also experienced at the communal level, whereas all the other psalms we have considered reflect this issue in the experience of the individual. As we shall see, the individual's experience is not absent from these poems, but they now extend this to the nation. Unlike the other groups we have considered, the Asaph psalms are comparatively easy to recognize as a collection, with all mentioning Asaph in the title.[21] Nevertheless, the Psalter's final shape has separated Psalm 50 from the rest of the collection so that although its connections to the rest of the Asaphic collection are evident, the collection now functions as a bridge between the first group of Korahite poems (Pss 42–49) and the Prayers of David (Pss 51–72). Our primary focus therefore will be the Asaphic psalms in Book III, that is, Psalms 73–83.

---

21. For a general introduction to the Asaphic collection, see Firth, "Asaph."

Within this block,[22] the question of God's presence is immediately raised by Psalm 73, highlighting this as a key issue through Book III.[23] There is also a marked shift from the confidence expressed in Psalm 72 which looks to the king as the one through whom God brings about the justice expected from Psalms 1–2, so this psalm becomes an extended reflection on a world that anticipates God's justice but which does not currently experience it.[24] The psalm itself is presented as a word of testimony from a speaker who begins by asserting the fundamental position of Psalm 1, that God is good to the pure in heart. However, despite the frequently made emendation that parallels this with "the upright" (cf. NRSV), the text reads "to Israel." Within the Psalter, this reading is important because it introduces a corporate dimension to the issue of God's presence with which the balance of the psalm wrestles, as this reading is also found in the versions it is to be retained, and also matches with the plural for the "pure of heart" (לברי לבב). God's presence is expected to be experienced by the individual and the community. As such, even though the balance of the psalm reports an individual's struggle with this issue because of the prosperity (שלום) of the wicked, we are to read the psalm as equally applicable to the individual and the nation. The wicked who trouble the psalmist may not assert "there is no God" but they do ask (v. 11):

> How can God know?
>
> Is their knowledge with the Most High?[25]

In context, the question suggests that the wicked have freedom to act as they wish because they do not believe God will act against them. God may well exist, but the question indicates the belief that even if this is true, it would not make any difference to them. The wicked effectively reject the claims of Psalms 1–2, though as with Psalms 9–14 and 52–55, such perspectives are voiced by the wicked. In the case of Psalm 73, this view is ultimately rejected as the psalmist testifies to an experience in worship that leads to a new insight (v. 17). Exactly what happens is not reported, and neither does the psalm explain this insight beyond providing reassurance that the wicked do come to an end. This leads to

---

22. This block can be further divided into two sub-units, Pss 73–78 and 79–83, but for our purposes it is sufficient to note the larger block.

23. See Foster, *Heard*, 83.

24. See Cole, *Shape*, 15–17.

25. My translation.

Yahweh becoming the psalmist's refuge, placing the poet in the position of blessing from Psalm 2:12.

Psalm 73 provides a grid through which to read the remaining Asaph psalms, with two of the communal complaints again providing instances where God's presence is denied. In Psalm 74, this occurs in a context where the nations are destroying the sanctuary, perhaps in the events leading up to the fall of Jerusalem. These nations are said to have decided on the destruction of the sanctuary, thus profaning the dwelling place of God's name. Here, the denial of God's presence is more nuanced, but it is still implied in their speech in verse 8 since it assumes that God will not act against them. Similarly, the community appeals to God to act against these enemies in verse 18 because they are a "foolish" (נבל) people, a label that echoes both Psalms 14 and 53. Their speech denies God's presence as making a meaningful difference. This theme recurs in Psalm 79, another communal complaint, which notes how the community has become an object of disgrace to their neighbors (v. 4) such that the adversaries believe they can act against the community with impunity. This reaches a climax in the enemy citation in verse 10, "Where is their God?" The implication here is either that God is absent or that his presence makes no discernible difference, so why should they honor him?

Psalm 79 introduces an important element—the community's sin—in verse 8. Whether this refers to the iniquities of the current generation or former generations might be debated (though Psalm 78 has shown the sinfulness of previous generations at some length). What matters here is that these elements are brought together at this point, noting that the perceived absence of God's good presence might not represent a failure on God's part but rather on the part of the community. This is, in fact, consistent with Psalm 73, where the poet's testimony up to verse 17 indicates a faulty understanding of God, which is challenged in worship, even if it is not called sin there. The presence of this note in Psalm 79 prepares for Psalm 80, in which the community now asks for God to restore them in the hope that they will not then turn from God (Ps 80:18). Psalm 81 then invites the community to worship (just as Ps 73 indicates they should), because here they hear God speaking from verse 6, explaining how the nation could have experienced his blessing. While the alternate views that question God's presence are voiced by others, it is God's speech that matters, which is why the Asaphic psalms conclude by asking for God to continue to speak (Ps 83:1). God's presence can be challenged, but the Asaphic psalms continue the interaction with Psalms 1–2 by also asking those who pray to ponder the nature of their relationship to God.

In short, the Psalter takes its readers on a literary journey as it wrestles with the question of God's presence, only part of which has been considered here. Nevertheless, three key observations can be made. First, as is widely recognized, the balance of the Psalter engages in a dialogue with Psalms 1–2, one in which the issue of God's presence is central. Second, although the Psalter allows for the possibility of questions about God's presence to be raised, these questions are always voiced by those whose views are automatically questionable, whether because they are the wicked, fools, or nations other than Israel. Readers know that such opinions are voiced, but within the Psalter, they are never voiced by the righteous. Finally, although not introduced until the Asaphic psalms (at least in terms of explicit questioning of God's presence), the possibility is raised that the failure to experience God's presence might be because of the community's sin rather than God's failure to demonstrate the care for the righteous indicated by Psalm 1.

Habakkuk 3

As a text which is demonstrably a psalm, though not in the Psalter, Habakkuk 3 provides an intriguing additional perspective. Although there are other poems in the Old Testament which could reasonably be considered "psalms" (e.g., Jonah's prayer in Jonah 2 or the Song of the Sea in Exod 15:1–18), none are as closely linked to the Psalter as Habakkuk 3. As with many psalms, it includes a title ("A prayer of Habakkuk" [תפלה לחבקוק], Hab 3:1),[26] one that is similar in form to numerous psalms, especially Psalms 17 and 86, which are identical save for the presence of the name "David" rather than "Habakkuk," and Psalm 90, which has "Moses the man of God" (תפלה למשה איש־האלהים). The title clearly represents a standardized liturgical form. That it is "according to Shigionoth" (על שגינות) most probably links it to Psalm 7, which uses the singular form of this term,[27] and is the only other place where it occurs. The chapter also includes "*selah*" (Hab 3:3, 9, 13), an enigmatic term that appears elsewhere only in Psalms, the vast majority in Books I–III

---

26. We may pass over the question of the correct translation of the preposition ל here.

27. Albeit the meaning of שגיון is uncertain.

where we have also noted instances of explicit questioning of God's presence.²⁸ Finally, though somewhat enigmatically, the chapter also includes a colophon that places the chapter in the director's collection, noting that the chapter was performed with stringed instruments (Hab 3:19b). Although placing this information in a colophon is unusual, this again represents information that is typical of various psalm titles, with a close match to Psalm 4:1. Again, this information provides a closer link to Books I–III, since all but three of the sixty-three mentions of the director's collection occur in these books.²⁹ Habakkuk 3 is thus not only a psalm, it is one for which Habakkuk's compilers have felt it important to point to the close connections between it and Books I–III of the Psalter, enabling it to both echo and extend the Psalter's themes.

Although Habakkuk 3 has often been read as a distinct text with little attention to its present literary setting,³⁰ it fits its current setting very well once we recognize that the poem proper only begins in verse 2.³¹ Nevertheless, attention to the editorial notes is important since it provides pointers to the Psalter. Accordingly, the chapter is to be read both in its current literary context within Habakkuk and also in dialogue with the Psalter, especially Books I–III. Since most commentaries read the chapter within Habakkuk,³² our comments on this element can be brief. However, it is important to note that the rest of the book is cast in the form of a series of dialogues between the prophet and Yahweh. The prophet is initially troubled by the presence of violence in Judah—"the wicked surround the righteous" (Hab 1:4)—to which Yahweh has not responded. The prophet has cried out, but Yahweh has not responded. The prophet does not assert "there is no God" but he does ask about God's presence if God does not act against violence that leaves the law (תורה) numb (פוג). Since Psalm 1

---

28. In all, *selah* (סלה) occurs seventy-one times in Psalms, all in Books I–III save for four occurrences in Ps 140 (vv. 3, 5, 8) and Ps 143:6. The presence of this term in the closing Davidic collection may be an intentional mechanism for linking these psalms to Books I–III, especially as the Psalms 144–145 also have numerous links to Psalms 1–2. See Snearly, *Return*, 161.

29. The other three are all in Book V: Pss 109, 139, 140. Again, two of these are in the closing Davidic collection (Pss 138–145), pointing to the links between these psalms and Books I–III.

30. E.g., Hiebert, *God*, 144–49, reads it in its current setting only as evidence of secondary interpretation that occurs in the formation of the book and is therefore of lesser importance for exegesis than his own proposed setting.

31. With Roberts, *Nahum*, 148.

32. See especially Firth, "Habakkuk," 552–59.

insists that Yahweh watches over the righteous, Habakkuk's opening does question the reality of God's presence.

But as with the Asaph psalms, Habakkuk also reports direct speech from God. Admittedly, this is not explicitly marked at first, but the switch to plural imperative verbs in 1:5 indicates a change of speaker, while the fact that the "I" who speaks is able to raise up nations (Hab 1:6) indicates that it is God. Yahweh responds to Habakkuk's plea by indicating that he is present, and the way he will respond to the problem in Judah is by raising up the Chaldeans. Yahweh is then directly addressed again in Habakkuk 1:12, indicating that he has indeed been the speaker in the previous section. Here, the speaker is again the prophet who, in essence, complains that Yahweh's solution is worse than the problem. Habakkuk then announces that he would take his stand and see how Yahweh responds (Hab 2:1), with an explicit response given in 2:2–5. Much of the interpretation of these verses is debated, but for our purposes, it is sufficient to note that Habakkuk 2:4[33] makes clear that the righteous are to live faithfully, perhaps both living by faith in Yahweh and the kind of faithful life that Yahweh desires. The balance of chapter 2 contains five woes against those who act against the righteous, though without ever pointing to the time when the reversal motif explored here will transpire. What is certain, though, is that Yahweh is in his holy temple so that all the earth should be silent before him (Hab 2:20). Yahweh is definitively present, but the wicked also remain. Accordingly, the faithful need to wait for the "appointed time" (מועד) of the vision, a time known to Yahweh but not to the righteous. Eschatology thus becomes a mechanism for resolving the issue of Yahweh's presence with the righteous, though if so, it is an inaugurated eschatology because of the temple's presence.

Habakkuk 3 then emerges from this literary setting. It is important to note that, as with the Psalter, Psalm 1 has been an important intertext precisely because Habakkuk has expected Yahweh to know the way of the righteous in a way that means the wicked do not flourish more than the righteous. But the book's opening chapters have also established the need for the righteous to live by faith, even though they live in a world that is marked by violence. It is in this world, where violence is prevalent and yet the righteous hope in Yahweh's justice, that Habakkuk prays. As the various elements noted above suggest, this is a prayer that engages with the Psalter, drawing on its themes and language. In verse 2, Habakkuk asks that

---

33. Snyman, *Nahum*, 69, calls this the "turning point" of the book.

Yahweh revive his work so that the themes that Habakkuk has heard in the past might now be experienced. That is, the prayer understands the sort of affirmation that can be made considering Psalm 1, but it urges Yahweh to make these affirmations real in lived experience. Strikingly, the prayer is also prayed in the context of a theophany in verses 3–7. As is typical of theophanies, Yahweh comes from the south (Teman) and moves north.[34] Somewhat remarkably, the imperfect verbs at this point suggest that Yahweh is coming (יבוא) even as Habakkuk prays. The glory in which God comes evokes a similar description to Psalm 18:12. Here, as God comes, all else is shown to be powerless, so that creation bows before him, while the nations are powerless before him (Hab 3:4–7). Much of the description of God's coming in verses 4–7 evokes the exodus, but in verses 8–15 this is also linked to the conquest under Joshua.[35] God's power in both these settings also appears to overcome various mythological figures,[36] demonstrating that all of the forces that might oppose God are finally powerless before him. Moreover, the presence that was clear from the temple in Habakkuk 2:20 is here experienced by all creation.

However, the striking conclusion that is reached in Habakkuk 3:16–19 does not report a resolution where Yahweh's justice is now revealed so that the righteous experience his presence as positive care. Rather, Habakkuk needs to wait (נוח) for trouble to come on the nation's invaders. Justice is coming, but it has not yet come in full. Rather, it has been announced, reassuring Habakkuk that Yahweh's caring presence is retained, but also insisting that it might not be experienced by the righteous. They may discover that their crops all fail, and livestock die, removing the very things that were meant to mark the presence of God's blessing (cf. Deut 28). But even so, Yahweh is the one who makes the prophet walk like a deer on the high places. In Psalm 18:33, the poet reports being able to do this as evidence of God's approval and presence in which God watches over the way of the psalmist. But the prophet does this in a setting where the hoped-for blessing has not yet come. It is anticipated because God has promised it, but it has not yet happened. God has been challenged and has responded, just as we saw also in Psalms, but the prophet now looks beyond present experience and understands that although God's presence does mean he looks over the righteous for their good, that good may well be future. Yet, like the psalmists, Habakkuk holds Yahweh to account, calling for God's

---

34. A similar pattern occurs in Ps 68.
35. See Firth, "Habakkuk," 557.
36. See Perlitt, *Nahum*, 87.

justice to be worked out in lived experience while knowing that it may come later than the righteous might want.

Conclusion

Both the Psalter and Habakkuk record individuals and communities wrestling with the issue of God's presence and how that presence is experienced. Both know that God's presence can be reduced to simple slogans that attempt to resolve challenging circumstances by cutting the gordian knot rather than holding to both the God of justice and the presence of violence and injustice in the world. The Psalter, especially in Books I–III, works hard to hold Yahweh to account. It knows the orientation to the world and life provided by Psalms 1–2 and wants to see it enacted in experience. Yet it also knows that this is not always true to lived experience and that some will therefore seek to live as if God is not actively involved in the world. It is not that such people deny God, but they live as if he makes no difference. The Psalter only allows this voice as an opinion by those whose views are automatically questionable, but by giving voice to them it accepts that some will believe this. Yet, it does allow that the presence of sin in the community might mean that it does not receive the blessing of God's presence as might be wished. What it does not introduce, at least not in the psalms that explicitly address the question of God's presence, is the thought that this might be resolved eschatologically. This does not mean that there is no eschatology in the Psalter since at least one function of the royal psalms is to point to the ways in which God's reign is to be experienced ultimately, something that would be of particular importance as these psalms were still prayed after the exile. But of more importance for the Psalter is the task of holding God to account in prayer and asking that his justice be expressed. Here, Habakkuk offers an important extension to the Psalter. Habakkuk also holds Yahweh to account, and like the Asaph psalms, reports points where God speaks in response. But while still holding Yahweh to account, Habakkuk introduces an eschatological dimension, insisting both that God's justice will finally be seen and that there would also be instances of this justice, which can be seen and which continue to give hope even in a world of violence. Within the canon, neither the Psalter nor Habakkuk has the final word. Rather, each offers a potential resource to wrestle with this issue, and the challenge is always to know which is most appropriate at any one time.

Bibliography

Auffret, Pierre. "Sur ton peuple ta bénédiction!: Étude structurelle du Psaume 3." *ScEs* 50 (1998) 315–34.
Botha, Phil J. "The Ideological Interface between Psalm 1 and Psalm 2." *OTE* 18 (2005) 189–203.
———. "Intertextuality and the Interpretation of Psalm 1." *OTE* 18 (2005) 503–20.
———. "Ironie as Sleutel tot die Verstaan van Psalm 14." *SK* 16 (1995) 16–27.
———. "Psalm 53 in Canonical Perspective." *OTE* 26 (2013) 583–606.
———. "Psalm 55 Interpreted in View of its Textual, Metatextual and Intertextual Connections." *SJOT* 31 (2017) 118–41.
Brueggemann, Walter. *The Message of the Psalms: A Theological Commentary*. Minneapolis: Augsburg, 1984.
deClaissé-Walford, Nancy L., et al., *The Book of Psalms*. NICOT. Grand Rapids: Eerdmans, 2014.
Cole, Robert L. *Psalms 1–2: Gateway to the Psalter*. Sheffield: Sheffield Phoenix, 2012.
———. *The Shape and Message of Book III (Psalms 73–89)*. LHBOTS 307. Sheffield: Sheffield Academic, 2000.
Firth, David G. "Asaph and Sons of Korah." In *Dictionary of the Old Testament: Wisdom, Poetry and Writings*, edited by Tremper Longman III and Peter Enns, 24–27. IVP Bible Dictionary Series 3. Downers Grove: IVP Academic, 2008.
———. "Habakkuk." In *Daniel–Malachi*, edited by Iain M. Duguid et al., 533–69. Vol. 7 of *ESV Expository Commentary*. Wheaton: Crossway, 2018.
Firth, David G., and Brittany N. Melton. "In A World without God: Reading Esther Alongside Psalms." In *Reading Esther Intertextually*, edited by David G. Firth and Brittany N. Melton, 99–108. London: T&T Clark, 2022.
Foster, Robert L. *We Have Heard, O Lord: An Introduction to the Theology of the Psalter*. Lanham, MD: Lexington/Fortress, 2019.
Goldingay, John. *Psalms 1–41*. Vol. 1 of *Psalms*. Baker Commentary on the Old Testament Wisdom and Psalms. Grand Rapids: Baker Academic, 2006.
Grant, Jamie A. *The King as Exemplar: The Function of Deuteronomy's Kingship Law in the Shaping of the Book of Psalms*. Academia Biblica. Leiden; Boston: Brill, 2004.
Hartenstein, Friedhelm. "'Schaffe mir Recht, JHWH!' (Psalm 7,9): Zum theologischen und anthropologischen Profil der Teilkomposition Psalm 3–14." In *The Composition of the Book of Psalms*, edited by Erich Zenger, 229–58. BETL 238. Leuven: Peeters, 2010.
Hiebert, T. *God of My Victory: The Ancient Hymn in Habakkuk 3*. Atlanta: Scholars, 1986.
Ho, Peter C. W. *The Design of the Psalter: A Macrostructural Analysis*. Eugene, OR: Pickwick, 2019.
Hossfeld, Frank-Lothar, and Erich Zenger. *Psalms 51–100*. Minneapolis: Fortress, 2006.
Kraus, Hans-Joachim. *Psalms 1–59: A Commentary*. Minneapolis: Augsburg, 1988.
Perlitt, Lothar. *Die Propheten Nahum, Habakuk, Zephanja*. Göttingen: Vandenhoeck & Ruprecht, 2004.

Roberts, J. J. M. *Nahum, Habakkuk, and Zephaniah: A Commentary*. OTL. Louisville: Westminster John Knox, 1991.
Schaefer, Konrad. *Psalms*. Berit Olam. Collegeville, MN: Liturgical, 2001.
Seybold, Klaus. *Die Psalmen*. HAT I 15. Tübingen: Mohr Siebeck, 1996.
Snearly, Michael K. *The Return of the King: Messianic Expectation in Book V of the Psalter*. LHBOTS 624. London: T&T Clark, 2016.
Snyman, S. D. *Nahum, Habakkuk and Zephaniah: An Introduction and Commentary*. TOTC. London: IVP, 2020.
Vesco, Jean-Luc. *Le psautier de David: Traduit et commenté*. 2 vols. Paris: Cerf, 2006.
Wilson, Gerald H. *The Editing of the Hebrew Psalter*. SBLDS 76. Chico: Scholars, 1985.

CHAPTER 9

"In That Day"

*Holism and the Eschatologies of
the Book of the Twelve*

Daniel C. Timmer

THIS CHAPTER DRAWS ON recent discussions of conceptual coherence in linguistics to evaluate the different kinds and degrees of unity and diversity in the eschatologies of the Book of the Twelve. It begins by defining eschatological material and developing understandings of coherence and cohesion that are suitable to ancient Israelite literature and informed by contemporary linguistics. It then explores eschatological material in Amos, Zephaniah, Micah, and Malachi and considers the degree to which these perspectives complement or compete with one another and whether compositional explanations of the texts' origins are necessary. The chapter concludes with a comparison of the eschatological profiles of these four books with those found in the Psalter to explore holism in and between two multi-author collections, then briefly brings the eschatological horizons of the Twelve into dialogue with those of the rest of the Hebrew Bible and the New Testament.[1]

---

1. On the relation of the Twelve to the rest of the HB/OT and the NT from the perspective of authorship as conveying macro-level coherence, see Petrovich in this volume.

Defining Eschatology

The eschatology of ancient Israelite literature, especially as it appears in prophetic books, is a rare gem in the ancient Near East.[2] This is due to several factors, including differences between YHWHism and other religions, most notably the belief that YHWH is the only creator and lord of history.[3]

> There are two conditions . . . that give shape to the Hebraic understanding of history. First is the creation of the world by God *ex nihilo*, and second is God's direction of history towards its goal. . . . The principle of *creatio ex nihilo* implies that the world is invested with a *telos*. There is a reason for its being; and history, in consequence, is to be understood as the space and time opened up for the world to become what it is intended to be. Second, the idea of creation out of nothing means that the world is fully God's world. . . . History may be confessed to have an overall coherence under the creative, providential and redemptive care of God.[4]

Since creation and teleological history go together, eschatology as the "end" of history (in both senses of the word) is part of the same reality. Eschatology involves both continuity as the culmination of God's creative and redemptive purposes and discontinuity as a radical departure from the world as it now is under the variegated effects of sin.[5] The element of discontinuity is impossible without the direct involvement of a transcendent God,[6] and is essential to an inductive definition of eschatology in the HB/OT. While it might seem preferable to define as eschatological only those passages with terminology such as the Day of YHWH, that phrase and many similar ones are quite rare in the OT, and not all of their uses are clearly eschatological (e.g., Ezek

---

2. Arnold, "Eschatology," 31, concludes that "we have at present no evidence outside of Israel for an eschatological notion of a glorious *Endzeit*, or a culminating and meliorative end to the historical process."

3. Balzer's non-ontological, non-future eschatology (as presented in Balzer, "Eschatological Elements") is thus ill-suited to the HB/OT.

4. Rae, "Creation and Promise," 284–85.

5. Arnold, "Eschatology," 25, contends, "The course of . . . salvation history follows a trajectory of promises" that reaches its endpoint in eschatology, which is thus "a culmination of history, rather than an annulment of it."

6. Bauckham, "Eschatology," 310.

13:5).[7] Although these and other phrases do often occur in eschatological material, such material is *inherently* eschatological, regardless of the chronological markers it uses, because it presents scenarios that are "significantly discontinuous from the present" and which represent "the culmination of Yahweh's purposes."[8]

This inductive definition allows us to place eschatological texts on a spectrum, with some being more discontinuous than others with respect to the status quo that they interrupt. In all cases, however, such texts speak of decisive breaks between the present and the future.[9] As mentioned earlier, this discontinuity is complemented by the texts' dynamic continuity with earlier material in the HB/OT, especially the covenants and promises associated with Abraham, Israel, and David (see the chapter by Sweeney in this volume); the tabernacle, temple, and divine presence; and the identity and nature of Israel, Judah, and the nations.[10]

Methodology and Eschatological Diversity in the Book of the Twelve

Even a glance at the Twelve reveals that its depictions of the end of history are presented in diverse ways and use a wide variety of terms and concepts.[11] Other aspects or dimensions of diversity include authorship, historical context, and the particular situations in which God's eschatological intervention brings decisive change.[12] This study will deal with the relationship of unity to diversity at three levels: within individual books of the Twelve, across the Twelve, and then in relation

---

7. See the discussion in Arnold, "Eschatology," 27. Nogalski, "The Day(s) of YHWH," proposes that the term denoted significant divine intervention, whether for or against Israel/Judah and/or the nations, but overstates the literary cohesion that this gives to the corpus by proposing that each usage was influenced by others in the Twelve rather than being part of a discrete context and book (one of twelve).

8. Martens, "Eschatology," 178.

9. In Peterson, "Eschatology," 575, the definition is slightly more demanding, requiring that the eschatological scenario be "an entirely new state of reality." The contested distinction between eschatology and apocalyptic literature does not bear on the arguments made here. Barton, "Day of Yahweh," 71, 73, is less demanding, defining "a new world order" established by "vengeance on this or that nation . . . not of the world itself made new" as "fully eschatological."

10. Some of these, especially the patriarchal, Sinai, and Davidic covenants, are noted by Peterson and Arnold. On the nations, see Timmer, "Nations."

11. See Macchi, "jour de YHWH"; Williamson, "Day of the Lord."

12. For a more detailed defense of this approach, see Timmer, "Unity and Diversity."

to other corpora, especially the Psalter (see the chapters by Maxwell and Ayers in this volume).

Whether dealing with the relation between units within a single book or between books or groups of books, the fundamental issue concerns the presence of diversity and its implications for the whole (or wholes). For the past century and more, scholars commonly approach this question under the rubric of synchronic/diachronic opposition, transposing a perspective from de Saussure's linguistic work to the nature of text production.[13] In studies of this nature, a sometimes small number of texts or pericopae within a book that possess a high degree of conceptual, lexical, or theological homogeneity are attributed to a single author or redactor, while the rest are thought to be the result of successive steps of redaction, modification, or supplementation.[14]

The synchronic/diachronic polarity unfortunately obscures several important points. First, the nature of the diachrony at issue is multifaceted, including not only text production but text-internal references to contemporaneous and future scenarios.[15] Second, although the synchronic/diachronic pair is deployed dichotomously, no language system, and no text, is entirely one or the other. Transposed to biblical interpretation, this artificial polarity frequently generates readings that interpret merely potential indicators of textual development as probative evidence of redaction.[16]

To avoid such problems, the case studies below focus on historical, literary, conceptual, theological, rhetorical, and other dimensions of the texts they examine in an effort to capture the multifaceted nature of their coherence. The case studies begin as acts of critical reading that attempt to make sense of the whole, in this case a single book, as more than the sum of its disjointed parts.[17] Eschewing a polarized approach, the nature and degree of coherence of the texts studied will be evaluated as an incremental phenomenon and measured using criteria from

---

13. See Moor, *Synchronic or Diachronic?*; Hong, "Synchrony and Diachrony"; and Pavan's overview of interpretative approaches to the Twelve in this volume.

14. For a sketch of this method, see Werlitz, *Studien zur literarkritischen Methode*, esp. 90–92.

15. As Paul House observes, the books' superscriptions are "diachronic markers" (House, "Endings," 317).

16. See the helpful discussion of this problem by Berman, "Empirical Models."

17. Jacobs, *Conceptual Coherence*, 194, argues that "the coherence of the whole cannot be determined by the observation of only parts of that whole." Barton, *Biblical Criticism*, 44, also avers that "critics try to read each text as cohering."

linguistics, especially reference, causation, and other semantic relations that the hearer or reader "computes" or infers as she or he processes the text in an effort to understand it holistically.[18] If the features holding the book's eschatology together outweigh those that would atomize it, the book will be considered coherent to that degree and on that level.[19] If that is not the case, compositional explanations for the diversity can be cautiously proposed.

The unity of a corpus, particularly a multi-author corpus such as the Book of the Twelve or the Psalter, must be evaluated on rather different grounds, since it is not a single text but a collection of texts.[20] The holistic nature of the Twelve will thus be evaluated primarily by conceptual, pragmatic, and thematic means, and complementarity or similarity will be a sufficient criterion of coherence in the absence of cross-book redactional layers.[21]

Amos

YHWH's leonine roar that begins the book of Amos (1:2) sets the tone for much but not all of its message, including its eschatology (cf. 3:8).[22] Much of the book develops the theme of punishment focused on various people groups, both within Israel/Judah and beyond their borders. The theme of punishment focuses on Israel from 2:6 onward, and moves beyond a "day" in which YHWH will exercise judgment in a general way and to an unspecified degree (e.g., 2:13–16), to increasingly clear depictions of *radical* judgment that threatens to completely destroy Israel. Although these events will affect the material surroundings of Israel/Judah (e.g., 3:13–15), their focus and their strongest language concerns YHWH's people. Hence the population of Samaria will effectively cease to exist (2:12), with the

---

18. Hellman, "Notion of Coherence," 194–97. Teeter and Tooman, "Standards of (In)coherence," is especially insightful.

19. Landy, "Three Sides."

20. Ben Zvi and Nogalski, *Two Sides*.

21. With Hagedorn, *Anderen im Spiegel*, 294–95, I conclude that the evidence for such redactions across the Twelve is weak.

22. See Strawn, *Lion*, 286, who summarizes the significance of the leonine metaphor as used in the OT in terms of "power, threat, ferocity, dominance, predation, violence, fear," and similar elements.

very idea of a remnant being apparently excluded (unlike a sheep without an ear, an ear without a sheep cannot survive).[23]

These devastating covenant sanctions are announced only after Israel has repeatedly failed to respond with repentance, changed behavior, and submission to YHWH's discipline and calls to covenant faithfulness (4:1–11). Once God's remarkable patience is exhausted by Israel's incorrigibility, more radical means are called for. This *potentially* eschatological complex of events, which could spell Israel's abrupt end, is described as "meeting your God," who as the Creator maintains moral order in his world (4:12–13). The radical nature of these punishments is also evident in the pre-mortem dirge of 5:1–17, which by announcing Israel's "death" in advance (5:1) invites repentance (5:4–6, 14–15) and holds out the hope that a repentant remnant might survive (5:3, 15). Here, as in 4:12, judgment is summarized in terms of YHWH's presence, which "passes through" his people (עבר, 5:17).

The "Day of YHWH" in 5:18–20 is thus moderately eschatological not primarily by virtue of its use of that phrase, but because the context and the passage itself present radical changes with respect to Israel's relatively stable existence in the early eighth century. Even exile does not go as far as the assertions that Israel will be almost entirely wiped out and that God's intervention will be entirely without "light" or reprieve, at least in its initial phase.[24] The repeated mention of exile (4:2–3; 5:27; 6:7; 7:17) indicates the definitive rupture of the covenant relationship that has bound YHWH to his people (cf. Exod 19:4–5; Deut 28:15–68). The sanctions of the Sinai covenant listed in Deuteronomy 28 contain no mention of relief, and the same tone is struck by Amos's announcements of judgment and reinforced by the divine statement that, despite some past reprieves (7:1–3, 4–6), God will "no longer" refrain from judgment (7:7–9; 8:1–3; 9:1–6). This judgment will affect the land, the king, and those among the elite who act as if YHWH has neither the right nor the ability to hold accountable (7:9, 17) both the elite and all others who persist in sin (8:4–6).

---

23. Pfeiffer, "Rettung," 276.

24. Barton's contention ("Day of Yahweh," 76–78) that juxtaposition of future judgment and deliverance creates incoherence that is best explained by attributing these views to different literary strata overlooks the rhetorical nature of some apparently unqualified statements and unnecessarily imposes a dichotomous relationship between "threat" and "divine promise" of deliverance. Notably, a number of ancient Near Eastern texts juxtapose these two elements without any indication of incoherence, as do many biblical psalms and prophetic texts. See Millard, "From Woe to Weal."

The picture of the heaving earth and darkened sky in the penultimate oracle of judgment (8:7–14) juxtaposes these highly discontinuous images (8:7–10) with the more mundane punishments of 8:11–14. There is no reason to presume that all of these punishments are simultaneous or equal in scope, so we are warranted in concluding that there are various phases or stages of divine judgment in view here, with some being less severe and less eschatological than others.[25] Those described in seismic or cosmic terms, by contrast, present a divine intervention that upends the world and the created order upon which continued human existence depends.[26] The final section, which spans all of 9:1–15, begins once again with an image of an ostensibly inescapable divine judgment (9:1–6). YHWH's rejection of an apparently illegitimate cultic site (9:1) entails the destruction of the worshipers gathered there, as does his hunt for any escapees in 9:2–4.

Over against this tide of judgment stand divine mercy as well as YHWH's covenantal promises to Abraham. These interwoven elements prevent divine judgment from destroying Israel entirely. For the first time in Amos, YHWH states in 9:10 that he will destroy only "the sinners" from among his people, preserving those whose belief in his ability to judge and save (contrast "won't act") and whose trust in his mercy (cf. 5:4–6, 14–15) drive a lifestyle of conformity to his will and humble repentance from sin (4:6, 8, 9, 10, 11). This is arguably the most focused judgment of the whole book, likely because its consequences reach farthest into the eschatological future.[27] Only those whom YHWH's morally-focused judgment spares will survive, which surely means that this divine intervention cannot be identified with the exile or any other event in which human beings are the primary actor.

The salvation of the faithful that follows this judgment of "sinners" has three features which are also possible only with divine intervention. First, the restoration of the Davidic dynasty places the Israelites who survive the divine judgment once again under the leadership of a Davidide and maintains YHWH's commitment to that covenantal promise (9:11; cf. 2 Sam 7). Second, this restoration leads to Israel's peaceful exercise of supremacy over a number of surrounding peoples, all of whom are defined by YHWH's name having been called over them as a

---

25. It is better to allow for a spectrum than a binary non/eschatological opposition, as Arnold, "Eschatology," 28, seems to do with regard to Amos.

26. Here I draw upon Timmer, *Jonas, Amos*, 222–27.

27. Timmer, *Nations*, 51–53.

sign of covenantal ownership (9:12).²⁸ Like the remnant of Israel, these non-Israelites have been spared divine judgment and become part of the Israel that YHWH's judgment has created and that he will richly bless (Gen 12:1–3). The shift from the nations' antagonism and outright violence against Israel to their peaceful incorporation into renewed Israel is as radical a change as can be imagined. This superlative blessing also radically undoes the covenant sanctions of famine, drought, and other judgments that had fallen upon Israel (4:6–11). Cast in terms of the national Sinai covenant (Lev 26:4–5; contrast Deut 28:30, 39) and the promise of land to Abraham (Gen 15:18–21), YHWH's deliverance and renewal produce agricultural abundance and his people's peaceful, permanent existence in the land.

This eschatological conclusion of Amos's message demonstrates the importance and value of eschatology in the book of Amos. Otherwise insoluble problems, sin in particular, are resolved by YHWH's world-changing intervention. In the place of Israel's protracted disobedience in the author's past and present comes an obedient remnant that is so aligned with God's will that another exile is impossible.²⁹ Similarly, the paradigm in which a homogeneous Israel and the nations around her are habitually in conflict is replaced by a new paradigm in which subgroups of (some) Israelites and (some) non-Israelites willingly submit to the rule of an eschatological Davidide. Their respective national and ethnic identities are thereby subordinated to a shared identity defined by submission to the eschatological Davidide who will rule over this newly constituted people. In the same way, tenuously held covenant blessings, and even the covenants themselves, are consummated and yield their blessings without interruption. In place of the broken Sinai covenant comes a new, final reality that constitutes the fulfillment of YHWH's promises and purposes for his world and his people. The Creator whose justice threatened Israel and the nations and brought about the destruction of some among them is also the one who (re-)creates a world and a people who are without sin and enjoy life to a degree never realized before.³⁰

---

28. See Kessler, "Natanweissagung"; Timmer, "Possessing Edom."

29. Paul, *Amos*, 289–95, carefully explores the dimensions of this "ideal" scenario.

30. McCann's discussion of righteousness in Amos, in this volume, reaches similar conclusions with respect to the role of eschatology in Amos.

Micah

The theophanic appearance of YHWH that begins the book of Micah sets the non-eschatological material later in chapter 1 in the context of a divine intervention that will have destructive, cataclysmic effects on the created order (1:3–4).[31] For the moment, this future reality remains *in nuce*, and the rest of chapter 1 predicts a number of non-eschatological events: a military invasion that will decimate Judah and lead to the exile of some of its citizens (1:16), destruction for those guilty of oppressive economic practices (2:3–6), and the exile of all, with only those who do not persist in such sins surviving exile and eventually regaining possession of the land.

The return from exile described in 2:12–13 is sufficiently discontinuous with Micah's present and with the exile that it can be termed semi-eschatological.[32] The liberation and return of the remnants from both Israel ("Judah" here) and "Jacob" (the northern kingdom) involve the reunification of God's restored people, who form a single flock, noisy by virtue of its large size (2:12). This section stresses the pastoral and royal role of YHWH as "their king" who leads them out toward their destination. YHWH's kingly role complements descriptions of the Messiah elsewhere in Micah, but is distinct from them because elsewhere in Micah the Davidic king is distinct from YHWH.

The next eschatological passage, 4:1–8, follows the condemnation of Judah's and Israel's oppressive rulers. Several serious punishments are announced against these elites, with the destruction of Jerusalem and the temple coming last as the most significant (3:12). However, after this destruction God will radically remake and exalt his temple and repopulate the restored Jerusalem city with very different inhabitants than those in chapter 3. The prominence of the exalted temple and the word of YHWH will attract non-Israelites who want to know YHWH (4:2). This change leads to peace between the nations and holistic well-being, with ample food and shelter for all (4:4) under God's unending reign (4:7).[33] The rest of Micah 4 looks toward the near future and thus toward exile. However, the restoration of the exiles entails YHWH's decisive divine intervention in favor of his people and against their

---

31. Timmer, *Obadiah, Jonah, Micah*, 109–11.

32. Dempster, *Micah*, 104–7, who notes that "deliverance from exile" by the Messiah is at the center of this passage.

33. Smith-Christopher, *Micah*, 150–51.

enemies, and this is sufficiently discontinuous with Israel/Judah's situation in exile that it is at least semi-eschatological.

Coming after the Davidide who is humiliated in 5:1, the eschatological Davidic messiah establishes a worldwide kingdom that welcomes the returning exiles (5:3, cf. 4:12–13) and repels all assaults, typified by Assyria in 5:5–6, on the basis of God's covenant made with David "long ago."[34] The similarity of this human messiah to YHWH, with whom he shares the kingly role of shepherd-protector (cf. 2:12–13), makes both figures central in Micah's eschatology.

The Israelite-Judean remnant is the main subject in 5:8–15, and its presence among the nations and its purification (5:10–14) are such striking developments that they are at least semi-eschatological. Among the nations, the remnant has either a beneficial or a deleterious effect, depending on how each audience responds to its testimony to YHWH or its identity as his people. In terms of its internal or spiritual reformation, the remnant loses military infrastructure in which it might wrongly trust (5:10–11), its dependence on divination in order to control or account for the future (5:11), and all cult images and statues. The fate of the nations, which remain disobedient to YHWH here, contrasts with their identity and fate in 4:1–4, but this tension does not threaten the book's coherence because the opposing fates of the nations in each passage are correlated with their radically different behavior toward YHWH and his people. In short, YHWH creates remnants within both Israel/Judah and the nations, destroying those who remain rebellious but transforming those who abandon their autonomy. The end result of these divine interventions is a world characterized by righteousness in which YHWH rules from Zion and the messiah ensures the perfect well-being of YHWH's people under his oversight.[35]

Micah's final eschatological section shifts from the near future and exile to a radically changed condition and experience. Daughter Zion speaks from her current condition of humiliation and divine punishment but anticipates a radical change in that condition (7:7–10). God will vindicate and exalt her and make his righteousness serve her justification (7:9), shaming her enemy for the last time. This vindication leads to the radical expansion of the city and people, as part of which new inhabitants come from all directions (7:12) while the rest of the earth (outside

---

34. Timmer, *Obadiah, Jonah, Micah*, 176–78.

35. Renaud, *Michée, Sophonie, Nahum*, 116, notes the "tableau idyllique des nations converties et adoratrices de YHWH."

Zion) and its rebellious inhabitants suffer the consequences of their sin (7:13). The summary of YHWH's full deliverance at the end of the section includes the subjugation of the nations (7:16) and their worship of YHWH (7:17) alongside the full pardon of God's people, in fulfillment of the Abrahamic and Davidic covenants (7:20).[36]

Zephaniah

The Book of Zephaniah makes extensive and effective use of eschatology, which brackets the book (1:2–3, 14–18; 3:8–20) and appears repeatedly within it. The author's repeated allusions to creation or creational categories give his eschatology a cosmic dynamic in which a new creation takes the place of the old, which was subject to judgment because of human sin.[37] This creational theme unites the poles of judgment and salvation, underlines the global significance and scope of YHWH's future interventions, and interprets YHWH's actions as the reestablishment of moral righteousness and order by the Creator whose world sin and sinners have corrupted.[38]

All of these points are present in the book's first announcement of judgment, which reuses phrases from Genesis 7:4, 23 to describe the global scope of YHWH's intervention. The use of categories from Genesis 1, albeit in inverted order, simultaneously emphasizes the undoing of creation and the many domains this eschatological intervention will affect: humankind and animals (day 6, Gen 1:24–27), and even birds and fish (day 5, Gen 1:20–22), which survived the primeval deluge.

The reason behind this apparently unlimited destruction of created life has to do with "the wicked" (1:3).[39] Notably, this group is not tied to any particular nation at this point, so all humanity is potentially threatened by this cataclysmic display of divine justice. This global perspective continues in 1:14–18, where the "Day of YHWH" is described as imminent and its central element is again destruction focused on humankind ('*adam*), whose "blood" (cf. Gen 9:6) will be poured out like

---

36. Wendland's extended discussion of Micah 7:14–20 in this volume explores some of these points in more detail.

37. It thus exemplifies the "weal—woe—weal" pattern identified by Millard, "From Woe to Weal."

38. Irsigler, *Zefanja*, 99, 376.

39. Renz, *Books*, favors retaining "wicked" as original; cf. Sweeney, *Zephaniah*, 64–65.

the dust from which Adam was made (Gen 2:7). It is hard to imagine a more fully eschatological event than this.[40]

By contrast, the rest of Zephaniah 1 is not eschatological, its horizon being limited to Judah's religious and political spheres near the end of the seventh century. The sins that are enumerated in 1:4–13 will be met with non-eschatological consequences, the worst of which is exile or a devastating invasion (1:13). Yet these events, although not eschatological in nature, are literarily and thematically inseparable from their context (1:2–3, 14–18), which insists that YHWH will also punish sin in definitive, irreversible ways. This overlapping or blending of far and near temporal horizons is very clear from the placement of the "Day of YHWH" in 1:7, where it is explained as a feast at which sinful Judeans (the intended present audience) will be consecrated as the sacrificial meal rather than partaking of it.[41] YHWH distinguishes between those Judeans who are guilty of these sins and those who are not, ensuring that his punishment is warranted and just (1:5, 6, 8, 9, 12).

In 2:4–10, Judah's post-judgment remnant appears rather abruptly (2:7, 9). The proximity of the call to repentance in 2:1–3 hints that repentance *here and now* is the only way to avoid the *future* judgment that will eventually fall on sinners in Judah. Here the remnant finds itself on the far side of judgment, and thus in the semi-eschatological restoration phase of the Day of YHWH. The remnant's restoration is inseparable from the punishment of (some) non-Israelites, exemplified by Nineveh and Assyria in particular (2:15), whose arrogance and autonomy have led them to disparage and act violently against God's people.

Zephaniah 2:4–10 is the first of several passages in Zephaniah in which the fates of Judah and the nations are explicitly intertwined. Quite often, this creates a focus on the results of the different ways that non-Israelites respond to Israel and her God, pairing animosity with cursing and submission with blessing (see Gen 12:3). While 2:4–10, 12–15 explores the former (animosity → cursing), 2:11 interrupts that portrayal with a stunning prediction that connects YHWH's judgment against "them," that is, the non-Israelites who have opposed him and his people in 2:9–10, with his radically positive divine intervention among other non-Israelites. This intervention's destructive element is limited to the *gods* of these groups, whom YHWH will "starve" or "famish" with the result that

---

40. Timmer, "Political Models," 319–20.
41. See Jong, "Sanctified or Dedicated?"

an unknown number of non-Israelites will "bow down to him" wherever they are. The distinction between Judah and its remnant in the first half of the book is thus mirrored by the creation of a remnant within the nations, with the primary characteristics of both remnants being worship of YHWH and acceptance of his claims upon them.[42]

The review in 3:1–7 of Judah's holistic failure to follow YHWH and his will reveals that Judah is beyond help—at least at present. Things have reached a critical point, with Judah failing to learn even from God's punishment of the nations around her. This creates significant dramatic tension: YHWH's presence among his sinful people (3:5) cannot continue indefinitely, yet this dire situation can only be changed by his radical, monergistic intervention, announced in 3:8. In keeping with Zephaniah's global horizon, the scope of the action that God announces is not limited to Judah. In sharp contrast to the nations of Zephaniah's day, roundly condemned in most of chapter 2, some of them (as in 2:11) will be radically transformed. YHWH will "purify" their speech, effecting a change that is not linguistic but spiritual and holistic, as the link between lips and heart in the OT suggests and as their unanimous worship of YHWH shows (Pss 12:2–4; 16:4; 31:18; 34:13; 140:3; 141:3–4; Prov 8:7; 15:7; Isa 6:7). While until now these nations had called on their own gods, they will soon turn from their gods and serve YHWH, ending their conflicts at the same time.[43]

The "dispersed ones" in 3:10 are most likely Israelites, and 3:11–13 describes the creation of the Judean remnant in detail.[44] As is the case with non-Israelites in 3:9, this change is internal and radical, and so can be termed eschatological. The remnant itself is contrasted with those who are proud and self-exalting, who are "removed" from God's people (3:11; cf. Amos 9). God will also remove the smallest vestiges of pride and independence from the remnant itself (3:12). YHWH will even remove from their hearts and lives injustice and dishonesty, creating a sinless, perfected remnant that enjoys a life undisturbed by external threats (3:13). God's presence with his restored people in this future scenario is intimate, relational, and unencumbered, and YHWH celebrates his successful rescue of his people and their perfected relationship with him

---

42. Despite its interruptive nature, the content of 2:11 thus coheres well with themes and dynamics elsewhere in the book, and it should not be identified as a redaction. See Timmer, *Theology*, 177–78, 205.

43. See the careful discussion in Irsigler, *Zefanja*, 372–79.

44. So Gärtner, "Jerusalem—City of God."

(3:17). Elements of discontinuity with the previous status quo include the end of his people's shame and reproach, the removal of the oppressor, and the elevation of the lame and marginalized.

The dynamic of judgment and salvation, with YHWH's justice and grace harmoniously interlinked, is at the heart of Zephaniah's shift from a present in which Judah's sin and the nations' opposition to YHWH and his people are dominant to a radically different eschatological endpoint. The flood of divine justice announced in 1:2–3 thus saves as well as destroys, much like the deluge itself. The radical changes predicted in Zephaniah often involve human actions such as repentance (2:1–3) but are fundamentally a divine work. Only YHWH can destroy evil and those who practice it, and he alone changes the hearts of Israelites and non-Israelites (3:9–13). These radical discontinuities are at the same time fulfillments of YHWH's earlier promises to Abraham and Israel to be their God and, through them, the God of the whole earth.[45] YHWH's unmediated presence among his people is similarly a superlative fulfillment of the promise partially realized in the Tabernacle and the Jerusalem temple. One final discontinuity must be appreciated. Unlike the first creation in which sin is all too possible, YHWH himself has removed sin from the human inhabitants of his new creation, and Zephaniah gives every indication that the new status quo will be absolutely permanent. This brings the creation itself to its intended telos: "There must be redemption if creation is to be itself."[46]

Malachi

The first eschatological horizon that greets the reader of Malachi sees YHWH being worshiped "among the nations" (1:11, 14). In contrast to the post-exilic present, non-Israelites will worship God acceptably without coming to Jerusalem, a scenario that presupposes the worldwide expansion of his kingdom. Particularly in the context of Malachi's focus on the Jerusalem temple, this assertion is radically new.[47] The arrival of YHWH's messenger in 3:1 is so closely connected to the arrival of YHWH himself that it too must be considered to be at least semi-eschatological, since God will remove sin from the Levites so that they can offer

---

45. Renz, *Books*, 630–33.
46. Gunton, *Triune Creator*, 167.
47. Timmer, *Nations*, 207–14.

acceptable sacrifices to him, while his judgment will condemn those who persist in sin against him and fail to recognize his unique deity (3:5).[48] This judgment of Israelites produces a remnant in the most direct, empirical way possible, a process that is described in more detail in the book's final disputation (3:13–4:3). To undo the moral chaos that has led many Israelites to abandon God and seek well-being elsewhere, God promises that in a future "day" he will make "those who revere him" his "treasured possession," sparing them but by implication destroying those who do not revere and serve him (3:16–18).[49] The language used here is drawn from key passages in Exodus, especially the initial invitation to enter into covenant with YHWH at Sinai (Exod 19:4–5), and so significantly modifies the definition of God's people. This day also includes or leads to the destruction of "all evildoers," with no specification of their nationality. The fate of those who "revere" YHWH's name is the very opposite, and they will thrive under his righteousness and healing.

Malachi's overview of YHWH's eschatological interventions is thus two-sided. God's people, defined as those who revere and serve him faithfully, will be purified, whereas those who refuse to honor and submit to him as God will be destroyed. In parallel with the salvation of the Israelite remnant, an unspecified number of non-Israelites will effectively be made priests and worship YHWH acceptably in their homelands, paralleling the purification of the Levites in chapter 3. Judgment and salvation, exercised on a global scale for and against Israelites and non-Israelites, lead to the elimination of sin and sinners and to the deliverance and holistic, permanent well-being of those who revere YHWH.[50]

Coherence, Complementarity, or Contradiction?

We are now ready to consider the degree to which the eschatologies of the four prophetic books surveyed above are consistent in themselves (each book considered individually) and as a collective whole. The syntheses of each book's eschatology, presented above, have demonstrated the predominance of factors that give it coherence. As a result, it is unnecessary to propose a compositional history in which a given book's

---

48. Merrill, *Commentary*, 431.

49. Snyman, *Malachi*, 160–62, notes the prominence of antitheses throughout this unit, especially regarding the un/righteous distinction.

50. Kessler, *Maleachi*, 298–300.

unwieldy diversity presumably came into being as successive redactors added supplements and made changes that revealed their disagreement or dissatisfaction with the earlier form of the text and attempted to create a new synthesis more acceptable to them.

As for the books taken together, global coherence exists because the same things happen to the same kind of people for the same reasons. Further, these events are a fulfillment of the same promises by the same God. Of course, these events come about in different historical circumstances. Each book focuses first or primarily on YHWH's relationship with Israel/Judah, which has come under immense pressure due to its sin. God's intervention inevitably involves punishment, but that is never the last word, although not all those who are punished will enjoy the deliverance that appears sooner or later. The interrelated fates of Israel/Judah and the nations consistently involve non-Israelites in similar dynamics. Just as some in Israel/Judah come to constitute a remnant that will survive and enjoy full, eschatological deliverance, so likewise some from among the nations will turn to YHWH and join his people in worshiping him.[51]

Within this joint presentation of God's present and future involvement with his people and with all of humanity, each prophet exhibits unique emphases that enrich but do not disrupt the main lines of their collective message.[52] The Davidic messiah plays a minor role in Amos and a major role in Micah, but is absent from Zephaniah and Malachi. The cosmic, creational dimensions of YHWH's salvation and judgment are more explicit in Zephaniah than elsewhere; Micah emphasizes forgiveness of sins in ways that the other three books do not; Amos's presentations of the future are almost entirely negative as he seeks to correct the tragically flawed and overly rosy eschatology of his audience; and Malachi presents a clearer redefinition of Israel than the other books using several unique images and mechanisms.[53] Despite these distinguishing features, the substantial homogeneity of the eschatologies of these four books is clear.

---

51. See the related conclusions in the study by Maxwell in this volume.
52. For a contrasting view, see Schmid, "Kosmische Weltgericht."
53. The significance of this point is overemphasized by Himbaza, "L'eschatologie," 359, 363.

The Twelve and the Psalter

Here we can undertake only a brief comparison of the eschatologies of the Twelve and the Psalter. Our cursory probe will highlight the prominence of similar themes in both corpora that favor their fundamental complementarity while preserving their less weighty differences in tone, topic, and audience.

YHWH as Judge and Deliverer of the Nations

Although some interpreters adopt a geopolitical definition of the nations in the Psalter, and so see its "final, definitive expression of God's kingship in relationship to foreign nations" as exclusively negative or punitive,[54] such conclusions are arguably reductionist. Some psalms clearly announce judgment against those nations who scorn YHWH and his people (Pss 79, 83, etc.), but the very definition of these "nations" is theological rather than geopolitical. In the same vein, other psalms make "the boundary between friend and enemy of YHWH more porous" than a simple Israel-foreigner dichotomy.[55] This perspective is reinforced by the Psalter's consistent distinction between the anonymous righteous and wicked.[56] In the gateway to the Psalter, Psalm 2 envisions two types of non-Israelites: those that continue in rebellion against YHWH and his anointed and those that submit to him.[57] Similarly, non-Israelites that turn to YHWH figure prominently in the first Korahite collection (Psalms 42–49), in the prayer of Psalm 72, and in the list of Zion's restored citizens in Psalm 87.[58] Furthermore, the Psalter's strong missional emphasis, in which the speakers regularly invite non-Israelites to rejoice in YHWH and submit to him, reinforces the Abrahamic trajectory (Gen 12:1–3)[59] and parallels the prophets' frequent inclusion of non-Israelites in YHWH's deliverance and their insistence that YHWH's reign encompasses the whole world.[60]

54. Wittman, "Let Us Cast Off."
55. Cornell, *Divine Aggression*, 201.
56. See Creach, *Destiny of the Righteous*, 126–34.
57. Compare the similar conclusions of Ayars regarding Psalms 1–2 in his essay in this volume.
58. Maier, "Israel und die Völker."
59. Boda, "Declare His Glory."
60. Cornell, *Divine Aggression*, 147.

The Faithful (Remnant) in Israel

The condemnation of (some) non-Israelites on religious and moral grounds in some of the Psalms is paralleled by references to Israelites who oppress the psalmists.[61] In Psalm 1, the author identifies the wicked, whose company the wise in Israel must avoid, exclusively in terms of their behavior.[62] Psalm 10 presents a clear picture of an Israelite "enemy" who is fully committed to a life in opposition not only to the psalmist, but to YHWH and his law (10:5), and who commits violence in Israel (10:8–10). No clearer example of the distinction between the righteous and the wicked *within Israel* can be found than that in Psalm 50, where the "wicked" person has intimate knowledge of YHWH's law and covenant while testifying falsely against his (Israelite) "brother" (50:16–20).[63] This bifurcation parallels the remnant concept as developed in Amos, Micah, Zephaniah, and Malachi.

YHWH as Universal King

YHWH's royal glory illuminates the Psalter. "The Psalter refers extensively to the reign of God, to God as the one who reigns. Creation and the ruling over . . . what he has made, especially his wayward covenant people, are the two main acts of God described in the Psalter."[64] Like Amos, Micah, and Zephaniah, the Psalter looks beyond David and his line to YHWH's reign. McCann and many after him underline the importance of Psalm 2 as part of the gateway to the Psalter and find in it "primarily . . . an affirmation of God's sovereignty rather than the sovereignty of the Davidic monarch."[65] This eschatological orientation is clearer still in Book IV of the Psalter, which reorients readers after the apparent "failure of the Davidic covenant" by "calling their attention to the continued reign of God" despite that loss.[66] This perspective culminates in the celebration of YHWH as creator and king in Psalms

---

61. Creach, *Destiny of the Righteous*, 7–8.

62. Craigie and Tate, *Psalms 1–50*, 60–61.

63. Whether or not this psalm is (part of) a liturgy for covenant renewal, it is clear that it addresses the Israelites (50:7); cf. Craigie and Tate, *Psalms 1–50*, 363–66.

64. Holmes, *Lord is Good*, 81.

65. McCann, *Theological Introduction*, 43.

66. McKelvey, *High Kingship of Yahweh*, 16.

146–150,⁶⁷ although the Psalter connects this hope to the restoration of the Davidic line in Psalm 110 and elsewhere.⁶⁸ As such, the rule of YHWH as described in the Psalms closely parallels the Davidic element in Amos and especially Micah as well as the prophetic books' unanimous attribution of all rule and authority to YHWH.

The World Remade

It is significant that Psalm 104 "anticipates an eschatological restoration of God's creation, when the wicked will be no more."⁶⁹ Psalm 72 moves in the same direction, if not quite as far, as it describes the submission of the nations to YHWH's messianic king, the elimination of injustice, and agricultural fecundity. The YHWH *malak* psalms likewise predict the arrival of perfect righteousness (96:13; 98:9) and the elimination of idolatry worldwide (97:7), two realities quite discontinuous with the present age but very close to the images of eschatological renewal in the prophetic books studied above.⁷⁰

Summary

This brief glance at the eschatology of the Psalter reveals a fundamental alignment with the Twelve. The primary actors (YHWH, Israel, and the nations) play their respective roles in YHWH's gradual establishment of his kingdom, with justice or mercy exercised toward both Israelites and non-Israelites (judgment/salvation). These dynamics have the same goal as the eschatology of the writings we considered from the Twelve: the full establishment of YHWH's rule, the elimination of his enemies, and the consummation of his relationship with faithful, penitent Israelites and non-Israelites.

---

67. Scaiola, "End of the Psalter." See also Ayars on the ideal David and ideal Zion, in this volume.

68. Mitchell, "Lord, Remember David," 538, correctly observes that "the kingships of YHWH and David are not mutually exclusive."

69. McKelvey, *High Kingship of Yahweh*, 302.

70. Note also Psalms 144 and 145, discussed by Barbiero, "Messianismus und Theokratie."

The Twelve and the Rest of the Jewish and Christian Scriptures

HB/OT

Other parts of the HB/OT pick up the same threads seen in the eschatologies of the Twelve. The Davidic promise of 2 Samuel 7 is developed in Chronicles, Isaiah (9:2–7; 11; 55:3), Jeremiah (17:25; 23:1–8; 30:1–11; 33:14–18), and Ezekiel (34:20–31; 37:21–28). The same is true of the elimination of sin and sinners from YHWH's remade world (Isa 24; 66), the radical renewal of Zion and the remnant (Ezek 37:23), and the creation of a radically remade world (Isa 25:1–6; 65:17–25). These developments bring the covenants with Abraham and David to their eschatological fulfillment and usher in the full establishment of YHWH's kingdom.[71]

The New Testament

Here we can treat only summarily the NT's pervasive claim that the eschatological kingdom of God prophesied and foreshadowed in the HB/OT comes into existence with Jesus Christ (Mark 1:15). It is evidenced by his miracles and exorcisms (by him or in his name),[72] but is only inaugurated, not consummated, during his earthly ministry. From the moment of his resurrection, Christ is presented as the final messianic agent of God's rule (Rom 1:1–4). The Christian church is born among Jews, and an increasing number of non-Jews join it (Acts 15, cf. Amos 9:11–12) as Christ's reign gradually extends to the ends of the earth (Rom 16:26; Col 1:6, 23).

The resurrection of Jesus Christ is also the harbinger and "enacted promise" of the new creation foretold by the prophets: "His ministry, death, and resurrection constitute God's definitive promise for the eschatological future of all things."[73] In the NT, Christ's return coincides with the full realization of the new heavens and the new earth through the punishment and elimination of evil (1 Thess 5:3–4; Titus) and the initiation of eternal fellowship between God and his redeemed, perfected people (1 John 3:2; Rev 21:3–8): "that single, perfect reality

---

71. The study of Marvin Sweeney in this volume develops further the importance of the covenants in the eschatology of the Twelve, especially their integration.

72. See Twelftree, *Name of Jesus*.

73. Bauckham, "Eschatology," 309.

which is the basis and end of all realities."[74] The prominence of the risen Christ in Revelation as the only one able and worthy to open the scroll of God's plans and to exercise his unlimited power in bringing them to realization in time and space confirms Murray Rae's observation that "Christian faith holds that it is within the framework of divine creation and promise, and particularly within its Christological articulation, that the true *telos* of history is disclosed."[75]

Bibliography

Arnold, Bill T. "Old Testament Eschatology and the Rise of Apocalypticism." In *The Oxford Handbook of Eschatology*, edited by Jerry L. Walls, 23–39. Oxford: Oxford University Press, 2008.

Balzer, H. R. "Eschatological Elements as Permanent Qualities in the Relationship between God and Nation in the Minor Prophets." *OTE* 4 (1991) 408–14.

Barbiero, Gianni. "Messianismus und Theokratie: Die Verbindung der Psalmen 144 und 145 und ihre Bedeutung für die Komposition des Psalters." *OTE* 27 (2014) 41–52.

Barton, John. "The Day of Yahweh in the Minor Prophets." In *Biblical and Near Eastern Essays: Studies in Honour of Kevin J. Cathcart*, edited by Carmel McCarthy and John F. Healey, 68–79. JSOTSup 375. London: T&T Clark, 2004.

———. *The Nature of Biblical Criticism*. Louisville, KY: Westminster John Knox, 2007.

Bauckham, Richard. "Eschatology." In *The Oxford Handbook of Systematic Theology*, edited by John Webster et al., 306–22. Oxford: Oxford University Press, 2007.

Ben Zvi, Ehud, and James D. Nogalski. *Two Sides of a Coin: Juxtaposing Views on Interpreting the Book of the Twelve / the Twelve Prophetic Books*. Analecta Gorgiana 201. Piscataway: Gorgias, 2009.

Berman, Joshua. "Empirical Models of Textual Growth: A Challenge for the Historical-Critical Tradition." *JHebS* 16 (2016) 1–25.

Boda, Mark J. "'Declare His Glory among the Nations': The Psalter as Missional Collection." In *Christian Mission: Old Testament Foundations and New Testament Developments*, edited by S. E. Porter and C. L. Westfall, 13–41. MNTS. Grand Rapids: Eerdmans, 2010.

———. "The Future in the Twelve." In *The Oxford Handbook of the Minor Prophets*, edited by Julia M. O'Brien, 146–58. Oxford: Oxford University Press, 2021.

Boloje, B. O., and A. Groenewald. "Malachi's Eschatological Day of YHWH: Its Dual Roles of Cultic Restoration and Enactment of Social Justice (Mal 3:1–5; 3:16–4:6)." *OTE* 27 (2014) 53–81.

Cathcart, K. "Day of Yahweh." In *ABD* 2:84–85.

Cornelius, Izak. "Paradise Motifs in the 'Eschatology' of the Minor Prophets and the Iconography of the Ancient Near East." *JNSL* 14 (1988) 41–83.

Cornell, Collin. *Divine Aggression in Psalms and Inscriptions: Vengeful Gods and Loyal Kings*. SOTSMS. Cambridge: Cambridge University Press, 2021.

---

74. Webster, *Culture of Theology*, 53.
75. Rae, "Creation and Promise," 287.

Craigie, Peter C., and Marvin E. Tate. *Psalms 1–50*. Word Biblical Commentary. 2nd ed. Nashville: Thomas Nelson, 2004.

Creach, Jerome F. D. *The Destiny of the Righteous in the Psalms*. St. Louis, MO: Chalice, 2008.

Dempster, Stephen G. *Micah*. The Two Horizons Old Testament Commentary. Grand Rapids: Eerdmans, 2017.

Gärtner, Judith. "Jerusalem—City of God for Israel and for the Nations in Zeph 3:8, 9–10, 11–13." In *Perspectives on the Formation of the Book of the Twelve: Methodological Foundations, Redactional Processes, Historical Insights*, edited by Rainer Albertz et al., 269–86. BZAW 433. Berlin; Boston: de Gruyter, 2012.

Goswell, Greg. "The Eschatology of Malachi after Zechariah 14." *JBL* 132 (2013) 625–38.

Gunton, Colin E. *The Triune Creator: A Historical and Systematic Study*. Grand Rapids: Eerdmans, 1998.

Hagedorn, Anselm C. *Die Anderen im Spiegel: Israels Auseinandersetzung mit den Völkern in den Büchern Nahum, Zefanja, Obadja und Joel*. BZAW 414. Berlin; Boston: de Gruyter, 2011.

Hellman, Christina. "The Notion of Coherence in Discourse." In *Focus and Coherence in Discourse Processing*, edited by G. Rickheit and C. Habel, 190–202. Research in Text Theory. Berlin: de Gruyter, 1995.

Himbaza, Innocent "L'eschatologie de Malachi 3." In *Les prophètes de la Bible et la fin des temps*, edited by J. Vermeylen, 359–66. ACFEB. Paris: Cerf, 2010.

Holmes, Christopher R. J. *The Lord Is Good: Seeking the God of the Psalter*. Downers Grove: IVP Academic, 2018.

Hong, Koog P. "Synchrony and Diachrony in Contemporary Biblical Interpretation." *CBQ* 75 (2013) 521–39.

House, Paul. "Endings as New Beginnings: Returning to the Lord, the Day of the Lord, and Renewal in the Book of the Twelve." In *Thematic Threads in the Book of the Twelve*, edited by Paul L. Redditt and Aaron Schart, 313–38. BZAW 325. Berlin; Boston: de Gruyter, 2003.

Irsigler, Hubert. *Zefanja*. HTKAT. Freiburg: Herder, 2002.

Jacobs, Mignon R. *The Conceptual Coherence of the Book of Micah*. JSOTSup 322. Sheffield: Sheffield Academic, 2001.

Jong, John Hans de. "Sanctified or Dedicated? הקדיש in Zephaniah 1:7." *VT* 68 (2018) 94–101.

Kealy, Sean P. *An Interpretation of the Twelve Minor Prophets of the Hebrew Bible: The emergence of Eschatology as a Theological Theme*. Lewiston: Edwin Mellen, 2009.

Kessler, Rainer. "Die Natanweissagung (2 Sam 7) und die 'Zerfallene Hütte Davids' (Amos 9:11)." *Caminhos* 13 (2015) 353–64.

———. "The Unity of Malachi and Its Relation to the Book of the Twelve." In *Perspectives on the Formation of the Book of the Twelve: Methodological Foundations, Redactional Processes, Historical Insights*, edited by Rainer Albertz et al., 223–36. BZAW 433. Berlin; Boston: de Gruyter, 2012.

Kraus, Hans-Joachim. *Theology of the Psalms*. Translated by Keith Crim. Continental Commentaries. Minneapolis: Fortress, 1992.

Landy, Francis. "Three Sides of a Coin: In Conversation with Ben Zvi and Nogalski, *Two Sides of a Coin*." *JHebS* 10 (2010) 1–21.

Macchi, J.-D. "Le thème du 'jour de YHWH' dans les XII petits prophètes." In *Les prophètes de la Bible et la fin des temps: XXIIIe congrès de l'Association catholique française pour l'étude de la Bible (Lille, 24–27 août 2009)*, edited by J. Vermeylen, 147–81. LD 240. Paris: Cerf, 2010.

Maier, Michael P. "Israel und die Völker auf dem Weg zum Gottesberg: Komposition und Intention der ersten Korachpsalmensammlung (Pss 42–29)." In *The Composition of the Book of Psalms*, edited by E. Zenger, 653–65. BETL 238. Leuven: Leuven University Press, 2010.

Martens, Elmer A. "Eschatology." In *Dictionary of the Old Testament Prophets*, edited by Mark J. Boda and J. Gordon McConville, 178–85. Downers Grove: IVP Academic, 2012.

McCann, J. Clinton, Jr. *A Theological Introduction to the Book of Psalms*. Nashville: Abingdon, 1993.

McKelvey, Michael G. *Moses, David, and the High Kingship of Yahweh: A Canonical Study of Book IV of the Psalter*. Gorgias Dissertations 55. Piscataway: Gorgias, 2013.

Merrill, Eugene H. *An Exegetical Commentary: Haggai, Zechariah, Malachi*. Chicago: Moody, 1994.

Millard, Alan. "From Woe to Weal: Completing a Pattern in the Bible and the Ancient Near East." In *Let Us Go Up to Zion: Essays in Honour of H. G. M. Williamson on the Occasion of His Sixty-Fifth Birthday*, edited by Iain Provan and Mark J. Boda, 193–201. VTSup 153. Leiden; Boston: Brill, 2012.

Mitchell, David C. "Lord, Remember David: G. H. Wilson and the Message of the Psalter." *VT* 56 (2006) 526–48.

Moor, Johannes C. de, ed. *Synchronic or Diachronic? A Debate on Method in Old Testament Exegesis*. OtSt 34. Leiden; Boston: Brill, 1995.

Nogalski, James D. "The Day(s) of YHWH in the Book of the Twelve." In *Thematic Threads in the Book of the Twelve*, edited by Paul L. Redditt and Aaron Schart, 192–213. BZAW 325. Berlin; Boston: de Gruyter, 2003.

Paul, Shalom M. *Amos: A Commentary on the Book of Amos*. Hermeneia. Minneapolis: Augsburg Fortress, 1991.

Peterson, David L. "Eschatology (OT)." *ABD* 2:575–79.

Petterson, Anthony R. "The Shape of the Davidic Hope across the Book of the Twelve." *JSOT* 35 (2010) 225–46.

Pfeifer, Gerhard. "'Rettung' als Beweis der Vernichtung (Amos 3,12)." *ZAW* 100 (1988) 269–77.

Pury, Albert de. "Le Dieu qui vient en adversaire: de quelques différences à propos de la perception de Dieu dans l'Ancien Testament." In *Ce Dieu Qui Vient: Mélanges offerts à Bernard Renaud*, edited by B. Renaud and R. Kuntzmann, 45–67. LD 159. Paris: Cerf, 1995.

Rae, Murray. "Creation and Promise." In *"Behind" the Text: History and Biblical Interpretation*, edited by Craig Bartholomew et al., 267–99. SHS. Grand Rapids: Zondervan, 2003.

Renaud, Bernard. *Michée, Sophonie, Nahum*. SB. Paris: Gabalda, 1987.

Renz, Thomas. *The Books of Nahum, Habakkuk, and Zephaniah*. NICOT. Grand Rapids: Eerdmans, 2021.

Scaiola, Donatella. "The End of the Psalter." In *The Composition of the Book of Psalms*, edited by E. Zenger, 701–10. BETL 238. Leuven: Leuven University Press, 2010.

Schmid, Konrad. "Das kosmische Weltgericht in den Prophetenbüchern und seine historischen Kontexte." In *Nächstenliebe und Gottesfurcht*, edited by H. Jenni and M. Saur, 409–34. AOAT 439. Münster: Ugarit Verlag, 2016.

Smith-Christopher, Daniel L. *Micah: A Commentary*. OTL. Louisville: Westminster John Knox, 2015.

Snyman, S. D. *Malachi*. HCOT. Leuven: Peeters, 2015.

Strawn, Brent A. *What Is Stronger than a Lion? Leonine Image and Metaphor in the Hebrew Bible and the Ancient Near East*. OBO 212. Fribourg: Academic Fribourg; Göttingen: Vandenhoeck & Ruprecht, 2005.

Teeter, David A., and William A. Tooman. "Standards of (In)coherence in Ancient Jewish Literature." *HebBAI* 9.2 (2020) 94–129.

Timmer, Daniel C. *Jonas, Amos*. CEB. Vaux-sur-Seine: Edifac, 2022.

———. "The Nations in the Minor Prophets." In *The Oxford Handbook of the Minor Prophets*, edited by Julia M. O'Brien, 131–45. Oxford: Oxford University Press, 2021.

———. *The Non-Israelite Nations in the Book of the Twelve: Thematic Coherence and the Diachronic-Synchronic Relationship in the Minor Prophets*. BibInt 135. Leiden; Boston: Brill, 2015.

———. *Obadiah, Jonah, Micah*. TOTC 26. Downers Grove: IVP Academic, 2021.

———. "Political Models and the End of the World in Zephaniah." *BI* 24 (2016) 310–31.

———. "Possessing Edom and All the Nations over Whom YHWH's Name Is Called: Understanding ירש in Amos 9:12." *BBR* 29.4 (2019) 468–87.

———. *The Theology of the Books of Nahum, Habakkuk, and Zephaniah*. Old Testament Theology. Cambridge: Cambridge University Press, 2024.

———. "Unity and Diversity in the Book of the Twelve." In *The Law, The Prophets, and the Writings: Studies in Evangelical Old Testament Hermeneutics in Honor of Duane A. Garrett*, edited by Andrew M. King et al., 187–200. Nashville: B & H Academic, 2021.

Twelftree, Graham H. *In the Name of Jesus: Exorcism Among Early Christians*. Grand Rapids: Baker Academic, 2007.

Webster, John. *The Culture of Theology*. Edited by I. J. Davidson and A. C. McCray. Grand Rapids: Baker Academic, 2019.

Werlitz, Jürgen. *Studien zur literarkritischen Methode: Gericht und Heil in Jesaja 7,1–17 und 29,1–8*. BZAW 204. Berlin: de Gruyter, 1992.

Williamson, Hugh. "The Day of the Lord in the Book of Isaiah and the Book of the Twelve." In *Isaiah and the Twelve: Parallels, Similarities and Differences*, edited by Richard J. Bautch et al., 223–42. BZAW 527. Berlin; Boston: de Gruyter, 2020.

Wittman, Derek E. "Let Us Cast Off Their Ropes from Us: The Editorial Significance of the Portrayal of Foreign Nations in Psalms 2 and 149." In *The Shape and Shaping of the Book of Psalms: The Current State of Scholarship*, edited by Nancy L. deClaissé-Walford, 53–69. SBLAIL 20. Atlanta: SBL, 2014.

CHAPTER 10

The Choir of the Nations in the Psalter

An Intertextual Characterization of "the Nations" in the Book of the Twelve and the Psalter

NATHAN MAXWELL

From One Book to Another

THIS STUDY EXPLORES INTERTEXTUALITY between the Psalter and the Book of the Twelve, a focus that implies from the outset the coordination of a few established hermeneutical paradigms. Each of these methodological dependencies constitutes a storied corpus in its own right, with its own progenitors and detractors, insights and caveats, and continued development. Rather than rehearsing the justification for their theoretical underpinnings, however, the merit and utility of these approaches are, in large part, taken for granted. They are deployed in concert here, working together to draw a higher-resolution portrait of "the nations" and their role in the eschatological vision of the Psalter.

Chief among these methodological assumptions is the internal coherence of literary collections. Neither the *Sepher Tehillim* nor the Book of the Twelve are, in the usual sense, "books." Over the last thirty years, however, both collections have occasioned a din of scholarly interest in their intentional ordering and internal linkage. For the psalms, this era dawned with the effort to discern the editorial purpose behind the Psalter's final canonical form.[1] Today, the "shape and shaping of the canonical Psalter," as it has come to be dubbed, represents a major paradigm for Psalter interpretation that is especially dominant in North American scholarship.[2] In its synchronic ("shape") expressions, interpreters observe linguistic and thematic links at both the macro- and micro-exegetical levels. Thus, for example, the "seam" between Psalms 89 and 90 (and so Books III and IV) is the catalyst for a hermeneutical chemistry that these psalms could not have afforded originally or independently—namely, that Book IV provides a kind of theological response to Book III.[3] Likewise, Psalms 93–100 are each connected in series through "lowest-level lexical links" and comprise a "unified, coherent" structure that places emphasis on the expression יהוה מלך ("YHWH reigns") and the theme of divine kingship.[4] The aggregate effect, achieved in large part through the redactional activity ("shaping") of the Psalter's final editors, moves beyond simple logical organization—the Psalter's present arrangement is *meaningful*. In this way many interpreters approach the Psalter very much like a "book" that poetically recounts Israel's covenantal story. Books I–III retell the rise and fall of the Davidic dynasty, celebrating divine provision but ultimately lamenting the fall of the kingdom and the pain of exile. Books IV–V in turn provide a response to the anguishing problem of exile, recalling that "YHWH reigns."[5]

While interpreters have riffed extensively off this basic tune, the most essential observation is that once the Psalter is in fact deemed

---

1. The first inklings came with the publication of Gerald Henry Wilson's dissertation, *The Editing of the Hebrew Psalter*, along with a number of articles by Wilson in the same orbit: Wilson, "Evidence," 337–52; "'Untitled' Psalms," 404–13; "Royal," 85–94. Wilson's work was not immediately recognized as a watershed moment for Psalms interpretation. By the time Wilson found himself reminding interpreters of his approach in "Shape," 129–42, interest in the "editorial purpose of the Psalter" had collected enough momentum to warrant the now-classic collection of essays in McCann, *Shape and Shaping*. From there it did not take long before Wilson's theory had become robust enough to provide a suitable basis for new studies and a working exegetical strategy for commentaries. Examples are nearly inexhaustible here, but we may note McCann, "Book of Psalms," 639–1280; deClaissé-Walford, *Reading*. The "canonical shape and shaping of the Psalter" has long since trickled down into introductory textbooks and become standard fare for commentaries. See Bellinger, *Psalms*; deClaissé-Walford et al., *Psalms*.

2. Prinsloo, "Reading," 145–77.

3. See Wilson, *Editing*, 215; deClaissé-Walford, *Reading*, 5.

4. See for example, Howard, *Structure*, 19–22.

5. deClaissé-Walford, *Reading*, 5.

to have a purposeful, meaningful shape, interpreters cannot help but ask, "What is the theology of the Psalter?" That is to say, the "editorial purpose of the Psalter" affords the inference that the Psalter therefore harbors some central thesis or hermeneutically-organizing principle, such as the problem of exile (Gerald Wilson), the reign of God (J. Clinton McCann), divine faithfulness (Rolf Jacobson), the destiny of the righteous (Jerome Creach), and so forth.[6] Our interest here is not to indulge one of these "centers" over against the others, or to suggest a new one. We do not even intend to assert that only one key unlocks the Psalter (indeed, the central themes noted here exhibit some cooperative if not overlapping properties). Instead, it is necessary to recognize what sort of "intertextual surface area" we have in the Psalter. When the Book of the Twelve illuminates a particular refrain or character in a psalm (as I suggest below), that interaction does not occur in isolation. To the extent that the Psalter is read as a poetic whole, intertextual connections from the Twelve have this same horizon.

The story of the Twelve is not dissimilar. As Jakob Wöhrle observes, thirty years ago "Old Testament scholarship found a new object: The Book of the Twelve."[7] The seminal moment came with the effort to retrace the historical process by which the twelve Minor Prophets evolved together "as a single corpus," disrupting the widely-accepted view that these texts had essentially reached their final form independently, prior to their incorporation as a collection.[8] The "Book of the Twelve" approach began by making sense of the so-called "catchwording phenomenon"—a freestyle anadiplosis of sorts that daisy chains much of the Twelve together.[9] An oft-cited example of this phenomenon is found in Joel 3:16 and Amos 1:2, in which "YHWH roars from Zion/utters his voice from Jerusalem"—forming a link between the rhetorical context of Joel's conclusion and Amos's opening oracle. As intertextual connections of various kinds continued to aggregate over the years, biblical interpreters became nearly overwhelmed with potential examples and needed

---

6. Wilson, *Editing*, 215; McCann, "Book of Psalms," 1040; Jacobson, "Faithfulness," 125–52; Creach, "Destiny," 64–76.

7. Wöhrle, "Cross-References," 3.

8. This paradigm takes shape with two successive works. See Nogalski, *Literary*; *Redactional*. Today this approach is even more ubiquitous than the corresponding paradigm concerned with the editorial purpose of the Psalter.

9. See Nogalski, *Literary*, 6. One of the earliest references to the "Stichwortverkettung" ("catchword chain") phenomenon in the Twelve appears in Delitzsch, "Wann," 92–93.

to fashion (or import) additional methodological tools to sort through them.[10] The aggregate effect of this scholarship on the Book of the Twelve over the last three decades has been to demonstrate "that this corpus is not just a collection of twelve prophetic books. It is rather a coherent work with a common history of formation and, based upon this, with an overall message and intention. The individual books of the Book of the Twelve are part of a larger whole in which they can be interpreted in a fruitful manner."[11] Like the Psalter, then, the organizational logic in the Twelve moves well beyond a common genre and comparable length; these prophetic texts are *meaningfully* arranged together.

So, too, interpreters have asked, "What is the center of gravity in the Book of the Twelve, sufficient to hold all the individual volumes in its orbit?" The answer may lie in a freighted refrain echoing (and evolving) across the Twelve, such as the "Day of the Lord."[12] Candidates also include broader themes like the character of God or the call to repentance (שׁוב), or even particular books such as Micah or Joel.[13] Yet again, our goal here is not to champion whatever theological center appears to consolidate the most explanatory power. Instead, it is essential to recognize that insofar as the Book of the Twelve may be received and interpreted as a unity, so its individual books may also function in unison to illuminate other domains in the canon—namely, the Psalter. The portrayal of a given character or theme does not occur in isolation, but corporately. In this manner the Book of the Twelve can "speak" into the Psalter.

The affinity between these two domains of the Hebrew canon is underappreciated. The lyrical verse of the psalms and the vivid oracular imagery of the prophets descend from the same poetic ancestry. Both books exhibit a similar modular literary architecture, in which the whole is composed of a dynamic matrix of interconnected parts. This complex design has been the central discovery and keen interest of researchers in both fields over the last few decades. Finally, both function in the biblical canon as a kind of chorus in the divine epic, weighing in as the covenantal drama between Israel and her God unfolds.

10. Wöhrle, "Cross-References," 3.

11. Tiemeyer and Wöhrle, "Introduction," ix.

12. Nogalski, "Day(s)," 212–13; House, "Endings," 338; Rendtorff, "How to Read," 77–86; Schart, "Reconstructing," 41.

13. For the "full-orbed" portrait of God as the sustaining focus in the Book of the Twelve, see House, "Character," 144–45. For the theme of "return," see LeCureux, *Thematic*, 233–37. For Joel as the "literary anchor" of the Twelve, see Nogalski, "Joel," 91–109; Jeremias, "Function," 78–87. For Micah, see Zapff, "Micah," 130–46.

Describing the mechanisms through which the Book of the Twelve and the Psalter connect is more perilous. Despite a flourishing life in biblical studies, scholars have regarded intertextuality almost like a hermeneutical palantír, expressing caution or outright reservation over using the tool.[14] Part of the problem is that "intertextuality" was imported from literary critical theory and subsequently repurposed into a bewildering range of methodological permutations.[15] Most broadly, intertextuality in biblical studies refers to a methodological umbrella for any possible connection between texts.[16] Intertextual relationships can therefore include direct quotations, allusions, echoes, catchwords, or themes.[17] In practice, intertextuality can be difficult to distinguish from what is usually recognized as inner-biblical exegesis—prompting Ellen van Wolde to characterize the borrowed term as little more than a "literary theoretical coat of veneer" over the traditional methodology.[18] Richard Schultz, however, offers the distinction that "intertextuality offers an alternative to the traditional approach to inner-biblical allusion that is *synchronic* rather than *diachronic* in emphasis, *reader*-focused rather than *author*-focused, and thus explores the *effect* rather than the *purpose* of such interconnections."[19] Drawing on the work of Schultz, Will Kynes argues that intertextuality is *both* diachronic and synchronic in nature.[20] For example, mapping out the redactional evolution of a given text and the way in which one author or editor might have influenced another can provide a "necessary limit for the infinite potential meanings" that a synchronic approach might detect.[21] But the coordination between

---

14. Schultz, "Ties," 28. See also Schart, "Reconstructing," 41–43; Nogalski, "Intertextuality," 109; Radine, "Dating," 21–22.

15. Wöhrle, "Cross-References," 5–6. Not surprisingly, intertextuality meant something different in its original context of literary theory. There, a "text" includes any "readable" object or event, and every text essentially absorbs and transfigures the extant corpus. Biblical scholarship has generally followed a narrower interpretation of the term. Finding such stricter applications boring, the literary theorist who coined the term eventually abandoned it, so it would seem the academy is not without its little ironies. See Wöhrle, "Cross-References," 6. For a summary of the controversy over the meaning of intertextuality in biblical studies, see Kynes, *Psalm*, 17–27; Tull, "Intertextuality," 59–90.

16. Schultz, "Ties," 29. See also Miscall, "Isaiah," 44.

17. Schultz, "Ties," 27–28.

18. Wolde, "Trendy," 29.

19. Schultz, "Ties," 29 (emphasis original).

20. Kynes, *Psalm*, 27–30. Schultz takes a similar position in Schultz, *Search*, 332–33.

21. Kynes, *Psalm*, 25.

diachronic and synchronic intertextuality runs deeper. Kynes portrays interpreters as naturally alternating between both approaches, integrating their insights in a symbiotic manner such that the method is "more than a sum of its parts, because the interaction between the two offers more insight than both do individually."[22]

Kynes is especially important to the discussion about intertextuality because his work reflects a trend in biblical studies to explore intertextual relationships across subdivisions, genres, and even Testaments. For example, Kynes has rallied interpreters to the cause of dissolving the Wisdom Literature category altogether, liberating those books from the isolation imposed by an artificial taxonomy and allowing for their "intertextual reintegration . . . back into the canon."[23] Together, Kynes and his mentor Katharine Dell have made an enterprising effort to document the rich intertextual tapestry that exists between Proverbs, Job, Ecclesiastes, and the rest of the biblical canon.[24]

In these ways, intertextuality has evolved in biblical studies. Our focus is the evocative effect one corpus (the Book of the Twelve) may have on a reader's sensemaking of another (the Psalter), even if they are members of different canonical domains. At the same time, we remain attendant to how their redactional histories and editorial influence might intersect. What usually follows from the natural reaction to intertextuality's infamy for being unwieldy and difficult to control[25] is the curation or adoption of a set of rules—criteria for sorting and weighing the spectrum of intertextual relationships. Among the many options one can hardly do better than the careful work of Kynes, which has occasioned nearly a decade of fruitful intertextual analysis. The strategy proposed here, however, is to restrict our attention to a specific subcategory of intertextual analysis.

Intertextual characterization may be broadly described as "a form of indirect, metaphorical characterization; traits and dispositions are inferred from a contrast or comparison with the same character . . .

22. Kynes, *Psalm*, 29.

23. Kynes, *Obituary*, 3.

24. Dell and Kynes, *Reading Job*; *Reading Ecclesiastes*; *Reading Proverbs*. Dell and Kynes have published similar volumes for Esther and Lamentations. While scholarship in the Book of the Twelve has tended to pursue intertextuality within the confines of prophetic literature, interpreters of the Psalter have demonstrated a greater inclination to explore intertextual relationships with other parts of the canon. See, e.g., Botha, "Intertextuality," 503–20.

25. Cf. Schart, "Reconstructing," 41.

or another character in a different text."[26] More explicitly, intertextual characterization occurs when a character who is portrayed in one text appears in another. Such intertextual comparison may be especially fruitful when one text affords a more fully developed, higher-resolution portrait of the same character who appears elsewhere. This benefit is compounded if the interpreter can infer a flow of influence *from* the more richly characterized text into a different setting, because it means the later author or editor was able to tap into a robust resource when deploying that character into a new context.

Biblical interpreters have already utilized intertextual characterization to traverse canonical domains. Ruth Sheridan, for example, has utilized the Old Testament to flesh out the portrayal of "the Jews" in the Gospel of John. "Methodologically and theoretically," she observes, "it is sound to argue that the Gospel of John invites the ideal reader to characterize the Johannine characters, including 'the Jews,' in light of the OT."[27] Sheridan subsequently notes that an "illustrative case of intertextual characterization can be found in studies on the relation between Moses and Jesus in John's Gospel. For a long time scholars argued that the portrait of Moses in the Torah informed the Johannine picture of Jesus. . . . Just as an OT character can find a place within John's Gospel as a character, so can 'the Jews' of John's Gospel be characterized with reference to other OT characters."[28]

It is noteworthy that the example above identifies a group as a functional character in John's Gospel. Our focus here is to consider the intertextual characterization of "the nations" between the Book of the Twelve and the Psalter. Specifically, our intent is to register the evocative potential of the rich, detailed role of the nations in the Book of the Twelve within the Psalter—where "the nations" are acknowledged with striking regularity while remaining relatively ambiguous and thinly portrayed. To the extent that we may infer that the final editors of the hymnbook were also ancient readers of the prophetic corpus, we may also surmise their ability to tap into that abundant repository of traits and dispositions that characterize the nations in the Twelve. Given the way in which interpreters have come to regard the Book of the Twelve and the Psalter, this intertextual relationship is drawn, as it were, from one book to another.

---

26. Temmerman and Emde Boas, *Characterization*, xiv.
27. Sheridan, *Retelling*, 94.
28. Sheridan, *Retelling*, 94–95n208.

Intertextual Characterization of "the Nations" in the Book of the Twelve and the Psalter

The characterization of the nations in the Book of the Twelve is well documented. Perhaps one of the most important studies is Daniel Timmer's *The Non-Israelite Nations in the Book of the Twelve*, which develops the nations as a highly complex but conceptually coherent literary theme within the Twelve.[29] Informed by the work of Kenneth Cuffey, Timmer describes thematic coherence not as "a theme that is itself coherent," but rather as "a complete text that is united by means of a common theme."[30] In this way the non-Israelite nations constitute an element in the literary infrastructure that makes the Book of the Twelve a unity. Like Kynes, Timmer is dubious of a dichotomy between diachronic and synchronic analyses and sees his work as an integration of both approaches.[31]

Timmer heuristically consumes a spectrum of signifiers to develop his portrait of the nations in the Twelve. As such, the study resists any attempt to reduce "the nations" to a simple, static definition. Nevertheless, Timmer recognizes the need to sketch the main lines of the semantic fields used to express the concept. These lines include proper nouns such as Philistia, Edom, Ammon, etc.; political/social language, especially עם ,גוי,, and ממלכה ("nation," "people," and "kingdom," respectively) but also rarer items like אי ("coast, island"); and generic nouns, especially enemies (איב, Zeph 3:15), remnant (שארית, Amos 9:12), and remainder (יתר, Zech 14:16). Additional complexity arises from the fact that not only are these labels sometimes dynamic and other times static, but these same texts create other aspects of the identity of the "nations" by using other semantic fields such as language (Zech 8:23), genealogical descent (Amos 9:7), national citizenship (Hos 9:6), and religion (Nah 1:14).[32]

In addition to this basic sketch, two additional details are essential. First, rendering the non-Israelite nations as a "coherent theme" is not contingent on a uniformly aligned perspective across the Twelve (or even within an individual book). A reader may encounter opposing perspectives "as long as there exists a unifying conceptual basis that frames the

---

29. Timmer, *Non-Israelite*, 1–11. A more recent essay-length explanation of Timmer's work may be found in Timmer, "Nations," 131–46.

30. Timmer, *Non-Israelite*, 4. See also Cuffey, *Literary*, 100–101.

31. Timmer, *Non-Israelite*, 2. Instead of diachronic and synchronic, Timmer suggests the alternate terms compositional and holistic, respectively. In practice, Timmer's analysis seems to afford some measure of primacy to a holistic reading of the Twelve.

32. Timmer, *Non-Israelite*, 15.

particularities of the various occurrences of the subject in the text."[33] Second, a characterization of "the nations" does not need to account for the entire textual corpus of the Twelve; the thematic focus of individual books can and does vary.[34] Put differently, Timmer explains, "thematic complexity does not necessarily entail thematic incoherence."[35]

It is a small travesty, in my view, to extract selectively from a thorough and nuanced analysis like Timmer's. One aspect of his findings, however, is critical to our discussion here. Specifically, the theme of "the nations" coheres within the Book of the Twelve according to the relationship between a given nation's characterization and its fate:

1. The fate of non-Israelite nations is never determined according to their ethnic otherness vis-à-vis Israel.
2. Groups with the same characterization are not assigned different fates.
3. Groups with different characterizations are not assigned the same fate.
4. Groups that are assigned two different fates are also characterized in two different ways.
5. Groups characterized by restored relationship with YHWH are assigned a positive fate.
6. Groups characterized by opposition to YHWH are assigned a negative fate.[36]

In other words, when "the nations" are reconciled to the reign of YHWH and are no longer in opposition to YHWH's people, theirs is a future of well-being. Likewise, punishment is the destiny of "the nations" who oppose YHWH and YHWH's people. In this way the fate of the nations is contingent on their relationship to YHWH, and this theme is expressed at both the individual book and collection levels.[37] Although not eschatological in every case, it is striking how many individual books (Joel,

33. Timmer, *Non-Israelite*, 8.
34. Timmer, *Non-Israelite*, 8–13.
35. Timmer, *Non-Israelite*, 8.
36. See Timmer, 231–33.
37. Timmer, *Non-Israelite*, 232–33. See also Escobedo, "Gather," 158. Escobedo argues that the fate of a given nation on the "Day of the Lord" is contingent on their dealings with Israel/Judah and whether the nation was the Lord's instrument of judgment for Israel/Judah.

Amos, Jonah, Micah, Zephaniah, Haggai, Zechariah, Malachi) Timmer classifies as depicting some part of the nations entering into "a positive relationship with Israel/Judah and YHWH" and so avoiding punishment.[38] The ideal reader's doppelgänger might superficially perceive "the nations" as a relatively flat character in the Book of the Twelve, provisioned only as a receptacle for pronouncements of divine judgment or as a tool for exacting divine judgment on Israel. It is clear, however, that the role of the nations is decidedly—if not dramatically—more evolved. The fate of the nations in the Twelve provides an eschatological beacon signaling the scope of YHWH's mission among the peoples of the earth.

Other studies confirm the relationship between the characterization of the nations and their fate in the Book of the Twelve. In his theological reading of the Book of the Twelve, Rolf Rendtorff also establishes a connection between reconciliation and eschatological salvation.[39] Jerry Hwang has argued that the Twelve's major themes—"land, kingship, the move from judgement to salvation, and the relationship of Israel to the nations—find a uniting link in the *missio Dei*."[40] In his analysis the individual books collectively depict a redemption history that culminates with all nations acknowledging the greatness of YHWH (Mal 1:11) and climaxes in eschatological salvation for all nations.[41] In this way the theological theme of *missio Dei* provides a means for "interpreting the collection as a unified Book of the Twelve."[42] Although he ultimately resists the "Book of the Twelve" paradigm, Anselm Hagedorn does acknowledge that the "ubiquity of the theme of the nations may suggest that we have a unifying theme here that binds the collections of twelve individual books together," and suggests that that unifying theme is substantial enough to compare with more widely recognized themes such as the Day of YHWH.[43] Hagedorn also recognizes "a handful of passages in the Minor Prophets where the nations are explicitly included in the salvation (Zeph

---

38. Timmer, *Non-Israelite*, 227.

39. Rendtorff, "How to Read," 86.

40. Hwang, "My Name," 161.

41. Hwang, "My Name," 161, 162, 179. It is admittedly difficult to include Edom in this scenario; see Hadgedorn, "Nations," 562 and Timmer, *Non-Israelite*, 75.

42. Hwang, "My Name," 161. Likewise, Goswell sees the eschatological salvation of the nations as a prominent feature of the wider nations theme in the Book of the Twelve. See Goswell, "Making," 90.

43. Hagedorn, "Nations," 556, 573.

3:9–10; Joel 3:1–5; Mic 4:1–4; 5:6–7; Zech 2:15–16; 8:20–23; 14:16–19) as they now also worship YHWH."[44]

Composition-minded interpreters regard such passages as a distinct redactional layer. Dubbed the "Salvation for the Nations" corpus, this focus on the eschatological redemption of the nations was likely added at a very late stage in the formation of the Twelve.[45] Even at this late stage, however, the final formation of the Twelve comfortably pre-dates the final formation of the Psalter. If we assign the final redactions of the Twelve to the Persian or early Hellenistic periods, and likewise observe the continued fluidity of Books IV–V of the Psalter until (and perhaps into) the first century CE, then we may regard the final editors of the Psalter as ancient readers of the Book of the Twelve.[46]

The role of the nations in the Psalter is a curious matter. On one hand, their presence in the Psalter is inconspicuous; at first glance referents seem to play a secondary role the psalms in which they appear.[47] The psalmist frequently invokes the nations in the worship of YHWH:

> All the ends of the earth shall
> remember and turn to the LORD,
> and all the families of the nations shall
> worship before you. (Ps 22:27)

> Praise the LORD, all nations!
> Extol him, all peoples! (Ps 117:1)

The casual reader might be tempted to dismiss such examples simply as an exuberant ornament of praise. After all, the Psalter is in some sense an artifact of Israel/Judah's national cult, making the non-Israelite nations a third wheel of sorts in the rhetorical setting between a

---

44. Hagedorn, "Nations," 572.

45. Tiemeyer and Wöhrle, "Introduction," 3; Tiemeyer, "Haggai–Zechariah," 57–59; Ebach, "Joel," 134; Lux, "Zechariah," 251. It is the sixth step in Wöhrle's eight-stage reconstruction. See Wöhrle, *Sammlungen*; Wöhrle, *Der Abschluss*.

46. See Nogalski, "Completion," 66; Nogalski notes that American interpreters gravitate toward a Persian-period dating, while their continental counterparts tend towards a later Hellenistic dating (70). On the late stages of the formation of the Psalter, see deClaissé-Walford, *Reading*, 34–35; Willgren, *Formation*, 8. Books I–III likely solidified around 300 BCE. See Zenger, "Mother," 159.

47. The inherent ambiguity of the Psalter is also a factor here. Like "the enemy" that occasions some unspecified distress, "the nations" rarely wear a name tag in the Psalter. There are, of course, exceptions. Pss 45; 68; 72; 87; 105; 114; 135 all include proper nouns referencing place names or people groups.

supplicant and YHWH. Yet even a secondary reference to "the nations" is sharpened by an intertextual characterization link to the Book of the Twelve. Can we really treat any reference to the nations as an incidental prop on the poetic stage—a simple silhouette the psalmist addresses in apostrophe? Can we imagine ancient readers (or final editors) of the Psalter recognizing the presence of "the nations" in each psalm *without* evoking the rich theological backstory from the Book of the Twelve? Even if the nations are not usually the central focus in the Psalter, the higher-resolution portrait from the Book of the Twelve informs ancient (and intertextual) readers, and as a result, they recognize far more than a superficial reading affords.

Although the nations in the Psalter may seem inconspicuous, they nevertheless appear in the Psalter with striking regularity. Approximately one third of the psalms include some reference to the nations.[48] In the largest category, the nations are portrayed in some form of opposition to YHWH or Israel/Judah. The psalmist frequently calls on YHWH to judge the nations:

> Arise, O Lord! Let not man prevail;
> let the nations be judged before you! (Ps 9:19)

> You, Lord God of hosts, are God of Israel.
> Rouse yourself to punish all the nations;
> spare none of those who treacherously plot evil. (Ps 59:5)

> Pour out your anger on the nations that do not know you,
> and on the kingdoms that do not call upon your name! (Ps 79:6)

In other examples YHWH subdues the nations on behalf of Israel/Judah (or the psalmist solicits YHWH to do so):

> Ask of me, and I will make the nations your heritage,
> and the ends of the earth your possession. (Ps 2:8)

---

48. A relatively conservative list, restricted to social and political terms (e.g., "nations," "peoples") would include Pss 2; 7; 9; 10; 18; 22; 33; 44; 45; 46; 47; 49; 56; 57; 59; 65; 66; 67; 68; 72; 77; 78; 79; 80; 82; 86; 87; 89; 94; 96; 97; 98; 99; 102; 105; 106; 108; 110; 111; 113; 115; 117; 118; 126; 135; 138; 144; 147; 148; 149. Appending expressions that depict the proclamation or praise of YHWH "to the ends of the earth," etc., we would also add Pss 8; 19; 48; 83; 107.

> Your arrows are sharp in the heart of the king's enemies;
> the peoples fall under you. (Ps 45:5)

> The nations rage, the kingdoms totter;
> he utters his voice, the earth melts. (Ps 46:6)

> He drove out nations before them;
> he apportioned them for a possession
> and settled the tribes of Israel in their tents. (Ps 78:55)

Just as the nations are depicted as the possession of YHWH or Israel/Judah, however, YHWH's people are also delivered into the hands of the nations:

> You have made us like sheep for slaughter
> and have scattered us among the nations.
> You have made us a byword among the nations,
> a laughingstock among the peoples. (Ps 44:11, 14)

> [H]e gave them into the hand of the nations,
> so that those who hated them ruled over them. (Ps 106:41)

The frequent characterization of the nations as in opposition to YHWH or Israel/Judah is illuminated intertextually by the Book of the Twelve, where the prophets have "named names" and recounted the deeds for which the nations are indicted. Compositionally, the so-called "Foreign Nations I–II" corpora constitute the redactional layers that most directly provide intertextual characterization for this thread in the Psalter.[49]

The most interesting portrayal of the nations in the Psalter, however, is found in their destiny as the subjects and supplicants of YHWH. We find hints of this thread early in Book I:

> All the ends of the earth shall
> remember and turn to the Lord,
> and all the families of the nations shall
> worship before you.
> For kingship belongs to the Lord,
> and he rules over the nations. (Ps 22:27–28)

---

49. Tiemeyer and Wöhrle, "Introduction," 3.

Book II builds on this idea and characterizes YHWH's reign over the nations as one that is conducted with equity:

> God reigns over the nations;
> God sits on his holy throne.
> The princes of the peoples gather
> as the people of the God of Abraham.
> For the shields of the earth belong to God;
> he is highly exalted! (Ps 47:8–9)

> Let the nations be glad and sing for joy,
> for you judge the peoples with equity
> and guide the nations upon earth. *Selah*
> Let the peoples praise you, O God;
> let all the peoples praise you! (Ps 67:4–5)

Book III includes Psalms 82 and 87, which both play a critical role in characterizing the YHWH-nations thread. Interpreters have described Psalm 82 as "one of the most spectacular texts" in the Old Testament, and even "the most important text in the entire Christian Bible."[50] The singularity of the psalm lies in its depiction of YHWH dethroning all the deities of the nations—who have failed to practice justice among their peoples—and assuming a universal throne of sovereignty. In this way the psalm makes justice the definitive criterion for divinity and the basis for YHWH's claim on the nations.[51] Although a number of interpreters have rebuffed any eschatological reading of Psalm 87, Erich Zenger suggests that the psalm envisions a "great 'world family'" in which Zion is the "mother of all humanity" and becomes "the 'capitol' of the king of the world, YHWH."[52] Thus the psalm contributes to the Messianic Psalter (Books I–III or Psalms 1–89), which "bathes Zion in an eschatological light as the mother of the nations."[53]

The role of the nations in the eschatological vision of the Psalter climaxes in Book IV. This pattern is noteworthy for two reasons. First, Books IV–V exhibit fluidity after the Book of the Twelve was relatively complete. This redactional history strengthens the connection between

---

50. McCann, "Single," 64; Hossfeld and Zenger, *Psalms 2*, 337; Crossan, *Birth*, 575–76.
51. McCann, "Single," 81–83.
52. Zenger, "Mother," 160.
53. Zenger, "Mother," 160.

the characterization of the nations in the Book of the Twelve and the final shape of the Psalter. Second, many interpreters consider Book IV, and especially Psalms 93–100, to be the "theological heart" of the Psalter.[54] The coinciding culmination of "the nations" with the editorial and theological apex of the Psalter intensifies the significance of the nations in the macro-poetic design of the Psalter.

Book IV of the Psalter presents readers with "the largely hymnic . . . sketch of the universal royal reign of YHWH, which YHWH brings about in a grandiose theophany on Zion. Israel with these psalms once again invites the nations to experience this theophany of YHWH, the ruler of the world, who will bring to fruition YHWH's system of justice against all chaos."[55] The central movement in Book IV is found in Psalms 93–100, and the theme of the nations is most explicitly developed in Psalms 96 and 98. The close semantic ties of these psalms invite interpreters to read them together, with Psalm 98 intensifying Psalm 96.[56] Together these psalms portray the summoning of the nations to Zion to accept "YHWH's universal rule over the world and YHWH's justice."[57] This pilgrimage to Zion essentially affords the nations an opportunity to witness YHWH's salvation of Israel, and understand it as the basis for their own redemption in YHWH's world-encompassing reign:

> Say among the nations, "The LORD reigns!
> Yes, the world is established; it shall never be moved;
> he will judge the peoples with equity." (Ps 96:10)

> The LORD has made known his salvation;
> he has revealed his righteousness in the sight of the nations.
> He has remembered his steadfast love and faithfulness
> to the house of Israel.
> All the ends of the earth have seen
> the salvation of our God. (Ps 98:2–3)

It is a remarkable moment for the nations in the Psalter because the YHWH-nations theme here reveals the aim of "YHWH's reign: YHWH is not interested in annihilation and death but in deliverance and life.

---

54. See for example McCann, "Single," 83; Zenger, "Reign," 168. The view originates with Wilson.

55. Zenger, "Reign," 161–62.

56. Zenger, "Reign," 172.

57. Zenger, "Reign," 172.

Therefore, the nations should and can acknowledge YHWH's reign and submit to it. If this happens the world will at the same time be wonderfully transformed, as the cosmic imagery of the two psalms . . . indicates" (cf. 96:11–13; 98:7–9).[58] This key series in the Psalter finally achieves its apex in Psalm 100, which "calls Israel and the nations to the *common* acknowledgement of YHWH's reign over the world."[59]

> Make a joyful noise to the Lord, all the earth!
> Serve the Lord with gladness!
> Come into his presence with singing!
> Know that the Lord, he is God!
> It is he who made us, and we are his;
> we are his people, and the sheep of his pasture.
> Enter his gates with thanksgiving,
> and his courts with praise!
> Give thanks to him; bless his name!
> For the Lord is good;
> his steadfast love endures forever,
> and his faithfulness to all generations. (Ps 100:1–5)

Although "the nations" are not predominantly a central character in the Psalter, their fate ends up playing a crucial role in the eschatological vision of the Psalter. Although they are often characterized in the Psalter as the enemy of YHWH and so the recipients of divine wrath and judgment, the nations ultimately testify to a peaceful kingdom, comprising all the families of the earth, established by the just rule of YHWH. As we imagine the nations answering the call to sing praise to YHWH, they become a kind of hermeneutical choir, reprising the theological (and eschatological) melody that crescendos in Book IV. One cannot help but observe the intertextual relationship between the *missio Dei* and the fate of the nations in the Book of the Twelve. Amos, Haggai, Zechariah, and Malachi provide the most illuminating intertextual links to the characterization of the nations in Psalms 93–100. Each of these prophetic texts develops a complex portrait of the reconciliation between the nations and YHWH.[60] The so-called "Salvation for the Nations" corpus, apparently a keen interest for redactors during

---

58. Zenger, "Reign," 173.

59. Zenger, "Reign," 178–79 (emphasis original).

60. See Timmer, *Non-Israelite*, 222–25; Hwang, "My Name," 168–70, 176–79.

the Book of the Twelve's late stages of development, most directly connects to this critical moment in the Psalter.

The nations are not the editorial or theological center of either the Book of the Twelve or the Psalter, and we do not here intend to propose any new "center" or organizing principle. The characterization of the nations does, however, contribute to the theological unity of both books. Through the intertextual characterization of the nations, the complex portrait in the Book of the Twelve affords a remarkable depth and fidelity to the hymn of the nations in the Psalter.

Bibliography

Bellinger, W. H., Jr. *Psalms: A Guide to Studying the Psalter*. 2nd ed. Grand Rapids: Baker Academic, 2012.

Botha, Phil J. "Intertextuality and the Interpretation of Psalm 1." *OTE* 18 (2005) 503–20.

deClaissé-Walford, Nancy L. *Reading from the Beginning: The Shaping of the Hebrew Psalter*. Macon: Mercer, 1997.

deClaissé-Walford, Nancy L., et al. *The Book of Psalms*. NICOT. Grand Rapids: Eerdmans, 2014.

Creach, Jerome F. D. "The Destiny of the Righteous and the Theology of the Psalms." In *Soundings in the Theology of Psalms: Perspectives and Methods in Contemporary Scholarship*, edited by Rolf A. Jacobson, 64–76. Minneapolis: Fortress, 2011.

Crossan, John Dominic. *The Birth of Christianity: Discovering What Happened in the Years Immediately after the Execution of Jesus*. San Francisco: HarperSanFrancisco, 1998.

Cuffey, Kenneth H. *The Literary Coherence of the Book of Micah: Remnant, Restoration, and Promise*. LHBOTS 611. London: T&T Clark, 2019.

Delitzsch, Franz J. "Wann weissagte Obadja?" *Zeitschrift für die gesammte Lutherische Theologie und Kirch* 12 (1851) 92–102.

Dell, Katharine, and Will Kynes, eds. *Reading Ecclesiastes Intertextually*. LHBOTS 587. London: T&T Clark, 2014.

———. *Reading Job Intertextually*. LHBOTS 574. London: T&T Clark, 2013

———. *Reading Proverbs Intertextually*. LHBOTS 629. London: T&T Clark, 2019.

Ebach, Ruth. "Joel in the Book of the Twelve." In *The Book of the Twelve: Composition, Reception, and Interpretation*, edited by Lena-Sofia Tiemeyer and Jakob Wöhrle, 124–38. VTSup 184. Leiden; Boston: Brill, 2020.

Escobedo, Mario, II. "'I Will Gather the Nations': The Fate of the Nations on the Day of Yahweh in the Book of the Twelve." PhD diss., Baylor University, 2011.

Goswell, Gregory. "Making Theological Sense of the Prophetic Books of the Old Testament Canon." *JETS* 64 (2021) 77–94.

Hagedorn, Anselm C. "The Nations in the Book of the Twelve." In *The Book of the Twelve: Composition, Reception, and Interpretation*, edited by Lena-Sophia Tiemeyer and Jakob Wöhrle, 554–80. VTSup 184. Leiden; Boston: Brill, 2020.

Hossfeld, Frank-Lothar, and Erich Zenger. *Psalms 2: A Commentary on Psalms 51–100*. Translated by Linda M. Maloney. Hermeneia. Minneapolis: Fortress, 2005.

House, Paul R. "The Character of God in the Book of the Twelve." In *Reading and Hearing the Book of the Twelve*, edited by James D. Nogalski and Marvin A. Sweeney, 124–45. SBL Symposium Series 15. Atlanta: SBL, 2000.

———. "Endings as New Beginnings: Returning to the Lord, the Day of the Lord, and Renewal in the Book of the Twelve." In *Thematic Threads in the Book of the Twelve*, edited by Paul L. Redditt and Aaron Schart, 312–38. BZAW 325. Berlin; Boston: de Gruyter, 2003.

Howard, David M., Jr. *The Structure of Psalms 93–100*. Edited by William Henry Propp. BJSUCSD 5. Winona Lake: Eisenbrauns, 1997.

Hwang, Jerry. "'My Name Will Be Great Among the Nations': The *Missio Dei* in the Book of the Twelve." *TynBul* 65 (2014) 161–80.

Jacobson, Rolf A. "'The Faithfulness of the Lord Endures Forever': The Theological Witness of the Psalter." In *Soundings in the Theology of Psalms: Perspectives and Methods in Contemporary Scholarship*, edited by Rolf A. Jacobson, 125–52. Minneapolis: Fortress, 2011.

Jeremias, Jörg. "The Function of the Book of Joel for Reading the Twelve." In *Perspectives on the Formation of the Book of the Twelve: Methodological Foundations, Redactional Processes, Historical Insights*, edited by Rainer Albertz et al., 77–87. BZAW 433. Berlin; Boston: de Gruyter, 2012.

Kynes, Will. *An Obituary for "Wisdom Literature": The Birth, Death and Intertextual Reintegration of a Biblical Corpus*. New York: Oxford University Press, 2019.

———. *My Psalm Has Turned into Weeping: Job's Dialogue with the Psalms*. BZAW 437. Berlin; Boston: de Gruyter, 2012.

LeCureux, Jason T. *The Thematic Unity of the Book of the Twelve*. HBM 41. Sheffield: Sheffield Phoenix, 2012.

Lohfink, Norbert, and Erich Zenger. *The God of Israel and the Nations: Studies in Isaiah and the Psalms*. Translated by Everett R. Kalin. Collegeville, MN: Liturgical, 2000.

Lux, Rüdiger. "Zechariah in the Book of the Twelve." In *The Book of the Twelve: Composition, Reception, and Interpretation*, edited by Lena-Sophia Tiemeyer and Jakob Wöhrle, 238–54. VTSup 184. Leiden; Boston: Brill, 2020.

McCann, J. Clinton, Jr. "The Book of Psalms." In *1 & 2 Maccabees; Introduction to Hebrew Poetry; Job; Psalms*, edited by Leander E. Keck et al., 639–1280. Vol. 4 of *New Interpreter's Bible*. Nashville: Abingdon, 1996.

———. *The Shape and Shaping of the Hebrew Psalter*. JSOTSup 159. Sheffield: Sheffield, 1993.

———. "The Single Most Important Text in the Entire Bible: Toward a Theology of the Psalms." In *Soundings in the Theology of Psalms: Perspectives and Methods in Contemporary Scholarship*, edited by Rolf A. Jacobson, 63–75. Minneapolis: Fortress, 2011.

Miscall, Peter D. "Isaiah: New Heavens, New Earth, New Book." In *Reading Between Texts: Intertextuality and the Hebrew Bible*, edited by Danna Nolan Fewell, 41–56. Louisville: Westminster John Knox, 1992.

Nogalski, James. "The Completion of the Book of the Twelve." In *The Book of the Twelve: Composition, Reception, and Interpretation*, edited by Lena-Sophia Tiemeyer and Jakob Wöhrle, 65–89. VTSup 184. Leiden; Boston: Brill, 2020.

———. "The Day(s) of YHWH in the Book of the Twelve." In *Thematic Threads in the Book of the Twelve*, edited by Paul L. Redditt and Aaron Schart, 192–213. BZAW 325. Berlin; Boston: de Gruyter, 2003.

———. "Intertextuality and the Twelve." In *Forming Prophetic Literature: Essays on Isaiah and the Twelve in Honor of John D. W. Watts*, edited by James W. Watts and Paul R. House, 102–24. JSOTSup 235. Sheffield: Sheffield Academic, 1996.

———. "Joel as 'Literary Anchor' for the Book of the Twelve." In *Reading and Hearing the Book of the Twelve*, edited by James D. Nogalski and Marvin A. Sweeney, 91–109. SBL Symposium Series 15. Atlanta: SBL, 2000.

———. *Literary Precursors to the Book of the Twelve*. BZAW 217. Berlin; Boston: de Gruyter, 1993.

———. *Redactional Processes in the Book of the Twelve*. BZAW 218. Berlin; Boston: de Gruyter, 1993.

Prinsloo, Gert T. M. "Reading the Masoretic Psalter as a Book: Editorial Trends and Redactional Trajectories." *CurBR* 19 (2021) 145–77.

Radine, Jason. "The Dating of Prophetic Books and the Persian-Period 'Turn.'" In *The Oxford Handbook of the Minor Prophets*, edited by Julia M. O'Brien, 17–28. New York: Oxford University Press, 2021.

Rendtorff, Rolf. "How to Read the Book of the Twelve as a Theological Unity." In *Reading and Hearing the Book of the Twelve*, edited by James D. Nogalski and Marvin A. Sweeney, 74–87. SBL Symposium Series 15. Atlanta: SBL, 2000.

Schart, Aaron. "Reconstructing the Redaction History of the Twelve Prophets: Problems and Models." In *Reading and Hearing the Book of the Twelve*, edited by James D. Nogalski and Marvin A. Sweeney, 33–48. SBL Symposium Series 15. Atlanta: SBL, 2000.

Schultz, Richard L. *The Search for Quotation: Verbal Parallels in the Prophets*. JSOTSup 180. Sheffield: Sheffield Academic, 1999.

———. "The Ties that Bind: Intertextuality, the Identification of Verbal Parallels, and Reading Strategies in the Book of the Twelve." In *Thematic Threads in the Book of the Twelve*, edited by Paul L. Redditt and Aaron Schart, 27–45. BZAW 325. Berlin; Boston: de Gruyter, 2003.

Sheridan, Ruth. *Retelling Scripture: 'The Jews' and the Scriptural Citations in John 1:19–12:15*. BibInt 110. Boston: Brill, 2012.

Temmerman, Koen de, and Evert van Emde Boas, eds. *Characterization in Ancient Greek Literature*. Vol. 4 of *Studies in Ancient Greek Narrative*. Mnemosyne Supplements Monographs on Greek and Latin Language and Literature 411. Edited by C. Pieper. Boston: Brill, 2018.

Tiemeyer, Lena-Sofia. "The Haggai–Zechariah 1–8 Corpus." In *The Book of the Twelve: Composition, Reception, and Interpretation*, edited by Lena-Sophia Tiemeyer and Jakob Wöhrle, 38–64. VTSup 184. Leiden; Boston: Brill, 2020.

Tiemeyer, Lena-Sofia, and Jakob Wöhrle. "Introduction." In *The Book of the Twelve: Composition, Reception, and Interpretation*, edited by Lena-Sophia Tiemeyer and Jakob Wöhrle, 3–11. VTSup 184. Boston: Brill, 2020.

Timmer, Daniel C. "The Nations in the Minor Prophets." In *The Oxford Handbook of the Minor Prophets*, edited by Julia M. O'Brien, 131–46. New York: Oxford University Press, 2021.

———. *The Non-Israelite Nations in the Book of the Twelve: Thematic Coherence and the Diachronic-Synchronic Relationship in the Minor Prophets*. BibInt 135. Boston: Brill, 2015.

Tull, Patricia K. "Intertextuality and the Hebrew Scriptures." *CurBS* 9 (2000) 59–90.

Willgren, David. *The Formation of the "Book" of Psalms: Reconsidering the Transmission and Canonization of Psalmody in Light of Material Culture and the Poetics of Anthologies.* FAT II 88. Tübingen: Mohr Siebeck, 2016.

Wilson, Gerald H. *The Editing of the Hebrew Psalter.* SBLDS 76. Chico: Scholars, 1985.

———. "Evidence of Editorial Division in the Hebrew Psalter." *VT* 34 (1984) 337–52.

———. "The Shape of the Book of Psalms." *Int* 46 (1992) 129–42.

———. "The Use of the Royal Psalms at the 'Seams' of the Hebrew Psalter." *JSOT* 35 (1986) 85–94.

———. "The Use of 'Untitled' Psalms in the Hebrew Psalter." *ZAW* 97 (1985) 404–13.

Wöhrle, Jakob. *Der Abschluss des Zwölfprophetenbuches: Buchübergreifende Redaktionsprozesses in den späten Sammlungen.* BZAW 389. Berlin; Boston: de Gruyter 2008.

———. *Die frühen Sammlungen des Zwölfprophetenbuches: Entstehung und Komposition.* BZAW 360. Berlin; Boston: de Gruyter 2006.

———. "So Many Cross-References! Methodological Reflections on the Problem of Intertextual Relationships and their Significance for Redaction Critical Analysis." In *Perspectives on the Formation of the Book of the Twelve: Methodological Foundations, Redactional Processes, Historical Insights,* edited by Rainer Albertz et al., 3–20. BZAW 433. Berlin; Boston: de Gruyter, 2012.

Wolde, Ellen van. "Trendy Intertextuality?" In *Intertextuality in Biblical Writings: Essays in Honour of Bas van Iersel,* 43–49. Kampen, Netherlands: J. H. Kok, 1989.

Zapff, Burkard M. "The Book of Micah—The Theological Center of the Book of the Twelve?" In *Perspectives on the Formation of the Book of the Twelve: Methodological Foundations, Redactional Processes, Historical Insights,* edited by Rainer Albertz et al., 129–46. BZAW 433. Berlin; Boston: de Gruyter, 2012.

Zenger, Erich. "The God of Israel's Reign over the World (Psalms 90–106)." In *The God of Israel and the Nations: Studies in Isaiah and the Psalms,* edited by by Norbert Lohfink and Erich Zenger, 123–60. Translated by Everett R. Kalin. Collegeville, MN: Liturgical, 2000.

———. "Zion as the Mother of the Nations in Psalm 87." In *The God of Israel and the Nations: Studies in Isaiah and the Psalms,* edited by Norbert Lohfink and Erich Zenger, 161–90. Translated by Everett R. Kalin. Collegeville, MN: Liturgical, 2000.

CHAPTER 11

Micah the Prophet's Psalm (7:14–20) and Its Basis in the Psalter

Ernst R. Wendland

The closing, climactic pericope of the prophecies of Micah (7:14–20) forms an encouraging conclusion to the entire book yet includes a final word of warning to the wicked. This text, like Habakkuk 3,[1] is noticeably psalm-like in nature and one that is reminiscent of many passages found in the Hebrew Psalter. A selection of these crucial intertextual connections will be noted in the following discussion. It is also important to observe the cohesive way in which many of the salient topics of the preceding chapters are poetically and emotively reprised at the end of this prophecy to effectively summarize the essentials of Micah's positive pastoral message to the faithful people of God. However, there is also a stern warning levied here at the unrighteous leaders of Israel and to all hostile foreigners. The purpose of the present essay is to demonstrate how Micah, as a memorable representative of the prophetic Book of the Twelve, manifests three prominent psalmic macro-characteristics with respect to discourse structure, literary style, and thematic significance. This manifold correspondence in turn suggests the potential importance of applying the results of scholarly expositions of the Psalms when

1. The psalm ("prayer") of Habakkuk is packed with psalmic allusions and references. See Wendland, *Habakkuk*, 25.

seeking to interpret holistically the individual books as well as the entire corpus of the so-called "minor prophets."[2]

1. Discourse Structure

When analyzing the larger textual organization of Micah as a whole and 7:14–20 in particular,[3] essentially the same basic ten-step, literary-structural discourse analysis methodology was employed as in my studies of the Psalms and prophetic literature:[4]

> These ten steps are: *delimitation* (boundary determination), *spatialization* (text diagramming), *text-criticism* (major issues addressed), *segmentation* (demarcation of strophic units), *confirmation* (detailed linguistic examination), *distinction* (identification of peak points), *contextualization* (recording instances of intra- and inter-textuality), *conversation* (speech-act analysis), *summarization* (proposing a topical and/or rhetorical outline), and *translation* (communicating the text in another language).

The preceding text-oriented procedures are often combined, re-ordered, or augmented in actual practice; in the following discussion of this concluding pericope of the book, space allows for only a partial application and description.

In terms of its contextual delimitation, we observe that the psalm of Micah (7:14–20) forms the resounding close of a longer discourse

---

2. For an excellent study of intertextual quotation within the prophetic corpus, see Schultz, *Quotation*, 1999.

3. This closing section expressing Micah's "prayer" is entitled "Let the history of salvation resume" (Mays, *Micah*, 162). Mays considers this text to be a "lament" (163), but its primary illocutionary functions would seem to be more accurately classified as trust and praise. Hoyt classifies the larger portion of chapter 7 (vv. 7–20) as a "hope oracle." She notes that "Two verses vary from this pattern with mixed hortatory elements (vv. 8, 14)" (Hoyt, "Discourse," 169). Some scholars exclude most of chapter 7 from the authorship of Micah on alleged stylistic grounds, for example, Wood, in her consideration of "speech and action in Micah's prophecy." See Wood, "Speech." However, as R. K. Harrison astutely observes: "Arguments from style are never particularly strong at best since style can be altered so easily with a change of subject matter. Furthermore, it is not easy to see why 7:7–20 should be assigned to a post-exilic period, since there is nothing in the context which is in the slightest degree at variance with the language or theology of the eighth-century prophets" (Harrison quoted in Woodall, *Minor Prophets*, 92).

4. For further details of this analytical approach with regard to the Psalter, see Wendland, *Psalms*, 9–26; for an application to a selection of prophetic works, see Wendland, *Prophetic Rhetoric*; for a definition of some of the basic terminology used in the present study, see Wendland, *Micah*, 206–8.

unit that begins in 7:8. A major break in chapter 7 at verse 8 is preceded by Micah's lament—a mournful complaint that begins with "What misery is mine!" (v. 1). However, this passage concludes contrastively with the prophet's outburst of faith-filled hope for the future: "But as for me, I watch in hope for the LORD . . ." (v. 7). Commentators, beginning with Hermann Gunkel, have termed the subsequent and final portion of the book a type of "prophetic liturgy,"[5] which "moves from lament to final praise and describes the success of God's salvific plan for the world."[6] Two poetic sections precede the concluding psalm—a personified song of Zion that proclaims God's penitent people's joy over the righteous victory that Yahweh will win over their enemies (vv. 8–10),[7] followed by a salvation oracle pronounced by Micah on behalf of the LORD, which figuratively predicts worldwide expansion for Zion in contrast to the fate of all the wicked (vv. 11–13). An overlapping transition between these two poetic units is formed by the references to time— "now" (עַתָּה) in v. 10b and [that] "day" (יוֹם) in v. 11a (see also v. 12a). The "shameful" (בּוּשָׁה) defeat of the wicked predicted at the end of Zion's song in v. 10 is referred to again at the close of the following salvation oracle (v. 13) and set in graphic contrast to the description of the dramatic expansion of Zion's messianic kingdom (vv. 11–12; cf. the parallel passage in vv. 8–9). Allen notes the psalm-like character of 7:8–20 with general reference to the stylistic features of Psalms 12, 27, 44, 50, 62, 75, 77, 80, 81, 82, 90, and 95.[8]

The focus of our study, Micah's psalm, begins then in v. 14 where the prophet once again addresses Yahweh "as a representative of the faithful remnant."[9] The text divides structurally into three strophes (poetic paragraphs) that clearly differ with respect to their content and rhetorical function—though they all in one way or another recall the Exodus salvation history and hymn (Exod 15) as well as earlier passages in the prophecy of Micah:[10]

5. Gunkel, "Micah."
6. Dempster, *Micah*, 496.
7. "Lady Zion" as speaker of this (see 4:2–13) is implied by the feminine singular pronominal suffix on *"your God"* (אֱלֹהָיִךְ) in v. 10. She addresses "my enemy" (vv. 8, 10)—a figurative reference to the capital city of one of Israel/Judah's perennial enemies—in this case, probably Nineveh of Assyria. See Waltke, *Commentary*, 433; Soenksen, *Micah*, 571.
8. Allen, *Micah*, 393.
9. Waltke, "Micah," 758. See also 2:12.
10. For a corresponding application of discourse analysis procedures to the similar, triple-structured Psalm 30, see Wendland, *Psalms*, 40–60.

1. The first (*Strophe A*, vv. 14–15) is represented as an initial prayer to Yahweh, requesting beneficial provision for his people (cf. 2:12–13; 4:6–10; 5:2–6). This ardent plea is immediately followed, as it were, by God's affirmative response in a promissory oracle of direct speech (v. 15).

2. *Strophe B* (vv. 16–17) is a final prophetic judgment decree, warning all the ungodly among the nations (implicitly including the impenitent in Israel, 5:10–15) that God's blessings that bring joy to his people will have the opposite effect on them. In fact, they will experience a shameful, fearful recognition of the tragic consequences of their wicked ways and sinful attitude towards Yahweh (cf. 1:5–2:11; 3:1–4:12; 4:11–5:1; 5:9; 6:9–16; 7:1–6, 13).

3. The third and concluding segment (*Strophe A'*, vv. 18–20) climaxes Micah's collection of prophetic oracles with a wonderful word of praise echoing the voice of a psalmist (e.g., Ps 103:6–13). Here the prophet reminds readers/hearers of all nations about the amazing attributes of a unique "God" of proven covenant faithfulness, who eagerly desires to show steadfast love to the forgiven, and fidelity to all his gracious covenant promises (cf. 4:1–5; 7:7–12).

Micah's lyrical conclusion is thus arranged in the form of a tripartite "ring structure," each section of which is dominated by a specific "speech act" (shown in italics below). This strikingly psalm-like construction and mode of communication may be summarized as follows:[11]

A. *Petition* to Yahweh: care for your people, as in the past (vv. 14–15)

B. *Warning* to the ungodly: turn in penitence to Yahweh (vv. 16–17)

A' *Praise* of Yahweh: show forth your covenantal characteristics, as in the past (vv. 18–20)

In this rhetorically effective way, Micah sums up the essence of the urgent theological and ethical message that has been proclaimed throughout his prophetic text: Our God is gracious and good (A); he fervently desires a close and loving fellowship with his people (A').[12]

---

11. See, for example, a very similar patterning in Psalm 28, an individual petitionary prayer: A, vv. 1–2; B, vv. 3–5; A', vv. 6–9.

12. This includes the faithful believers of all nations (4:1–5)!

However, the LORD is also a holy and righteous God; all those who refuse his mercy will have to confront his justice—and this alternative can only result in total shame and disaster (B)!

2. Literary Style

The following examination of the psalm's principal stylistic features and thematic topics combines the annotated display of the Hebrew text of Micah 7:14–20 along with a formally correspondent English translation (ESV). The inserted lettered notes, situated after each of the three sections, correspond to the superscripts in the ESV and provide a close running commentary on some (but not all) of the significant formal, semantic, and functional (literary-structural) aspects of this lyric-prophetic composition, including a selection of significant psalmic intertextual references (a subject to be discussed more fully in section 3 below).

English Standard Version[13]	SBL Hebrew Text[14]

Strophe A: Prayer to YHWH and Response

14 Shepherd your people[a] with your staff,[b] the flock of your inheritance,[c] who dwell alone in a forest in the midst of a garden land;[d] let them graze in Bashan and Gilead as in the days of old.[e] 15 "As in the days when you[f] came out of the land of Egypt,[g] I will show them marvelous things."[h]	14 רְעֵה עַמְּךָ בְשִׁבְטֶךָ צֹאן נַחֲלָתֶךָ שֹׁכְנִי לְבָדָד יַעַר בְּתוֹךְ כַּרְמֶל יִרְעוּ בָשָׁן וְגִלְעָד כִּימֵי עוֹלָם׃ 15 כִּימֵי צֵאתְךָ מֵאֶרֶץ מִצְרָיִם אַרְאֶנּוּ נִפְלָאוֹת׃

(a) Introducing a prominent metaphoric theme to initiate a new strophe and section (discourse "aperture"), Micah calls upon Yahweh to "shepherd" (רעה) his faithful people, namely, those who follow the ethical principles of 6:8 and have the same theological perspective expressed by Micah in 7:7. The verb, a common metaphor for kings and rulers in the ANE (2:12; 4:6–7; 5:3), refers literally to the supply of food, water, and protection for the flock, but the reference here is to God's spiritual provision for those who follow him (cf. 5:3, 5, clearly reflecting Ps 23).

(f) Micah ("you"-singular) may be regarded here as a prototypical representative of the LORD's faithful "remnant" of covenant-keeping believers (v. 18)—or, more strikingly, the "you" could refer to Yahweh himself marching at the head of his army of liberated people (Exod 12:51; 13:3; 18:1).[15] As frequently occurs in his poetic style, the pronoun suddenly shifts in the second line of v. 15, i.e., "I (Yahweh) will show *him*" (אַרְאֶנּוּ)—with reference to Micah and his people, Israel—hence the translation "them." Similarly, the verb is again best interpreted as a "prophetic perfect," that is, with reference to a *future* event divinely assured of happening.

---

13. Obtained from: https://www.biblestudytools.com/esv/micah/7.html. I have slightly modified this translation in view of my interpretation of the Hebrew text.

14. *Biblia Hebraica Stuttgartensia*, Mic 7:14–20. The MT has been re-lineated into a sequence of rhythmic shorter cola that putatively better approximate psalm texts. Here is a summary: The Hebrew text is delineated into posited poetic lines or "cola" (i.e., utterance units, normally 2–5 lexical items) marked mainly by the accents *silluq* and *athnakh*, but also by *zaqeph* (e.g., נַחֲלָתֶךָ in v. 14b), less so by *tiphkhah* (יַעַר in 14c). Many authors divide poetic verses into "lines" with a break at the *athnakh*; however, often these are too long to achieve rhythmic balance when composed of 2–3 cola. In any case, 2–3 such lines usually form a complete verse as demarcated in the MT (occasionally monocola are inserted for special structural or rhetorical purposes). For a different, Gestalt-based, cognitive approach to BH lineation, see Grosser, *Unparalleled Poetry*, 51–222.

15. See Soenksen, *Micah*, 606; Clark and Mundhenk, *Micah*, 189. For a defense of retaining the MT in v. 15 "as YHWH's response to the prayer offered in v. 14," see Hagstrom, *Micah*, 101–2; Waltke, *Micah*, 760.

(b) The word (שֵׁבֶט), which can be rendered "staff" or "scepter" according to the context, connotes royal power and authority (Ps 45:6) in addition to protective and providential care (Ps 23:4).

(c) The key covenantal term "inheritance" (נַחֲלָה) "essentially refers to an inalienable, and therefore a permanent, possession that falls to an individual or group either through its awarding in the transmission as an inheritance or through its expropriation from the preceding owner."[16]

(d) The wild, unproductive "forest, thicket" (יַעַר) is apparently intended to contrast with bountiful "orchards, plantations" (כַּרְמֶל) all around them (cf. 3:12; also Isa 10:18; 16:10; 29:17; 32:15–16).[17] Hence there is a plea for the people to be restored to their promised, blessed state in the next line (cf. Deut 33:28). "The point seems to be that Israel is in a vulnerable position, like sheep in a 'thicket' populated by predators, while rich 'pastureland' (their homeland and God's blessings) is in view."[18] On the other hand, even in such an inhospitable place, God's Spirit is still poured out upon his faithful people in gracious blessings (Isa 32:15–16; Jer 50:19).

(g) We note here a rhetorical temporal reversal that signifies a period encompassing the entire Exodus salvation event. However, the time reference begins at the end at Israel's entrance into Canaan (v. 14d) and moves to the beginning when Yahweh undertook this great deliverance by bringing the nation out of Egypt (15a). In any case, the implied comparison moves prophetically from the lesser to the greater—from the "days" of the Exodus event to a much longer and more significant period in the future history of God's covenant people.

(h) The LORD immediately (and dramatically!) responds to Micah's petition of v. 14 with this brief, historically-based promise of deliverance in v. 15. "[M]arvelous things" (נִפְלָאוֹת) (see Ps 106:21–22 with reference to the Exodus) designates what human beings regard as "miraculous"—that is, things/events made possible by God's direct or indirect intervention and enablement.[19]

---

16. Dempster, "Micah," 440; cf. Ps 78:71.
17. Allen, *Micah*, 398–99; Clark and Mundhenk, *Micah*, 187; Smith, *Micah*, 59.
18. *NET Bible*, study note; cf. Ps 83:11–12.
19. Sweeney, *Twelve Prophets*, 412.

(e) "Micah prays for the restoration of these fertile expansions of Israel ('Bashan'; cf. Ps 68:15–16). The extended metaphor for *I AM*'s beneficent rule in the messianic era emphasizes the petition for new Israel's restoration to its original prosperity and security, 'as in the days of old,' when God chose his inheritance."[20] This covenantal relationship graciously established between Yahweh and his "chosen" people has been enlarged to include believers from all nations (see 4:1–5; 7:11–12; Ps 22:27–28).

Strophe B: The Effect upon the Ungodly

16 The nations shall see[i]	16 יִרְאוּ גוֹיִם
and be ashamed of all their might;[j]	וְיֵבֹשׁוּ מִכֹּל גְּבוּרָתָם
they shall lay their hands on their mouths;[k]	יָשִׂימוּ יָד עַל־פֶּה
their ears shall become deaf;	אָזְנֵיהֶם תֶּחֱרַשְׁנָה׃
17 they shall lick the dust like a serpent,[l]	17 יְלַחֲכוּ עָפָר כַּנָּחָשׁ
like the crawling things of the earth;	כְּזֹחֲלֵי אֶרֶץ
they shall come trembling out of their strongholds;[m]	יִרְגְּזוּ מִמִּסְגְּרֹתֵיהֶם
unto the LORD our God they shall turn in dread,[n]	אֶל־יְהוָה אֱלֹהֵינוּ יִפְחָדוּ
and they shall be in fear of you.[o]	וְיִרְאוּ מִמֶּךָּ׃

---

20. Dempster, "Micah," 459.

(i) An asyndeton and the presence of a different subject (גּוֹיִם) mark the onset of a new strophe. Yet there is also a structural connection ("juncture") forged with the close of the preceding strophe. Thus, in contrast to what God's people "will see" (רָאָה, v. 15b), all those among "the nations" who refuse to trust him and live according to his covenant principles "will see" (יִרְאוּ, v. 16a) a just punishment, thereby paying the price for personal pride in rejecting Yahweh and/or rebelling against him (vv. 16–17). The imperfective verbs of vv. 16–17 may be interpreted as futures or jussives;[21] I prefer the future in concordance with my interpretation of the verbs also in vv. 15 and 19–20.

(j) In this case, to be "ashamed" (בּוֹשׁ) of one's personal power is a litotes, an understatement for effect; that is, all their supposed worldly or religious "strength" (גְּבוּרָה) means nothing in comparison with that of almighty God. Unbelievers and apostates alike will have nothing at all to boast about when his judgment falls upon them (vv. 10–12, cf. 4:11–13; 5:15)![26]

(m) The verb of motion "they will come" is added for clarification. But the focus of this line and the next two is clearly upon the devastating distress being emotionally experienced by these sinful people ("trembling" [רָגַז] in "dread" [פַּחַד] and "fear" [יָרֵא]) as they appear like "condemned prisoners of war"[22] in the presence of their holy Judge, the LORD God Almighty. The various material, social, intellectual, or religious "strongholds, fortresses" (מִסְגְּרֹת), the sources of pride upon which they depended on in life, will profit them nothing in the end. Whether or not their awful experience is viewed as motivating their repentance, as I conclude, is debatable. Some commentators agree;[23] others do not;[24] while still others are uncertain.[25]

(n) The fronted locative phrase (אֶל־יְהוָה אֱלֹהֵינוּ) is striking—it not only serves to foreground the psalm's central participant and agent, but also implicitly responds to the enemies' taunt of 7:10 and sets up audience expectation for the concluding strophe in exuberant praise of Yahweh.

---

21. For the latter, see Soenksen, *Micah*, 600.

22. DeRouchie, *Old Testament*, 292.

23. Dempster, "Micah," 186, 189; Smith, *Micah*, 59; Soenksen, *Micah*, 601; cf. Hos 3:5.

24. See, e.g., Mays, *Micah*, 166; Sweeney, *Twelve Prophets*, 413; Waltke, *Commentary*, 461–62.

25. Barker and Bailey, *Micah*, 132; Clark and Mundhenk, *Micah*, 190; Leslie, *Micah*, 400–401.

26. Waltke, *Commentary*, 460–62.

(k) The final two lines of v. 16 give culturally specific, symbolic bodily expression to the shame and reproach that the ungodly will feel on the day of God's judgment. Not only will they have nothing to say in their defense but, more than this: "'their ears will be deaf'; apparently this means the opposing nations will be left dumbfounded by the LORD's power. Their inability to respond will make them appear to be deaf mutes."[27] Thus, these "enemies" of Yahweh will no longer be able to blaspheme him or taunt his people in their times of trial by saying, "Where is the LORD your God?" (v. 10).

(l) Vivid emotive imagery describing the humiliated state of the unrighteous continues in the first three lines of v. 17, now depicting them as defeated, ritually unclean, dust-eating serpents (נָחָשׁ) (see Gen 3:15; Ps 44:25; Isa 65:25). There is a probable messianic reference in conjunction with the mention of dust-licking enemies, as intimated in Ps 72:1–2, 9–10.[28]

(o) The sudden, final shift in pronominal reference "from you" (מִמֶּךָ) at the close of Strophe B (the last two lines being arranged in a syntactic chiasmus: adjunct-verb/verb-adjunct) reminds the faithful that, in contrast to the wicked (v. 17), they have nothing to "fear" (יָרֵא). Rather, they are the rescued, covenant-bound followers ("your people") of the good "Shepherd" (רֹעֶה), Yahweh, their God (vv. 14, 18), and will one day "see" (רָאָה) his salvation (vv. 15–16; note the cohesive paronomastic sequence). On the other hand, could the abject "fear" of pagans be graciously transformed by the wondrous works of an almighty God into an awesome reverence for an utterly exceptional deity who desires to show mercy (v. 18; see Exod 14:31; 15:14; Isa 49:22–23; Hos 3:5)? Surely, with the LORD all things are possible (4:1–2; 7:18)!

---

27. *NET Bible*, study note.

28. Peter C. W. Ho, personal correspondence. See also DeRouchie, *Old Testament*, 66; Soenksen, *Micah*, 608.

Strophe A': Praise for Yahweh's Forgiveness

18 Who is a God like you,ᵖ pardoning iniquityq
and passing over transgressionʳ
for the remnant of his inheritance?ˢ
He does not retain his anger forever,ᵗ
because he delights in steadfast love.ᵘ
19 He will again have compassion on us;ᵛ
he will tread our iniquities underfoot.ʷ
Youˣ will cast into the depths of the sea
all our sins.
20 You will show faithfulness to Jacob
and steadfast love to Abraham,ʸ
as you have sworn to our fathers
from the days of old.ᶻ

18 מִי־אֵל כָּמוֹךָ נֹשֵׂא עָוֺן
וְעֹבֵר עַל־פֶּשַׁע
לִשְׁאֵרִית נַחֲלָתוֹ
לֹא־הֶחֱזִיק לָעַד אַפּוֹ
כִּי־חָפֵץ חֶסֶד הוּא׃
19 יָשׁוּב יְרַחֲמֵנוּ
יִכְבֹּשׁ עֲוֺנֹתֵינוּ
וְתַשְׁלִיךְ בִּמְצֻלוֹת יָם
כָּל־חַטֹּאותָם׃
20 תִּתֵּן אֱמֶת לְיַעֲקֹב
חֶסֶד לְאַבְרָהָם
אֲשֶׁר־נִשְׁבַּעְתָּ לַאֲבֹתֵינוּ
מִימֵי קֶדֶם׃

(p) The final Strophe A' dramatically leads off with the exclamation מִי־אֵל כָּמוֹךָ, which initiates a climactic credo in praise of יהוה that brings the prophecy to a rousing covenantal conclusion. This initial positive personal exclamation corresponds to, but also transforms, Micah's negative assertion in 7:1: "Woe is me!" (אַלְלַי לִי).

(v) The initial verb "he will return" (שׁוּב), used adverbially, suggests also 'graciously' here ("again") in conjunction with the second verb "he will have mercy" (רחם). Verse 19a (mercy) thus stands as the result of v. 18d (steadfast love) in the covenantal relationship that links Yahweh with his faithful followers. We note a "twofold movement" here as v. 18 "describes what YHWH is like" and v. 19 "project[s] that knowledge in expectation of what he will do."29

---

29. Mays, *Micah*, 167.

(q) Literally, "one [YHWH] lifting up guilt" (נֹשֵׂא עָוֹן)—that is, "forgiving"—those who do not deserve it. "Guilt" refers to both the sin/sinfulness and its deserved punishment (compare Zion's confession in 7:9; cf. Isa 53:4, 12). The prophet's prayer moves from direct address (second person) in v. 18 to a descriptive style (third person) in vv. 18–19 and then back to direct address (second person) in vv. 19–20 (cf. Exod 34:6–7). To every believer, YHWH is the God of intimate personal relationship, who may always and immediately be addressed "you"!

(r) Literally: "who passes over rebellion"; this attribute figuratively restates and emphasizes the preceding notion of Yahweh's unmerited forgiveness and more—his incomparable "mercy" (*chesed*)—freely remitting on behalf of the penitent "remnant" the very sins that Micah had earlier accused the nation of (1:5; 3:8).

(w) The preceding thoughts of vv. 18–19a are reiterated figuratively (anthropomorphically) in the last three lines of v. 19. Furthermore, there is the likelihood that in this verse Micah is intertextually alluding to "God's forgiveness of his people's sins through the metaphor of his subduing the Egyptian army in the Red Sea"[30]—the "sea" (יָם) itself also being symbolic of chaos (and evil!) in the cultural world of the ANE. "Sins are personified as a physical enemy as daunting and oppressive as Pharaoh and his armies in Egypt," and "Micah presents Yahweh as a warrior fighting for his people,"[31] with Moses's "Song at the Sea" (Exod 15) patently resounding in the intertextual background of this passage.

(x) In defense of the MT's shift to the second person form here, see Soenksen, *Micah*, 614. Clark and Mundhenk suggest that "responsive reading or chanting" may be the reason for the sudden pronominal shifts in vv. 18–20.[32]

(y) The core covenantal correlates "truth" (אֱמֶת) and "steadfast love" (חֶסֶד) are emphatically recalled in this concluding verse via a reversal of their normal collocational order[33]—and in conjunction with Israel's illustrious patriarchs,[34] who are similarly mentioned in inverted historical order (perhaps to highlight the latter, the father of all the faithful, "Abraham").

---

30. Dempster, "Micah," 447. See also Zech 9:15.
31. Soenksen, *Micah*, 619.
32. Clark and Mundhenk, *Micah*, 191. See also *NET Bible*, translation note 38.
33. Waltke, "Micah," 448; cf. Hos 4:1; Zech 7:9.
34. DeRouchie, *Old Testament*, 60.

(s) The opening rhetorical question sets the stage for the subsequent litany of divine attributes which characterize Yahweh, the divine Shepherd who protects and provides for his flock, itself typified in familiar relational terms as "the remnant of his inheritance" (לִשְׁאֵרִית נַחֲלָתוֹ) (cf. 2:12; 4:7; 5:6–7; 7:14). "*I AM*'s incomparability pertains to his unique character to forgive sinners by his intervention in salvation history, not to his surpassing military power as we might expect [or foolishly depend on, as in this twenty-first century]."[35]

(t) Yahweh does not "hold fast to, retain" (חָזַק, *hiphil* perfect of customary action) his anger (אַפּוֹ), i.e., threat to punish sin, "forever"; one concept metonymically refers to its polar opposite: "not long at all." In other words, God is ever ready to forgive the penitent.

(u) This final line of the verse gives the reason or motivation for the preceding forbearing actions of the Lord: "He" (הוּא—emphasized by word order, with reference to אֵל, which began this verse) delights (חָפֵץ) in manifesting his "unending mercy/unfailing faithfulness." The latter term (חֶסֶד) encapsulates Yahweh's unfailing-faithful love as the eschatological Shepherd of his devoted flock. We note the close connection that the various key concepts of v. 18 have with correspondents in the most evangelical, messianic chapter of the Hebrew Bible—Isaiah 53 (vv. 6, 8, 10, 11). "Transgression" (פֶּשַׁע) and "grace" (חֶסֶד), the key thematic terms that contrast within v. 18, recall the beginning and conclusion of Psalm 32 (vv. 1, 10).

(z) Thus, in summary, Yahweh's past covenant fidelity to the "fathers" of faith "from the days of old" (מִימֵי קֶדֶם) (v. 20; see also v. 14 [inclusio]; 5:2; cf., e.g., Ps 132:11–18) form the foundational basis and guarantee of all his current promises to "us"—his "people" (v. 14), who are "the remnant of his inheritance" (vv. 18). The prophet's faith shines forth brightly in the end as he expresses his fervent hope in a divinely affirmed promise that the Lord will shepherd his faithful flock throughout the future, just like he did during the great patriarchal age of yesteryear. These ancient messianically focused promises "are as relevant today as then, because [God's] sublime attributes of fidelity and unfailing love guarantee their fulfilment in the church, which inherits them (Gal 3:29; Eph 2:19)."[36]

---

35. Waltke, *Commentary*, 463.
36. Waltke, "Micah," 764.

3. Thematic Significance

In this section I will progressively trace more explicitly some of the especially noteworthy (partial) quotations, allusions, and echoes that the concluding lyric of Micah references from the Psalter and the psalm of Moses in Exodus 15.[37] How does the prophet employ these thematic and precatory intertextual antecedents to bring his pastoral work to a grand finale of communal petition, reassurance, and praise?

The beginning of Strophe A (vv. 14–15) is quite striking: Yahweh as a shepherd for the flock of his people (7:1; cf. 2:12; 4:6; 5:4) is a strategic metaphor in the wider Psalter, and not only in Psalm 23. Thus, we hear in this poetic corpus several appeals not unlike Micah's opening petition: "Hear us, Shepherd of Israel, you who lead Joseph like a flock" (Pss 80:1a; see also 74:1; 95:6–7; 100:3), "be their shepherd and carry them forever" (Ps 28:9b). The rich fertility of the pasturelands of Bashan was also a familiar poetic commonplace (Ps 22:12). The miraculous, divinely enabled and directed departure of God's "inheritance" (Pss 33:12; 94:14) from Egypt, highlighted by the Lord himself (Mic 7:15; cf. Ps 68:7–10; 114), features prominently in the great paired historical psalms, 105:37 and 106:10–12, while the shock-and-awe effect on Israel's enemies is also noted (105:38), thus providing a historical context for Micah's next verse (7:16). Yahweh's vigilant, protective shepherding of his human "inheritance" is embodied in the kingship of David, a prophetic type of the Messiah (Ps 78:70–72; cf. Micah 5:2–4).

Strophe B (vv. 16–17) plainly recalls the pathetic response of the ungodly to the amazing manifestation of Yahweh's miraculous "wonders" performed in the deliverance and defense of his people at the time of the Exodus and their wilderness wanderings. The most ostensive, publicly demonstrated salvific event occurred at the Sea of Reeds, moving Moses to proclaim: "The nations will hear and tremble; anguish will grip the people . . . [they] will be terrified . . . will be seized with trembling . . . terror and dread will fall on them" (Exod 15:14–16a; see also Ps 18:45). Instead

---

37. English Bible versification and the NIV are followed in the quotations of this section. For a study of Moses's "Psalm of the Sea," see Wendland, *Psalms*, 323–80; for the "Exodus typology" in Micah, see Soenksen, *Micah*, 502–8, 615. It is also interesting to note that in the poetic section immediately preceding Micah's psalm, i.e., 7:7–13, immediately after his expression of "hope" in v. 7, there are a number of other psalmic references of varied overtness, e.g., v. 7 (Pss 4:3; 130:5), v. 8 (Pss 37:24; 112:4; 119:54–55), v. 9 (Pss 37:6; 107:10–14), v. 10 (Pss 18:42; 35:26; 42:3), v. 11 (Pss 89:40; 102:16), v. 12 (Ps 87:4).

of Israel being "brought down to the dust" due to their sinfulness (Ps 44:25), it will be the formidable foes of God's faithful who will be forced to "lick dust like a snake" in abject defeat (7:17a). The LORD will righteously deliver his people, with all hostile nations made to serve as witnesses (Pss 23:5, 46:9–10, 98:2, 126:2)—could it be also to this prophetic testimonial of who the true God and Lord of all really is (v. 18; cf. 1:2)?

The hostile character and actions of Israel's enemies, serving as Yahweh's punitive agents, are vividly described in Psalm 44:9–16 (cf. Mic 7:8–10). Whether the trembling and turning to the LORD of these hostile forces refers to their final judgment and punishment, or allows for their ultimate repentance, must remain an open question. Reputable commentators stand on both sides of this issue, as already noted. The crucial and central thematic text of Micah 4:1–3 would favor the latter option (see also Pss 18:44–45; 102:15). On the other hand, Micah's typical contrastive treatment of the righteous and the wicked, often with sudden shifts from one perspective to the other (e.g., 2:8–3:3), might lead one to favor the former hermeneutical conclusion, that is, with the enemies' inevitable condemnation in view.[38]

The concluding verses of Micah (Strophe A′, vv. 18–20) read as if they were deliberately composed by the prophet on behalf of the people of Zion as a psalm of praise—a paean lauding their incomparable God (cf. Pss 71:19; 77:13; 89:6, 8). This is a doxology that significantly, in addition, provides a clear confession of faith in the "covenantal correlates" of the God who gave birth to Israel as a nation and who will continue to sustain the believing remnant among them through the ministry of their coming Messianic Shepherd (2:12–13; 5:8). The initial rhetorical question highlighting Yahweh's incomparability echoes a string of psalms (Pss 35:10; 71:19; 77:14; 89:7–9; 113:5; cf. Exod 15:11). Whether for pagans (v. 17) or for the members of Yahweh's faith community (v. 9), "the sole ground of their hope [of sin's forgiveness] lies in the noble character of God as one who forgives, forgets, and offers a fresh beginning"[39]— precisely the message of Psalm 103.

It is interesting to observe how the literary structure of the opening passage significantly highlights its content. Thus, the theologically significant assertions of vv. 18–19 form a memorable chiastic pattern, so common also in the Psalms,[40] where God is prayerfully praised:

38. For further discussion, see Soenksen, *Micah*, 609–10.
39. Allen, *Micah*, 401.
40. See Ho, "Macrostructural Design," 40–62.

296 PART 2: THEMATIC APPROACHES

> [You are someone] who pardons sin
>
> and forgives the transgression of the remnant of [your] inheritance[.]
>
> > You do not stay angry forever
> >
> > > but delight to show *chesed*.
> >
> > You will again have compassion on us;
> >
> > you will tread our sins underfoot
> >
> > and hurl all our iniquities into the depths of the sea.

The initial description of Yahweh's distinctive merciful character, first declared in Exodus 37:6–7 and paraphrased in Micah 7:18–19, is reiterated in three of the so-called "books" of the Psalter (Book III, 86:15; Book IV, 103:6–13; Book V, 108:4 and 145:8–9).[41] Not only is the replication more extensive and semantically developed in Psalm 103, but this text also emphasizes the forgiveness of sins, which is the special focus also in Micah's psalm: "[Yahweh] does not treat us as our sins deserve or repay us according to our iniquities" (Ps 103:10).[42] It would seem that Micah does have Psalm 103 firmly in mind for a thematic emphasis, as we observe how he figuratively re-expresses 103:11b–12 in 7:19:

> [S]o great is his love for those who fear him;
>
> > *You will again have compassion on us;*
>
> as far as the east is from the west,
>
> > *you will tread our sins underfoot and hurl*
>
> so far has he removed our transgressions from us.
>
> > *all our iniquities into the depths of the sea.*[43]

---

41. Psalm 86 is a petitionary psalm; 103, a didactic psalm of praise; 108, a mixed psalm of praise and petition; 145, a pure hymn of praise. Exodus 37:6–7 has resonant echoes throughout the Tanakh—the Law, the Prophets, and the Writings—in addition to the Psalms; for example, in Numbers (14:18), Nehemiah (9:17), Jeremiah (15:15), Jonah (4:2), and Nahum (1:3).

42. "But where sin abounds, there grace abounds all the more (Rom 5:20). Micah's final proclamation illustrates this truth by the variety of statements of grace in these verses" (Soenksen, *Micah*, 616). Yahweh's "anger" is tempered with "mercy" (v. 18c–d; cf. Pss 30:5; 103:9) and the desire to forgive where repentance is forthcoming (Ps 51:1–9)—as the prophet has already expressed on behalf of the penitent people of Zion in 7:8–9 (Sweeney, *Twelve Prophets*, 413). In short, divine "covenantal faithfulness" (חֶסֶד in v. 18d) motivates God's "constant compassion" (רחם in v. 19a; cf. Ps 86:5–6).

43. There is quite a different application of similar figurative language in Ps 68:22, which includes a reference to "Bashan" (Mic 7:14). Here the psalmist depicts the enemies of God's people being dragged from high and low for retributive punishment on account of their inveterate opposition: "The Lord said, 'I will bring them back from

The psalmic testamental resonance in Micah continues right to the very end of Micah in verse 20 as the intertextual reference to the patriarchal fathers, Jacob and Abraham, features prominently from its probable source text in Psalm 105. We hear, for example, in verses 5–7a and 8–10 (see also vv. 23, 42–43) explicit mention being made of Yahweh's everlasting covenant with Abraham (cf. Gen 12:3; 18:18; 22:18; 26:4; 28:14) and the patriarch's descendants' exodus from Egypt (cf. Exod 15:17; Mic 7:15, 18):

> Remember the wonders he has done . . .
>
> you his servants, the descendants of Abraham,
>
> his chosen ones, the children of Jacob.
>
> He is the Lord our God . . .
>
> He remembers his covenant forever . . .
>
> the covenant he made with Abraham,
>
> the oath he swore to Isaac.
>
> He confirmed it to Jacob as a decree,
>
> to Israel as an everlasting covenant . . .

This then is the stirring, grace-based, hope-filled (cf. Mic 7:7, 20) thought-complex that Micah leaves in his listeners' minds: Our faithful God's covenant stands undisturbed and unalterable despite the many sins of the majority, both clergy and lay, that currently plague their society. But before forgiveness and restoration with the Lord can occur, genuine repentance must be publicly exhibited in a life of obedience to his directive moral laws (Mic 3:8; 4:2; 6:8; cf. Ps 105:45) and divine forgiveness received through faith in the promised Messiah-Shepherd-Savior (Mic 5:2, 4; cf. Pss 2:7–8, 12c; 16:10–11; 22:1–31; 23:5–6; 49:15).

Conclusion: The Psalter's Influence on Micah's Prophecy

I will close with a summary of the main psalmic characteristics observed in the preceding analysis of Micah 7:14–20, which demonstrates the crucial relevance of the Psalter in multifaceted, discourse-oriented studies of this nature, not only for Micah, but presumably also for all prophetic

---

Bashan, I will bring them back from the depths of the sea . . .'" In fact, this passage could also lie within the punitive cognitive framework of Mic 7:17.

works collected in the Book of the Twelve. The "psalm" of Micah overtly displays the following seven representative attributes:[44]

- There is a clearly defined *strophic structure* that demarcates a larger textual division.

- We have an unbroken sequence of *poetic parallelism* of various types, both conjunctive and disjunctive in nature.[45]

- Familiar *psalmic diction* permeates the passage from beginning to end.

- The preceding facet is associated with a thick lexical and conceptual *intertextuality* that can be readily traced back to one or more psalms (as noted in the earlier analysis).

- The prophet, as a priestly representative of his people, "prays" this entire pericope in *direct speech*, except for the short, inserted divine oracle cited in 7:15b.[46]

- Typical *stylistic* (literary-structural) *devices* are evident everywhere, such as metaphor and simile, "free" (non-metrical) rhythm, evocative imagery, rhetorical questions, historical allusion, punning, and other types of phonological play.

- We also note the presence of a distinctive thematic *peak* (vv. 18–19) plus an emotive *climax* (v. 19) that occur together in closing (end-stress)—discourse features that are prominent also in the Psalter.

---

44. See also Wendland, *Psalms*, 4–10.

45. On the subject of separated "disjunctive parallelism," see Zogbo and Wendland, *Hebrew Poetry*, 303–28. Regarding parallelism, Grosser argues, "Regular rhythms and parallelism are the wrong starting places for understanding the biblical poetic line." Instead, we must seek to understand "poetic structure in the free-rhythm biblical versification system: lines that fit to each other in organized part-whole relationships of lines and line-groupings, *emerging aurally as they unfold* in time. This cognitive approach is *oriented toward listener perception*, not abstract line forms or rules" (Grosser, *Unparalleled Poetry*, 294 [emphasis added]). However, there are two major problems with this method: (a) how does it enable one to discern and validate larger structures of poetic organization if author- (orator-) intended top-down SL stylistic shaping and marking is not first taken into consideration; as she herself admits, (b) "how to best format biblical poetry in Hebrew [the received MT] and in translation" for any contemporary readership (Grosser, *Unparalleled Poetry*, 300; see an example of such "paralleled" formatting below).

46. The psalm-like "dialogical character" of Micah 6–7 is highlighted in Hagstrom, *Micah*, 106–13.

As we have seen, Micah's psalm forms the theological and rhetorical high point of his impressive prophetic work, one that is heavily dependent upon the Psalms, with which the prophet must have had pronounced familiarity. Clearly, such extensive cross-textual influence is, or should be, of great interest to Bible students, interpreters, scholars, and commentators, for it substantially affects our understanding of what the prophet had to say and how he said it. But what is the relative significance of the Psalter today to other readers and hearers of the Scriptures, the laity, as well as all clergy? To what degree do the Psalms really impact and influence God's people in the twenty-first century, whether reading the text of Scripture silently to themselves or singing and reciting it in corporate worship?

In the interest of more effective Christian communication generally, and specifically as a concluding test of the earlier exegesis and an application of my method of discourse analysis,[47] I prepared a new "functional equivalence" translation of Micah 7:14–20.[48] In this rendition (*which stands to be critiqued and corrected*), I have made an effort to reflect more of the literary poetics and dynamics of the text in a meaningful manner and in a contemporary English style that is at the same time liturgically acceptable for use in public worship.[49] Thus, there is an emphasis upon the oral-aural qualities of the translation, which also through the printed typographical format of the text (including three strophic segments) aims to enhance the effective proclamation of the prophet's dynamic, dramatic, demanding, but also delightful message from the LORD to all the people of his flock, of every age and location.

> LORD, be a Shepherd for your people,   14
> guarding them with your mighty staff,
> leading your flock, your choice possession.
> Though they now live all alone in a forest,
> surrounded by the fruitful orchards of others,

---

47. See also Zogbo and Wendland, *Hebrew Poetry*, 281–302.

48. See Wendland, *MICAH*, 274–98. I do not claim that this rendition will be suitable for every audience and every setting. As Hamilton states: "Different translations have different goals, and those goals set the parameters and priorities for the work" (Hamilton, *Psalms*, 64). His case for "a very literal translation" is cogently expounded (Hamilton, *Psalms*, 64–70).

49. The next and ultimate step would be a recreated poetic composition that is also readily singable in pleasing psalmic unison or even as the basis for a professional "contemporary Christian musical" (CCM) production.

let them graze anew in fertile pastures,
like those of Bashan and Gilead long ago.
"Most surely,"[50] declares the Lord, our God,   15
"I will do mighty miracles for you,
    just as I did when I rescued your ancestors
       from their land of slavery in Egypt."

All nations of the world will see this;   16
they will look completely amazed
    at what the Lord God will do for you.
They will be greatly humiliated,
They have no power to oppose it, so—
    they will shut their mouths in silence;
    they will stop their ears in total shock.
Like serpents emerging from their dens,   17
creatures crawling in the dust of earth,
    they will come out to meet the Lord.
Yes, they will fearfully turn to our God,
trembling in terror at his very presence.

Is there, Lord, another God like you—*I say*,[51]   18
One who freely pardons all guilt of the penitent,
    forgiving the offenses of his faithful followers?
You never stay angry with your own people
since you delight in showing us reliable love.
You will continue in mercy to be forgiving,   19
trampling all our sins under your feet,
hurling them into the depths of the sea![52]

    50. The added emphasis intends to mark the vow-like nature of this divine assertion.
    51. The translation aims to explicitly mark the apparent pun on Micah's name (מִי־אֵל כָּמוֹךָ).
    52. The Haftarah for Yom Kippur Afternoon: Micah 7:18–20—"May you cast to the sea-depths all our sins!"—These words are well-known to observant Jews because they form the basis of the Tashlikh ceremony of the afternoon of the first day of Rosh HaShanah in which this text is symbolically re-enacted. It is of course an excellent practice to inflect a text not only on a verbal level, but on a physical level. Kinetic learning is a trait of all full-bodied religion (pun intended). Sephardic Jews recite Micah 7:18–20 together with Hosea 14:2–10 on Shabbat Shuvah (the Sabbath before Yom Kippur). All Jews recite it, together with the entire book of Jonah, as a Haftarah on Yom

> Truly, LORD, you will show us your faithfulness,   20
> your unfailing love just as you have promised,
> to our fathers Abraham and Jacob long ago!

May we all join the ancient "fathers" of Israel and the global remnant of the faithful followers of our Shepherd-LORD (2:12–13; 5:4) in professing and proclaiming these final three verses, even as we recommit ourselves to responding appropriately to his covenantal grace (7:18–19) in our personal lives as Micah fervently enjoins (6:8)!

Bibliography

Allen, Leslie C. *The Books of Joel, Obadiah, Jonah, and Micah*. Eerdmans Classic Biblical Commentaries. Grand Rapids: Eerdmans, 1976.

Barker, Kenneth L., and Waylon Bailey. *Micah, Nahum, Habakkuk, Zephaniah*. New American Commentary. Nashville, TN: Broadman & Holman, 1998.

Biblia Hebraica Stuttgartensia: with Westminster Hebrew Morphology. Logos electronic ed. Stuttgart; Glenside, PA: German Bible Society; Westminster Seminary, 2001.

Clark, David J., and Norm Mundhenk. *A Translator's Handbook on the Books of Obadiah and Micah*. London; New York: United Bible Societies, 1982.

Dempster, Stephen G. *Micah*. Two Horizons Old Testament Commentary. Grand Rapids: Eerdmans, 2017.

———. "Micah." In *Daniel—Malachi*, edited by Iain M. Duguid et al., 425–502. Vol. 7 of *ESV Expository Commentary*. Wheaton: Crossway, 2018.

DeRouchie, Jason S. *How to Understand and Apply the Old Testament*. Phillipsburg, NJ: Pilgrim & Reformed, 2017.

Grosser, Emmylou J. *Unparalleled Poetry: A Cognitive Approach to the Free-Rhythm Verse of the Hebrew Bible*. Oxford: Oxford University Press, 2023.

Gunkel, Hermann. "The Close of Micah: A Prophetic Liturgy." In *What Remains of the Old Testament and Other Essays*, 115–49. London: MacMillan, 1928.

Hagstrom, David Gerald. *The Coherence of the Book of Micah: A Literary Analysis*. Atlanta: Scholars, 1988.

Hamilton, James M., Jr. *Psalms 1–72*. Vol. 1 of *Psalms*. Evangelical Biblical Theology Commentary. Bellingham: Lexham, 2021.

Ho, Peter C. W. "The Macrostructural Design and Logic of the Psalter: An Unfurling of the Davidic Covenant." In *Reading the Psalms Theologically*, edited by David M. Howard Jr. and Andrew J. Schmutzer, 36–62. SSBT. Bellingham, WA: Lexham, 2023.

Hoyt, JoAnna M. "Discourse Analysis of Prophetic Oracles: Woe, Indictment, and Hope." *HS* 60 (2019) 153–74.

Mays, James Luther. *Micah: A Commentary*. Philadelphia: Westminster, 1976.

NET Bible: New English Translation. 2nd Beta ed. 2003. https://netbible.com.

Kippur Afternoon (https://ancienthebrewpoetry.typepad.com/ancient_hebrew_poetry/2007/09/the-haftarah-fo.html; see also Barker and Bailey, *Micah*, 133).

Schultz, Richard L. *The Search for Quotation: Verbal Parallels in the Prophets.* JSOTSup 180. Sheffield: Sheffield Academic, 1999.

Smith, Ralph. *Micah—Malachi.* Word Biblical Commentary 32. Waco: Word, 1984.

Soenksen, Jason R. *Micah.* Concordia Commentary. St. Louis: Concordia, 2020.

Sweeney, Marvin A. *The Twelve Prophets.* Vol. 2. Berit Olam. Collegeville, MN: Liturgical, 2000.

Waltke, Bruce. *A Commentary on Micah.* Grand Rapids: Eerdmans, 2007.

———. "Micah." In *The Minor Prophets*, edited by T. E. McComiskey, 2:591–764. Grand Rapids: Baker, 1983.

Wendland, Ernst. "'I Stand in Awe of Your Deeds'—A Study of Habakkuk's Psalm." Unpublished paper, 2023. https://www.academia.edu/106391925/I_stand_in_awe_of_your_deeds_A_Study_of_Habakkuk_s_Psalm.

———. "MICAH: Exegetical and Translational Guide Questions." Unpublished manuscript, 2019. 8th ed. https://www.academia.edu/38565341/MICAH_Exegetical_and_Translational_Guide_Questions_version_8_0.

———. *Prophetic Rhetoric: Case Studies in Text Analysis and Translation.* Dallas, TX: SIL International, 2014.

———. *Studies in the Psalms: Literary-Structural Analysis with Application to Translation.* Dallas: SIL International, 2017.

Wood, Joice Rilett. "Speech and Action in Micah's Prophecy." *CBQ* 62.4 (2000) 645–62.

Woodall, Chris. *Minor Prophets in a Major Key.* Kindle ed. Eugene, OR: Wipf & Stock, 2018.

Zogbo, Lynell, and Ernst Wendland. *Hebrew Poetry in the Bible: A Guide for Understanding and for Translating.* 2nd ed. Miami: United Bible Societies, 2020.